DATE DUE

DEMCO 38-296

Advances in Aggregates and Armourstone Evaluation

Geological Society Engineering Geology Special Publication No. 13

Advances in Aggregates and Armourstone Evaluation

EDITED BY

J.-P. Latham
Queen Mary and Westfield College
London University, UK

1998
Published by
The Geological Society
London

...GEOLOGICAL SOCIETY

...eological Society of London and is the oldest geological society in the ...or the purpose of 'investigating the mineral structure of the Earth'. The ...gy with a membership of around 8000. It has countrywide coverage and ...s. The Society is responsible for all aspects of the geological sciences including professional matters. The Society has its own publishing house, which produces the Society's international journals, books and maps, and which acts as the European distributor for publications of the American Association of Petroleum Geologists, SEPM and the Geological Society of America.

Fellowship is open to those holding a recognized honours degree in geology or cognate subject and who have at least two years' relevant postgraduate experience, or who have not less than six years' relevant experience in geology or a cognate subject. A Fellow who has not less than five years' relevant postgraduate experience in the practice of geology may apply for validation and, subject to approval, may be able to use the designatory letters C Geol (Chartered Geologist).

Further information about the Society is available from the Membership Manager, The Geological Society, Burlington House, Piccadilly, London W1V 0JU, UK. The Society is a Registered Charity, No. 210161.

Published by The Geological Society from:
The Geological Society Publishing House
Unit 7 Brassmill Enterprise Centre
Brassmill Lane
Bath BA1 3JN
UK
(*Orders*: Tel. 01225 445046
        Fax 01225 442836)

First published 1998

British Library Cataloguing in Publication Data
A catalogue record for this book is available from the British Library.

ISBN 1–86239–000–2
ISSN 0267–9914

Typeset by Aarontype Ltd, Unit 47, Easton Business Centre, Felix Road, Bristol BS5 0HE, UK.

Printed by The Alden Press, Osney Mead, Oxford, UK.

Distributors
USA
AAPG Bookstore
PO Box 979
Tulsa
OK 74101-0979
USA
(*Orders*: Tel. (918) 584-2555
        Fax (918) 560-2652)

Australia
Australian Mineral Foundation
63 Conyngham Street
Glenside
South Australia 5065
Australia
(*Orders*: Tel. (08) 379-0444
        Fax (08) 379-4634)

India
Affiliated East-West Press PVT Ltd
G-1/16 Ansari Road
New Delhi 110 002
India
(*Orders:* Tel. (11) 327-9113
        Fax (11) 326-0538)

Japan
Kanda Book Trading Co.
Tanikawa Building
3-2 Kanda Surugadai
Chiyoda-Ku
Tokyo 101
Japan
(*Orders*: Tel. (03) 3255-3497
        Fax (03) 3255-3495)

Contents

Foreword

The maintenance and upgrading of our built environment including large sections of our coastal defences relies heavily on natural construction materials. Hundreds of millions of tonnes of land-won aggregates and marine-dredged sand and gravel are used each year in the UK and throughout the world, typically in highways and in concrete but also in land reclamation and on our coasts.

Since the UK is an island nation faced with rising sea-levels, armourstone is playing an increasingly important role in erosion protection and flood defence structures along its coastline. Wave-energy dissipating structures (e.g. revetments, groynes and offshore breakwaters), seen as extensive placements of massive armourstone blocks in layers which slope towards the sea, have become well known coastal features. Nowadays, these rock-armoured structures are typically used in conjunction with 'soft defences' and beach management. The main tasks for this soft engineering approach to be effective are beach-level monitoring and the replenishment, when necessary, of relatively large volumes of sand and shingle: a kind of health-care service for beaches, excluding the obligatory water quality checks. This is coordinated through shore-line management plans founded on scientific understanding of physical processes, urbanization pressures and human responsibilities within each coastal region. Not surprisingly, such high material demand is not without environmental consequences.

Ever since the UK Department of the Environment published its Minerals Planning Guidance Note MPG6, 1994 ('Guidance for Aggregates Provision in England'), the projected resources and huge demands for these construction materials have been increasingly scrutinized by government strategic planners. In particular, MPG6 expressed a need to ease pressure on primary sources of aggregates (crushed rock, marine-dredged and land-won sand and gravel) by increasing the use of secondary aggregates (e.g. pulverized fly ash, slags, slate and china clay wastes) and recycled aggregates (crushed concrete and demolition waste). The technical potential of secondary and recycled aggregates is being actively investigated in response. More recently, the environmental sustainability debate has intensified under pressures to conserve the landscape and to minimize sea-bed disruption in sensitive areas.

Research is vital in helping to underpin a dredging industry seeking (i) effective exploration methods, (ii) accurate evaluation of survey results and (iii) sensitive management of the marine sand and gravel resources. To complete the picture, firm data on what 'could' be extracted from the sea-bed without causing long-term environmental damage is also needed to add to the quarrying opportunities on land that are better circumscribed. Predictions of the available marine aggregates resources, and the likely demands from the various user sectors are urgently needed to assist responsible planning within the industry.

Users of concreting aggregate and constructional fill, the coastal authority 'beach rechargers' and many overseas users often compete for the same marine aggregate supply. However, with the exception of some sand deposits, these resources are considered to be non-renewable, and the wisdom of extraction in certain locations has consequently become a complex matter to resolve. The circulation of sediment within nearshore cells generally remains poorly understood; as a result it is not always clear at what point sediment extraction at sea is no longer detrimental to the health of nearby beaches. Leaving aside the environmental problems of high material demand, another set of problems afflicting the construction materials sector of the extractive industries concerns the testing and specification of materials quality. This has been recently highlighted by the activity surrounding the introduction of Eurostandards required for the specification and testing of aggregates in their various unbound (e.g. construction fill) and bound (e.g. bituminous roads and concrete) applications, as well as for armourstone and building stone. The search for a single favoured European test method for each important aggregate or armourstone property has been ongoing where the sole aim has been one of reducing trade barriers. The micro-Deval test used to determine the resistance of aggregate to wear is one such chosen test which, until recently, was little known outside France. A comparison between competing alternative test methods is necessary before rational decisions can be reached amongst the various European nations, each of which have their different established practices, and their numerous varieties of rock types and prevailing climates. Published quantitative studies that compare chosen new or unfamiliar tests with older nationally established tests form essential data sources. It is these that give the industry the confidence to adopt new practices. More pressing perhaps, is the need for specification of tests that can predict in-service performance more successfully.

A further problem that is readily apparent when materials quality is a key issue is the question of reliability. For example, what is the probability that site concrete will be made from significantly contaminated aggregate, on the basis of routine testing of a continuously delivered product? Clear explanations of how to apply statistics to rock quality data is wantonly lacking at present and many results are presented in a manner that can easily confuse or mislead. The potential benefits to industry from clear explanations would include realistic confidence bounds, enabling structures to be built that are more economic and safe.

One sector of construction activity that is the subject of great uncertainty and risk for the designer and/or contractor is that surrounding armourstone operations. The risk is linked not only to the sheer scale and rigours of armourstone production, handling, transportation, construction and unpredictable weather conditions, but also to the high variation in the possible shapes, sizes and rock types for the blocks themselves. The physical awkwardness of this massive material and the relative lack of expertise with its design and construction has in recent years motivated greater study of this increasingly important quarry product, in spite of its relatively small volume share in the market. What makes one quarry better than another in terms of the quality of armourstone it produces is a question facing many users evaluating the various sources. Even though challenging to a geologist, the question remains totally baffling to the non-specialist because of the current lack of systematic guidelines.

European standardization has helped focus the minds of potential producers of armourstone, who appear eager to analyse predicted armourstone demands and the latest trends on how it will be specified. In contrast to the material needs of the developed countries of Northern Europe, the coastal engineering materials needed in many parts of the world may be produced under very different economic and environmental constraints. For example, the massive quantities involved (such as for a substantial breakwater) requires that material transport costs have to be minimized, thereby putting pressure on the need to open a local quarry dedicated to the project. The key technical and planning issues are then down to assessing the suitability of alternative local sources and to the efficient planning and development of the new quarry should one be necessary. The lack of case-history accounts and guidance on the technical principles governing the successful operation of a dedicated quarry has contributed to numerous cases of costly delays, over-production resulting in wasted quarried rock, and environmental problems.

These examples illustrate the background facing a major part of today's natural construction materials industry, albeit with a slant to coastal engineering materials. As implied by the word 'advances' in the title, this book is based on recent research. It contains a unified selection of research papers presented to the Extractive Industries Geology Conference (EIGC) at Warwick, UK on 15 and 16 April 1996, held under the umbrella of the Geological Society's first biennial Applied Geoscience Conference.

From among the eight EIGC sessions, the book draws upon four sessions: marine sand and gravel resources, armourstone evaluation, aggregate testing and engineering and mining rock waste. The recurrent themes which feature most prominently in this volume are: construction material resources, production, demand, testing, evaluation, specification and performance.

Papers selected for the book were presented by speakers invited by the plenary session convenors and include papers imparting both American and European expertise.

This book aims to highlight a range of pressing research issues in natural construction materials of direct relevance to an industry facing growing pressures for environmental sustainability and standardization of product quality within Europe. It is presented as a catalyst for furthering research and it is hoped that it will serve as an excellent reference on certain aspects of aggregates and armourstone.

Part 1 is on marine sand and gravel resources. One paper deals largely with sources of glacial and/or fluvial Quaternary origin that extend across the Northern European shelf and gives details of their production volumes from dredging. These sources are clearly identified and explained in relation to the major post-glacial sea-level rise of some 5000 years ago which submerged these terrestrial deposits. Another paper illustrates the use of geophysical exploration and interpretation techniques in sea areas around Hong Kong. Such methods can also help mitigate environmental impacts. The ways in which the dredging industry is harnessing an understanding of Quaternary depositional processes in its management of current and future licensed areas is also presented. A summary of the collaborative project with cosponsors (including the DoE, MAFF, NRA, Crown Estates, English Nature and representatives of the dredging industry), which led to the CIRIA report on beach recharge materials is also presented. Future demands for coast protection sand and shingle, as compared with demand for construction aggregates, can be seen alongside the resources for the offshore regions around England and Wales.

Part 2, on armourstone evaluation, continues the coastal theme, with a keynote paper on the outlook for coastal protection materials. The main physical and economic factors driving the use of armourstone and beach recharge materials are explained while a warning is sounded that despite high estimated demands, the extractive industry must also respond sensitively to environmental considerations.

The producers and users of armourstone have, since 1991, generally benefited from the availability of the CIRIA/CUR Manual on the use of rock in coastal and shoreline engineering and its armourstone specification but, have now to become accustomed to a new European specification for armourstone rock quality. This situation, and the many difficult issues surrounding armourstone quality testing and specification, are reviewed in a paper which gives the rationale for recent specification developments and describes the extensive comparative analysis of both familiar and new abrasion tests and intact strength tests which have influenced the new specifications. The testing and specification of European standard armourstone gradings and possible ways of controlling them at source are described in another paper which focuses on the annual pattern of armourstone usage in the UK in recent years. This provides the kind of market research data that potential producers and others have long been trying to obtain, but often with little success.

To rely on a single factor to evaluate the suitability of a rock source is clearly foolish. In one paper, from the USA, a rock-engineering systems approach is applied that considers most conceivable factors of influence. It gives a systematic and comprehensive rating system for assessing the suitability of armourstone sources. Indeed, it provides an 'expert system' for others with less experience. This paper is complimented by one which presents a case-history examination of the key technical and logistical factors leading to the opening and efficient running of a dedicated armourstone quarry in Malaysia.

The final paper of Part 2 describes a field and laboratory study to compare the long-term wear performance of different rock types for use as beach recharge shingle, thereby providing a link with Part 1. The approach and results presented bear upon assessing the degree to which quarried or sea-dredged rock sources are technically suited for such purposes in sites of differing prevailing weather conditions.

Part 3, on aggregate testing, has two papers on the micro-Deval test for aggregate wear. One pulls together the recent favourable Canadian experience of the micro-Deval test when applied to specification for several end uses which, perhaps surprisingly, include concrete. The second paper closely compares the micro-Deval test with the British Aggregate Abrasion Value test in the context of highway surfacings. Another paper focuses on the Polished Stone Value test for aggregates in the gritstone trade group, showing how increases in PSV are often at the expense of other important aggregate properties. A much-awaited and authoritative statistical study of aggregate testing data is also provided. The

basis upon which engineers apply judgement from consideration of their test results is thoroughly overhauled, with the help of examples of typical materials-testing problems whose interpretation is often the task of the engineer.

Preliminary results from an investigation of concrete made using slate waste, china clay waste and pulverised fly ash are also presented. Strength results and polished sections of these new mixes show how substantial technical achievements can be made with cheap processing, novel mix-design and the use of admixtures.

Finally, reflecting the breadth of the conference session on aggregate testing, a technical note is presented on a new method for abrasion testing, a subject which recurs throughout this book. A test procedure is outlined for assessing wear rates of planar rock or concrete surfaces subjected to grinding-wear typical of foot traffic. The test has been used to examine the surface laitance of pre-cast concrete slabs and calculation is by means of a reference material whose response enables the calculations to yield a more reliable index for comparing geomaterials.

The editor expresses his appreciation to all those who attended the conference sessions, to Dick Thomas for his keynote address, to session convenors Andy Bellamy and Bill French, to session chairmen Richard Fox, Alan Clark and Professor Peter Fookes, to all the authors who prepared and presented papers in this volume, especially Dave Lienhart, Chris Rogers and Jan van Meulen who came from overseas, to the reviewers of the submitted papers and to the organizing committee of the Extractive Industry Geology Conference 1996. Their efforts have enabled this volume to reach the quality for which the Geological Society Engineering Geology Special Publication Series is respected.

John-Paul Latham
Engineering Department
Queen Mary & Westfield College
July 1997

Acknowledgements

The editor wishes to express his thanks to David Ogden of the Geological Society Publishing House for his excellent work in preparing this volume.

SECTION 1

MARINE SAND AND GRAVEL GEOLOGY AND RESOURCES

Sources of sand and gravel on the Northern European Continental Shelf

D. J. Harrison[1], C. Laban[2], J. O. Leth[3] & B. Larsen[3]

[1] British Geological Survey, Keyworth, Nottingham NG12 5GG, UK
[2] Netherlands Institute of Applied Geoscience TND – National Geological Survey, PO Box 157, 2000 AD, Haarlem, The Netherlands
[3] Geological Survey of Denmark and Greenland, Ministry of Environment and Energy, Thoravej 8 DK 2400, Copenhagen NV, Denmark

Abstract. The extraction of marine sand and gravel has taken place in a number of countries around the North Sea, the Baltic Sea and English Channel for several centuries, but large-scale dredging for aggregates only began in earnest in the 1960s. Today, marine sands and gravels have an increasing role to play in maintaining European supplies of concreting aggregates as well as material for beach nourishment and constructional fill. The distribution of sand and gravel resources offshore is uneven. They vary in their thickness, their composition and grading, and their proximity to the shore. Many deposits lie in places that are currently inaccessible to the dredging industry.

This paper outlines the production of marine sand and gravel in northern Europe and describes the distribution, composition and Quaternary origins of the most important marine sand and gravel resources in northern Europe. Examples are given for the UK, the Netherlands and Denmark, and in summary form for France, Belgium, Norway, Sweden, Ireland and Germany. Most marine sand and gravel deposits are of fluvial or glacial origin and have been reworked to varying degrees by marine and coastal hydrodynamic processes. They represent a range of former depositional environments, including fluvial channel-fill or terrace deposits, glacial meltwater plain deposits, seabed lag gravels and degraded shingle beach or spit deposits, as well as modern marine tidal sandbanks and sandwave deposits.

Sand and gravel is located at the seabed in many parts of the North Sea, the English Channel, the Irish Sea and the Baltic Sea, and dredging for aggregates takes place in several countries in northern Europe, chiefly the Netherlands, United Kingdom, Belgium, France and Denmark, with limited extraction in Norway. The aggregates dredging industry has expanded rapidly since the 1960s and continues to grow as acceptable land-based sources of sand and gravel for the construction industry are being diminished.

The principal uses of marine sand and gravel are as concreting aggregates and in beach nourishment schemes. Marine aggregates are also used as constructional fill in land reclamation schemes or in the creation of artificial islands.

Resources of sand and gravel are not evenly distributed on the continental shelf but are similar to their land-based equivalents, occurring as small patches separated or covered by extensive areas of uneconomic deposits. Sand deposits are much more extensive than gravelly sediments. Offshore areas of the Netherlands and Belgium are almost devoid of gravels and here dredging is solely for sand. In contrast, the inner continental shelf around the UK is mostly covered by both sand and gravel deposits, and most dredging is for gravel aggregates which, as well as supplying the UK market, are also exported to Belgium, the Netherlands, Germany and France.

In most cases the sands and gravels are former Quaternary fluvial or fluvioglacial deposits reworked to varying degrees by marine wave and tidal current action. The distribution, composition and depositional environment of the most important marine sand and gravel resources on the northern European Continental Shelf are outlined in the following text.

Marine aggregate resources in the UK

The general distribution of seabed sediments around the coast of the UK is well known due to the reconnaissance surveys of the British Geological Survey (BGS), and the subsequent production by BGS of a series of geological maps at a scale of 1:250 000 (e.g. Harrison 1989), supported by regional reports detailing the offshore geology of the UK continental shelf (e.g. Cameron et al. 1992).

The regional mapping programme does not, however, provide in-depth information on potential resources of marine aggregates, although in recent years resource surveys of specific areas (Humber, the South Coast of England and off East Anglia) have been commissioned by the Department of the Environment and the Crown

HARRISON, D. J., LABAN, C., LETH, J. O. & LARSEN, B. 1998. Sources of sand and gravel on the Northern European Continental Shelf. *In*: LATHAM, J.-P. (ed.) 1998. *Advances in Aggregates and Armourstone Evaluation*. Geological Society, London, Engineering Geology Special Publications, **13**, 3–13.

Estate and carried out by BGS (Balson & Harrison 1986; Hamblin & Harrison 1988, 1989; Harrison 1988, 1990, 1992; James *et al.* 1994). These studies have assisted government in their considerations for marine aggregates dredging licensing, for assessing the potential for supply of these materials and also for drafting aggregates planning guidance. The techniques and procedures developed in these resource surveys (Harrison & Ardus 1989) have attracted widespread interest internationally and have for the most part been adopted as standard surveying practice by the UK aggregates dredging industry. BGS has also recently contributed to a major study by CIRIA on resources of marine sediments suitable for beach recharge materials (Arthurton 1998).

Deposits of sand and gravelly sand are extensive off the coast of England and Wales but sandy sediment is greatly in excess of gravel-sized sediment. Areas of mud or muddy sand are generally not widespread. Figure 1 shows the general distribution of gravel in the surface seabed sediments around England and Wales. At first sight this may appear to suggest that marine resources of gravel in the UK are huge as extensive areas of seabed such as the English Channel or off the Humber are covered by gravelly sediment. Unfortunately these deposits are mostly very thin and are typically a pebble-lag (often of single pebble thickness) directly overlying bedrock. Other areas, such as parts of the Irish Sea, are in waters deeper than those accessible by current dredging technology (i.e. >50 m) or are mixed with muddy sediment. It is therefore estimated that only around 10–15% of the total gravel-bearing areas shown on Fig. 1 can be considered for potential resources of gravels, although the percentage area varies with offshore location. Most of the potential gravel resource areas are known and have been prospected to varying degrees of detail by the dredging industry; most are also, at least in part, currently licensed for dredging.

Most dredging takes place in coastal waters less than 25 km offshore and in depths of between 18 and 35 m (Fig. 2). The majority of sands and gravels are dredged from areas between Great Yarmouth and Southwold (east coast region) and from Hastings to the Isle of Wight (south coast region). Currently the east coast contributes around 40% and the south coast over 20% of the total production (26 million tonnes in 1995) of marine dredged sand and gravel (Fig. 3). The outer

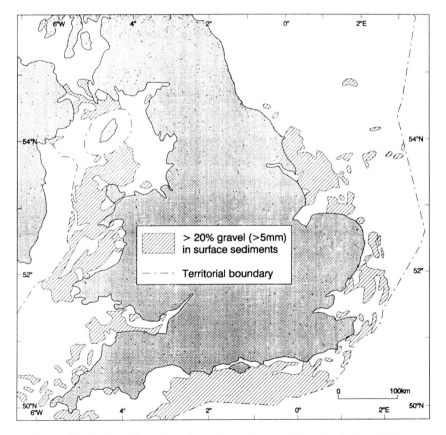

Fig. 1. Distribution of gravel-bearing seabed sediments offshore England and Wales.

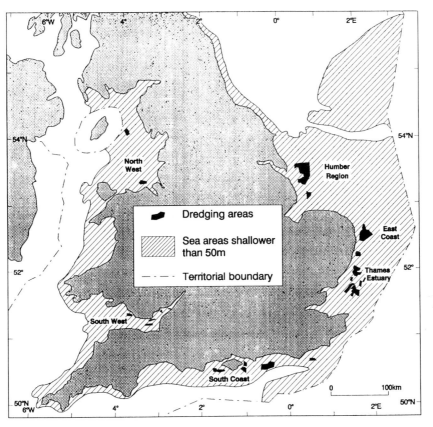

Fig. 2. Dredging areas off England and Wales.

Thames Estuary used to be the major producing area but reserves have declined and the estuary now contributes less than 10% of the total production. The Bristol Channel is a major local source of sand to the construction industry and currently contributes over 10% of the UK dredging total. Sand is also dredged in Liverpool Bay and gravels and sands are dredged in several areas off the Humber. Gravel is not mobile in the offshore area but sand is readily transported in the tidal current regime. This often results in extensive, thick (>15 m) accumulations of mainly medium-grained quartz sand as sand banks or ridges (such as the Norfolk banks and Thames Estuary banks) resting on a substrate of thin, gravelly, winnowed deposits, termed lag gravels. In areas of weaker tidal currents, deposits of fine- or medium-grained sands are more extensive at sea bed. In the nearshore zone wave action results in movement of both sand and gravel with transportation of sediment, particularly of the finer-grained fractions, into the offshore regime. It is important to note that the gravelly sediments offshore are relict deposits whose origins are comparable with those of terrestrial gravels. They are Quaternary deposits formed by fluvial or fluvioglacial processes but modified by the major post-glacial sea level rise that took place up to 5000 years ago and reworked by tidal currents. The gravels are therefore not replenished after extraction, although specific sand deposits, depending on the local sediment transport regime, may be replenished. The finite nature of gravel resources offshore requires that their extraction is rationally managed with a clear view to the anticipated demands and the locations of resources that could meet them.

Sand and gravel resources are not evenly distributed around the inner continental shelf of the UK but occur in discrete areas separated by extensive zones barren of workable resources. There are also considerable regional variations in the composition of the offshore sands and gravels and this is directly related to their origin and degree of reworking by marine processes.

Fluvial sediments

During the colder episodes of the Pleistocene, sea level lowstands were some 100 m below today's level and large areas of the continental shelf were crossed by rivers

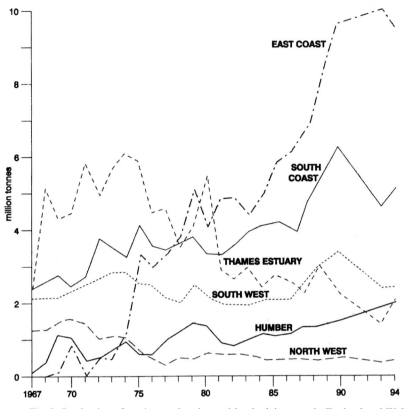

Fig. 3. Production of marine sand and gravel by dredging area in England and Wales.

flowing outwards from England and Wales. The climatic conditions of the glacial periods and associated periglacial activity led to high rates of erosion and high rates of river discharge, resulting in the deposition of large quantities of coarse grained sediment in the contemporary river channels and coastal zone. Gravel terraces were formed by the rivers downcutting during climatic cold episodes and these were later covered by temperate climate estuarine sediments as sea level rose. Sea level fluctuated considerably during the Quaternary and rising sea levels resulted in the reworking of the fluvial sediments, probably on several occasions. Not all of these sand and gravel deposits, however, were significantly reworked and some remain as terrace or channel-fill deposits of these former river systems.

Marine aggregate resources associated with former fluvial systems occur in several areas off the east and south coasts of England. The sediments of the modern Thames Estuary area are underlain by remnants of the late Pleistocene course of the Thames–Medway–Stour river systems. These palaeovalleys are mostly filled with silts, clays or fine to medium sands between 10 and 20 m in thickness. Former fluvial terrace deposits of sand and gravel locally flank the palaeovalleys and these degraded

and redistributed terrace deposits are the source of the Thames sands and gravels. The gravels are dominantly composed of flint (derived from the Chalk), of pebble size, with scattered encrusted flint cobbles. An area of particularly thick (often over 8 m thick) gravelly terrace deposits occurs extensively under Maplin Sands, but the gravels are considered to be uneconomic as they are covered by around 20 m of soft, fine sand and mud. The aggregates dredged off East Anglia are principally derived from fluvial sediments deposited in river channels during the late Pleistocene and reworked to varying degrees by Holocene coastal and shallow marine processes. This is reflected in the composition of the gravels which are dominantly (>90%) of flint. Most of the flint gravel is of pebble size (<64 mm) and particle shape varies from well-rounded to angular. Quartzite pebbles are relatively common (up to 25% of the gravel fraction) in the seabed sediments off Great Yarmouth (where they are believed to be fluvially derived from central England), whereas the gravels further south off Southwold contain large amounts of locally derived black phosphorite and reddish brown ironstone.

The floor of the eastern English Channel is marked by a number of palaeovalleys formed during the Pleistocene by fluvial systems draining southern England. The sediment bodies infilling the palaeovalleys record a complex history with multiple cut-and-fill events. Fine-grained sands, organic muds and silty clays predominate but gravel-bearing deposits also occur. Interpretation of these channel systems (Bellamy 1995) reveals a range of former sedimentary environments including fluvial, estuarine, nearshore and sub-aerial. The south coast gravel deposits are dominated by flint, but chalk and sandstone are also major constituents. Other rock types represented in the gravels include igneous and meta-morphic rocks, limestone, mudstone, ironstone and phosphorite.

Glacial sediments

During the last glacial maximum glacial sediments (chiefly tills and fluvioglacial sands and gravels) were deposited on parts of the continental shelf now covered by the North Sea, north of the Wash. The gravels in the Humber area, therefore, are of different origin to those off East Anglia, and are derived from reworking of the underlying late Pleistocene till units and fluvioglacial outwash. They are lithologically varied although hard sandstone and igneous or metamorphic rock types predominate, reflecting both local and distant source rocks. Flint, chalk and limestone (Carboniferous and Jurassic) are also important constituents. The gravels are variable in grain size and locally contain large cobbles or boulders.

The marine sand and gravels in the northeast Irish Sea area (Liverpool Bay–Isle of Man) also were largely originally deposited at the glacier margins as tills and other glacial sediments. These gravels are composed of a wide range of lithologies, presumably derived from both local and distant sources. The largest expanse of gravelly sediment covers an area between Anglesey and the Isle of Man, but elsewhere gravel is confined to small, discontinuous deposits in Liverpool Bay. The gravelly sediments are mostly thin (<0.5m) and directly overlie till from which the gravel is derived.

Coastal sediments

Relict, now submerged, beach and spit deposits are recognizable in several offshore areas around the UK. Parts of the Cross Sands flint gravel deposits offshore Great Yarmouth represent former spit deposits and the shingle deposits of Owers Bank off the south coast are also relict coastal spits. Drowned beach deposits are more difficult to recognize, but the localized accumula-tion of flint gravel at Shingle Bank off Hastings is presumed to be a former beach deposit.

Marine sediments

During the Holocene the continental shelf around England and Wales was invaded by the sea, and the Pleistocene and older sediments were subject to erosion and transportation to form seabed veneers, beach deposits or related nearshore deposits. By approximately 5000 years BP sea level had stabilized near to the present level. Repeated reworking of the seabed sediments by tidal and wave action has facilitated a gradual removal of the fine-grained fractions, leaving the coarser-grained sediments (gravels, coarse- and medium-grained sand) spread over the seabed. Large areas of the English Channel and the southern North Sea are covered by these lag gravels.

The floor of the English Channel is mostly covered by a lag deposit of gravel or sandy gravel which is typically less than 30 cm thick, although thicker deposits (up to 2 m thick) are locally developed. Flint gravels occur mainly in the Owers Bank (off Selsey Bill) and eastern Solent area, whereas chalky gravels occur in areas south of the Isle of Wight and southeast of Beachy Head. The gravels occurring southwest of the Isle of Wight contain high proportions of sandstone and siltstone derived from local outcrops of the Cretaceous strata. Winnowed gravel lag deposits also occur beneath and between the tidal sandbanks of the Thames Estuary and offshore East Anglia. These gravels are dominantly composed of flint and are mostly very thin (between 0.1 m and 0.5 m in thickness) although small areas of thicker gravelly sediment are patchily developed. The seabed sediments over most of the Humber area occur as a veneer of sandy gravels less than 1 m thick directly overlying stiff glacial clays (tills). Gravelly sediments are generally restricted to an irregular, broad zone which occurs in-shore of a line drawn between Flamborough Head and Haddock Bank (around 75 km offshore Skegness), although patchy areas of lag gravels also occur further offshore (e.g. Indefatig-able Banks–Markhams Hole area).

Since the sea level was established at its present position, very little sediment has been introduced into the seas around England and Wales from river sources. The main source of sediment at the present time, other than from the reworking of older seabed deposits, comes from cliff erosion, particularly the soft cliffs of parts of eastern and southern England. The Holderness cliffs, north of Spurn Head, for example, are eroding at rates of up to 2 metres/year and this is releasing large volumes of gravel, sand and mud into the marine environment. Gravels, however, although mobile in the wave-induced currents of the nearshore zone, are not transported out to sea. Sand is mobile under present-day hydrodynamic conditions and sandy sediments are widespread offshore. Strong tidal currents have swept the mobile sediments into large sandbanks in many parts of the southern North Sea, eastern English Channel, Bristol Channel and Liverpool Bay. Sand thickness in these tidal banks may locally exceed 20 m, although in many cases the banks are around 10 to 15 m thick. The sands form-ing the tidal sandbanks are quartzose and are mostly of medium grain size, although banks within the inner Thames Estuary are mainly composed of fine sand. In upper parts of the Bristol Channel the sand is also mostly fine-grained, but further offshore the sands are medium-grained.

Marine sand is dredged for fine aggregate and constructional fill as well as for beach recharge purposes in several areas around the coast of the UK. Where sand is extracted from the tidal bank systems, there is a particular environmental concern to ensure that sand extraction will not significantly change the morphology of the bank, affecting local inshore wave climate and threatening coastal erosion. All dredging of marine sediments in the UK is assessed for potential environmental impact, particularly the effect on fisheries and coasts, and production licences are not issued if there is judged to be any significant negative impact on the environment.

Marine aggregate resources in the Netherlands

In the Dutch sector of the North Sea only fine sand for beach nourishment and landfill is currently extracted. Total sand extraction in 1994 was 13.5 million cubic metres (Table 1). The sand is dredged along the 20 m isobath or at a distance of 20 km from the coast. The maximum permitted dredging depth below seabed is 2 metres. Sand used for concrete and mortar is not

Table 1. *Production of sand dredged from the Dutch continental shelf since 1975. The increase of extraction since 1990 is a result of the Governmental decision to maintain the coastline at the position of 1990. The sand has been extracted for beach nourishment*

Year	Quantities in cubic metres
1975	2 230 899
1976	1 902 409
1977	757 130
1978	3 353 468
1979	2 709 703
1980	2 865 907
1981	2 372 337
1982	1 456 748
1983	2 252 118
1984	2 666 949
1985	2 724 057
1986	1 955 491
1987	4 346 131
1988	4 346 131
1989	8 426 896
1990	13 356 764
1991	12 710 467
1992	9 667 958
1993	15 376 480
1994	13 484 650

extracted at the moment. The Netherlands imports large amounts of aggregate materials and currently around 4 to 5 million tonnes of concreting aggregates are supplied each year from dredging grounds off the east coast of England.

Deposits of coarse sand (D50 of $>500\,\mu m$) in the Netherlands are only present at the crests of sand waves south of 52°N and west of 3°E. The gravel occurrence northwest of the island of Texel is too small for exploitation and the occurrence near the Cleaver Bank is at this time economically not of interest because of the great distance to the nearest Dutch harbour.

In the Dutch sector of the North Sea, three main types of seabed sediments can be distinguished as potential sources of marine sand and gravel. These are Holocene marine sediments and glacial and fluvial sediments of middle and late Pleistocene age.

Marine sediments

In the southern part of the Dutch sector, a huge area covered with sand waves is present in the area between *c.* 51°20′N and 52°40′N (Fig. 4). The amplitude of these sand waves reaches between 2 and 12 m above the sea bed but decreases in amplitude to the north to between 3 and 5 m. The wavelength varies between 200 and 400 m. Towards the coast the limit of the occurrence is formed by the −20 m isobath.

The steep slope of the sand waves is mainly north facing indicating sand transportation over the sand waves towards the north. The sand transportation takes place mainly by mobile megaripples varying in height between 0.25 and 0.70 m with wavelengths between 12 and 24 m. The axis of the crests of the sand waves is more or less NW–SE, perpendicular to the tidal current. The sand waves are mostly formed of coarse to medium-grained marine sand with shells and shell fragments and sparse fine gravel. North of 52° the sands are of finer grain size and north of 52°40′N sand waves are only locally present.

The grain size of the crest is much coarser than in the troughs between the sand waves. Differences of more than $100\,\mu m$ are present. The increase in grain size towards the crest is probably due to the winnowing effect of removal of finer material during storm periods which increase current velocity over the top of the sand waves (Stride 1970; McCave 1971; Nio & Nelson 1981).

The sands are derived from marine reworking of Pleistocene fluviatile deposits from deltas of the rivers Rhine and Meuse. The sand is referred to as the Bligh Bank Formation on marine geological maps (Cameron *et al.* 1984; Balson *et al.* 1991).

Linear sandbanks occur in an area more or less parallel to the southwestern Dutch coast, and are termed the Zeeland ridges. The crests of these banks occur at water depths varying between *c.* 18 and *c.* 5 m below mean sea-level. They are formed due to the tidal regime

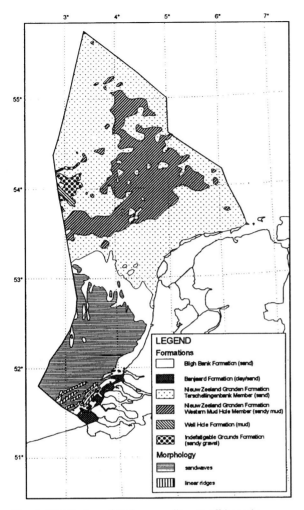

Fig. 4. Distribution of Holocene sediments offshore the Netherlands.

The Holocene and Pleistocene (Eemian) sediments covering the seabed in the area north of 53°N mainly consist of marine reworked glacial deposits of respectively the Saalian and Weichselian glaciations. They consist mainly of fine shelly sand with sparse gravel. The thickness varies from <1 m to >20 m. The Holocene sediments are referred to on geological maps (Fig. 4) as the Nieuw Zeeland Gronden Formation (Terschellingerbank Member) and the Eemian sediments are termed the Eem Formation.

Glacial deposits

The glacial sediments at or close to the seabed consist mainly of periglacial or morainic deposits, although fluvial deposits are locally recognized.

In the northeastern part of the Dutch sector, mainly east of 4°E, below a thin cover of Holocene deposits, fine to very fine sediments occur ranging in thickness from <1 to c. 12 m. Locally fine gravel is present. These periglacial sediments were deposited during the Weichselian glaciation and are referred to as the Twente Formation.

At two locations morainic deposits occur at or near the seabed. Northwest of the Dutch island of Texel gravelly deposits are present with gravel percentages varying from <2 to >70%. The average thickness of the deposit is 0.20 m. The sediments were deposited by ice during the Saalian glaciation and are referred to as the Indefatigable Grounds Formation.

A second area with gravelly sediments is present near the Cleaver Bank, southeast of the Dogger Bank. The gravel content varies between 30 and 70% and the deposit ranges in thickness between 0.1 and >2.0 m (Jeffery *et al.* 1989). The estimated amount of gravel is c. 40 million tonnes. The sediments were deposited by British ice during the Weichselian glaciation and on geological maps are referred to as the Indefatigable Grounds Formation.

In the southeastern part of the Dutch sector, below a cover of Holocene sediments (mainly sand waves), the remains of a Pleistocene delta occur consisting of fine- to coarse-grained fluviatile sand with sparse gravel and local thin gravel layers. The sediments were deposited during the late Pleistocene by the rivers Rhine and Meuse and are referred to as the Kreftenheije Formation (Fig. 5).

Marine aggregate resources in Denmark

The dredging of marine sand and gravel in Denmark represents 10–13% of total national production of materials for construction and reclamation. The amount has been more or less constant for the period 1990–1994, due to the general recession in construction activities (Table 2).

(Houbolt 1968) and mainly consist of fine- to medium-grained marine sands overlying cores of older Holocene sediments. Investigations have indicated that most of these banks are stable (Laban & Schüttenhelm 1981). The most western bank of this group is the Bligh Bank. The sediment transportation takes place by sand waves and megaripples migrating over the banks.

Isolated sandbanks northwest of the Zeeland ridges are the north–south trending Brown Bank and a number of smaller banks to the east. These banks consist of mainly fine to medium-grained marine sand which, in the case of the Brown Bank, overlies a core of Pleistocene clay. The sediment transportation takes place like the Zeeland ridges, by sand waves and megaripples migrating over the banks.

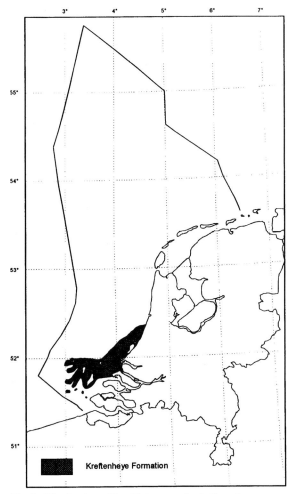

Fig. 5. Distribution of late Pleistocene fluviatile sediments (Kreftenheije Formation) offshore the Netherlands.

The dredging of sand for land reclamation has increased markedly over the last ten years due to several large construction works in the coastal areas. From 1989–1993 more than 9 million cubic metres of sandfill and till have been dredged for the Great Belt bridge and tunnel construction. In addition, about 3 million cubic metres per year of sand has been dredged for beach nourishment, mostly along the North Sea coast.

During the construction of the planned fixed link between Denmark and Sweden, it is expected that about 8 million cubic metres of sandfill and 1 million cubic metres of concreting sand will be dredged from the Kriegers Flak on the Baltic Sea over a four-year period.

No official forecast for the future extraction of marine aggregates has been prepared, but increasing use of marine materials at the expense of land-based aggregates is expected. This is mainly due to the future termination of a number of licences for land extraction together with increased environmental concerns and land use conflicts. In 1994, total marine aggregate production in Denmark was around 5.1 million cubic metres compared to a total land-produced output of about 19.6 million cubic metres.

Denmark is characterized by a glacial landscape of easily eroded tills and sorted meltwater deposits. These are the source of a wide range of sand, gravel and boulder deposits at the seabed. Marine aggregate resources are therefore, generally, of glacial origin or are marine deposits derived from glacial deposits.

Glacial deposits

Marine aggregates are similar to onshore deposits of sand and gravel in Denmark and are generally meltwater deposits washed out from glacial debris. They are mostly meltwater plain, valley fill or terrace deposits, although a few eskers and sand kames have been identified at the seabed. Ice margin deposits (proximal meltwater plains) tend to form banks which are highly variable in composition and structure, although locally they are very rich in boulder deposits and gravels. Large ice-marginal bank deposits are locally developed in inner Danish waters (Kattegat, the Danish Straits and adjacent Baltic Sea) and also in the North Sea off northern Jutland. The petrographic composition of the glacial derived materials is very complex including metamorphic gneisses, amphibolites, dense Palaeozoic

Table 2. *Extraction of marine sediments in Denmark*

Year	Sand 0–2 mm (million cubic metres)	Gravel 0–20 mm (million cubic metres)	Gravel/stones (6–300 mm) (million cubic metres)	Sand fill (million cubic metres)	Misc (till) (million cubic metres)
1990	1.0	0.2	0.6	3.9	0.1
1991	1.1	0.5	0.9	4.4	1.0
1992	0.7	0.5	0.9	1.2	0.8
1993	0.9	0.2	1.1	2.1	
1994	1.8	0.2	1.3	1.8	

limestones and sandstones, soft to hard Cretaceous and Danian limestones (chalk), and flint. The proportions of carbonates and flint vary considerably. Some of the flints may be porous and alkali-reactive.

Most of the glacial meltwater deposits infilling submarine valleys are covered by a thick blanket of late Pleistocene and Holocene deposits and are therefore seldom accessible for exploration and extraction.

During the last glaciation the southern part of the Danish sector of the North Sea was far from the ice margin and meltwater deposits here consist of fine-grained distal facies. Locally, however, older glacial deposits protrude these Weichselian fine sands/clays and form important marine resources of coarse grained-material.

In the northern part of the Danish sector of the North Sea at Jutland Bank/Little Fisher Bank widespread coarse sand and gravel lag deposits have accumulated. Many of these deposits consist of very mature glacial material. The deposits here, as well as at the Horns Rev, are interpreted as late Pleistocene coastal shingle beach deposits which later were remobilized by the rising sea level and spread as thin sheets of coarse sand and pebbles covering the surrounding sea floor.

Marine deposits

The marine deposits consist mostly of reworked glacial deposits eroded at the coast and at the seabed, but also they contain materials eroded from exposed Cretaceous and Danian limestone with flint. The marine deposits are therefore, either former coastal deposits formed during periods of marine lowstand or, deposits formed by marine processes at the seabed.

Most of the seafloor of the inner Danish waters (in water depths of less than 30 m) has been either a terrestrial or coastal environment in the lowstand period from the late Pleistocene to the early Holocene. There are, however, great regional differences in relative sea level through time due to differential isostatic rebound. In southeast Denmark, the Baltic Sea basin was dammed during the late Pleistocene and early Holocene, resulting in the accumulation of barrier coast deposits, which are now submerged but form valuable sand resources.

The most valuable marine gravel resources are related to ancient shorelines. Submerged shingle spits and other marine foreland deposits are frequently found on the lee side of submerged banks and are actively dredged for marine aggregates. Boulders derived from the eroded tills and lying on the wave-cut platforms, on the top of the banks or along the shoreline form important resources of coarse materials. However, many of these 'stone reefs' are now protected by environmental legislation.

The seafloor deposits in the Danish sector of the North Sea have only recently attracted attention as potential sources of marine aggregates, and extraction so far has been limited to the dredging of sandwave deposits for beach nourishment. Huge sandbank deposits have been identified in the area of Jutland Bank/Little Fisher Bank where they occur on the northern 'lee-side' of widespread glacial ablation areas. This very well-sorted sediment probably reflects processes of repeated sediment reworking. Most of the Danish continental shelf in the North Sea is an erosional platform covered by a thin lag deposit of sand and gravel with a mobile sand cover. In contrast, the coastal zone largely retains an irregular glacial morphology which provides a range of depositional environments. Marine sand deposits are therefore found on relatively protected slopes and mud deposits occur in sheltered, deeper water areas.

Many of the marine sand deposits in inner Danish waters are regarded as wavebuilt terraces, lateral accretions prograding on the seaward side of wave cut platforms. They are found on most steep submarine slopes at water depths of between 5 and 25 m depending on the local wave climate. The terrace deposits near the wave-cut platform contain gravel mixed with the sands, but in the more distal deposits the sand fraction predominates.

Marine sand deposits are also found in the funnel-shaped entrances to narrow straits and at other sites with occasional high current velocities.

Marine aggregates in other northern European countries

France

Marine aggregate resources are widespread off several parts of the French coast, particularly off the French Channel coast and offshore Brittany. These sands and gravels are predominantly of fluvial origin (similar to those off the south coast of England) but have been extensively reworked by marine action. They occur as degraded terrace or relict beach deposits and also as widespread gravel lags. Some palaeovalley deposits contain thick gravel layers, most notably in the Baie de la Seine, and many sandbanks contain thick accumulations of medium-grained siliceous marine sand.

In recent years there has been a considerable demand for marine dredging for sands and gravels from areas offshore the Seine and the Loire. There is, however, at present no extraction taking place in the French sectors of the southern North Sea, eastern Channel and Mediterranean, although there is some dredging of siliceous sands (currently 2 million cubic metres) in several areas between Dieppe and Bordeaux. In addition, there are several sites off Brittany where calcareous material (shell sand and Maerl) has been dredged for many years. Current production of calcareous material

Table 3. *Production of aggregates in France*

Year	Marine aggregates (million tonnes)	Total land-won sand and gravel (million tonnes)
1975	1.7	320
1977	3.4	345
1979	3.2	358
1981	4.2	369
1982	4.6	342
1987	3.3	335
1988	3.6	378
1991	3.9	399

Note: approximately 1 cubic metre of sand and gravel equates to 1.8 tonnes.

is 0.4 million cubic metres per year. Table 3 shows the production of marine aggregates in France compared with land-won sand and gravel production.

Belgium

The seabed sediments in the Belgian sector of the southern North Sea are predominantly sandy and sand dredging has occurred in two zones off the Belgian coast: the Zeeland Banks (zone 1) and on the Flemish Banks (zone 2). These sandbanks are relatively stable features and are formed by the tidal regime. They consist of fine- to medium-grained, siliceous marine sands.

There has recently been an increasing demand for marine sand in Belgium and marine production has increased steadily since the late 1980s. In 1994 a total of 1.6 million cubic metres of sand was extracted from zone 2 mostly from the Kwintebank (offshore Ostend) with smaller contributions from Oost Dyck Bank and Buiten Ratel. No dredging has taken place in zone 1 since 1987.

Sweden

There is little demand for marine aggregates in Sweden due to the large deposits of glacial sand and gravel on land in eskers. In 1989 a total of 70 500 cubic metres was extracted from the seabed in three areas off the west coast and in one area off the east coast of Sweden (Anon 1992). In 1992, marine dredging for aggregates in Sweden ceased when the sand extraction area in the Kattegat at Vastra Haken was included in the marine nature reserve established around the Falsterbo Peninsula. Applications have since been made to the Swedish Government for future marine aggregate extraction, but to date no permits for dredging have been granted.

However, large dredging operations are planned in the near future in the Sound between Sweden and Denmark for the construction of the bridge-tunnel Oresund link between Sweden and Denmark. The dredged material (around 7 million cubic metres) will be used for the construction of two islands south of Saltholm on the Danish side of the Sound.

Norway

In Norway, most aggregate for construction is produced from hard rock quarries or from land-won sand and gravel pits; the total amount of marine aggregates is less than 1% of total aggregates production. In 1994, around 100 000 cubic metres of marine sand and gravel was dredged in Norway. Carbonate sand extraction is an important industry in parts of Norway, especially in the southwest, and between 100 000 and 200 000 tonnes are dredged from the sea each year for local use as a fertiliser.

Ireland

There has been no significant dredging activity for marine aggregates off Ireland, although there has been recent interest in prospecting for suitable resources. There has also been occasional interest in deposits of Lithothamnium (Maerl) and small amounts (around 500 tonnes) are currently being extracted in a pilot scale project.

Germany

There is currently no dredging for aggregates in the FRG, although there are planned operations to extract sand from near the island of Sylt in the North Sea and also for sediment dredging in the Adlerground in the southern Baltic.

Future prospects

Marine sands and gravels are a valuable resource in many parts of northern Europe and make a significant contribution to national demands for constructional raw materials. Marine aggregates are also traded commodities within northern Europe; each year the UK exports about a third of total production to mainland Europe, primarily the Netherlands and Belgium with smaller quantities to France and Germany.

In most countries, the distribution, composition and geological history of marine sand and gravel deposits is well known at the reconnaissance level due to Government, academic or industry surveys, but detailed knowledge of specific deposits is not as widely available although many areas of seabed have been prospected in detail by the aggregates dredging industry.

Resources of marine sand and gravel are mostly finite and some of the traditional areas for gravel aggregates dredging, such as parts of the Thames Estuary, are virtually worked out. There are, however, substantial resources of marine aggregates in northern Europe and in the short term there should be no shortage of supply, assuming permissions are granted to extract these materials.

The dredging of aggregates, like all mineral extraction activities, has a potential environmental impact; particular concerns for the marine dredging industry are the effects of dredging on fishing, shipping navigation, coastal protection and benthic ecosystems. All dredging licences are subject to national Government consultations and are checked for their impact on adjacent coastlines and fisheries. In general, licences (similar to Planning Permissions for land-based mineral extraction) are issued only if the environmental assessment shows there will be little or no negative impact.

The management of marine sand and gravel resources is therefore fundamentally based on both assessment of resources and an assessment of environmental impact. Future research studies should encourage close cooperation and coordination of geological, biological and hydrodynamic investigations. There is also a need to ensure that extraction is managed within the context of the European market and to consider the issues of long-term sustainability and renewability of marine aggregate resources on the northern European continental shelf. In addition, because many environmental problems do not respect national boundaries, there is a need to safeguard marine habitats and coastal conservation areas. Research of this type can be carried out effectively only by a coordinated effort across frontiers.

Acknowledgements. The authors express their thanks to their colleagues in Europe who have contributed information on marine aggregates. Mr Harrison publishes with the approval of the Director of the British Geological Survey, and NERC.

References

ANON 1992. *Report of the ICES Working Group on the Effects of Extraction of Marine Sediments on Fisheries.* International Council for the Exploration of the Sea Cooperative Research Report No 182.

ARTHURTON, R. S. 1998. The CIRIA research project on beach recharge materials. *This volume.*

BALSON, P. S. & HARRISON, D. J. 1986. *Marine Aggregate Survey Phase 1: Southern North Sea.* BGS Report 86/38.

——, LABAN, C., SCHÜTTENHELM, R., PAEPE, R. & BAETMAN, C. 1991. *Ostend Sheet 51°N–02°E, SeaBed Sediments and Holocene Geology.* British Geological Survey and Rijks Geologische Dienst.

BELLAMY, A. G. 1995. Extension of the British landmass: evidence of shelf sediment bodies in the English Channel. *In:* PREECE, R. C. (ed.) *Island Britain: a Quaternary Perspective.* Geological Society, Special Publication, **96**, 47–62.

CAMERON, T. D. J., CROSBY, A., BALSON, P. S., JEFFERY, D. H., LOTT, G. K., BULAT, J. & HARRISON, D. J. 1992. *United Kingdom Offshore Regional Report: the Geology of the Southern North Sea.* HMSO, London.

——, LABAN, C. & SCHÜTTENHELM, R. T. E. 1984. *Flemish Bight Sheet 52°N–0.2°E, SeaBed Sediments and Holocene Geology.* British Geological Survey and Rijks Geologische Dienst.

HAMBLIN, R. J. O. & HARRISON, D. J. 1988. *Marine Aggregate Survey Phase 2: South Coast.* BGS Report 88/31.

—— & —— 1989. *The Marine Sand and Gravel Resources off the Isle of Wight and Beachy Head.* BGS Technical Report WB/89/41.

HARRISON, D. J. 1988. *The Marine Sand and Gravel Resources off Great Yarmouth and Southwold, East Anglia.* BGS Technical Report WB/88/9.

—— 1989. *Farne Sheet 55°N–0.2°W, Sea Bed Sediments.* British Geological Survey.

—— 1990. *Marine Aggregate Survey Phase 2: East Coast.* BGS Report WB/90/17.

—— 1992. *The Marine Sand and Gravel Resources off the Humber.* BGS Technical Report WB/92/1.

—— & ARDUS, D. A. 1990. Geological investigations for Marine Aggregates offshore East Anglia. *Journal of the Society for Underwater Technology,* **16**, 9–14.

HOUBOLT, J. J. H. C. 1968. Recent sediments in the southern Bight of the North Sea. *Geologie en Mijnbouw,* **47**, 245–273.

JAMES, J. W. C., HARRISON, D. J. & CIAVOLA, P. 1992. *Marine Aggregate Survey Phase 4: Irish Sea.* BGS Technical Report WB/92/10.

JEFFERY, D. H., FRANTSEN, P, LABAN, C. & SCHÜTTENHELM, R. T. E. 1989. *Silver Well Sheet 54°N–02°E. Quaternary Geology.* British Geological Survey and Rijks Geologische Dienst.

LABAN, C. & SCHÜTTENHELM, R. T. E. 1981. Some new evidence on the origin of the Zeeland ridges. Special Publications of the International Association of Sedimentology, **5**, 239–245.

McCAVE, I. N. 1971. Sand waves in the North Sea off the coast of Holland. *Marine Geology,* **10**, 199–225.

NIO, S. D. & NELSON, C. H. 1981. The North Sea and Northeastern Bering Sea: A Comparative of the occurrence and geometry of sand bodies of two shallow, epicontinental shelves. *Geologie en Mijnbouw,* **67**, 105–114.

STRIDE, A. H. 1970. Shape and size trends for sand waves in a depositional zone of the North Sea. *Geological Magazine,* **107**, 469–477.

Assessment of offshore sand and gravel bodies for dredging

Ian Selby[1] & Klaas Ooms[2]

[1] Coastal Geosciences, Salmon Road, Great Yarmouth, Norfolk, NR30 3QS, UK
[2] DEMAS (Dredging, Engineering and Management Studies), PO Box 2065, 2800 BE Gouda, Lekkenburg 2, Gouda, The Netherlands

Abstract. Reliable assessment of offshore sand and gravel resources permits efficient dredging, the maintenance of cargo quality control and the effective mitigation of environmental impacts. Site investigation should be based on the interpretation and correlation of high resolution seismic profiling and CPT/sampling data. A preliminary interpretation of the seismic data reveals the geological setting of the sand bodies and leads to the selection of appropriate sampling methods and the recognition of key sampling positions. Geologically complex sand bodies demand phased data acquisition to delineate geometry, physical properties and compositional variability. The alternative approach, of grid-based sampling using a predetermined sampling density, is costly at best and probably misleading. A three-dimensional model is created from the integration of acquired data and a resource volume calculated. Dredging constraints and overflow losses are applied to the model resulting in the determination of a reserve volume and critical dredging parameters. It is advisable to carry out a wide-ranging testing programme on the recovered samples to ensure compliance with relevant standards or requirements. The potential penalties for superficial site investigation include delay, unpredictable cargo quality and unforeseen environmental problems.

Offshore sands and gravels lying at depths of less than 60 m on the inner shelf form an important economic resource. The last 20 years has witnessed an escalation in the value of offshore deposits as demand and extraction rates have significantly increased for a wide range of uses. Sand and gravel deposits are dredged for four major applications:

- for use as fill in reclamations – pressures arising from population and development in many ports and coastal communities around the world, for example the Middle East, Hong Kong, Singapore and Taiwan, have lead to a demand for land through reclamations, (e.g. Ooms *et al.* 1994) together with the redevelopment of existing port sites
- for use as aggregates for construction and concrete – as land-based extraction has become environmentally less acceptable, an increased quantity of fine and coarse marine aggregate is being used in concrete and as fill. Currently in Japan about 85% of aggregates are supplied from marine sources, (Tsurusaki *et al.* 1988) compared with about 11–18% in the UK (British Marine Aggregate Producers Association 1995; Parrish 1987), while many other countries have investigated potential offshore resources, for example Suter *et al.* (1989)
- for beach replenishment – it is now recognized that soft, natural solutions, e.g. beach recharge, rather than costly, hard, structural solutions to coastal protection often offer significant environmental and economic advantages. Beach replenishment schemes around the world use a variety of methods (van Oorschot & van Raalte 1989) on a range of scales (for example Murray *et al.* 1994), typically resulting in the deposition of 0.5–10 million m³ of sand and gravel supplying starved and eroded beaches
- to extract placers – including precious stones and mineral sands (e.g. Hein *et al.* 1993), occurring in fluvial and marine sands and gravels

This paper examines the origins and assessment of sands and gravels dredged for fill, aggregates and beach replenishment. Dredged sand and gravel resources must satisfy a wide range of specifications for various uses. Sands dredged as fill for reclamations may contain up to 20% or more fines ($<63\,\mu m$), depending on the works programme and planned use of the area. If the area is to be developed upon completion of the reclamation works, a high bearing capacity is required at an early stage. This can be achieved by using a well-sorted, coarse-grained sand with a low fines content, although ground improvement methods are also used to enhance strength and stiffness characteristics. Reclamations allowing larger settlements over a longer period before construction begins may utilize sands with a higher fines content. Sands and gravels dredged as concreting aggregates require a very low fines content ($<5\%$), must satisfy colour and grading criteria and should not contain deleterious components. A wide range of gradings may be specified for beach nourishments, from fine-grained sands, encouraged as a

SELBY, I. & OOMS, K. 1998. Assessment of offshore sand and gravel bodies for dredging. *In*: LATHAM, J.-P. (ed.) 1998. *Advances in Aggregates and Armourstone Evaluation*. Geological Society, London, Engineering Geology Special Publications, **13**, 15–31.

beneficial use of sediments dredged for other projects (Permanent International Association of Navigation Congresses, henceforth PIANC, 1992) to well-sorted gravels.

Dredging is a large international business with over 1000 million m³ of sands and gravels being dredged annually. The advantages of dredging in comparison to quarrying have long been recognised, and dredging will continue in the foreseeable future to rapidly, reliably and economically deliver large volumes of sands and gravels to the developing areas of conurbations, thus ensuring good progress of projects. For example, at Chek Lap Kok airport in Hong Kong, over 70 million m³ of sand was delivered in about two years to form a platform measuring 2 km × 1 km, in an area of sea formerly 4–6 m deep. For the majority of these requirements, trailer suction hopper dredgers (TSHDs) are used to dredge sand from the licenced borrow areas and discharge their cargo at the site or wharf (Fig. 1). TSHDs used for capital projects typically have hopper volumes of 4000–10 000 m³, and are soon to be as large as 23 000 m³. Aggregate dredger hopper volumes are generally smaller, around 1000–3500 m³, largely due to

the restrictions imposed by tidal berths. This paper only considers dredging by TSHDs. In the past extraction by TSHD has been limited to depths of about −50 m, but several dredgers may now operate at −60 m and deeper as a result of outboard pump systems, and the trend towards deeper dredging continues.

Given the investment in TSHD technology, it is critical to maximize the utilization of finite geological resources. However during dredging operations (Bray 1979), production and quality problems often arise which can be directly attributed to a poor understanding of the geological context of the dredged deposit. This is often a result of an inadequate site investigation which has lead to an incorrect interpretation. Coupled with uncompromising restrictions being imposed as a result of the developing environmental awareness of dredging impacts, it is considered that the inefficiency arising from poor resource assessment is becoming increasingly unacceptable. This paper highlights the potential benefits of a thorough site investigation, which will result in a confident prediction and assessment of resources, permits optimal production and mitigation of environmental impacts. The methods outlined are based on

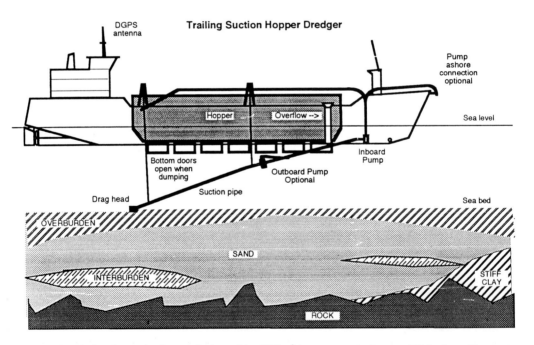

Fig. 1. A typical trailer suction hopper dredger with a 8000 m³ hopper capacity is around 125 m long, 21 m across and has a loaded draft of 9 m. Two dredge pipes permit rapid loading by a single inboard or two outboard pumps and the slurry is discharged in the rear of the hopper. Overflow from the hopper is regulated by adjusting the height of the overflow tubes. Discharge is through bottom doors, pump ashore or rainbowing. TSHDs dredging aggregates have a single dredge pipe, overflow through spillways in the top of the hopper above the waterline, and discharge by pump and bucket wheel or scraper and conveyor. Aggregate cargoes are often gravel-rich due to the screening off of sands and fines during loading.

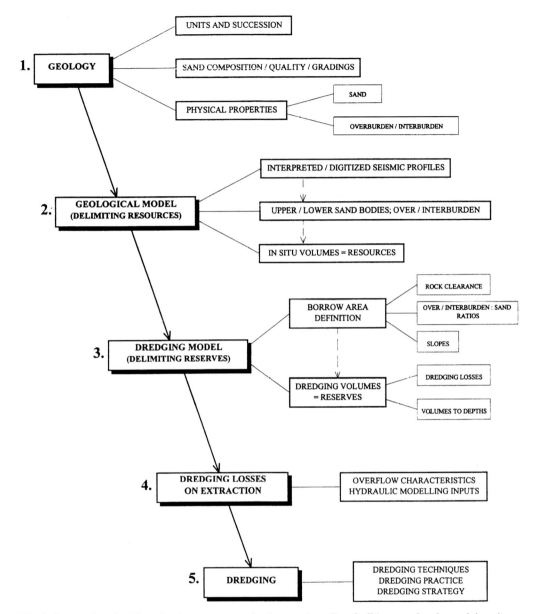

Fig. 2. Proposed methodology for the assessment of volume and quality of offshore sand and gravel deposits. When combined with physical and biological measurements and observations, the data derived from this assessment allows the prediction of environmental impacts.

experience of resource and reserve assessment in the UK and Hong Kong for sand and gravel deposits dredged for aggregates, fill and beach replenishment. Figure 2 illustrates the assessment methodology. Aspects of the geology of offshore sands and gravels, with examples from Hong Kong, and each stage in the assessment process are outlined in the following sections.

Occurrence of sands and gravels on the inner shelf

Offshore sands and gravels are a finite resource. The majority of the sands and gravels currently dredged from the inner shelf are relict and were deposited as a result of the numerous major sea level and climatic changes that have occurred during the alternating glacial and temperate episodes of the past 1–2 million years. Throughout this time sea levels have regularly fallen (lowstands), rarely to a maximum of around −120 m, sub-aerially exposing the shelf, and have risen (high-stands), occasionally above existing sea level (Shackleton 1987). In high latitudes during cold stages, glacigenic (subglacial, proglacial and glaciofluvial) and periglacial processes (Boardman 1987; Drewry 1986) have resulted in intensified erosion, transport and sedimentation rates of sands and gravels, which then may become available for reworking during the following warm stage highstand. In the lower latitudes, shifts in the climatic belts have resulted in changes in precipitation and vegetation leading to periods of intensified erosion of deeply weathered rocks and reworking of existing sand deposits. Throughout this time, climatic changes in hinterlands have resulted in changes in river sediment loads, composition and deposition rates.

Sands and gravels have been deposited in a wide variety of high energy, fluvial, coastal and marine settings which have been influenced by the numerous changes in relative sea level. Typically, sand and gravel bodies are characterized by complex depositional geometries and histories. Offshore, the shelf often slopes seaward at very low angles, e.g. 1 in 1000, and consequently even if a minor sea level fall occurs, wide expanses of shelf become sub-aerially exposed and rivers flow across the plains. Fluvial incision occurs as base levels fall and the channels of braided and meandering systems migrate and infill (Miall 1992). Coarse-grained sediments by-pass the exposed inner shelf during a lowstand. Terraces preserved along the channel margins (Bellamy 1995) provide evidence of further minor sea level changes and estuaries and deltas become sediment traps, where the rivers enter the sea (Orton & Reading 1993). Rising sea levels result in estuarine sedimentation backstepping coastwards, forming the late stage infills of

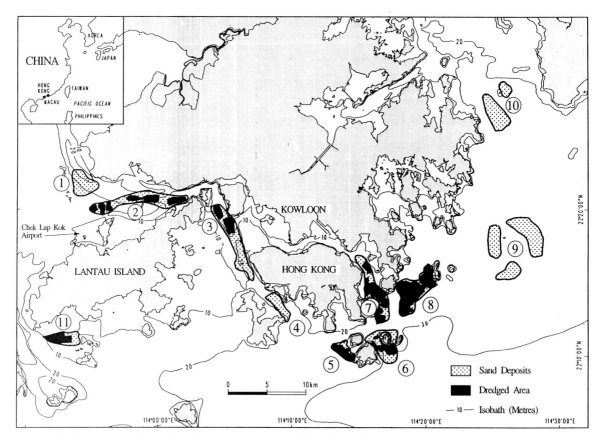

Fig. 3. Location of sand deposits and dredging around Hong Kong. The sands have been delivered to the reclamation at Chek Lap Kok and to projects in the centre of the harbour. The sand bodies are: (1) Urmston Roads, (2) Brothers, (3) Tsing Yi, (4) East Lamma Channel, (5) West Po Toi, (6) East Po Toi, (7) Tathong Channel, (8) West Ninepins, (9) Eastern Waters, (10) Mirs Bay and (11) Sokos. The sand deposits in Mirs Bay remain undeveloped for environmental reasons.

the fluvial channels, whilst concurrent erosion of the transgressed land surface forms a planar ravinement surface. The ravinement surface is commonly associated with overlying veneers of sand, locally up to a few metres thick, deposited in a nearshore, shallow shelf environment (Stride 1982). Stillstands in the transgression lead to the development of coastal depositional systems including beaches, bars and barriers, which may be partly preserved on the shelf (Nummedal *et al.* 1987), whilst shallow marine currents may lead to the formation of offshore sand banks.

Location and origin of sands dredged from the inner shelf around Hong Kong

The sands lying offshore Hong Kong provide a good example of the variety of inner shelf sand bodies. Around 250 Mm³ of sand has been dredged in Hong Kong to provide fill for the reclamation programme since 1985. Hong Kong lies on the stable passive margin forming the northern shelf of the South China Sea, on the eastern side of the mouth of the Zhujiang (Pearl) Estuary (Fig. 3). Within territorial waters, depths attain −33 m (all depths are below Chart Datum) and the sea bed is typically underlain by a 5–15 m thick mud sheet deposited during the final stages of the Holocene transgression (Fyfe *et al.* 1997). The mud sheet overlies a sub-aerially weathered succession of interbedded muds and sands incised by fluvial processes during at least two major sea level

lowstands. A significant difference between resources in Hong Kong and elsewhere, for example in the UK (Selby 1992), is that gravels are rare. This is attributed to the intensity and depth of the weathering of the bedrock in Hong Kong, which is dominated by silicic magmatic lithologies.

In Hong Kong, inner shelf submarine sands have been deposited in fluvial, estuarine and marine environments. However, two major types of sand body have been dredged to depths of −50 m: (i) sea bed marine sand sheets and (ii) fluvial channel sands, which have commonly required the removal of overburden. Examples of each type of sand deposit, which may be superimposed, are described in detail to illustrate the potential complexity of geological settings.

Sea bed marine sand sheets

The sea bed sands form mounds and sheets typically up to 5 m thick lying in restricted channels and around islands and headlands, e.g. East Po Toi, Tathong Channel and Urmston Roads (James 1993) at depths of −30 m (Fig. 3), and may grade laterally into mud sheets. These restricted tidal channels correspond with the highest existing tidal currents in Hong Kong, which reach about 1.0 m/s. Sand grain size varies across the sheets, whilst fines contents increase at the base of the sheets and channel margins where currents are reduced. For example, in the Tathong Channel (Fig. 4) the sands are grey, poorly sorted, fine to coarse-grained, shelly, occasionally gravelly with a fines

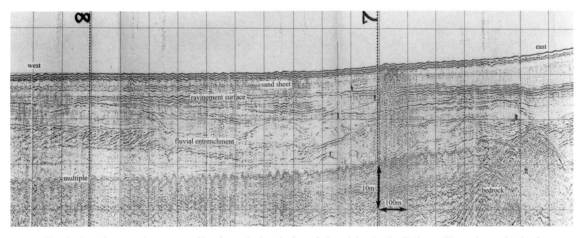

Fig. 4. A surface-tow boomer profile of a typical seabed sand sheet lying in the Tathong Channel at a depth of 25 m before dredging. The sheet is around 5 m thick, characterized by a moderate backscatter associated with occasional continuous reflectors and becomes seismically transparent towards the east as a result of an increased fines content. The continuous, flat lying, high amplitude reflector forming the base of the sand sheet is interpreted as a ravinement surface eroded during the Holocene transgression. The erosion associated with the Holocene transgression has truncated the infills of fluvially incised channels formed during the last glacial maximum lowstand. The channels are infilled by parallel, draping, continuous reflectors interpreted as a fine-grained deposits. The channels are eroded into a seismically homogeneous unit occasionally associated with prograding reflectors interpreted as sandy sediments.

content of 10–20%, but become very fine-grained with fines contents >30% at the margin of the sheet. The sheets were deposited in the final stages of the last transgression, probably as a result of current and tidal winnowing of coastal and sea bed sands by the enhanced currents flowing through the shallow channels, when sea levels were 15–25 m below present levels. Sandbanks formed locally (e.g. Evans 1988), and often became partly buried by the mud sheet that accumulated as sediment supply became predominantly fine-grained and current speeds reduced with increasing sea levels. As the sands overlie the flat-lying ravinement surface, dredging of underlying sand occurs below the erosion surface in places. Dredging has now removed the majority of the marine sand sheets in Hong Kong.

Fluvial channel sands

Two types of fluvial sand are present infilling channels:

(a) Type I channel sands lie in relatively narrow channels, often constrained by steep bedrock valley sides e.g. East Lamma Channel, Tsing Yi and Tathong Channel (Fig. 3). The sands have been deposited to depths of > −70 m, commonly within linear and continuous channels. Seismically, the sands are homogeneous and characterized by a high-amplitude backscatter, although prograding and flat-lying reflectors are occasionally present (Figs 4 & 5). In the East Lamma Channel, the very poorly sorted, medium to coarse-grained yellow sands and fine gravels (d_{50} 0.8–1.0 mm) are apparently massive and dense (SPT-N value 20–80), subangular-subrounded, of moderate sphericity and contain less than 5% fines. The fines contents increase towards the channel margins. Thin (<2.0 m), firm-stiff silt/clay lenses are rare, weathered yellow and red, and are generally overconsolidated due to desiccation (undrained shear strength up to 70 kPa). The sands are interpreted to be autochthonous and deposited in braided, possibly seasonal, fluvial channels characteristically infilled by deposition by lateral and downstream accretion and have been subjected to prolonged, possibly repeated periods of sub-aerial exposure. It is likely that the sands were deposited by the fluvial system that drained through Hong Kong, prior to the development of the Zhujiang (Pearl) Delta, since the last glacial maximum (Long & Huo 1990). Strong tidal currents in the areas restricted the deposition of the mud sheet and consequently these sands are associated with minor thicknesses of overburden.

(b) Type II channel sands infill fluvially entrenched channels and are often overlain by up to 10m of overburden deposited during the final stages of the Holocene transgression, for example at West Ninepins and Eastern Waters (Fig. 6). Seismic profiles reveal channels up to 3 km across incised to depths of −58 m and courses locally controlled by bedrock configuration. The sand bodies form lenses up to 15m thick lying at the channel margins. The sand lenses may coalesce and are char-acterized internally by a series of prograding packages of reflectors. Samples reveal the sands are often grey, well-sorted, medium-grained (d_{50} 150–220 μm), moderately dense, (cone resistance occasionally up to 40 MPa) subrounded and contain less than 2% comminuted shell. Fines contents are generally less than 10%, although occasional mud partings and interburden lenses are present in the uppermost and basal sections of the channels. The sand lenses at the margins contrast the final infilling of the centre of the channel, which consists of fine-grained sediments. The sand bodies are interpreted as lateral accretion deposits including giant point bars, deposited in fluvial and locally estuarine channels. Overlying sands associated with the ravinement surface add to the thickness of the dredgable resources, together with the underlying poorly sorted, fine to coarse-grained, angular sands containing less than 15% fines and up to 30% gravel (Type I sands). Type II fluvial sands lie within channels commonly incised during the last glacial maximum (18 000 years BP), although it is possible minor incision and limited deposition occurred during the other lowstands following the oxygen isotope stage 5e highstand of about 125 000 years BP.

Following this discussion of the type of sand resources dredged for fill in Hong Kong as examples of sand bodies, the most effective methods of investigating and quantifying these resources are described and evaluated.

Site investigation

Site investigation begins with a desk study of available data. Although this may include reconnaissance surveys, (for example Harrison 1988) and maps (for example Balson 1990), large areas of sea bed remain unexplored and it is reasonable to assume a comprehensive investigation will be required. However, the desk study does provide an indication of the characteristics of the local geological sequence to be expected and should be considered when planning the forthcoming surveys. Offshore site investigation consists of seismic acquisition, which is relatively cheap, and sampling, which is generally expensive. In the past, it has been common to drill boreholes on a pre-determined grid, e.g. a 500 m spacing, in an attempt to determine the geological structure, whilst the information provided by seismic data has been overlooked or ignored (see Orlic & Rösingh 1995). The previous section outlined the depositional environments and superimposition typically associated with sea bed sands and gravels which strongly suggests that grid sampling is only reliable for resource assessments of sea bed sand sheets and mounds. The complexities of variable bedrock levels, the courses of infilled channels, together with sand body geometry, internal structure, variability and deposit margins all remain undefined using the grid method.

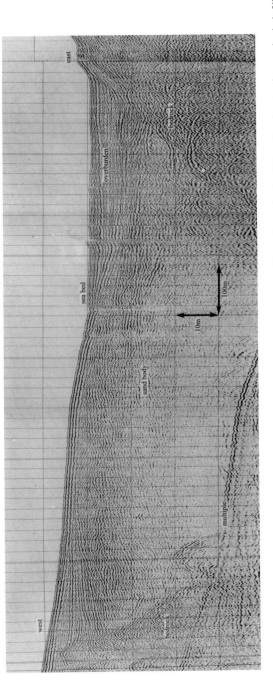
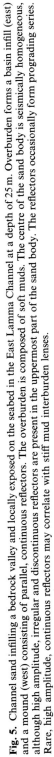

Fig. 5. Channel sand infilling a bedrock valley and locally exposed on the seabed in the East Lamma Channel at a depth of 25 m. Overburden forms a basin infill (east) and a mound (west) consisting of parallel, continuous reflectors. The overburden is composed of soft muds. The centre of the sand body is seismically homogeneous, although high amplitude, irregular and discontinuous reflectors are present in the uppermost part of the sand body. The reflectors occasionally form prograding series. Rare, high amplitude, continuous reflectors may correlate with stiff mud interburden lenses.

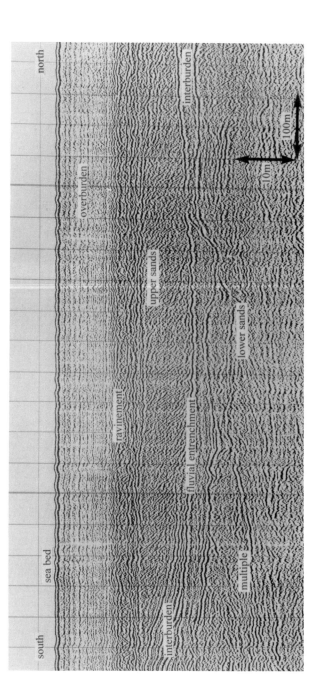

Fig. 6. A surface-tow boomer profile across sands infilling a north-south trending channel in the eastern waters of Hong Kong at a depth of 28 m. The overburden is characterized by a series of parallel, continuous, low amplitude reflectors and consists of soft silty clays. The flat lying discontinuous reflector, interpreted as a poorly defined ravinement surface, was formed during the Holocene transgression and truncates a 10 m thick channel infill forming the upper sands. The upper sands accreted following channel incision during the Last Glacial Maximum. The prograding reflector configuration is interpreted as representing lateral accretion. The interburden was deposited following an earlier phase of fluvial entrenchment.

Unfortunately the grid sampling concept persists, for example Stone (1992) and IADC (1995), demanding high sampling densities, and is therefore costly at best and probably misleading (Figs 7 & 8). It is proposed that the grid sampling technique has been superceded and this section describes the essential site investigation elements required for a confident resource assessment.

Although surveys should always begin with a seismic survey and an initial interpretation, further investigation should be designed to constrain the (i) quality and (ii) quantity of the reserve, as well as (iii) predicting the potential environmental impacts of dredging the reserve. Confident interpretation is reliant upon accurate positioning to define the limits of sand and gravel bodies offshore and it is assumed that all surveys and the majority of dredgers will utilize DGPS navigation systems offering positioning around ±1 m. Site investigation methods are briefly reviewed below and are discussed further by Le Tirant (1979) and Spigolon (1995a).

Survey strategy

If a survey is planned without consideration of geological structure, it is likely to prove expensive and unreliable in geologically complex areas. A phased approach guarantees cost effectiveness and achieves the level of detail required to plan a successful dredging strategy. Depending on the resource, it may only be necessary to complete part of the phases outlined below.

- Phase I consists of seismic acquisition on a grid size depending on the size and origin of sand bodies.

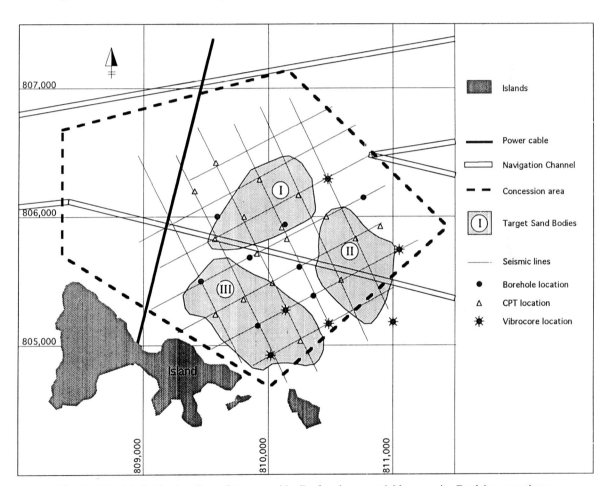

Fig. 7. A chart indicating locations of target sand bodies forming potential borrow pits. Dredging operations must consider adequate clearance for cables/pipelines, proximity to islands and exposed bedrock at sea bed and other shipping. The example site investigation consists of seismic profiling, sampling and CPTs, however the grid sampling at intersections of seismic lines is not likely to refine the understanding of the sand body. Rather, samples should be placed in geologically representative locations to assess the variability and limits of a resource.

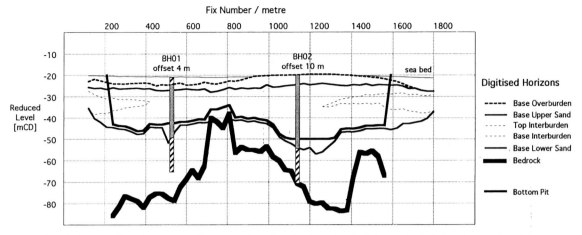

Fig. 8. Cross section of a proposed borrow pit based on horizons digitized from seismic data. The margins of the borrow pit are defined by the interburden and the base of the pit is locally controlled by channeling in the base of the sand and an irregular bedrock surface. For modelling purposes 1 m clearance is applied to the base of sand horizon and 2 m clearance is applied to the top of bedrock. Operational dredging constraints are also taken into account together with overburden to sand ratios. A very misleading interpretation would arise if the resource assessment was based solely on boreholes as shown on this figure.

A line spacing of 250–750 m may be appropriate, with lines transverse to the trend and internal structure of sand bodies. The opportunity should be taken to acquire as much sea bed and water column data as possible for use in forthcoming environmental studies and extraction plans. If possible, baseline suspended sediment concentrations should also be measured using siltmeters or water samples.
- Phase II is composed of sampling and establishing cone penetration test correlation with existing seismic data. Additional seismic acquisition, at a line spacing of less than 250 m, and sampling is carried out with the objective of understanding the small-scale variability, defining overburden/interburden and the margins of the sand body.

High resolution profiling and the sea bed

High resolution shallow seismic profiling forms the basis of a variety of offshore site investigations. Interpretation of the data reveals the configuration, relationships and a guide to the composition of the sedimentary units lying below the sea bed (Figs 4–6). The standard profiler used in sand and gravel assessment is the surface-tow boomer system (Sylwester 1983). The boomer provides a balance of penetration (up to 80 m) and resolution (around 0.5 m) in a wide range of sediments including gravels and can be processed if required. Pinger and existing chirp acoustic profiling systems often do not penetrate sands and gravels. A bathymetry survey should be carried out concurrently with the profiling using a multibeam system if required. Interpretation of side scan sonar data reveals

the configuration and composition of the sea bed sediments and provides baseline evidence for the pre-dredging condition of the sea bed. The identification of obstacles, including debris and bedrock exposures which could result in serious damage to dragheads and suction pipes, allows a dredging plan to be formulated. At a later stage interpretation problems may arise as a result of the susceptibility of acoustic systems to gas blanking in overlying muds. Geoelectric systems offer an alternative, if lower resolution, system to profile sub-sea bed successions.

Sampling

Coarse-grained clastic sea bed sediments are successfully sampled using hydraulic grabs (up to 0.5 m³ bucket) to ensure cargo quality for aggregates (coal is occasionally a deleterious contaminant) and provide baseline data for an environmental assessment and ensuing monitoring. Undisturbed sampling of the sedimentary succession underlying the sea bed is achieved by a variation on a vibrated tube, for example a vibrocorer, or a pushed/driven tube of varying length, for example a U76. The vibrocore consists of a frame with a sliding, vibrating pod and barrel which is lowered from an anchored or dynamically positioned ship to rest on the sea bed. Vibrocore samples are generally up to 6 m long (occasionally up to 9 m), recovered in a 70 mm diameter plastic liner; the system is quick and relatively cheap. However, vibrocore samples are compromised by variable recoveries. Vibrocoring to a greater depth using casing requires stable mooring. Boreholes may be drilled to depths

> −60 m for investigations of fill resources from rigs, barges or drillships. The borehole is formed using a bit and is cleaned using a bailer, pumped water or mud. Typically, 70 mm diameter samples are recovered: 1 m long, thin walled piston samples in soft silt/clays and sands, and pushed, driven, hammered or Mazier samples in loose sands and gravels. A variety of other methods have been developed, including airlift and reverse circulation (Browne 1994), for specialised sampling requirements. To complement the sampling programme, the relative density of the cohesionless sedimentary succession should also be assessed by the Standard Penetration Test (SPT) N value, whilst drilling the borehole.

Accurate compositional assessment of the sand body demands that the sampling is continuous, at least in the target sand body. Although disturbance of the samples should be kept to a minimum, two common problems often arise: the coarse gravel component of a deposit (>25 mm clast diameter) is difficult to establish due to the diameter of the sampling tube or vibrocore; and poor recoveries are typical with clean, medium to coarse-grained sands and gravels.

Cone penetration testing

The *in situ* physical properties of the sedimentary succession are commonly measured by the Cone Penetration Test (CPT) as outlined by Meigh (1987). Although of limited use within sea bed marine sand sheets, within complex channel infills and superimposed resources, the test provides additional information on consistency, type, relative density and strength of the sediment, together with refining the correlation and interpretation of seismic data. The CPT consists of a rod pushed into the sediment column, whilst measurements of cone resistance are recorded, together with the sleave friction and pore pressure. Interpretation of CPT data to provide lithological data is site specific and it is essential that the CPT is correlated with an adjacent borehole to establish the local relationship.

Testing and reporting

Site investigation reporting should be to established standards (see discussion in Spigolon 1995*b*), for example BS 5930 (1981), BS 1377 (1990) or PIANC (1984), adapted to the requirement of each project. Representative subsampling of cores for testing following extraction establishes several dredging characteristics of the deposits based on particle size distributions (PSDs) and geotechnical parameters. PSD testing should include sieves of particular importance to the project, for example the sand fraction retained on the 106 μm sieve provides additional resolution when calculating TSHD overflow. A tendency exists to concentrate subsampling in poten-

tial problem zones and this skews the data if combined PSD plots are used to define the sorting within sand units. Geotechnical parameters to be tested that may affect dredging production rates include moisture content, undrained shear strength, bulk density, compaction, index properties and carbonate content. Petrological analyses are required to assess compositional suitability of the aggregate for concrete mixtures (Gutt & Collins 1987) and to predict wear rates of dredging pumps and pipes. Grain sphericity and angularity also influence wear rates of dredge pumps and pipes. Finally, it should be recognized that the unconsidered application of standards may not always provide the information required to make decisions regarding production rates, quality and potential environmental impacts.

Data interpretation

Seismic interpretation is based on the establishment of a seismic stratigraphy, defining units which are characterised by their geometries, external relationships and the internal configuration of reflectors (Mitchum *et al.* 1977). The application of sequence stratigraphic concepts, based on sediment supply and sea level change (Posamentier *et al.* 1993; Swift *et al.* 1991), assists in placing units in their depositional context. Most importantly for the resource assessment, the interpretation of seismic units allows predictions of lithology and lithological variation within target sand and gravel bodies. Although minor modifications may arise following analysis of sample data, the geometry of the resource is delimited entirely by seismic data. It is clearly essential that the type of deposit constituting the target resource should be defined. As previously stated, for some projects the minimum acceptable sand content for fill may be as low as 60%, whereas aggregates for concrete may require as low a sand content as possible. In addition, the accurate identification of overburden and interburden forms an important component of the interpretation. Typically overburden forms sheets and interburden forms lenses.

Interpretation problems arise where gradual compositional changes occur within successions which are unlikely to result in the generation of a reflector on seismic records, but are clearly defined as resource horizons on the basis of sampling and testing. These horizons would not be picked in a geological assessment and indeed need not be reflectors, but are compositional and may cross-cut seismic units and geological structure. For the final interpretation horizons are marked on the seismic profiles. The records are digitized at every fix (assuming a velocity of sound in sediment of around 1600 m/s) and input files produced for use in the resource modelling (Fig. 8). The confidence of interpretation and assessment of risk associated with the geological aspects of dredging productivity, is therefore controlled by the geometry and composition of the resource and the quality of the site investigation data. It is clear from this analysis that the detailed understanding of the resources based on seismic interpretation and the recognition of critical horizons cannot be matched by the traditional, unrealistic method of assessment, joining levels of similar lithologies in boreholes and assuming geological units occur as flat layers.

Resource and reserve modelling

As outlined in the Introduction, it is the specification of the required sands and gravels that broadly defines the resource and reserve. Once the specification has been established, the resource is the volume of that grade of sediment lying within the offshore investigation area. Commonly, resources cannot be fully utilized due to constraints imposed by economics, extraction methodology, legal obstacles or the location of utilities (Fig. 7). The resource volumes are further reduced by pit slopes, interburden lenses and losses during the dredging process. Following deduction of all non-recoverable volumes from the resource, the reserve may be calculated.

Assessments of resources and reserves in potential dredging areas appear similar to assessments for mining and quarrying. However, there are major differences in the approach of each assessment. The developers of mines or quarries often carry out their own site investigation or hire specialist site investigation contractors to carry out a geological survey aimed at the delineation of the target resources. In-house knowledge of the developer guarantees that the survey is tailored to the mining practices to extract the target resources. This is not the case with the site investigations for dredging and reclamation works (BS 6349: 1991). Proponents typically do not have in-house capability to develop a project and seek consultants to carry out feasibility and detailed design studies. The consultants design the project according to the proponent's objective, for which the dredging or reclamation is often just a minor, although expensive detail. Therefore site investigations for dredging projects should assist the contractor to locate and quantify the resource, and establish the parameters which are relevant to assessment of settlement of sediment in the hopper and disintegration and transport of sediment as slurries through pipelines.

Use of a database

Depending on the scale of the planned marine dredging programme, individual site investigations may be considered, or the results of several investigations may have to be analysed to assess the resources. In both cases

a database may be used to structure the data collected during the site investigation and the laboratory testing. The collected data should be tailored to suit easy input, output and use. The stored data could be used to assess and manage the resources; assign dredging areas; provide contractors with the information collected during site investigations; study the production from dredging areas to reclamation or disposal sites and to study the recovery factors and production efficiency for differing sediment types and working conditions.

In order to make data input flexible, it should be possible to enter data from a keyboard, a data disk in a selected format, or by digitizing a graph or map. The output data should be available in any selected format and scaled to either a screen, a plotter (up to A0 size), a printer or disk. Data formats should be selectable to suit the importation of the information into other data processing applications, for example spreadsheets, CAD and survey programs and other databases.

Preparation of the data

It is necessary to store all of the information used during the assessment to quantify the reserve. This would normally consist of bathymetric, seismic, borehole, CPT, SPT, PSD and other geotechnical data. Other useful information includes the position of utilities, coastlines of local islands, navigation channels and marine traffic constraints. These data should be stored in a separate database. A record of all the changes that have been made to the original data during the assessment permits back analysis following exhaustion of the dredging area, if disputes arise about the volume and accessibility of the reserves.

Validation of the data

The raw data in a database are often unsuitable for the direct calculation of volumes of sand bodies, overburden and interburden. All data should be checked for their validity and compared with other sources of information before they are entered into the database. Interpreted seismic data and borehole logs form the basis of the geological assessment of the area, together with CPT, SPT, PSD and other data. As previously outlined, the data should be interpreted to suit the requirements of the dredging assessment. Resolution to 0.50 m is acceptable, as thinner layers generally cannot be worked independently by a dredger.

Although costs may be saved on site investigations if the collection of information from areas close to known features, such as rock outcrops, is avoided, these additional data should be entered into the database for the preparation of the ground model by a computer. In many site investigations the boundaries of a resource have been poorly investigated with boreholes or CPTs, although the seismic survey may be extended beyond the boundary of the target area. This seismic information then forms the basis of the ground model. PSDs, SPTs and CPTs are used to check that the borehole descriptions match with the laboratory results. If these indicate a relationship between the layer description and the values derived from the samples the system should be able to calculate an average and standard deviation of the respective values in that particular layer.

Ground model

Following the selection, addition and modification to the original data undertaken during the interpretation, the data are ready to build the ground model. To build a good ground model it is necessary to extend interpretation to areas where information is not available from the site investigation. The ground model may be generated by calculation of all relevant information on the basis of Thiessen polygons or a selected square grid. However, as soon as a connection to other systems is necessary it is advisable to have all information for the nodes or centres of a square grid.

The model should be able to generate depths to digitised horizons, isopachs for all layers and calculate the stripping ratio (the ratio of overburden over sand) for the base of each sand layer. The system should be able to present the contoured isopachs and ratios at a selected scale. Cross-sections through the multi-layered model are generated at selected lines and scales to compare the result of the modelling with the interpreted seismic lines. The grid size of the model may alter during the course of the assessment and for a feasibility study the model must be able to provide a quick estimate, although at a lower resolution. However, when detailed designs of pits need to be prepared, the model grid size has to be reduced, for example to 20 m. The larger the grid size, the greater the effect of smoothing the data, whilst computer running time will increase if the grid size is reduced. A reduced grid does not necessarily contribute to a greater accuracy in the assessment if the density of the data collected during the site investigation is spaced at greater intervals than the grid size. A grid spacing equal to, or half of, the average separation of the seismic lines is usually sufficient to build a reliable ground model. As SI information is typically much denser along seismic lines, the standard deviation of the horizons is smaller along the lines than between the lines, and depends on the horizon variability, for example a highly irregular bedrock compared with an even channel base.

Volume calculation

The ground model allows volumes of layers to be calculated as a resource in a block with the outer boundary of the dredging area as a limit. *In situ* volumes should be calculated without considering limitations caused by a maximum dredging depth or loss of material due to overburden and interburden. A second step is the calculation of volumes where a maximum dredging depth is imposed on the model. All resources below this depth should then be discarded in the volume calculation. Furthermore, a minimum layer thickness may be selected for exploitation, and thinner layers should not be considered. It is also important to recognize that utilities not only sterilize the underlying resource, but a large volume associated with a safety zone and stable slopes.

When calculating the reserves, the reliability and resolution of the data should be considered. TSHDs work to tolerances of several metres horizontally and a metre vertically. A sub-seabed layer less than 2 m thick should not be considered, as the horizons are defined to an accuracy of 1 m and the dredger requires a layer thickness of at least 2 m to make dredging worthwhile. Irregularities in the horizons also result in the dredging of unsuitable sediment before the reserve is exhausted. For the estimates, rock outcrops must be avoided with a 2 m safety margin due to the risk of damage to the draghead and the suction pipe.

Cross-sections through the area

In order to validate and to improve the model, it should be possible to generate cross sections along selected lines through the area which show all relevant information (Fig. 8). The offset of all boreholes and other data points selected should be given, along with the SI data. It is necessary to have the choice to change the maximum offset of the data points to be taken into account for each line. The effect of smoothing the data can be checked in this stage. PSD data and other soil properties should be correlated with the units defined in the assessment.

Slopes

In view of the fact that, especially in deep deposits, slopes cover a high percentage of the Marine Borrow Area (MBA), it is advisable to quantify the volumes that are found within the slopes. Therefore the system should be able to generate a borrow pit layout, to a chosen depth, with selected barter slopes for each soil type, for example 1 in 3 for sand and 1 in 5 for soft muds. Finally, the volumes for each of the selected layers within the boundaries of the selected borrow pit are calculated.

Overflow losses and assessment of environmental impacts

The environmental impacts associated with dredging form an important component of an increasing number of dredging projects and many are now subject to some form of Environmental Impact Assessment. Impacts from dredging arise from the physical disruption of the sea bed, which occurs over relatively small areas, and from sediments within the overflow mixture entering the water column.

Overflowing occurs from the keel or over spillways of a TSHD (Fig. 1) and has been briefly considered by Pennekamp & Quaak (1990). As a result of dredging trials, Whiteside *et al.* (in press) estimated that 80% of sediment contained in the overflow is transported to the seabed within a density flow and around 20% of the sediment forms a plume which becomes established around 250 m behind the dredger. Therefore high dredging production rates commonly lead to the rapid, proximal deposition of fine sands and silts on the sea bed from density flows close to the dredger, and fine silts and clays settling from suspension distally, perhaps up to

several kilometres downstream of the dredger. Consequently both proximal and distal sedimentation rates are likely to increase above background levels. Sensitive receivers around the dredging area may include corals, intertidal and sea bed communities, which may be often susceptible to increased sedimentation rates (Hodgson 1994), whereas fisheries are often considered to be more sensitive to variation in suspended sediment levels.

Realistic prediction of overflow rates is therefore of critical importance when predicting environmental impacts. Site investigation provides the required data for; (i) assessing baseline conditions in and around the dredging area and (ii) input into a dredging model.

Baseline conditions

Site investigation provides baseline suspended sediment and sea bed sediment data associated with the natural

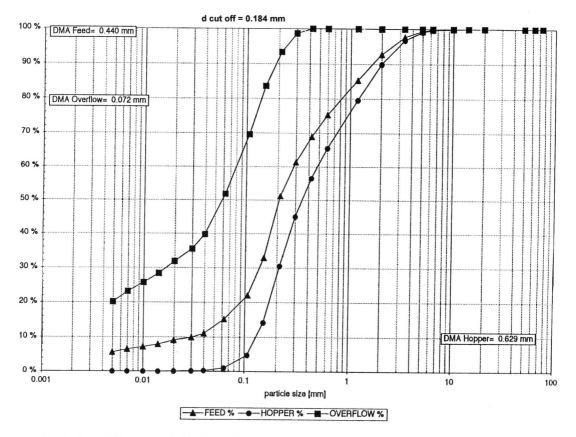

Fig. 9. *In situ* PSD compared with the predicted hopper and overflow PSDs following dredging of a moderately well-sorted, medium-grained sand with a typical 8000 m³ TSHD. The predicted hopper PSD indicates that a significant proportion of the sub-100 μm sediment present in the reserve is lost to the overflow and over 60% of the sediment in the overflow is coarser than 30 μm. The medium to coarse silt and very fine sand will form a density current which flows down onto the sea bed close to the dredging area. In this type of sand reserve, overall dredging losses are estimated to be around 25%.

sediment regime. In areas where benthic communities are adapted to high sedimentation rates, for example in deltas and estuaries, or disturbance of the sea bed, for example stormy or intensely trawled seas, it is possible that the impacts of overflowing will be insignificant. However in areas of low suspended sediment levels and depositional rates, mitigation measures should be taken.

Dredging model

The dredging process can be simulated using a dredging model. The dredging model developed by DEMAS takes into account all dredging parameters, e.g. pumping rates, mixture densities, loading level, hopper configuration and location of overflow, in combination with the characteristics of the dredged sediments, ie. the reserves. The model predicts overflow rates and overflow PSDs (Fig. 9) for the average or the range of deposits forming the reserves throughout the loading time. As an example, the sediment losses associated with the overflow occurring during loading of a typical 8000 m³ TSHD are shown in Table 1.

The information obtained from the dredging model may be combined with a hydrodynamic model and used in environmental impact studies to ensure that the potential impacts associated with dredging are assessed and mitigated through operational restrictions prior to the beginning of operations. Once a realistic input has been defined by the dredging model, the plume model predicts compliance with Target/Action/Trigger (TAT) levels established for environmental monitoring and audit. Alternatively, the contractor may propose and develop mitigation measures throughout the course of the dredging operation. Mitigation measures must accommodate all the factors described above and include working in conjunction with currents (tidal, oceanic and seasonal), controlling the dredging method (e.g. minimise overflowing) and restricting the dredging area. In conclusion, an unrepresentative site investigation can lead to unexpectedly high overflow losses, increased depositional rates and elevated suspended sediment levels. This may result in unacceptable environmental impacts and culminate in a restriction of production rates.

Conclusions

Offshore sands and gravels are finite resources and have been deposited in fluvial and marine environments. The sand and gravel bodies are often complex, superimposed and combine to form resources characterized externally by irregular geometries and internally by abrupt vertical and lateral compositional variation.

To assess and understand the variabilty of these resources and ensure efficient production of high quality cargoes, a dedicated site investigation should be designed. An effective investigation will consist of high resolution seismic profiling, sampling and CPTs, and designed to define the resource and its limits, together with the identification of overburden/interburden. Following interpretation and the establishment of a database, the resource and reserve assessment based on digitised horizons defines the dredging area, volumes and predicts losses. A dredging strategy based on this data is formulated and, if necessary, an environmental mitigation plan proposed.

Consequently a well-planned site investigation benefits both the contractor and the client through the development of an efficient and effective dredging programme. Compared to the cost of developing dredging technology, a site investigation is a cheap and cost-effective investment; it increases confidence in estimation of production rates, identifies possible sources of delay, permits dredging of marginal resources and ensures the quality of the dredged cargo. A thorough, integrated site investigation will enhance efficiency and hence profitability, as well as giving the opportunity to effectively mitigate against unacceptable environmental impacts. For these reasons the benefits of site investigation must become the focus of increased scrutiny within the dredging industry in the future.

Acknowledgements. This paper is published with the permission of the Director of Civil Engineering, Hong Kong Government. The authors are grateful for the critical reviews of Gerben Postma and John Scott together with the views of their other colleagues in DEMAS and the Geotechnical Engineering Office.

Table 1. *Overflow rates from a typical TSHD with an inboard pump loading in about 1.5 hours, dredging a moderately well-sorted sand containing 20% fines (Fig. 9) from a depth of 40 m and a cycle time of around 5 hours. The sorting and concentration of sediment in the overflow does not remain constant throughout loading. The sediment concentration increases and becomes increasingly poorly sorted as the hopper fills*

Payload per trip (net sand reserve, m³)	Sand production per week (net sand reserve, m³)	Overflow losses per trip (Mg)	Overflow losses per week (Mg)
6500	200 000	5000	150 000

References

ANON 1981. *BS 5930:1981. Code of Practice for Site Investigation.* BSI, London.
——1990. *BS 1377:1990. British Standard Methods of Test for Soils for Civil Engineering Purposes, Parts 1–9.* BSI, London.

——1991. *BS 6349:1991. Maritime Structures Part 5. Code of Practice for dredging and Land Reclamation.* BSI, London.

——1995. *Aggregates from the Sea – Why Dredge?* British Marine Aggregate Producers Association, London, 2nd Edition.

BALSON, P. S. 1990. *Spurn (53N-00W) Sea bed sediments.* 1 : 250 000 Offshore map series, British Geological Survey, Nottingham, UK.

BELLAMY, A. G. 1995. Extension of the British landmass: evidence from shelf sediment bodies in the English Channel. *In*: PREECE, R. C. (ed.) *Island Britain: a Quaternary Perspective.* Geological Society, London, Special Publication, **96**, 47–62.

BOARDMAN, J. 1987. *Periglacial Processes and Landforms in Britain and Ireland.* Cambridge University Press.

BRAY, R. N. 1979. *Dredging: A Handbook for Engineers.* Edward Arnold, London.

BROWNE, I. 1994. Placer drilling in Australia. *Sea Technology,* June 1994, 31–37.

DREWRY, D. 1986. *Glacial Geological Processes.* Edward Arnold, London.

EVANS, C. D. R. 1988. Seismo-stratigraphy of early Holocene sand banks. *In*: WHITESIDE, P. G. D. & WRAGGE-MORELY, N. (eds) *Marine Sand and Gravel Resources of Hong Kong.* Geological Society of Hong Kong, University of Hong Kong, Hong Kong, 45–52.

FYFE, J. A., NELLER, R. J., OWEN, R. B., SELBY, I. C. & SHAW, R. 1997. Sequence stratigraphy: refining the understanding of the offshore Quaternary succession of Hong Kong. *In*: JABLONSKI, N. G. *The changing face of East Asia during the Quaternary, Proceedings of the 4th International Conference on the Evolution of the East Asian Environment,* Centre of Asian Studies, University of Hong Kong, Hong Kong, 189–205.

GUTT, W. & COLLINS, R. J. 1987. *Sea-dredged Aggregates in Concrete.* Building Research Establishment Information Paper 7/87, Watford, UK.

HARRISON, D. J. 1988. *The Marine Sand and Gravel Resources off Gt. Yarmouth and Southwold, East Anglia.* British Geological Survey Technical Report WB/88/9C, Nottingham, UK.

HEIN, F. J., SYVITSKI, J. P. M., DREDGE, L. A. & LONG, B. F. 1993. Quaternary sedimentation and marine placers along the North Shore, Gulf of St. Lawrence. *Canadian Journal of Earth Science,* **30**, 553–574.

HODGSON, G. 1994. The environmental impact of marine dredging in Hong Kong. *Coastal Management in Tropical Asia,* **2**, 2–8.

INTERNATIONAL ASSOCIATION OF DREDGING COMPANIES (IADC) 1995. International Dredging Seminar.

JAMES, J. W. C. 1993. *The Offshore Geology of the Area around Lantau Island, Hong Kong.* British Geological Survey Technical Report WB/93/13R, Nottingham, UK.

LE TIRANT, P. 1979. *Seabed Reconnaissance and Offshore Soil Mechanics for the Installation of Petroleum Structures.* Institute Francais du Petrole Publications, Paris, Editions Technip.

LONG, Y. & HUO, C. 1990. The characteristics of sedimentation in Late Quaternary in Zhujiang (Pearl) River Delta. *In: Proceedings of the First International Conference on Asian Marine Geology,* China Ocean Press, Beijing, China, 213–223.

MEIGH, A. C. 1987. *Cone Penetration Testing: Methods and Interpretation.* CIRIA Ground Engineering Report: In-situ Testing, Butterworths, London, UK.

MIALL, A. D. 1992. Alluvial deposits. *In*: WALKER, R. G. & JAMES, N. P. (eds) *Facies Models: Response to Sea Level Change.* Geological Association of Canada, St. Johns, Newfoundland, Canada. 119–142.

MITCHUM, R. M. JR., VAIL, P. R. & SANGREE, J. B. 1977. Seismic stratigraphy and global changes of sea level, Part 6: Stratigraphical interpretation of seismic reflection patterns in depositional systems. *In*: PAYTON, C. E. (ed.) *Seismic stratigraphy – Applications to Hydrocarbon Exploration.* AAPG Memoir, **26**, 117–133.

MURRAY, R. J., ROBINSON, D. A. & SOWARD, C. L. 1994. Southern Gold Coast Nourishment project. *Terra et Aqua,* **56**, 12–24.

NUMMEDAL, D., PILKEY, O. H. & HOWARD, J. D. 1987. *Sea Level Fluctuation and Coastal Evolution.* Society of Economic Paleontologists and Mineralogists Special Publication, **41**.

OOMS, K., WOODS, N. & WHITESIDE, P. G. D. 1994. Marine sand dredging: key to the development of Hong Kong. *Terra et Aqua,* **54**, 7–16.

ORLIC, B. & RÖSINGH, J. W. 1995. Three-dimensional geomodelling for offshore aggregate resources assessment. *Quarterly Journal of Engineering Geology,* **28**, 385–391.

ORTON, G. J. & READING, H. G. 1993. Variability of deltaic processes in terms of sediment supply, with particular emphasis on grain size. *Sedimentology,* **40**, 475–512.

PARRISH, F. G. 1987. Management of UK marine aggregate dredging. *Underwater Technology,* **14**, 20–25.

PENNEKAMP, J. G. S. & QUAAK, M. P. 1990. Impact on the environment of turbidity caused by dredging. *Terra et Aqua,* **42**, 10–20.

PIANC 1984. *Classification of Soils and Rocks to be Dredged.* Supplement to Bulletin No. 47. Brussels, Belgium.

PIANC 1992. *Beneficial Uses of Dredged Material, A Practical Guide.* Brussels, Belgium.

POSAMENTIER, H. W., SUMMERHAYES, C. P., HAQ, B. U. ALLEN, G. P. 1993. *Sequence Stratigraphy and Facies Associations.* Special Publication of the International Association of Sedimentologists, **18**. Blackwell, Oxford.

SELBY, I. C. 1992. An introduction to marine aggregates and their Quaternary origin. *In*: GRAY, J. M. (ed.) *Applications of Quaternary Research.* Quaternary Proceedings No. 2 Quaternary Research Association, Cambridge, UK, 25–31.

SHACKLETON, N. J. 1987. Oxygen isotopes, ice volume and sea level. *Quaternary Science Reviews,* **6**, 183–190.

SPIGOLON, S. J. 1995a. *Geotechnical Site Investigations for Dredging Projects.* Dredging Research Technical Note DRP-2–12, US Army Engineer Waterways Experiment Station, Vicksburg, MS, USA.

——1995b. *Geotechnical Descriptors for Dredgability.* Dredging Resarch Technical Note DRP-2–13, US Army Engineer Waterways Experiment Station, Vicksburg, MS, USA.

STONE, M. J. 1992. Soil investigation. *Terra et Aqua,* **48**, 12–19.

STRIDE, A. H. 1982. *Offshore Tidal Sands.* Chapman and Hall, London.

SUTER, J. R., MOSSA, J. & PENLAND, S. 1989. Preliminary assessments of the occurrence and effects of utilisation of sand and aggregate resources of the Louisiana inner shelf. *Marine Geology*, **90**, 31–37.

SWIFT, D. J. P., OERTEL, G. F., TILLMAN, R. W. & THORNE, J. A. 1991. *Shelf Sand and Sandstone Bodies. Geometry, Facies and Sequence Stratigraphy*. International Association of Sedimentologists Special Publication, **14**. Blackwell, Oxford.

SYLWESTER, R. E. 1983. Single-channel, high-resolution, seismic-reflection profiling: A review of the fundamentals and instrumentation. *In*: GEYER, R. A. (ed.) *CRC Handbook of Geophysical Exploration at Sea*. CRC, Boca Raton, 77–122.

TSURUSAKI, K., IWASAKI, T. & ARITA, M. 1988. Seabed sand mining in Japan. *Marine Mining*, **7**, 49–67.

VAN OORSCHOT, J. H. & VAN RAALTE, G. H. 1989. Beach nourishment; execution methods and developments in technology. *Coastal Engineering*, **16**, 23–42.

WHITESIDE, P. G. D., OOMS, K. & POSTMA, G. M. 1996. The generation and decay of plumes from sand dredging overflow. *Proceedings of the XIV World Dredging Congress, Amsterdam, The Netherlands*.

The UK marine sand and gravel dredging industry: an application of Quaternary geology

Andrew G. Bellamy

United Marine Dredging Limited, Francis House, Shopwhyke Road, Chichester PO20 6AD, UK

Abstract. Marine sands and gravels currently contribute 24% (over 20 million tonnes/year) of the total sand and gravel aggregate consumption of Great Britain. To maintain or increase this contribution into the future, the identification, assessment and licensing of additional sand and gravel resource areas is of fundamental importance. Research into the Quaternary history of the continental shelf surrounding the UK assists in the prediction of sand and gravel resource locations. Similarly, resource assessment is significantly improved through an understanding of the origin and formation of these Quaternary deposits.

Geological considerations also feature strongly in the management of existing dredging licence areas and in the acquisition of future licences from the Crown Estate. Precise resource assessment, coupled with accurate dredger positioning and track recording systems, minimizes the extent of dredged sea bed, thereby limiting environmental impact and improving the consistency of dredged cargoes. Also important is the need to overcome marine aggregate prejudice which arises from the perception by some customers that marine dredged sands and gravels differ markedly from those obtained onshore. Central to this issue is the argument that some of the most substantial marine deposits originated in subaerial environments at similar times and by the same processes as their present-day terrestrial equivalents, having been deposited in Quaternary cold climate fluvial environments.

Marine dredged sand and gravel aggregates currently contribute 24% (over 20 million tonnes per year) of total aggregate consumption in Great Britain. This contribution is significantly higher in southeastern England (over 30%) due to the exhaustion of land-based supplies and because the advantages of relatively low marine transport costs apply. In densely populated southeastern England, the benefits of landing large aggregate tonnages close to the point of demand from distant sources and without the need for road transport are clear. Of equal significance nationally are the benefits to be gained through the reduction in the pressure to quarry land of residential, agricultural or conservational significance, avoiding disturbance, noise, dust and loss of amenity value. In 1996, taking into account UK construction demand, exports and other outlets, a total of over 26 million tonnes of marine sands and gravels were dredged from licence areas in UK waters (Crown Estate 1996). From UK demand alone, over 400 hectares of land will be saved from sand and gravel production each year (the British Marine Aggregate Producers Association (BMAPA), 1995). Whilst the majority of marine aggregate landings are concentrated in south-eastern Britain, there are other areas of considerable regional significance – for example 90% of sand supply to South Wales is derived from sources in the Bristol Channel. In this region, alternative land-based resources are sparsely distributed, commonly of poor quality and are largely inaccessible due to planning constraints in conservation and recreation areas (Liverpool University 1992). Significant quantities of aggregate are exported to northern Europe from UK licence areas, totalling 6.7 million tonnes in 1996. Recipient countries include Holland, Germany, Belgium and France.

UK marine dredged sands and gravels are predominantly used in the construction industry, notably in the production of concrete. Major projects to which marine aggregates have been supplied for concrete have included the construction of the Dartford Bridge, the National Stadium in Cardiff, Canary Wharf, the Thames Barrier, Sizewell B power station, the Second Severn Crossing and, still ongoing at the time of writing, the Jubilee Line Extension. In addition to the supply of aggregates for concrete, marine sand and gravel is used for various other civil engineering tasks such as beach nourishment and fill projects. It has been argued by Hydraulics Research (1993) that the supply of marine sands and gravels for beach nourishment can represent an environmentally beneficial solution to shoreline erosion since the sands and gravels dredged would not otherwise be transported onshore by natural processes. In addition, marine sediments are commonly readily available in the large volumes required for beach nourishment and may be selected to closely resemble the pre-existing beach sediments. In 1996, 7.2 million tonnes of marine sand and gravel was dredged for fill and beach nourishment projects (Crown Estate 1996).

BELLAMY, A. G. 1998. The UK marine sand and gravel dredging industry: an application of Quaternary geology. In: LATHAM, J.-P. (ed.) 1998. *Advances in Aggregates and Armourstone Evaluation*. Geological Society, London, Engineering Geology Special Publications, **13**, 33–45.

Fig. 1. The United Marine Dredging Limited trailing suction dredger MV 'City of Westminster' dredging sandy gravel in a licence area off East Anglia. The vessel has a cargo hopper capacity of 3000 m³ and can dredge in water depths of up to 45 m. The dredge pipe is deployed from the port side and sediment is pumped into the hold as a saturated slurry via two loading towers positioned on the starboard side. The objects in the foreground are the bucket scrapers which are used to offload the cargo on to a ship to shore conveyor belt at the landing point.

During the past ten years, the UK aggregate dredging industry has invested large sums of money to build and re-equip dredging vessels and to provide the associated wharves and aggregate processing facilities. The industry now operates over 35 dredgers, some capable of dredging in water depths of 50 m. The cargo capacities of UK offshore aggregate dredgers range from 600 to 8500 tonnes and hopper capacities of 5000 tonnes are now common (Fig. 1). The industry currently employs approximately 2500 personnel, including dredger crews, wharf and other shore-based employees.

The current process of obtaining a licence to dredge offshore aggregate begins with the granting by the Crown Estate of a Prospecting Licence through competitive tender for areas of interest. If a viable aggregate deposit is located, then a Production Licence Application is made to the Crown Estate who owns the mineral rights (excluding oil and gas) to the UK continental shelf. Decisions as to whether aggregate dredging can take place in an area (a Production Licence) are made by the Department of the Environment, Transport and the Regions (DETR), Welsh Office or Scottish Office after extensive consultation with interested parties. Studies of the potential effects of dredging on coastal processes are made by consultants (normally Hydraulics Research Wallingford Ltd) commissioned by the Crown Estate. Other important consultees include MAFF, English Nature, commercial fishermens' associations, local authorities and archaeological bodies. The consultative process whereby dredging licence applications are determined is known as the Government View Procedure and licences are normally issued by the Crown Estate to applicant companies provided that a favourable Government View is given either by the DETR or Welsh Office. This procedure is currently under review, although extensive consultation will remain a key feature.

Government forecasts state that provision should be made in England alone for marine dredged sources to supply 320 million tonnes of construction aggregate over the period 1992–2006 (DoE 1994). To achieve this level of supply, an annual average of 21.33 million tonnes of marine sand and gravel must be landed – twice current production levels. In addition to this, aggregate supply to Wales and exports to northern Europe must be considered together with projected needs for beach nourishment, which in total suggests an overall marine sand and gravel requirement of around *500 million tonnes* to 2006 (BMAPA 1995).

The application of Quaternary geology

Introduction

Given the increasing need for marine sands and gravels and the fact that they are a finite resource, the identification and accurate assessment of resource areas is of fundamental importance. Geological considerations are central to the future of the industry, with the need to define and quantify resources on the sea bed, assess their quality and predict possible future dredging areas. Research into the origins and formation of marine sands and gravels will lead to a better appreciation of the processes responsible for their transport and deposition. This in turn will play a significant role in determining the success of the industry in the future by subsequently allowing reasoned prediction and assessment of other sand and gravel resource locations.

The UK marine aggregate dredging industry extracts sands and gravels from the sea bed forming the inner continental shelf of northwestern Europe. The industry currently operates offshore southern Britain in water depths of less than 45 m (and commonly less than 30 m), generally within 25 km of the Welsh and English coastline (Fig. 2). The locations of dredging areas are determined not only by the position of a sand or gravel deposit but also by the water depth, the dredging depth capability of the vessels concerned, the distance of the deposit from the intended landing points and various environmental constraints. Whilst primarily a geological consideration, the choice of dredging area is therefore made by addressing a wide variety of separate issues. This paper will focus on the geological setting of the aggregate dredging industry, and its use in resource assessment, extraction operations and licensing.

Origins of marine sands and gravels

The origins and depositional history of marine sand and gravel deposits determine the location of aggregate resources on the northwest European continental shelf. Events during the most recent geological Period, the Quaternary, influenced the evolution of these sediments and included the repeated and large-scale climatic and sea level changes that are widely held to have affected the British Isles and adjoining continental shelf during the past 1–2 million years.

Glacio-eustatic sea level falls resulted in the subaerial exposure and subaerial linkage of parts of the continental shelf to the present British landmass under cold climatic regimes. Thus the southern North Sea basin and English Channel became exposed concurrently with the growth of ice sheets in the north and northwest of Britain (Jansen *et al.* 1979; Balson & Jeffrey 1991; Gibbard 1995). Pantin & Evans (1984) suggest from evidence of ice rafting that sea level during the Late Devensian (last glacial stage) was at least around −113 m in the Celtic Sea and Belderson *et al.* (1986) report from tidal current modelling that sea level was around −100 m when the now relict tidal sand ridges of the south-western Celtic Sea were formed. Jelgersma (1979) suggests a sea level of −120 m to −130 m during the last glacial maximum based on data from the continental shelves off the USA and from calculations of the volume of land-based ice caps. This figure is echoed by Baeteman *et al.* (1992) who also consider that relative sea level in the southern North Sea off Belgium was about −45 m during the early Holocene (<10 000 years).

Given these environmental conditions, the coastline of southern Britain has been located significantly seaward of its present position during the Quaternary and at times has possibly been close to the shelf break. Rivers and grounded ice masses therefore extended across parts of the continental shelf around southern Britain during Quaternary cold stages and were probably important agents in transporting and depositing sands and gravels onto the shelf. Since sands and gravels attributed to glacial and fluvial origins are well known on land, it is therefore likely that similar and related deposits occur on the adjoining continental shelf. Indeed, since the rivers which drained the inner continental shelf also

flowed from the present landmass of Britain, sands and gravels quarried in present river valleys on land commonly have the same origin and lithology as those offshore. This aspect of aggregate geology is commonly highlighted by the industry in demonstrating the similarity of marine aggregates to their land-based equivalents (e.g. BMAPA 1995) and is elaborated later.

The origins of marine sand and gravel resources on the north European continental shelf are discussed in more detail by Harrison *et al.* (1998).

The investigation, identification and exploitation of current sand and gravel aggregate resources

Reconnaissance surveying and subsequent mapping of the geology of the UK continental shelf by the British Geological Survey (BGS) and others over the last

Fig. 2. Current Crown Estate licensed dredging areas off the UK in relation to inner continental shelf bathymetry.

20 years or so has revealed some of the principle Quaternary features and deposits of the shelf (Holmes *et al.* 1993). Channels attributed to fluvial erosion have been detected both in the Thames Estuary and off the south coast of England and significant areas of diamictons interpreted as glacial tills have been mapped in the southern and central North Sea. Figure 3 shows that these areas correspond to some of the largest concentrations of current sand and gravel dredging licence areas and shows the link between the location of commercial deposits and centres of former fluvial, glaciofluvial and glacial activity on the inner shelf.

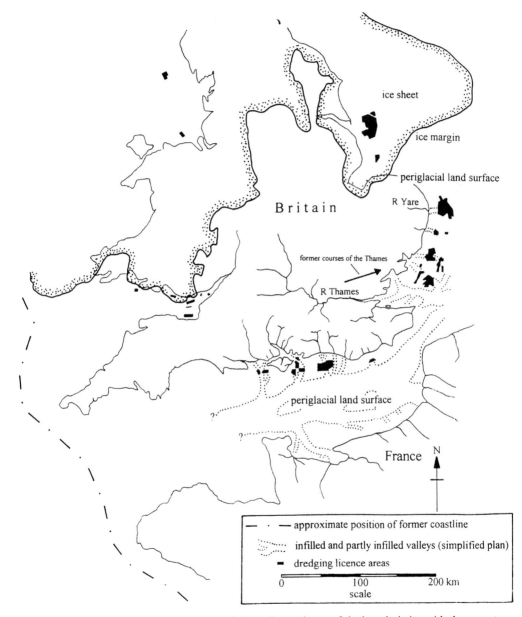

Fig. 3. Simplified reconstruction of southern Britain at the maximum of the last glaciation with the current Crown Estate licensed dredging areas superimposed. The ultimate source of much of the sand and, especially, gravel within these areas was glacial and fluvial erosion and deposition in a cold climate. Some reworking of shelf sands and gravels occurred during marine transgression.

Broad-scale regional maps are unfortunately insufficient on their own to define dredging areas and it is normally necessary for a dredging company to undertake detailed prospecting to establish the location of a viable deposit. These prospecting surveys employ high-resolution shallow seismic equipment commonly run at a line spacing of 100–500 m, followed by sea bed grab and core sampling with sample densities of commonly over 5 per km². The locations of the samples are normally determined by initial interpretation of the seismic data. The high cost of offshore sampling prohibits denser sampling. Samples generally assist seismic interpretation and summary core logs are shown on certain seismic profile examples below. Sampling also provides valuable information regarding sediment composition, aggregate quality and grading and can be used in conjunction with seismic data to calculate reserve volumes. Techniques of effective resource assessment are discussed further by Selby & Ooms (1998).

On the inner shelf offshore southeastern Britain, prospecting has concentrated along the courses of the channels depicted in Fig. 3 and has revealed complex channel infills and submerged terrace deposits considered to be associated with cold climate fluvial activity during periods of lower than present sea level on the inner shelf (e.g. D'Olier 1975; Bellamy 1995; Bridgland & D'Olier 1995). The channels typically contain highly localized but occasionally thick (>5 m) gravelly deposits lying in close association with finer-grained sands and

muds (Fig. 4). There is normally little evidence from seismic profiles for marine modification of these original fluvial deposits although, as shown in Fig. 4 the upper surfaces of the infills are commonly truncated at the sea bed by a ravinement surface considered to have been formed by shoreface erosion and marine planation during marine transgression(s). The resulting low relief of the sea bed commonly belies the complexity and irregularity of the deposits lying immediately beneath (Fig. 5) and limits the use of bathymetric data in locating former shelf valley systems. The locations of former valley systems may also be masked by overlying sandbanks and sandwave fields.

Seismic units within the infilled channels are commonly unconformably superimposed and display markedly contrasting geometries and seismic signatures. Geometries displayed include channel margin lenses, wedges or banks with erosional boundaries against underlying strata; basin or channel infills onlapping adjacent units and thin, discontinuous sheets or veneers which may be mounded. Stratigraphic analysis suggests that multiple phases of cut-and-fill have locally occurred to form the infills, e.g. Figs 5 & 6. In these examples, initial incision into bedrock has occurred followed by deposition of 'fine-grained sediments' in Fig. 5 and 'gravelly sediments' in Fig. 6. Further subsequent erosion and sedimentation occurred to form the remainder of the deposits resulting in a complex channel infill. Cut-and-fill events with associated deposit truncation and 'blanketing' of gravels

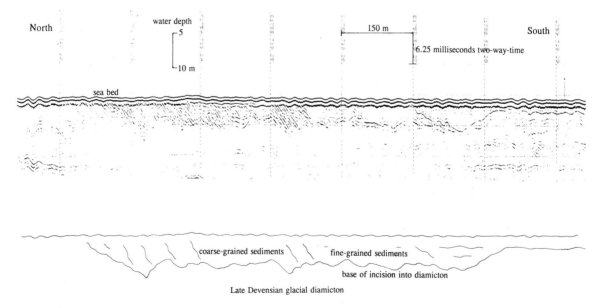

Fig. 4. Interpreted seismic (boomer) profile of a completely infilled depression located in a dredging area off the Humber Estuary. The upper surface of the infill is considered to be truncated by a ravinement surface formed during marine transgression. Note the considerable vertical exaggeration on this and on the other seismic profiles in this paper.

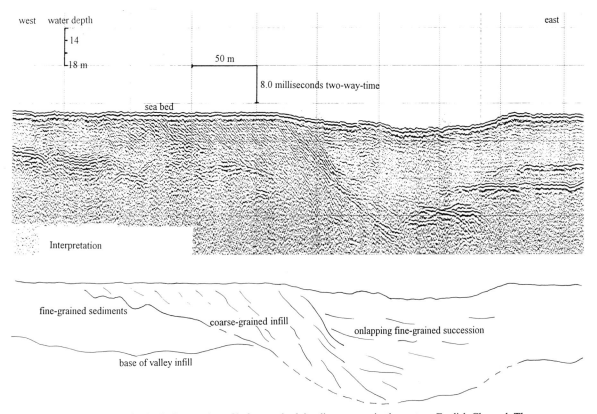

Fig. 5. Interpreted seismic (boomer) profile from a dredging licence area in the eastern English Channel. The sea bed 'outcrop' of the coarse-grained infill (indicated by the high amplitude dipping reflectors) is only about 100 m wide and would necessitate accurate dredger positioning if it were to be dredged without contamination from the adjacent fine-grained sediments. Such positioning is possible using modern navigation and track display systems.

by onlapping fine-grained sediments commonly result in the development of overburdens and interburdens (Selby & Ooms 1998) which significantly constrain the 'dredge-ability' of a possible resource given current technology and environmental considerations. This is illustrated in Fig. 6 where a fine-grained channel infill forms an overburden up to 7 m thick over gravelly sediments, restricting their sea bed occurrence to a small area in the southwest of the profile.

The coarse-grained (commonly gravelly) sediments can generally be distinguished by high acoustic amplitude irregular or dipping reflectors which infer high energy sedimentation. Reflector patterns can also suggest specific depositional styles, such as progradation or lateral accretion in the case of dipping reflectors (Fig. 5), although caution should be exercised in interpretation given that similar patterns can be the product of acoustic backscatter (or artefacts) from gravel clasts, notably cobbles or boulders. By contrast, fine-grained sediments are commonly distinguished either by low amplitude, low angle and continuous reflectors which onlap bounding

reflectors or by reflector-free areas and homogeneous backscatter (Figs 6 & 7).

It is suggested that the coarse-grained elements of the channel infills originated mainly in cold climate (periglacial) fluvial environments, possibly in braided rivers, in which gravelly sediments were transported in high energy flows. These were fed either by glacial meltwater or by seasonal snow and ground ice melt in areas more distant from glacial margins, for example in southern England and the English Channel. Infills of finer-grained sediments which onlap the gravelly deposits are suggested to be the products of lower energy environments and sedimentation, possibly in abandoned river channels, meandering single channel rivers or estuaries which developed during climatic amelioration and associated marine transgressive phases on the inner continental shelf.

Bedrock seismic signatures in high resolution shallow seismic data vary according to the rock type and structure but are commonly distinguished by either homogeneous backscatter or by high ampitude continuous reflectors which may be interpreted to provide

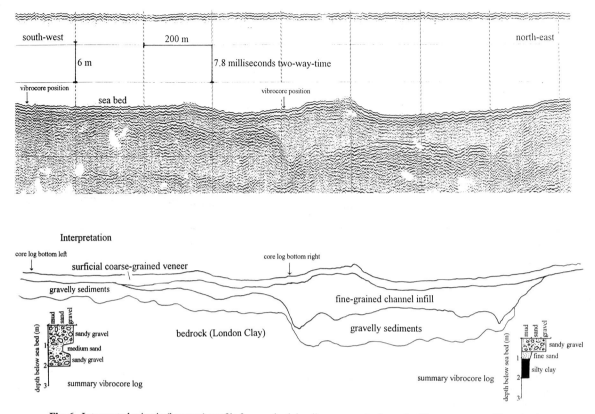

Fig. 6. Interpreted seismic (boomer) profile from a dredging licence area in the outer Thames estuary. The seismic data is interpreted to show a completely infilled channel which trends generally west to east across the area. Most of the gravelly sediment is not extractable by conventional aggregate dredging techniques because of the extensive and thick overburden of fine-grained sediment infilling the channel. Vibrocoring has assisted (and confirmed) the seismic interpretation.

evidence of dipping, folded or faulted strata. Bedrock reflectors are commonly truncated either at sea bed or by the bases of infilled channels (Fig. 6).

The location, geometry and thickness of potential aggregate resources determines the operation of the dredging vessels within the area and it is the role of the geologist to define dredge runs or patches which are worked either by the dredger trailing over an extensive deposit or anchoring over a thick but localised deposit. The location adopted for dredging is also influenced by the sediment required for the cargo. For example a 60% gravel, 40% sand content is the typical requirement for concrete production, whilst a beach recharge contract might specify a pure sand or gravel depending on specific requirements.

Figure 8 depicts an area of sea bed to the east of the Isle of Wight where anchor dredging has formed a shallow depression in gravels thought by their location to have been deposited by the former Solent River (Dyer 1975). This particular deposit is worked repeatedly at the

same locality to a depth of about 5 m below the general level of the sea bed. The size and accessibility of the extractable resource (the reserve) is however constrained by a localised, mounded overburden veneer of silty fine-grained sands up to about 2.5 m thick which unconformably overlies thick sandy gravels (Fig.8).

Relatively thin deposits may be worked by trail dredgers which remove deposits to create a furrow 1–2 m wide and typically 20–25 cm deep across an area. Here, care must be taken to avoid dredging into areas of contamination, such as clay or peat deposits, which are also highlighted during prospecting surveys. Again, it is the geologists' role to determine the location of potential areas of comtamination and to locate extractable aggregate reserves within or between them. One such example lies 10 km offshore the mouth of the River Yare, Great Yarmouth, Norfolk, where there is a large cluster of dredging areas (Fig. 3). Detailed surveying has shown that the gravelly deposits in this region are locally interspersed with overlying peat and clay-filled basins or

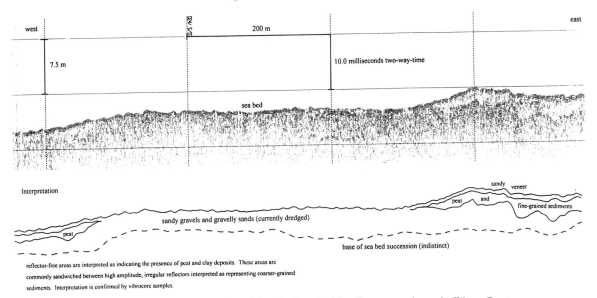

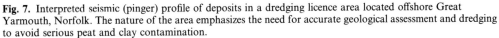

reflector-free areas are interpreted as indicating the presence of peat and clay deposits. These areas are
commonly sandwiched between high amplitude, irregular reflectors interpreted as representing coarser-grained
sediments. Interpretation is confirmed by vibrocore samples.

Fig. 7. Interpreted seismic (pinger) profile of deposits in a dredging licence area located offshore Great
Yarmouth, Norfolk. The nature of the area emphasizes the need for accurate geological assessment and dredging
to avoid serious peat and clay contamination.

channels creating a complex, irregular pattern of contrasting sea bed and near-sea bed sediments (Fig. 7).
These sediments are tentatively suggested to be the inner
shelf correlatives of the Quaternary Yare Valley and
Breydon Formations mapped by Arthurton *et al.* (1994)
within the infilled valley of the River Yare in eastern
Norfolk and immediately offshore. The coarse-grained
Yare Valley Formation was identified from boreholes
and tentatively from seismic profiles and was ascribed a
Pleistocene fluvial origin by these workers. The overlying Breydon Formation consists of muddy organic-
rich sediments including peat and was interpreted as a
nearshore/tidal flat/marshland sequence deposited
during the Holocene. The sequence detected offshore
broadly matches this succession, in terms of sediment
types, general stratigraphy, locality and trend of the
infilled former Yare valley onto the continental shelf.

The complex distribution of the possible correlative
sediments in the dredging areas necessitated a detailed
seismic survey utilizing a pinger profiler run at 50 m line
spacing to define the extent of the peat and clay filled
(?Breydon Formation) basins. Subsequent vibrocoring
revealed that the peats were commonly over 1 m thick
and locally overlain by a gravelly sea bed veneer <0.3 m
thick (Fig. 7). Figure 9 shows the results of the survey
within the dredging licence area in question, and Fig. 10
illustrates the information given to the dredging vessel
on the navigation computer, allowing peat-free aggregates to be dredged. The area provides an example of
how regional geological information is used to suggest

potential dredging areas with detailed surveying per-
mitting accurate identification, characterization and
quantification of resources and potential areas of
contamination.

The prediction and identification of future sand and gravel resources

Investigation of the origin of sand and gravel deposits
on the inner shelf off southern Britain has an applied as
well as an academic rationale, since the ability to define
the characteristics of offshore sediment bodies enables
accurate assessment of marine aggregate resources to be
made. Geological mapping of sediment bodies on the
inner shelf represents resource mapping and character-
isation in an industrial context. The view emphasized
here that cold climate subaerial (mainly fluvial) environments were chiefly responsible for the initial transport
and deposition of sands and gravels onto the inner
continental shelf off southern Britain (D'Olier 1975;
Dyer 1975) suggests that resources may be identified
within the courses of former fluvial channels and valleys
and so will be only well developed within the confines of
these inner shelf Pleistocene drainage networks. Areas
between former drainage systems (interfluves) are characterized by an absence of thick resources and instead
are marked by marine sea bed sediment veneers overlying planated, commonly bedrock, surfaces. Furthermore, within submerged valley systems (considered to

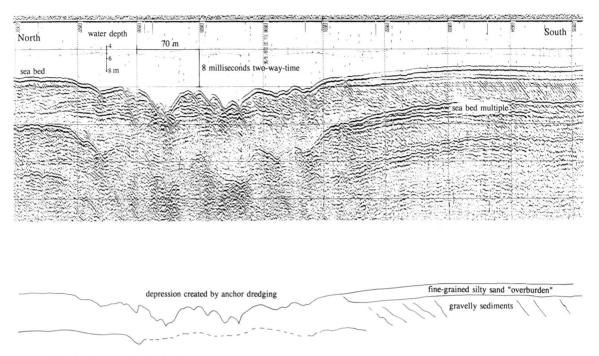

Fig. 8. Interpreted seismic (boomer) profile across dredged sea bed in a licence area located immediately east of the Isle of Wight. Extraction at this locality has occurred by anchor dredging which creates a depression on the sea bed. Note the vertical exaggeration on the profile.

have been estuarine sediment sinks during transgression) muddy sediments commonly overlie or lie adjacent to gravel bodies such that significant seabed occurrences of gravel resources within former fluvial channels are usually of limited extent.

In certain areas, former coastal features such as beaches or spits may be preserved as submerged, elongate mounds overlying bedrock, and aggregate resources also occur in localized areas as lags which infill bedrock depressions.

Given the complex cut-and-fill histories which are thought to have characterized the evolution of fluvial drainage systems offshore southern Britain, notably off the south coast, together with repeated marine planation of infilled channels, then the outcrop of submerged fluvial gravel resources will be further restricted. Much of the gravel on the inner shelf lies at depth beneath mud and fine-grained sand 'overburdens' while also occupying the irregular courses of the former river channels. Whilst seabed veneers represent more laterally extensive and more easily accessible deposits, it is suggested that the longer-term future of the gravel dredging industry lies in the exploitation of thicker but highly irregular and/or localized Pleistocene fluvial sands and gravels. The workability of seabed veneers as aggregate resources is

restricted due to the higher risk of clay contamination and seabed environmental change, produced by altering the seabed sediment types. Overall therefore, the most substantial aggregate reserves offshore southern Britain exist in localized areas which demand accurate dredging techniques to ensure consistent cargo quality.

It is also likely that coastal landforms which formed on the continental shelf during marine transgression, including beaches and spits, represent potentially significant gravel deposits, being reworked from pre-existing fluvial or glaciofluvial deposits. The configuration of the former coastline during marine transgression together with hydrographic factors and preservation potential would clearly have been important in determining the present location of such features. The development of sandbanks and bars during and after marine transgression has led to the accumulation of significant sand deposits which are locally important as fine-grained marine aggregates, for example in the Bristol Channel.

The aggregate dredging industry in the future

The high degree of precision applied to the characterization of sand and gravel reserves, both in terms of

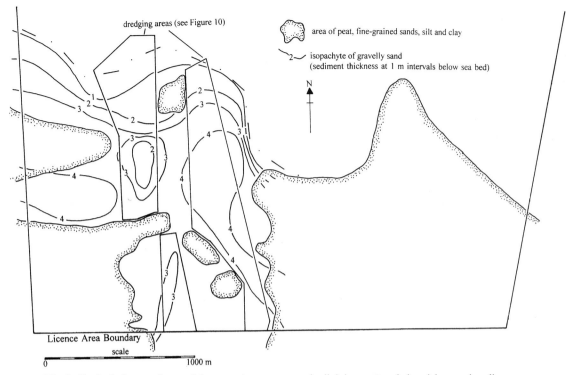

Fig. 9. Geological map of potential aggregate resources and adjoining peat and clay-rich areas in a licence area off Great Yarmouth, Norfolk. The demarcated dredging areas correspond to those in Fig. 10.

navigation, positioning control and geological appraisal, means that dredging areas need to be carefully defined and will be commonly of limited extent, being governed by the distribution of the resource. While resources may exist throughout a dredging licence area, individual deposits can be repeatedly worked at the same locality thereby minimizing the extent of dredged sea bed and hence environmental impact. Many of the present dredging licences were granted before detailed, accurate surveying had been undertaken and so do not necessarily reflect the smaller extent of the reserve. The Owers licence area (Fig. 2) is an appropriate example since parts of this licence area are largely unworkable or difficult to work due to areas of Palaeogene strata and transgressional clays at or near sea bed. Indeed, detailed seismic and sampling surveys in the eastern half of the licence (the area most commonly dredged at the time of writing) have demonstrated that substantial sand and gravel 'outcrops' are limited in extent relative to the rest of the licence area and are commonly irregular in outcrop pattern thereby necessitating care while dredging.

It is therefore suggested that future dredging licence areas could be smaller than many of those currently in existence since accurate surveying techniques coupled with the use of the geological approach discussed here will enable the best resource areas to be well defined, allowing areas containing poor quality, thin or unworkable deposits to be discarded. Furthermore, future licence applications to the Crown Estate and DETR for additional dredging areas may in some cases be assisted by applicant companies first proposing compact application areas and then offering to exchange areas within existing licences which are either worked out or contain no significant resources. Again, the geological considerations examined here are fundamental in deciding which areas to relinquish. Another factor which has limited the overall area of seabed affected by dredging is the development of modern dredging vessels with the ability to dredge highly localised or deep water deposits, perhaps across the tidal current direction, due to advancements in manoeuvrability, ship power, increased dredging depth capability and increased position fixing accuracy due to satellite navigation and computerised plotting techniques (Fig. 10). These advancements combined with geological appraisal also assist in the precise choice of dredging locality to yield aggregate of an appropriate quality for a certain end use,

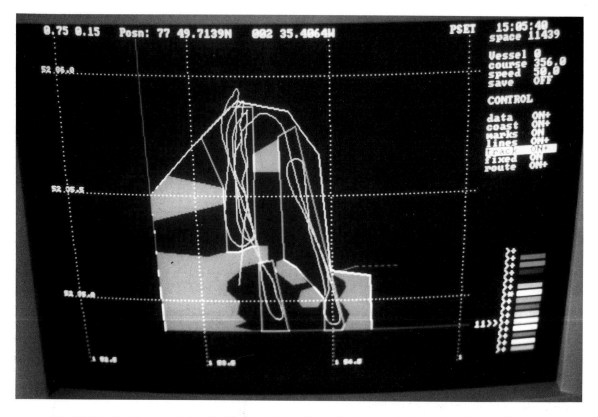

Fig. 10. The dredging area depicted in Fig. 9 as displayed on a dredgers' navigation and track recording computer. The lines within the dredging boxes represent the tracks of the dredger while working across the extraction area.

specification or contract –for instance concrete production, beach nourishment, reclamation or fill.

On the whole, therefore, geological considerations are crucial for the success of the dredging industry in the future and will lead to the licensing of smaller dredging areas, those containing the resources of greatest long term potential. Geologists, through a well informed scientific stance, have an important role to play in enhancing the public perception of the offshore aggregates industry, especially with regard to its effect upon fishing and coastal protection which are commonly highlighted as areas of concern in relation to dredging. In the case of the fishing industry for example, potential conflicts of interest can be minimized through the accurate definition of dredging areas and zoning of licence areas, often using geological criteria, thereby cutting down the area of dredged seabed. Such arrangements are promoted through the licencing procedure and by regular liaison.

Of equal importance is the need to overcome marine aggregate prejudice which arises from the perception by some customers that marine dredged sands and gravels are markedly different from those obtained onshore. Research findings summarized here have shown that some of the most substantial offshore reserves originated in subaerial environments at similar times and by the same processes as their present-day terrestrial equivalents, having been deposited in former cold climate glaciofluvial and fluvial environments. Prejudice against marine aggregates may be more easily overcome by demonstrating this aspect of aggregate geology to concerned parties, the only difference between the two equivalent deposits being a commonly higher chloride content in marine aggregates which is reduced to acceptable levels by washing at the wharf (BMAPA 1995). In addition, marine reworked sands and gravels can contain detrital shell fragments which are another source of reservation held against marine aggregates. However, research has demonstrated that the quantities of shell fragments normally found in marine aggregates are not detrimental to the end use of the product (Gutt & Collins 1987). Marine sands and gravels also have distinct advantages over their land based counterparts, being commonly winnowed of their silt and clay content by marine currents and having had their 'soft' rock (e.g. chalk) components removed through reworking, leaching or by abrasion due to longer distance transport. For the same reasons, marine gravels are frequently more rounded than terrestrial deposits, enabling a more workable concrete for the same water content.

Concluding remarks

With recent investment and increasing pressures against land-based quarrying, the UK marine sand and gravel dredging industry is well established (Hollinsworth 1994). The industry faces a challenging future in which the predicted increase in marine aggregate provision will be accompanied by the need to licence additional reserves to meet requirements. As Fox (1993) points out, geologists will have an important role to play in this future, providing input into resource exploration, assessment, extraction, environmental impact assessment and licensing. It is considered that significant improvements have been made throughout the industry in the exploration, assessment and management of UK marine sand and gravel resources and licence areas as recommended in the mid 1980s by Nunny & Chillingworth (1986, Chapter 6). Enhanced performance in these areas, coupled with the availability of modern dredging technology (including precision positioning systems and computerised track recording) has led to more effective controls on aggregate cargo quality, consistency and predictability. In addition, improved survey techniques, environmental assessment, environmental monitoring and controlled and regulated dredging has, and continues to, enhance the control on the environmental performance of the industry in licensed dredging areas. It is clear that the application of Quaternary geology in dredging licence management and in continued research into the evolution of the sediments on the northwest European shelf forms a basis for these industry improvements and will remain a key element in the development of the industry in the future.

Acknowledgements. Figures 1, 4, 5, 6, 7, 8, 9 and 10 appear courtesy of United Marine Dredging Limited.

References

ARTHURTON, R. S., BOOTH, S. J., MORIGI, A. N., ABBOTT, M. A. W. & WOOD, C. J. 1994. *Geology of the Country around Great Yarmouth*. Memoir of the British Geological Survey, Sheet 162 (England and Wales).

BAETEMAN, C., DE LANNOY, W., PAEPE, R. & VAN CAUWENBERGHE, C. 1992. Vulnerability of the Belgian coastal lowlands to future sea level rise. *In*: TOOLEY, M. J. & JELGERSMA, S. (eds) *Impacts of Sea Level Rise on European Coastal Lowlands*. Institute of British Geographers Special Publication Series. Blackwell, Oxford, 56–71.

BALSON, P. S. & JEFFREY, D. H. 1991. The glacial sequence of the southern North Sea. *In*: EHLERS, J., GIBBARD, P. L. & ROSE, J. (eds) *Glacial Deposits in Great Britain and Ireland*. Balkema, Rotterdam, 245–253.

BELDERSON, R. H., PINGREE, R. D. & GRIFFITHS, D. K. 1986. Low sea level tidal origin of Celtic Sea sand banks – evidence from numerical modelling of M2 tidal streams. *Marine Geology*, **73**, 99–108.

BELLAMY, A. G. 1995. Extension of the British Landmass: evidence from shelf sediment bodies in the English Channel. *In*: PREECE, R. C. (ed.) *Island Britain: a Quaternary Perspective*. Geological Society, London, Special Publication, **96**, 47–62.

BRITISH MARINE AGGREGATE PRODUCERS ASSOCIATION 1995. *Aggregates from the Sea – Why Dredge?* London, British Marine Aggregate Producers Association, Second Edition.

BRIDGLAND, D. R. & D'OLIER, B 1995. The Pleistocene evolution of the Thames and Rhine drainage systems in the southern North Sea Basin. *In*: PREECE, R. C. (ed.) *Island Britain: a Quaternary Perspective*. Geological Society, London, Special Publication, **96**, 27–45.

CROWN ESTATE 1996. *Marine Aggregate Licences Summary of Statistics 1996*. The Crown Estate, London.

DoE 1994. *Minerals Planning Guidance: Guidelines for Aggregates Provision in England*. Minerals Planning Guidance Note 6. London, HMSO.

D'OLIER, B. 1975. Some aspects of late Pleistocene–Holocene drainage of the River Thames in the eastern part of the London Basin. *Philosophical Transactions of the Royal Society*, **A279**, 269–277.

DYER, K. R. 1975. The buried channels of the 'Solent River', southern England. *Proceedings of the Geologists' Association*, **86**, 239–245.

FOX, R. A. 1993. The Offshore Aggregate Industry in the U. K. *Underwater Technology*, **19**, 17–23.

GIBBARD, P. L. 1995. The formation of the Strait of Dover. *In*: PREECE, R. C. (ed.), *Island Britain: a Quaternary Perspective*. Geological Society, London, Special Publication, **96**, 15–26.

GUTT, W. & COLLINS, R. J. 1987. Sea dredged aggregates in concrete. *Building Research Establishment Information Paper*, London, Building Research Establishment.

HARRISON, D. J., LABAN, C., LETH, J. O. & LARSEN, B. 1998. Sources of sand and gravel on the Northern European Continental Shelf. *This volume*.

HOLLINSWORTH, C. C. 1994. Marine aggregates today and into the 21st Century. *Quarry Management*, August 1994, 17–27.

HOLMES, R., JEFFREY, D. H., RUCKLEY, N. A. & WINGFIELD, R. T. R. 1993. *Quaternary Geology around the United Kingdom (South Sheet)*. 1:1,000,000 (Edinburgh, British Geological Survey).

HYDRAULICS RESEARCH 1993. *South coast sea bed mobility study*, summary report EX2795. Wallingford, Hydraulics Research Limited.

JANSEN, J. H. F., VAN WEERING, TJ. C. E. & EISMA, D. 1979. Late Quaternary sedimentation in the North Sea. *In*: OELE, E., SCHUTTENHELM, R. T. E. & WIGGERS, A. J. (eds), The Quaternary History of the North Sea, *Acta Universitatis Upsaliensis, Symposium Universitatis Upsaliensis Annum Quingentesimum Celebrantis*, **2**, 175–187.

JELGERSMA, S. 1979. Sea level changes in the North Sea basin. *In*: OELE, E., SCHUTTENHELM, R. T. E. & WIGGERS, A. J. (eds), The Quaternary History of the North Sea, *Acta Universitatis Upsaliensis, Symposium Universitatis Upsaliensis Annum Quingentesimum Celebrantis*, **2**, 233–248.

LIVERPOOL UNIVERSITY 1992. *An Appraisal of the Land Based Sand and Gravel Resources of South Wales*. Unpublished report for the DoE and Welsh Office, Department of Earth Sciences, University of Liverpool.

NUNNY, R. S. & CHILLINGWORTH, P. C. H. 1986. *Marine Dredging for Sand and Gravel*. Department of the Environment Minerals Division, London, Her Majesty's Stationery Office.

PANTIN, H. M. & EVANS, C. D. R. 1984. The Quaternary history of the Central and South-western Celtic Sea. *Marine Geology*, **57**, 259–293.

SELBY, I. & OOMS, K. 1998. Assessment of offshore sand and gravel bodies for dredging. *This volume*.

The CIRIA research project on beach recharge materials

Russell Scott Arthurton

British Geological Survey, Keyworth, Nottingham NG12 5GG, UK

Abstract. A CIRIA report presenting a regional review of the marine resources of sand and gravel around the coasts of England and Wales assesses the capacity of these resources to meet the anticipated demands for these materials by the aggregate industry and for beach recharge over the next 20 years. In an analysis of the demand for the materials required specifically for beach recharge – shingle and sand – the report identifies a shortfall for shingle in five of the twelve defined sub-regions, though there appears to be capacity within adjoining sub-regions to meet the demands. The report indicates a huge capacity at the regional level for satisfying the combined demands of beach recharge and the aggregate industry for sand, although at the sub-regional level some shortfalls have been identified off the coasts of northern England.

Marine-dredged sand and gravel are preferred to land-won materials for beach recharge purposes. In most cases such marine materials can be delivered directly to the point of use, and the grading and cosmetic specifications can usually be matched easily with those of the existing beach material. While beach recharge is a management option that has been adopted in the United States particularly over the last 40 years or so (Davison *et al.* 1992), its use in England and Wales has developed significantly only within the last 20 years (Babtie Dobbie 1991).

The beach recharge option for coastal defence schemes in England and Wales is increasingly favoured over the more traditional hard defence systems. Such a preference is based largely on the grounds of cost, but also on the belief that so-called soft-engineered defences are more acceptable environmentally, have an enhanced recreational value, and are less likely to cause problems downdrift than rigid defence structures (Simm *et al.* 1996). The growth in the implementation of beach recharge options, and the consequent growth in the use of marine materials for such schemes, has led to concerns as to the availability of suitable materials for recharge in England and Wales over the long-term, say the next 20 years, assuming that coastal management policies favouring a soft-engineered approach remain in place.

The seabed around England and Wales is an important source of sand and gravel for aggregates and fill materials used by the construction industry. Indeed about 18% of the present total annual requirement for the South East Minerals Planning Region is estimated to come from marine sources (Department of the Environment 1993). Government policy encourages the development of marine-dredged materials, planning constraints making the development of land resources increasingly difficult. In addition to the marine-dredged materials

landed at wharves in England and Wales, some are exported to the European mainland. As well as supplying these aggregate markets, commercial production licence areas off the coasts of England and Wales supply beach recharge schemes with sand and shingle.

The dependence of these markets upon licensed aggregate production areas off the coasts of England and Wales may lead to problems of supply over the long term. Certain materials required for beach recharge may become scarce, and, while there may be alternatives, such as crushed rock, available for use as aggregates, there may be no other economic supply source for beach recharge schemes. The shipping distance from the dredge site to the point of placement is an important factor in considerations of viability, as is the cosmetic specification, ensuring that recharged material is compatible with the naturally occurring beach material. Thus the question has been raised as to whether the estimated demand for beach recharge materials in England and Wales over the next 20 years can be met from marine-dredged sources in view of the likely growth in aggregates demand from England and Wales as well as the maritime nations of northwest Europe.

The CIRIA research project

With the support of funding from Government departments and agencies, the Crown Estate and the marine aggregate industry, CIRIA commissioned this study examining the relationship between the demands for marine-dredged materials (sand and gravel), and their resources at the seabed in water depths to 60 metres (Fig. 1). In particular, the study examined the potential for meeting the specific demand for beach recharge material over the next 20 years. The study report

ARTHURTON, R. S. 1998. The CIRIA research project on beach recharge materials. *In*: LATHAM, J.-P. (ed.) 1998. *Advances in Aggregates and Armourstone Evaluation.* Geological Society, London, Engineering Geology Special Publications, **13**, 47–56.

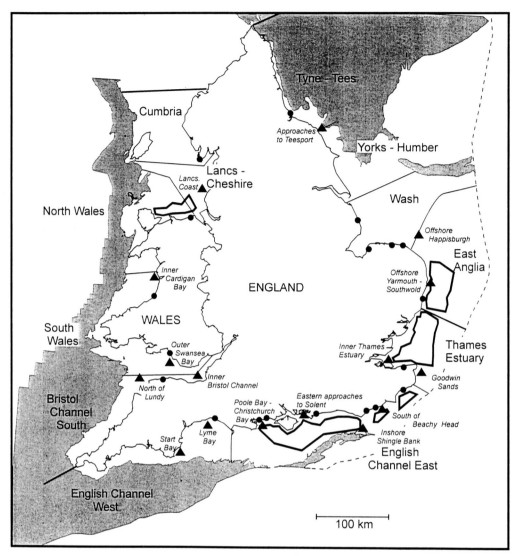

Fig. 1. Sub-regional division of the coast of England and Wales and its adjoining shelf to water depths of 60 m. Locations of beaches assessed in the calculation of the demand for recharge materials are indicated by spots. The general extents of the principal areas densely sampled by the aggregate industry are bold-outlined and the locations of the additional areas selected for study as part of the resource assessment are shown by solid triangles.

(Humphreys *et al.* 1996) has provided, for the first time, quantitative regional estimates of recharge demand for England and Wales, in terms of shingle and sand, and the resources of suitable material to meet that demand in the context of the likely requirements for aggregates.

The estimates of demand and resources are of relevance in the determination of policy on coastal defence and minerals planning in England and Wales. The report provides information on the distribution and quality of the resources of potential recharge materials,

both within existing licensed prospecting and production areas and in selected areas outside. Some of these additional resource areas extend into the nearshore zone. The information on the distribution and quality of the resources provides guidance to minerals planning at the more local level, and informs coastal authorities of the likely resource options to be considered in planned or proposed schemes. The report deals with the possibilities for use in beach recharge of materials other than marine-dredged sand and gravel. It also refers to navigational dredgings, and provides a brief review of the environmental considerations relating to the extraction of marine sand and gravel.

The study was carried out for CIRIA by a consortium led by the British Geological Survey (BGS), and including HR Wallingford Ltd, who calculated the recharge demand, and Posford Duvivier Ltd, who compiled information on aggregate demand as well as facilitating the use of resource information contained in the Crown Estate database.

This paper summarizes the approaches used to estimate the demands for marine-dredged materials for recharge and aggregate use, and provides a brief review of the results and their caveats. Its main aim, however, is to describe the methodology and results of the assessment of the resources of sand and gravel on the shelf around the coasts of England and Wales to water depths of 60 metres. The assessment considers areas that are currently inaccessible to the aggregate industry. These include sterilized ground in the vicinity of seabed cables, pipelines and wrecks; and the nearshore zone, where there are particular concerns over the impact of extraction on the stability of nearby shorelines. The paper reviews the main findings of the report in terms of resource distribution and regional demand.

Demand estimation

The demand estimates for marine-dredged materials for beach recharge and aggregates for England and Wales over the next 20 years are divided in the report into 12 coastal/seabed areas. These areas are referred to as sub-regions (Fig. 1) and, for convenience, are grouped into three regions for the purposes of the resource assessment. The sub-regions are divisions within the five dredging areas defined by the Crown Estate. Their coastal boundaries are, as far as possible, conformable with the seaward limits of the onshore Minerals Planning regions of the Department of the Environment, while there is only broad correspondence with MAFF's littoral cells and sub-cells (Brampton & Motyka 1993).

Recharge materials

In estimating the demand for recharge materials, the approach adopted was to apply simplified standard numerical modelling procedures to determine the demands for a representative set of 19 beaches from around England and Wales (Fig. 1), and then to extrapolate the results to all the lengths of coastline for which beach recharge schemes may be implemented. The estimates presented in the report are shown as ranges, reflecting the uncertainty of the methods, the sensitivity to sediment sizes and to wave and water level conditions, the potential for climate change and the

effect of using beach control structures or other methods of coastal defence.

The beach sites chosen were selected to meet a range of criteria. The sites had to lie within the areas for which HR Wallingford had relevant synthetic wave climate data. Other criteria were the provision of a representative distribution around England and Wales, representation of both sand and shingle beaches, the recognition of erosion or flood defence problems, the potential for the implementation of a recharge scheme, the representation of different risk categories, and the size of the recharge scheme. A simplified beach material classification was adopted; the material with D_{50} within the ranges 125 μm–2 mm was classified as Sand and that with $D_{50} > 5$ mm was classified as Shingle. Material with D_{50} of less than 125 μm is not considered suitable for beach recharge. That with D_{50} between 2 mm and 5 mm is uncommon, except as mixed beaches with bimodal grading, and is beyond the scope of the available numerical models.

The recharge demand estimates for sand and for shingle quoted in the report include both initial and maintenance volumes. Maximum and minimum values for each region are an indication of the large potential errors inherent in the simplified approach to the site predictions and their extrapolation.

Estimated recharge demand for sand over the next 20 years is greatest in the Wash sub-region with a range of 8 to 15 million cubic metres (Mm^3), followed by Tyne–Tees (6 to 13 Mm^3), Yorkshire–Humber (6 to 10 Mm^3) and North Wales (4 to 9 Mm^3). The lowest demands for sand are in the English Channel East and West sub-regions (1 to 2 Mm^3). The total demand for sand over 20 years in all sub-regions in England and Wales is estimated to be within the range 36 to 83 Mm^3. The estimated recharge demand for shingle shows a markedly contrasting distribution. The greatest demand by far, 11 to 22 Mm^3, is in the English Channel East sub-region. This is followed by that in the Thames Estuary at 6 to 12 Mm^3. Nine of the remaining ten sub-regions have a maximum demand of less than 3 Mm^3, while in four sub-regions, Tyne–Tees, Yorkshire–Humber, South Wales and Lancashire–Cheshire, there is no demand identified. Over England and Wales as a whole the potential increase in the demand for sand due to climate change is estimated as about 10%, while the demand for shingle may show a slight decrease as a consequence of reduced rates of longshore drift.

Aggregate materials

Estimates of the total demand for marine-dredged aggregates in England and Wales over the next 20 years have been based on Department of the Environment (DoE) figures as published in the revised version of the Minerals Planning Guidance Note 6 (MPG 6) (Department of the Environment 1994). However, the figures quoted (in millions of tonnes, Mt) apply to

England only and cover only the 15-year period to 2006. For the purposes of the CIRIA report the demand has been estimated to include Wales and to cover the 20-year period to 2015. This estimate shows a total demand for marine aggregates of 565 Mt.

The overall demand figure for England and Wales is derived from estimates of the likely demands from the individual Minerals Planning regions. To meet those demands, the likely supply from the English Channel East, Thames Estuary and East Anglia sub-regions is estimated as 435 Mt, with about two-thirds being supplied to wharves in the Thames Estuary; that from the Wash, Yorkshire–Humber and Tyne–Tees sub-regions is estimated as 30 Mt. Almost all of this material is gravel with sand in the proportions required for concrete. The total 465 Mt of gravel with sand can be assumed to comprise 280 Mt (equivalent to 140 Mm^3) >5 mm, 40 Mt (22 Mm^3) 2 to 5 mm, 125 Mt (78 Mm^3) 125 μm to 2 mm and 20 Mt (13 Mm^3) below 125 μm. Of the remaining sub-regions, Bristol Channel South, South Wales, Lancashire–Cheshire and North Wales are estimated to supply a total of 100 Mt (64 Mm^3), entirely for sand in the range 125 μm to 2 mm. The assignation of estimated supply volumes to specific sub-regions

Table 1. *Demand volumes over the next 20 years for beach recharge and aggregate (Mm^3) by region and sub-region for shingle and sand shown in relation to the calculated resources of these materials in densely sampled areas (D) and additional selected areas (A). The limits of the sub-regions and locations of the resource areas studied are shown in Fig. 1*

Region	Sub-region		Resources (Mm^3)		(Max.) Recharge demand (Mm^3)		Aggregate demand (Mm^3)	
			Shingle	Sand	Shingle	Sand	Shingle	Sand
Off South Coast	English Channel East	D	225	496	22	2	42	24
		A	1	266				
	English Channel West	D	–	–	3	2	–	–
		A	–	43				
	All region	D	225	496	25	4	42	24
		A	1	309				
Off East Coast	Thames Estuary	D	86	2 053	12	5	86	48
		A	5	1 321				
	East Anglia	D	144	661	6	8	3	2
		A	80	4 892				
	The Wash	D	76	434	2	15	–	–
		A	–	–				
	Yorkshire–Humber	D	–	–	–	10	3	2
		A	–	–				
	Tyne–Tees	D	–	–	–	13	6	3
		A	–	30				
	All region	D	306	3 148	20	51	98	55
		A	85	6 243				
Off Wales and Western England	Bristol Channel South	D	24	67	1	3	–	16
		A	126	3 399				
	South Wales	D	6	134	–	4	–	41
		A	–	122				
	North Wales	D	9	296	2	9	–	1
		A	–	29				
	Lancashire–Cheshire	D	–	–	–	5	–	6
		A	–	128				
	Cumbria	D	–	–	1	6	–	–
		A	–	–				
	All region	D	39	497	4	27	–	64
		A	126	3 678				
	Exports						60	31
	Totals	D	570	4 141	49	82	200	174
		A	212	10 230				

(Table 1) should be interpreted as only a general indication of anticipated production. The volumes shown in relation to the main resource regions may serve as a more useful indicator of overall expectations.

Marine gravel with sand, almost all for concrete, is currently supplied from licensed dredging areas off the coasts of England and Wales to four countries in northwest Europe – France, Belgium, the Netherlands and Germany. The estimated demand over the next 20 years totals some 200 Mt and comprises 120 Mt (60 Mm^3) >5 mm, 20 Mt (11 Mm^3) 2 to 5 mm, 50 Mt (31 Mm^3) 125 μm to 2 mm, and 10 Mt (7 Mm^3) below 125 μm. The sources of these exported materials are not specified in the report.

Resource assessment

A main objective of the CIRIA report is to present a review of the resources of sand and gravel on the continental shelf around the coasts of England and Wales to water depths of 60 m (Fig. 1). The review covers mainly the areal distribution of the resources and their estimated volumes. For the purposes of the assessment, the study area has been divided into three regions: Off the south coast of England, Off the east coast of England, and Off the coasts of Wales and western England. The assessment is constrained by the availability of data, and by the variable quality of the data, which come from a variety of sources. In some areas the existing survey coverage is inadequate to permit meaningful assessment.

Data sources and assessment methodology

Seabed sediment data have been collected extensively over the past 30 years or so for a variety of purposes. BGS has its own database for samples and shallow seismic records collected between 1967 and 1992 as part of its Offshore Regional Mapping Programme. In addition the BGS database includes a wealth of data from other sources, in particular the marine sand and gravel resource assessment data collected by BGS in projects co-funded by the DoE and the Crown Estate. A principal source of information is the Crown Estate database, maintained by Posford Duvivier Ltd. This database contains data generated by the marine aggregate industry. Its conditions of use for the project were agreed between the Crown Estate, the aggregate industry as represented by the British Marine Aggregate Producers Association (BMAPA), and CIRIA, through its project steering group. Another important source of data is the Hydrographic Office (HO), who have modern survey cover for much of the area of interest comprising echo-sounding, side-scan sonar and sediment sampling. The HO data

extends into parts of the nearshore zone, an area covered poorly by the BGS database and not at all by the Crown Estate database.

The seabed sediment data from their disparate sources have been integrated in a common database, the majority of the information on sediment thickness and lithology coming from the BGS and Crown Estate databases. The code system used by HO to describe lithologies has been used to assess the dominant lithology where no other data are available. To protect the confidences of the data owners, lithology and thickness information has been manipulated into a grid square format. The data are generalized to refer to 4 km-a-side grid squares where commercial considerations are paramount, and to 2 km-a-side grid squares where the data are not commercially constrained. The integrated database on which the report is based holds over 14 400 points of data which have been manipulated in some 2800 2 km-a-side grid squares of averaged data. Areas where data are considered inadequate for the purposes of resource assessment are indicated in the report.

The report presents the resource information in relation to two types of resource area. The most detailed information comes from areas that are referred to as *densely sampled* by the marine aggregate industry. The data within these areas are largely commercially constrained and thus indications of their resource distribution are generalized to 4 km-a-side grid squares. The other type of resource area is referred to as an *additional selected area*. The selection of additional areas as likely to have a resource potential has followed a general review of seabed sediment data within the BGS Offshore Database. The data in these areas are not commercially constrained, and their resource distribution is presented in the report generalized to grid squares of 2 km-a-side.

So that there can be a useful comparison between the results of the recharge material demand study and those of the resource assessment, a size classification has been determined in which the size ranges of materials in greatest demand for recharge can be identified. The full range of size categories and nomenclature used in the report are:

>5 mm	Shingle;
2 to 5 mm	Mixed sand and gravel;
125 μm to 2 mm	Sand;
<125 μm	Fines.

Shingle is in demand both for coarse aggregate and beach recharge, mixed sand and gravel is in demand from the aggregate industry, especially for concrete, sand is required for fine aggregate and beach recharge while fines are in no particular demand.

A key element in the assessment of resources is the estimation of sediment thickness. Boreholes and vibrocores yield the most reliable information, especially when supported by seismic data. Modern techniques of high-resolution shallow seismic profiling can resolve thicknesses to between 0.5 and 2 m at best and require seabed samples to assist in data interpretation. In areas where only grab sample data are available, a default thickness of 0.1 m has been applied, except where bedrock is known to be extensively exposed, where a default thickness of 0.05 m is considered to be more realistic for the purpose of volume calculations.

In areas densely sampled by the marine aggregate industry, where volume estimates are derived entirely from the Crown Estate database, the percentage of each size category has been estimated for each core, based on grain size analyses. The volumes for each 2 km-a-side grid square are calculated by multiplying the average percentage of each lithology by the mean thickness of sediment in the grid square, multiplied by the area of that square. Generalization of the data to 4 km-a-side grid squares is achieved by adding together the data from the component 2 km-a-side squares, but only those which are known to contain a resource. In the additional selected areas of study the volumetric estimates are shown in 2 km-a-side grid squares, without a necessity for further generalization.

The grid squares indicate by their tone the dominant lithology across the square as a whole. Calculated volumes of the various size categories (shingle, sand and gravel and sand) within each grid square are included. Grid squares over which the resource thickness averages over 0.5 m are highlighted. The resource maps shown in the report incorporate totalled volumetric estimates for the size categories by sub-region and provide figures for the estimated total potentially workable resources for that sub-region, calculated on the assumption that the lowest 0.5 m of the deposit and the material in grid squares dominated by fines would not be extracted. Where the additional selected areas straddle sub-regional boundaries, they have been assigned wholly to one or other of the specific sub-regions. A summary of the estimated workable shingle and sand resources within each sub-region is given in Table 1.

Resources suitable for recharge off the south coast of England

The report considers the region off the South Coast as two sub-regions; English Channel West, between Land's End and Portland; and English Channel East, between Portland and South Foreland, Dover (Fig. 1). For the region the project database holds over 8000 points of data and these have been manipulated into 935 2-km-a-side grid squares of averaged data. The region has been widely, though not comprehensively, covered by geological surveys and extensively prospected for marine aggregates. With the exception of a few intensely investigated areas, survey cover in the nearshore zone is poor.

Much of the sea floor is covered by material that is potentially suitable both for beach recharge and aggregate purposes. Muddy sediments are generally uncommon on account of the strong tidal current activity, and tend to be confined to some sheltered nearshore areas. Palaeovalleys are a special feature of the region, and these may contain sand and gravel resources. The seabed sediments are generally less than 0.5 m thick, resting on bedrock, although thicker deposits occur as palaeovalley infills and mobile sand bodies resting on shingle lag deposits. The shingle lag veneer is a product of marine transgression over terraced fluvial deposits. Its distribution generally reflects depositional processes no longer active at the present day. Exposed shingle is commonly encrusted with serpulids, bryozoa and barnacles, indicating that it is immobile under today's tidal regime. In a few places substantially thicker shingle deposits occur, representing relict, now submerged, beaches and spits (e.g. Owers Bank). Unlike the shingle lags, the distribution of sand reflects contemporary tidal current transport paths. Sand waves, dunes and ribbons occur scattered on the lag, but the most substantial resources are in sand banks and sand ridges with thicknesses ranging up to 20 m. Bedrock is widely exposed at the seabed over much of the English Channel West sub-region.

English Channel East

In the English Channel East the shingle comprises mostly flint. Around parts of the Isle of Wight, however, sandstone clasts form an important component, and locally these may dominate. Where the lag is underlain by a Chalk outcrop, clasts of chalk may be the main component, as in areas south of the Isle of Wight and offshore Beachy Head. Shell content is generally low but may be more significant offshore Shoreham–Newhaven. Within areas densely sampled by the marine aggregate industry, the report indicates a workable shingle resource of 225 Mm^3, the bulk of this occurring off the coasts of Sussex, Hampshire and the Isle of Wight. Of the additional areas selected for assessment, only one, South of Beachy Head (Fig. 1), appears to carry a significant shingle resource – some 60 Mm^3 – though nearly all of this would be excluded by applying the criterion of workability (see above). The workable sand resources in the densely sampled areas are estimated at nearly 500 Mm^3, while 266 Mm^3 are indicated in the additional areas.

English Channel West

None of this sub-region has been densely sampled by the aggregate industry. The available data show that resources of shingle are sparse. Where shingle does occur it commonly has a large shell component. Palaeovalley fills may include some shingle, but these need further investigation. In the additional areas assessed, some 10 Mm³ of shingle were identified in Lyme Bay, but none of this is likely to be workable. While bedrock is exposed at the seabed over much of this sub-region, sands are known to occur in Start Bay and Lyme Bay, both of which were selected as additional study areas (Fig. 1). Palaeovalley fills may also include sand resources. In Start Bay some 41 Mm³ of workable sand has been estimated, while in Lyme Bay there is believed to be a total sand resource of about 40 Mm³, of which only perhaps 2 Mm³ are workable.

Resources suitable for recharge off the east coast of England

The report assesses the resources off the east coast in five sub-regions which accord with coastal divisions for recharge material demand estimates: the Thames Estuary, East Anglia, Wash, Yorkshire–Humber, and Tyne–Tees (Fig. 1). Over 4700 data points were included in the database, and these have been manipulated into over 1300 2-km-a-side grid squares of averaged data. The region has been widely covered by geological surveys and extensively prospected for aggregates. With a few exceptions the survey cover of the nearshore zone is inadequate for resource assessment.

Much of the sea floor comprises material that is potentially suitable both for beach recharge and aggregates. Sandy sediment dominates over much of the region, much of it mobile under present-day hydrodynamic conditions. Extensive sandbank systems characterize much of the Thames Estuary and East Anglia sub-regions. The largest bank, Long Sand, is over 45 km in length. Shingle is widespread at the sea floor mostly as only a veneer, and, with a few exceptions, is immobile. Its component clasts range from being flint-dominant in the south, with some chalk or mudstone reflecting the underlying bedrock, to a more varied suite further north, including flint, sandstone, and igneous and metamorphic lithologies. Mud is mostly confined to intertidal areas in estuaries and tidal inlets. Palaeovalleys are a feature of the region but their fills are likely to consist largely of mud.

Thames Estuary

This area has traditionally supplied most of the marine sand and gravel produced off England and Wales. Although its reserves are depleted, it continues to be an important source of aggregates to the South East Minerals Planning region. There are some large shingle deposits, particularly on the north side of the estuary. Some of these extend into the shallower waters of the

nearshore zone. Within areas densely sampled by the industry, the project database indicates a workable shingle resource of some 86 Mm³. However, this and other estimates for this sub-region should be treated with caution in that significant dredging is likely to have occurred since the survey data were obtained. A further 5 Mm³ of workable shingle are indicated in an additional study area, the Inner Thames Estuary (Fig. 1). The sub-region represents a major sand resource. Within the densely sampled areas the potentially workable sand resource is more than 2000 Mm³, and in the additional areas of the Inner Thames and the Goodwin Sands (Fig. 1) further workable resources of more than 1300 Mm³ are indicated.

East Anglia

The sea floor of this sub-region is covered largely by sand and sandy shingle. The sediments occur mostly as a veneer less than 1 m thick. The Great Yarmouth–Southwold area includes some of the most important dredging grounds in the UK. Many of the resources are sterilized by the protective corridors of the many gas pipelines and cable routes that traverse the area. Some of these installations may be abandoned during the 20-year period under consideration. Within the areas densely sampled by the aggregate industry, the database indicates a workable shingle resource of 144 Mm³. Of the additional areas assessed, Offshore Happisburgh has an identified potentially workable shingle resource of about 80 Mm³. For sand, the data from the densely sampled areas indicate a workable resource of about 660 Mm³, while workable resources of some 280 and 4600 Mm³ have been calculated for additional areas Offshore Yarmouth–Southwold and Offshore Happisburgh respectively (Fig. 1). It should be noted that the Offshore Happisburgh area extends into the adjoining Wash sub-region (Fig. 1).

The Wash

The seabed sediments over most of this sub-region occur as a veneer less than 1 m thick resting on stiff glacial clays. Some much thicker sand bodies also occur, including banks up to 20 m thick. Mud is generally confined to the estuarine inlets, though muddy deposits occur in the vicinity of clay or mudstone substrates. Almost all the area has been prospected for sand and gravel except the nearshore zone. The project database indicates a workable shingle resource of 76 Mm³ within areas densely sampled by the industry. No additional areas were assessed other than the overlapping part of the Offshore Happisburgh area (Fig. 1, see above). The workable sand resources within the densely sampled areas total some 435 Mm³.

Yorkshire–Humber

Seabed sediments over much of this sub-region are less than 1 m thick, with bedrock and glacial formations extensively exposed. Only reconnaissance geological survey data are available and only parts of the sub-region, which includes the Dogger Bank area, have been prospected by the aggregate industry. No quantitative data are available. There is a general paucity of shingle, and where present this is commonly shelly. Deposits are known off Flamborough Head and at Whitby, where they occur mostly in water depths greater than 50 m. Some areas of Dogger Bank have potential shingle resources in water depths of less than 40 m. Sand is present in banks around the Dogger Bank, rising to more than 20 m above the general seabed in water depths of 50 to 60 m.

Tyne–Tees

In this sub-region the area of interest is restricted to the nearshore zone, some 10 km wide. Elsewhere the waters are generally too deep for dredging operations. Over most of the sub-region the seabed sediments are either absent or of veneer thickness overlying glacial till or bedrock. Thicker accumulations are present in bays and in the lee of headlands. Only reconnaissance geological survey data are available and only a few areas have been prospected by the aggregate industry. On the Durham coast dumped colliery waste has been distributed by littoral and nearshore processes, tending to make any seabed sediments muddy. Shingle is a sparse resource, its deposits being generally thin (<0.5 m) and patchy. Minor amounts of shingle are indicated from an assessment of the additional area, Approaches to Teesport (Fig. 1). Study of this area shows the existence of sandwave fields occupying sea floor depressions between 35 and 55 m water depth. There are indications of a workable sand resource of some 30 Mm³, which might serve local recharge schemes.

Resources suitable for recharge off the coasts of Wales and western England

The report divides the western waters into five sub-regions: Bristol Channel South, South Wales, North Wales, Lancashire–Cheshire and Cumbria, corresponding to the coastal divisions for recharge demand (Fig. 1). The project database holds over 1700 points of data. The resource information has been manipulated into some 560 2-km-a-side grid squares of averaged data. The region has widespread reconnaissance geological survey cover, and much of it has modern HO survey cover. Detailed geological survey information is available for much of the Bristol Channel, while detailed prospecting

data have been acquired for parts of the Bristol Channel and the Liverpool Bay–Isle of Man area. Survey cover in the nearshore zone is generally inadequate for assessment purposes.

Water depths exceed 60 m over most of the area of the Celtic Sea west of Lundy and of St George's Channel west of St David's Head and the Lleyn Peninsula. The Bristol Channel, Cardigan Bay and the eastern part of the Irish Sea, by contrast, are generally shallower than 50 m. Over most of the region the seabed sediments comprise a widespread veneer of sandy gravel resting on glacial and glacio-fluvial deposits or bedrock, and covered in places by sand waves, ribbons and banks whose distribution reflects the contemporary tidal current regime. A belt extending from the northern part of Liverpool Bay to offshore Cumbria is dominated by muddy deposits.

Bristol Channel South

Deposits of shingle within this sub-region are mainly of veneer thickness (less than 1 m) and bedrock is widely exposed. The shingle clasts comprise chert, sandstone and siltstone, as well as igneous and metamorphic rocks. For areas densely sampled by the aggregate industry the project database indicates a potentially workable shingle resource of 24 Mm³. A further 126 Mm³ of workable shingle is estimated in the additional studied area of Inner Bristol Channel (Fig. 1). Workable sand resources as indicated in the densely sampled areas are 67 Mm³, while volumes in the additional areas of North of Lundy (Fig. 1) and Inner Bristol Channel are estimated as 2855 Mm³ and 545 Mm³ respectively.

South Wales

This sub-region is a major source of aggregate, mainly sand. The sand resources occur in well defined bank systems, including Nash Sand and Culver Sand. Areas between the sand banks are characterised by exposed bedrock or shingle lags. Some 6 Mm³ of workable shingle are estimated in areas densely sampled by the industry, while no shingle resource was identified in the only additional area studied: Outer Swansea Bay, off Porthcawl (Fig. 1). The workable sand resource within the densely sampled areas is estimated as 134 Mm³ and that in the additional area in Outer Swansea Bay as 122 Mm³.

North Wales

The major licensed dredging areas in Liverpool Bay lie within this sub-region; these are mainly for sand. A large though interrupted area of shingle-rich sediment, resting on glacial deposits, extends from Anglesey towards the Isle of Man. Shingle clasts comprise mainly Lower Palaeozoic rock types including metasediments and volcanics, or in southern Liverpool Bay, limestone and sandstone. Shingle (including coarse shingle) is present as shoals known as sarnau, up to 20 km long and 3 km wide, which extend from the coast into Cardigan Bay. Workable shingle resources within areas densely sampled by the industry are estimated to total some 9 Mm^3, while in the additional area of Inner Cardigan Bay (Fig. 1), no further workable resources are indicated. Workable sand resources in the densely sampled areas total some 296 Mm^3, while those in the Inner Cardigan Bay area are estimated to be of the order of 29 Mm^3.

Lancashire–Cheshire

The seabed is covered variously by sand and shingle-rich sediment in this sub-region. A large expanse of shingle-rich sediment covers the area between Anglesey and the Isle of Man and patches of shingle occur also in Liverpool Bay and Morecambe Bay. The shingle forms a veneer mostly less than 0.5 m thick which rests on glacial deposits. There are no densely sampled areas within this sub-region. In the additional studied area – the Lancashire Coast (Fig. 1) – there is no indication of a shingle resource while the workable sand resources are estimated as some 128 Mm^3.

Cumbria

Much of this sub-region is blanketed by mud or mud-rich sediments. Sand and coarser sediments are confined to the nearshore zone around Cumbria and in the vicinity of the Isle of Man. Sand is present in the Solway Firth as tidal sandbanks up to 20 m thick and similar banks occur off northeast Isle of Man. No volumetric resource data is available, either for shingle or sand.

Matching the demand and the resources

In comparing the demand for, and resources of, shingle and sand on the seabed around the coasts of England and Wales (Table 1), the report has adopted the following practice. Firstly, the quoted volumes of materials required for beach recharge are those at the estimated range maximum for each sub-region. Secondly, the resource volumes in each area assessed exclude the material that forms the lowest 0.5 m of the deposits.

The sub-regional and regional demand volumes quoted in the report have separate elements for recharge materials and aggregates. The recharge demands relate to the shorelines of the respective sub-regions. The aggregate demands, however, reflect the anticipated demands for marine materials from the DoE Minerals Planning regions. The assignation of such aggregate demands to specific sub-regions over the 20-year term is speculative, and the figures quoted in Table 1 provide

general guidance only. Neither the sub-regional nor regional sources of marine materials exported to continental Europe are specified in the report.

Despite the uncertainties and assumptions implicit in the methodologies for estimating demands and resources, the results provide a clear indication of the capacity of the marine resources around the coasts of England and Wales to meet the anticipated demands for those materials over the next 20 years, and, in particular, their capacity for providing suitable materials for beach recharge – shingle and sand, as defined above.

Shingle

Taking a regional view (South, East and Western coasts), the resources of shingle identified in the report are adequate to meet the combined demands of beach recharge and the aggregate industry (including exported material). Even in the most critical regions, the South coast and the East coast, the resources comfortably exceed the demands. Analysis at the sub-regional level, however, shows that, in some cases, the identified resources are inadequate or scarcely adequate. In the Thames Estuary sub-region, the combined demand is for 98 Mm^3 while the identified resources total 91 Mm^3. Shortfalls are also identified in the English Channel West, Yorkshire–Humber, Tyne–Tees and Cumbria sub-regions. With the exception of Cumbria, there appears to be capacity within adjoining sub-regions to meet the demands.

Sand

The report indicates a huge capacity at the regional level for meeting the combined demands of beach recharge and the aggregate industry for sand. Off the East coast the identified resource volume is nearly ninety times the demand, while, even at the base of the league – off the South coast – it is nearly thirty times. At the sub-regional level, however, the results indicate shortfalls in resources in Yorkshire–Humber and Cumbria, with the possibility of a problem in Tyne–Tees.

Further resource investigation

The indication in the report of resource shortfalls within specific sub-regions is based on the assessment of the available data. Many areas with a resource potential have yet to be investigated, and it is possible that further resources will be identified, even in the critical sub-regions. The resources indicated in the additional areas that were selected for detailed study require more detailed investigation.

Two areas considered to have a significant potential for shingle are Offshore Happisburgh (East Anglia) and Inner Bristol Channel (Bristol Channel South). The nearshore zone in many sub-regions is also considered to merit investigation, there generally being little systematic geological survey data and no prospecting data available. Other possible shingle-bearing deposits deserving attention are those known in the deeper waters (>50 m) off the southwest of the Isle of Wight (English Channel East) and those occuring generally as lags between and around offshore tidal sandbanks. A detailed survey of the additional selected areas in the English Channel West would provide a more reliable indication of workable shingle resources to meet the recharge demand of that sub-region. The possibility that infills of some of the palaeovalley systems, particularly those in the English Channel East and Thames Estuary sub-regions, include shingle is considered a priority for investigation.

The potential for supplying the sand recharge needs of Yorkshire–Humber and Tyne–Tees sub-regions with materials from Dogger Bank (within Yorkshire–Humber) merits attention, while the identification of local resources to meet the sand (and shingle) recharge needs of Cumbria would also be worthwhile.

Acknowledgements. The author is pleased to acknowledge the generous support from CIRIA (Construction Industry Research and Information Association) in the preparation of this paper, in particular Dr J. A. Payne and Ms S. John. The paper summarizes the recently published CIRIA Research Report 154, Beach recharge materials, demand and resources, with particular emphasis on the resource issues. The contributions of the main authors of that report, Mr B. Humphreys and Mr D. J. Harrison (British Geological Survey), Mr T. T. Coates (HR Wallingford) and Mr M. J. Watkiss (Posford Duvivier) have formed the essential basis of this paper and are warmly acknowledged. Figure 1 is based on figures in the CIRIA report and is reproduced with copyright permission from CIRIA. The paper is published with the permissions of CIRIA and the Director of the British Geological Survey (NERC).

References

BABTIE DOBBIE LTD 1991. *Artificial Beach Recharge.* CIRIA Report 444, London.

BRAMPTON, A. H. & MOTYKA, J. M. 1993. *Coastal Management: Mapping of Littoral Cells.* Report No. SR328, HR Wallingford.

DAVISON, A. T., NICHOLLS, R. J. & LEATHERMAN, S. P. 1992. Beach nourishment as a coastal management tool: an annotated bibliography on developments associated with the artificial nourishment of beaches. *Journal of Coastal Research,* **8**, 984–1022.

DEPARTMENT OF THE ENVIRONMENT 1993. *Guidelines for Aggregates Provision in England and Wales: Revision of MPG 6.* Draft consultation document/policy issues paper.

——1994. *Guidelines for Aggregates Provision in England.* Minerals Planning Guidance Note No. 6.

HUMPHREYS, B., COATES, T. T., WATKISS, M. J. & HARRISON, D. J. 1996. *Beach Recharge Materials – Demand and Resources.* CIRIA Report 154, London.

SIMM, J. D., BRAMPTON, A. H., BEECH, N. & BROOKE, J. 1996. *Beach Management Manual.* CIRIA Report 153, London.

SECTION 2

ARMOURSTONE EVALUATION AND SHINGLE PERFORMANCE ASSESSMENT

The outlook for rock armour and beach recharge

Richard Stephenson Thomas

Posford Duvivier Ltd, Rightwell House, Bretton, Peterborough PE3 8DW, UK

Abstract. Rock armour and beach recharge have been used increasingly over recent years as central elements of coastal defence and other forms of coastal construction. In attempting to define the outlook for rock armour and beach recharge, the context at the coastline, the background to coastal defence, the present need for coastal works and the environmental value of the coast are considered. The advantages of natural materials such as rock, sand and gravel compared with some of the more traditional forms of coastal construction are reviewed. The 'market' for rock armour and beach recharge materials, including the legal background and relevant economic factors, is considered and the actual demand for the materials estimated. Important environmental considerations are discussed.

The coast has for many centuries been an area of importance for human development. It is attractive in terms of its flat, fertile land, as a base for transport by boat and as a base for fishing. The UK has been no exception. Early coastal development consisted of the establishment of commercial ports, fishing ports and, in Roman times, the reclamation of low-lying mudflats and saltings. Over the centuries the reclamations were progressively extended in places such as the Wash, East Anglia and South Wales, and the ports grew larger.

In the 19th century the development of holiday resorts such as Brighton and Blackpool began. These involved the construction of extensive promenades, many involving reclamation along the seafront and the protection of that reclamation with vertical masonry walls. It is the maintenance of these vertical masonry walls on the one hand, and of the sea walls protecting low-lying land on the other, which now presents UK coastal defence engineers with one of their main tasks. Similar issues apply to the maintenance of breakwaters and harbours where many of the old masonry structures are in need of refurbishment. To this situation should be added the sometimes major demand for the construction of new harbour facilities to accommodate the changing needs of commercial shipping and recreational craft.

The context in which coastal engineering is carried out, however, is substantially different from that of the 19th century. It is now one of: (1) increasing basic understanding of physical processes, brought about by extensive research; (2) increasing ability to model and predict the behaviour of coastal defences and their inter-relationship with the coastal process regime, brought about by the understanding mentioned above, plus major advances in the power of computers and computer modelling; and (3) increasing public and political sensitivity with regard to environmental matters, and in particular the impact of coastal structures on the coastal process regime.

There is thus a strong demand to build environmentally compatible and sustainable coastal defences and this is combined with an improving understanding which enables us to do so. The use of natural materials such as rock and beach-fill (sand and gravel) is one of the potentially environmentally acceptable options. This paper therefore explores the future use of these materials in coastal engineering, the likely demand for them and the environmental impacts that they themselves may cause.

Context

As mentioned in the introduction, the early forms of coastal defence, whether flood defence of low-lying land or the protection of land from erosion, were largely in the form of sea walls. In the UK many of these are now well over 100 years old and stand as a testament to their designers. However, many more have long since collapsed. These old sea walls were built without the benefit of modern understanding and technology. Indeed, the foreshore is an extremely hostile place in which to build anything. The loadings produced by wave impact are extreme and regular tidal inundation does not facilitate good quality construction. In the UK, a large number of sea walls have lasted since the last century along the seafront of holiday resorts. This compares with the sea defences fronting low-lying lands, particularly in the major flood-prone areas of East Anglia, which were to a large extent built or rebuilt after the 1953 floods. In both cases many of the sea walls are fronted by beaches that are much lower than they were, say, 40 years ago. The sea walls themselves have in many

THOMAS, R. S. 1998. The outlook for rock armour and beach recharge. *In*: LATHAM, J.-P. (ed.) 1998. *Advances in Aggregates and Armourstone Evaluation*. Geological Society, London, Engineering Geology Special Publications, **13**, 59–63.

locations been blamed for causing this problem, by virtue of the fact that, unlike a beach, they reflect rather than dissipate wave energy.

When considering this erosion it must be remembered that erosion of the coast is a far more natural state than stability. It has been stated that more than 70% of the world's coastlines are eroding. The mere fact of building a wall, possibly to protect an eroding coast, does nothing to counter an erosion tendency seawards of it. Nonetheless, whether sea walls have exacerbated the problem or whether the problem was always there, there is undoubtedly erosion taking place and sea walls are definitely being undermined. In addition, sea levels are rising and in many places people expect higher standards of defence than were previously provided. Areas not previously requiring defence from flooding or erosion are being protected in response to natural coastal change or as a result of development in areas at risk.

What is certain is that the older forms of construction, vertical walls and sloping walls, reflect wave energy. This tends to increase wave action in front of the wall and, at least locally, will tend to increase sediment transport and thus cause erosion at the toe of the wall.

About 54% of England's coastline (MAFF 1994) is currently protected by artificial structures. Many of these structures require rehabilitation to provide increased standards or to counter toe erosion. These rehabilitation measures are taking place with an increased awareness of the value of the environment. The coastal environment is one of great importance in several areas.

- Landscape – along many stretches of coastline there is, to a large extent, an unspoilt natural landscape of great value to all.
- In areas of coastal erosion the exposed cliff faces give an intriguing and invaluable insight into geological formations. The very process of coastal erosion is of great geological interest in numerous areas.
- The natural coastal environment is important, with cliffs and the foreshore providing vital and often unique habitats for flora and fauna, e.g. seabirds, shellfish and invertebrates.
- The human environment is equally important. The beach is an amenity, generating tourism and providing walking areas for ramblers.
- The coastal process regime of erosion and deposition is dynamic and, even if it is in equilibrium, it may only be in a delicate state of balance. Erosion in one area will provide gravel, sands and muds for the building of beaches and intertidal flats in another area. The prevention of erosion in one place may well cause erosion somewhere else.

This is the context in which coastal engineering takes place. Although the preceding discussion refers largely to the UK, many of the considerations apply throughout the world. We now have a hard line of defence along much of our coastline. The problem is whether, and if so how, to sustain it within the environmental and economic constraints that apply. What is the advantage of natural materials in this context? Firstly, as mentioned earlier, vertical or sloping solid sea walls tend to reflect wave energy and to exacerbate an erosion problem. On the other hand, rock armour and natural beaches absorb wave energy by dissipating it to a far greater extent. Secondly, it is possible by careful choice of these natural materials to produce coastal defences which present far less of an unnatural visual intrusion into a otherwise natural landscape. Thirdly, in an area where the foreshore is falling in any case, the use of rock armour constitutes a flexible solution when used as toe protection. Further scour in front of the toe protection does not undermine the rock; the rock structure merely deforms to accommodate that settlement. Fourthly, in a situation where there is a requirement to increase the standard of the coastal defence or breakwater, placing rock or, for that matter, a beach in front of it, can, by virtue of increasing wave dissipation, reduce the amount of wave overtopping and thus improve the effectiveness of the structure. Finally, either by direct provision of an enhanced beach through beach nourishment, or by the contribution towards that by the reduction of reflection brought out by the use of rock armour, both the amenity value of a beach and its habitat value can be enhanced. It is fair to say that rock armour, shingle and sand provide attractive options to solve coastal engineering problems. This situation has been emphasized by improved techniques for the extraction and transportation of such materials, which have made them, in many cases, attractive from the point of view of cost.

Legal and economic background

Even the physical form of coastal defences can be a function of the legal framework within which those coastal defences are constructed and managed. In England and Wales coastal defences are administered under the Coast Protection Act 1949 and the Water Act 1991. Until recently these provided for grant aid from central government for capital schemes, but not for maintenance. Although those constructing sea defences were in many cases the recipients of more than 70% central government grant, the maintenance of those same sea walls was considered to be the sole financial responsibility of the operating authority and therefore subject to no grant whatsoever. This strongly militated against the use of low initial cost, high maintenance schemes, such as beach nourishment. Over the last few years the UK central government has seen the problems that this has caused along the coastline, and now encourages a more strategic approach where re-nourishment and beach monitoring are frequently the subject of grant aid.

In addition to this, in many countries where public expenditure is increasingly tightly controlled, coastal engineering works are no exception to the requirement for economic evaluation and justification. This is not to say that there is a problem with identifying such economic justification. The towns of Brighton, Blackpool and many other holiday resorts in the UK depend on the seafront for their livelihood as well as for protection of the promenade and adjacent properties from erosion. As another example, the flood defences of the 26 km long coast between Mablethorpe and Skegness in Lincolnshire are vital to the protection of 20 000 ha of land. When they were breached in the 1953 floods, 42 people died. In a recent appraisal (Posford Duvivier 1991), the benefits of continuing to maintain those flood defences 'at a once in 200 year' standard were estimated to be of the order of £350 000 000.

Such strong justification (often social more than economic) for coastal defences is not confined to developed countries such as the UK and the Netherlands. For example, in the Maldives, a group of islands largely made up of coral, there is little land more than 1 m above sea level. Significant sea level rise in an area such as this will lead, in the absence of major coastal defence work, to inundation of the entire country. In Guyana in South America the vast majority of the country's population lives in the coastal strip within 16 km of the sea, on land that is low-lying and at risk from flooding. The land is protected by clay banks along the coast and the coast itself is subject to periodic erosion on a massive scale. In Kenya, about 50% of the population live on the coastal belt, 60% of the country's protein comes from the coastal belt and 60% of the foreign currency earnings come from tourism (Odada 1995). Coastal defences and coastal structures are clearly important to many countries. Although in the UK the annual level of expenditure of around £100 000 000 is small by comparison with other areas of engineering such as transport, there will always be a demand for coastal defence in the UK and in many countries overseas. This situation is unlikely to change.

Demand

The future demand for rock armour and beach nourishment therefore appears to be fairly secure in terms of the need for coastal engineering works, plus the appropriateness of rock and beach materials as a major component of those works. However, these are not the only factors that define demand. A major factor is the available financial budget. As an example, in England and Wales the major part of coastal defence work is grant aided by central government. This work (including both central and local funds) amounts to £100 000 000 each year. It is the author's view that with the seemingly

Table 1. *Estimate of beach nourishment demand*

Based on coastal protection needs

The following figures in Mm^3 show the estimated total projected demand for beach nourishment in England and Wales for the period 1995–2095 (CIRIA 1996). The figures in parentheses are in Mt using recommended bulking factors

Shingle	47.43 (94.9)
Sand and gravel	No data
Sand	82.78 (132.5)
Total	130.21 (227.4)
Average per year	6.5 (11.4)

Based on available budget

Alternatively, the demand can be estimated on the basis of the likely available funding. If we assume that (1) the annual expenditure in England and Wales on grant-aided coastal defences is £100 million, (2) 50% of the expenditure (at maximum) is on beach nourishment and (3) the average beach nourishment costs are £6/m^3, then the total demand is $100\,000\,000 \times 50\%/6 = 8.3\,Mm^3$ or 15.0 Mt per year.

ever-increasing pressure to reduce public spending on the one hand and the continuing essential need for coastal defence on the other, the figure of £100 000 000 is unlikely, in real terms, to increase greatly in the foreseeable future.

On the basis of this and other data (CIRIA 1996), Tables 1 and 2 provide a number of estimates of future demand. Demand for rock armour is dealt with further, and on the basis of different estimates, by Rees-Jones & Storhaug (1998).

Table 1 deals with beach nourishment. Demand has been estimated by CIRIA (1996) on the basis of a review of all the coast of England and Wales and the consequent identification of where beach nourishment might be appropriate. This method suggests a total annual

Table 2. *Estimate of armour rock demand based on the available budget*

Demand can be estimated on the basis of the likely available funding in a manner similar to that used in Table 1, item 3. If we assume that (1) the annual expenditure in England and Wales on grant-aided coastal defences is £100 million, (2) 70% of this expenditure is on schemes involving the use of rock, (3) 50% of the cost of these latter schemes relates to rock (the other 50% being concrete, shingle, etc.) and (4) the average rock costs are (supply and place including general and preliminary items) £30/t, then the total demand is $100\,000\,000 \times 70\% \times 50\%/30 = 1.2\,Mt\,a^{-1}$.

This estimate does not include non-grant aided coastal defences (e.g. Towyn), where the responsibility for the defences lay with a private body nor other (non-coastal defence) coastal work, e.g. harbours (a breakwater could use $2000 \times 15 \times 50 = 2.7$ Mt.

demand of about 6.5 Mm³, or 11.4 Mt. This ties in reasonably well with figures derived from the available budget, which point to a possible demand of 15 Mt each year. It is understood from CIRIA (1996) that the actual demand for beach nourishment has yet to reach these forecast figures and that these figures are in excess of those available from existing licensed areas. However, CIRIA (1996) also shows that the actual physical resource (potentially available) is in excess of the forecast demand. Turning to armour rock, a similar approach can be used to estimate the demand for rock and Table 2 suggests an annual demand in the region of 1.2 Mt. This is not dissimilar to demand that has occurred in recent years (Rees-Jones & Storhaug 1998).

The demand estimates which are derived from grant aid figures do not make allowance for non-grant-aided works such as harbours and private coastal defences. A single large breakwater could double the demand for rock for a single year (Rees-Jones & Storhaug 1998). A large private coastal defence scheme could also increase the demand significantly. The scheme at Towyn, North Wales (by British Rail) used 400 000 t of rock, for example.

In view of these figures, the demand for beach nourishment in England and Wales does not yet appear to have reached its full potential, while that for rock may be more steady in the future. The demand for both materials will occasionally be influenced by large schemes.

Environmental aspects

This paper has discussed the environmental value of the coast and the environmental advantages of using natural materials (such as rock and gravel) for coastal defences. However, recent developments in the use of both rock and beach nourishment have shown another environmental aspect not yet mentioned. This is the environmental impact at the source. The Mablethorpe to Skegness Beach Nourishment Scheme, needing 25 million tonnes of sand, over a number of years (Posford Duvivier 1991), has been significantly delayed by the failure to obtain a dredging licence for the fill. This was largely the result of objections by fishermen, whose concerns could not be answered as a result of uncertainty with regard to the possible impact on crab fisheries. In a not dissimilar vein, plans for major new superquarries in Scotland have been substantially affected by environmental concerns. There are those who say that although the use of rock and beach nourishment is environmentally sympathetic at the site, it may be at the cost of environmental damage elsewhere.

Environmental awareness and concern is increasing everywhere. There are those who still hold the view that an environmental conscience is a luxury only to be afforded by wealthy countries, but nonetheless environmental legislation is increasing. Environmental protection is becoming ever stronger and more widespread. Environmental protection is no longer confined to the currently developed world.

The extraction of rock and beach material has the potential to cause major environmental damage. The extraction process, with respect to environmental impacts, often goes through four stages: (1) extraction starts in the belief that there will be no significant environmental damage, or in ignorance of any such risk; (2) as a result of clear or anecdotal evidence of environmental pressure, there is a recognition that there may be environmental damage; (3) attempts are made to understand the environment and define or quantify the damage and its seriousness; and (4) given an understanding gained in stage (3), the extraction can often continue or be amended to proceed in a managed, sustainable fashion.

It is unfortunate when the steps take place in this order. In such cases stage (3) can lead to a precautionary approach which requires that extraction is stopped until the environment is understood and stage (4) takes place. It is far better to achieve this understanding before extraction starts and to enable the operation to begin on a sound commercial and environmental footing.

For example, in the case of gravel extraction on land in the UK, historically permission was given without planning conditions. Conditions now require the extractor to landscape the sites when exhausted. In many cases the environmental impact is mitigated to the extent that the sites become of environmental benefit as, for example, wildlife habitats and recreational amenities resulting from the new water areas. In many parts of the UK it seems like the quarrying industry is already behaving in an environmentally sensitive manner.

There are, however, still areas where extraction is causing major environmental damage. Examples are the mining of beach sand and the coastal erosion it causes, or the mining of foreshore coral for construction and the consequent damage to the coast. We cannot avoid the conclusion that these are activities living on borrowed time, but in reality they will often not be stopped until viable alternative sources are found. This in itself offers considerable commercial opportunities for established extraction industries to export their talents.

Summary and conclusions

The preceding discussion has shown, drawing heavily on UK experience and practice, that there is and will be a continuing demand for engineering work at the coast.

The demand is taking place at a time of increased understanding of physical processes and increased awareness of the value and sensitivity of the environment. In this context rock armour and beach recharge are likely to be a major component of engineering structures because their characteristics are in many ways more environmentally acceptable than some of the alternatives, as well as being economically competitive. The fact that the extraction industries can potentially cause environmental damage at source is in many cases being addressed. Through extraction in a sustainably managed fashion such an approach offers opportunities for the export of skills to developing countries where they still have problems. In conclusion, the outlook for rock armour and beach recharge in the UK and overseas is good and not without substantial challenges and opportunities.

References

CIRIA 1996. *Beach Management Manual*. CIRIA Report 153. CIRIA, London.

DEPARTMENT OF THE ENVIRONMENT 1994. *Minerals Planning Guidance; Guidance for Aggregate Provision in England*. Report MPG6, April 1994, HMSO, London.

MAFF 1994. *Coast Protection Survey of England*. HMSO, London.

ODADA, E. O. 1995. Coastal change: its implications for Eastern Africa. Keynote address. *In: Proceedings, International Conference on Coastal Change – Bordomer 95*. IOC, Bordomer, 65–267.

POSFORD DUVIVIER 1991. *Mablethorpe to Skegness Sea Defences. Strategy Study*. Report on behalf of the National Rivers Authority Anglian Region.

REES-JONES, R. G. & STORHAUG, E. 1998. Meeting the demand for rock and armour and its grading specification. *This volume*.

Assessment and specification of armourstone quality: from CIRIA/CUR (1991) to CEN (2000)

J.-P. Latham

Department of Engineering, Queen Mary & Westfield College, Mile End Road, London E1 4NS, UK

Abstract. As a typical by-product to normal quarrying, armourstone has many attributes that make its objective specification and testing less straightforward than most producers would wish. Neither, it appears, has the market forces principle and tendering practices in the UK construction industry, leading to minimal forward planning of armourstone testing, helped to enhance quality control of materials. The undoubted advances heralded by the standardizing approach of the CIRIA/CUR *Manual on the Use of Rock in Coastal and Shoreline Engineering* and its model specification have done much to rationalize a previously over-simplistic view of armourstone specification. However, recent practical experience with many coastal contracts which have adopted the CIRIA/CUR specification has exposed a number of problems with the detailed implementation of the rock quality testing part of the model specification. In particular, this experience draws attention to a lack of published correlation studies between the various abrasion tests and between strength tests. Rock suppliers are reporting that designers are continuing to specify using the BS 812 suite of aggregate tests. The potential for bias in the taking and preparation of representative test portions has also remained a problem.

The manual specification's rationale, its strengths and weaknesses, are outlined. Correlation analysis of new research data from a suite of rocks is presented. A re-examination of the manual specification's acceptance criteria for resistance to wear and to breakage is presented. A way forward is offered for the continued use of the manual specification until its supersedence by the European CEN specification for armourstone. Improvements in the 16th draft of the CEN standard are briefly discussed, and it is found that certain problems that the manual began to address remain unsolved.

There can be little doubt that the publication of the CIRIA/CUR (1991) *Manual on the Use of Rock in Coastal and Shoreline Engineering*, hereafter referred to in this paper as the manual, has had a major impact on UK practitioners working with armourstone. Discussion of the manual's recommendations has figured centrally in a number of conferences and meetings dedicated to the subject of armourstone and attended by producers and suppliers of rock armour as well as designers and owners of rock-armoured coastal structures. For those less familiar with the manual, the overall aim of this Anglo–Dutch collaboration was to provide guidance on materials, hydraulics and the geotechnical design of rock structures. It was thus an opportunity to present best engineering practice and to unify within one volume the diversity and evident confusion that reigned over the subject of armourstone and its use.

One of the more novel, but also controversial, parts of the manual is that dealing with materials. An explanatory main text is supported by suggested protocols contained within appendices. One appendix, which is the main subject of this paper, outlines a suggested standard specification for rock properties and placement, now known in the industry as the CIRIA/CUR specification. A second appendix gives all the new test methods that are associated with the specification, but which cannot be found elsewhere as they are not national standard tests. The rationale behind the push towards standardization embodied in the manual's sections dealing with materials and specification was summarized by Simm *et al.* (1992). Tables and figures reproduced from the manual publicizing the standardized terminology and a test results guide to rock durability are given in Simm & Latham (1994). Using the recommendations of the manual, Gauss & Latham (1995*a, b*) reported the on-site quality control and the as-built armour layer geometry of a rock revetment that was designed and built following the manual's publication. However, the subject of rock quality testing was outside the scope of these two papers.

Now, with at least four year's experience of contracts, including that from various testing laboratories who have been presented with the full CIRIA/CUR specification for rock quality tests, it is timely to consider and wherever possible to rectify various shortcomings that

LATHAM, J.-P. 1998. Assessment and specification of armourstone quality: from CIRIA/CUR (1991) to CEN (2000). *In*: LATHAM, J.-P. (ed.) 1998. *Advances in Aggregates and Armourstone Evaluation*. Geological Society, London, Engineering Geology Special Publications, **13**, 65–85.

have come to light. The most important problems encountered with this new specification for rock quality are summarized below.

Bad planning of materials supply

The planning of materials procurement has often been poor and tendering periods are typically far too short. It would seem logical that the designer should allow the tendering contractors sufficient time to price offers that take account of alternative prices for rock of certified quality as well as the less well known sources that may be local to the site. However, the truth has been that testing laboratories have on a number of occasions been asked to test rock samples representing a 10 000 t barge consignment that is already loaded – perhaps to meet a narrow window of possible tides for beaching the barge and a pressing start date to beat a peak tourism period! The possible failure of the rock to meet test requirements is merely treated as an added risk, while understandably eager contractors try to solicit preliminary results from testing laboratories perhaps only two or three days after the laboratory has received the samples. It is often forgotten that certain mandatory tests (i.e. those required for source approval) take a minimum of three or five weeks to conduct.

It is, however, understandable that contractors will often not wish to incur the cost of a set of test results before winning the contract, unless perhaps it is a very substantial contract. Clearly, specification by quality and not by source must be facilitated in the tendering process and contractors must, among other matters, review the information on the availability and quality of materials continuously.

Lack of investment in quality control by supplier

The complete test suite is more expensive than in pre-manual days. This is compounded for the rock producer as the client usually interprets the manual as requiring new sample test results for each new contract. Certain tests such as density, according to the quality control section of the manual, should be reported several times for a large contract, especially those with a range of sources or variable geology in the source quarry. There has been a general lack of willingness of potential suppliers of armourstone to invest in a set of test results for a sample suite before tendering, although some leading Norwegian suppliers have done so to great competitive advantage. However, in spite of the status of armourstone as a by-product or waste product of aggregate or dimension stone production, there now appears to be a move towards annual or periodic test certification of approved armourstone sources, in recognition of the armourstone market. This is a helpful trend, but one which may disadvantage aggregate quarries who are

only small local suppliers of armourstone and therefore tend not to carry out special armourstone tests. In North Wales, for example, very few suppliers of Carboniferous limestone can see armourstone as a marketable product, preferring to sell it on as and when a particular scheme comes up that requires the particular size of stone that they have accumulated since the last job.

A national and European-wide database of historical test data and quarry working practices would help facilitate the free market approach. These data would give contractors the extra confidence required to delay selection and source approval until after winning a contract. Generally, both client and supplier would be rewarded for investment in such a database of testing and quality control as the risks with rock armour quality are reduced.

Lack of clarity in the manual

Sampling, testing and the requirements are presented in separate sections of the manual's text and appendices. This has left some degree of confusion, even with regard to which tests are mandatory. Specific instructions telling the sample taker what should be sent to the laboratory cannot be easily found.

Unavailability of apparatus for mandatory test

The apparatus for one of the mandatory tests, the QMW mill abrasion test, is of limited availability. This test has been described in detail, but in a US publication (Latham 1993). Published correlation studies comparing this test with more familiar tests are therefore not well known.

Need for published correlation studies for reference

There is a general lack of correlation study data relating aggregate test results (e.g. the BS 812 test suite, which was traditionally used for coastal structures in the 1970s and 1980s) to the intact rock strength test results now preferred for specifying armourstone strength.

Need for decision-tree staged approach to testing

The sheer waste of carrying out an expensive suite of tests on rock that an experienced geologist can immediately see would pass the requirements with flying colours has long been recognized. However, a staged 'decision-tree' approach to testing, allowing the possibility of fewer tests, is a delicate matter to specify correctly. This is especially so because representatives of the quarry industry have tended to resist (on the basis of possible subjectivity) the possibility of allowing a petrographer's techniques and judgement to influence source approval.

The producer's preference is for more objective tests than petrographic analysis, even though they may be less diagnostic.

Discussion

Despite the good intentions of the Anglo–Dutch manual, the above discussion clearly indicates that, in practice, it has not been possible to implement smoothly the methods of testing armourstone quality in the more objective manner intended in its suggested specification.

In the meantime, to facilitate European trade, the CEN (Comité de Européen Normalisation) commissioned in 1991 a 'Group of Experts' to develop a Euro-standard for armourstone as an offshoot of the activities of the technical committee TC154 covering aggregates. The group's aim was essentially to provide an objective means for the evaluation and testing of armourstone that is appropriate, both practically and scientifically, for this uniquely large class of materials with its particular performance requirements. However, the TC154 terms of reference did not include a research budget and the group's work has also been restricted to reaching majority agreement based on the use of existing specification practices and test methods of national standard status. As special tests and specifications for armourstone are a relatively new development, the existing national standards which are usually based on aggregate tests do not provide a wholly appropriate pool of tests to draw upon. Fortunately, lessons learned from using the manual specification have greatly influenced the shaping of the new draft CEN standard for armourstone and some particular test refinements to meet the needs of armourstone will be included in the Euro-standard, whereas certain others have been shelved. At the time of writing (in 1997), the 16th draft of the Euro-standard was about to be submitted as a prEN to CEN enquiry.

The purposes of this paper are: (1) to summarize the rationale behind the programme of sampling and testing of rock quality presented in the manual; (2) to present a selection of new results from testing carried out at Queen Mary and Westfield College (QMW) – the results will provide correlations between the new tests proposed in the manual specification and certain other popular aggregate tests; and (3) to propose a number of modifications and simplifications to the CIRIA/CUR 1991 suggested specification that would be appropriate for current contracts. These will take on board the 16th draft CEN standard for armourstone whose final widespread adoption may still take several years.

Proceeding from the above introduction, the paper now continues with an explanation of the rationale of the CIRIA/CUR (1991) test suite. The QMW research programme, designed to investigate the correlation between certain tests is then presented. It deals with two specific groups of tests: those for abrasion resistance and those for breakage resistance, as it is these properties for which new tests are specified in the manual. A full presentation and discussion of the results is given so that the confidence or lack of it is well understood when predicting one test result from another.

The CEN specification developments are also of interest to practitioners and so a short section is included which summarizes the key differences in requirements (and thus test methods and samples) that may be needed in the not too distant future using the forthcoming EN (European Norme or standard) as compared with the manual. Assessment of resistance to weathering of armourstone as proposed in the 16th draft CEN specification is then raised. The role that petrographic screening and service record is to play is also mentioned.

The paper ends with recommendations in the knowledge that there will otherwise be a few unguided years before the forthcoming CEN standards for armourstone are routinely referred to in contracts.

The needs of the sample taker regarding field examination, sample reduction procedures and the sample sizes involved in each test are also addressed. These are presented in an appendix in the form of a set of instructions recommended for use in connection with the manual specification and are based on several years' practical laboratory experience. These instructions may need slight adjustment when the final EN is in use.

Armourstone properties: CIRIA/CUR (1991)

The properties of armourstone that the designer aims to control by means of a contract specification can be divided into the following.

- Intrinsic properties which are the *in situ* geological properties of the source rock such as strength, density and resistance to weathering under given conditions.
- Manufactured properties (sometimes termed as-produced, or production-affected properties) –these are the geometric properties such as shape and grading and the integrity of materials ready for delivery.
- Execution-induced properties (sometimes called as-built, or as-constructed properties) which are the bulk properties of granular media after construction, such as layer thickness and bulk density.
- Durability, i.e. resistance to degradation in service, which in turn is a function mainly of (1), but also, as is all too often disregarded, the site environment and design of the structure.

This paper is primarily concerned with intrinsic properties and the tests associated with rock quality.

CIRIA/CUR test rationale

The rock quality requirements of the CIRIA/CUR suggested specification for armourstone divide, as shown in Table 1, with mandatory quantitative testing from within four types of properties given in the left-hand column. The following sections highlight what is recommended in the manual and propose improvements in the light of recent experience.

Role of petrography

A petrographic description is stated in the body of the manual text to be a vital early stage in a rock source evaluation. In a properly executed petrographic study, samples of the rock are examined in thin section. Ideally, the report should provide all the data required to indicate the rock type, the likely density and water absorption, the degree of weathering that has already taken place and the potential for further alteration, the potential for the development of planes of weakness and the potential for resistance to abrasion. The study would allow the categorization of the likely suitability of materials and obviously defective material would be recognized. For example, basalt liable to the Sonnenbrand effect (described later) should be identified in the petrographic assessment.

The role of petrography in the manual specification is in need of further clarification arising from the fact that petrographic description is not itemized as a mandatory

test and that no standard description method is referred to. Nonetheless, in the decision process for testing resistance to weathering stated in the manual specification, the rock type name must be established. Furthermore, 'a description' of the test sample or test pieces is required within the laboratory report on each particular test or test series for most of the CIRIA/CUR tests. This loose use of the term 'a description' has in some instances led to the suggestion that all samples tested by methods described in the manual specification should be supported by full petrographic descriptions of the samples even if not specifically requested. This was not the original intention, besides which a petrographic description method had not then been agreed upon. Rather, the description intended was more that of a geological classification into rock type that could be assumed to be sufficiently accurate and previously available for the purpose of commercial exploitation of the source. In hindsight, the mistake was not to give a simple test method for petrographic description and make it mandatory, a lesson now rectified in the 16th draft CEN specification, which refers to a simple EN test for the petrographic description of aggregates.

Physical property tests

Density
Oven dry density is a vital parameter for design purposes and, together with water absorption, gives essential stability information as well as an undisputed reference

Table 1. *Mandatory and optional tests in the CIRIA/CUR specification*

Type of properties	Mandatory tests	Further non-mandatory tests (can be specified depending on the specifier's judgement of conditions and risk)
Physical properties	Density Water absorption	

Resistance to weathering	Water absorption
	Presence of deleterious secondary minerals as indicated by either (I), test first by a petrographic examination to give a rock type name
	(a) if on a certain list of 'safe' rock types, no further testing required
	(b) if of basaltic type test (i) for methylene blue and (ii) for Sonnenbrand
	(c) if not basaltic, but not on 'safe' list, test (i) for methylene blue
	or (II), without rock type name, test (i) for methylene blue and (ii) for Sonnenbrand
		none, one or two from:
		    magnesium sulphate test
		    freeze–thaw test

Resistance to impact and mineral fabric breakage (type 2 breakage)	One from
	    Fracture toughness
	    Point load index
	    Wet dynamic crushing value
		None, one or two from
		    fracture toughness
		    point load index
		    wet dynamic crushing value

Resistance to abrasion	QMW mill abrasion	
Block integrity (type 1 breakage)	Visual examination (subjective)	Drop test breakage index

value for volume filling and weight relations for the execution-induced properties of the armour layer. With repeated testing between given periods of production (the manual suggests the choice of test frequency be between 5 and 20 000 tonnes of rock armour), variations in density within a quarry can give a warning of meeting weathered zones or suspect quality rock. Ten test pieces taken from ten armourstones are tested on a stone by stone rather than aggregate basis. The CIRIA/CUR test is therefore based on the quick submerged weight test principle, a brief submergence time (with some consequent increased variability due to differing amounts of initial saturation before testing) and individual pieces with a volume of at least 50 ml. In practice, the advantage of the rapidity of the test is often lost as the water absorption test (requiring saturation to constant weight) is usually performed together using the same test pieces. Thus the EN for density and water absorption for armourstone will involve a method with saturation to constant weight.

Resistance to weathering

The intention of the CIRIA/CUR specification was to guard against two breakdown mechanisms, one being cyclic cystallization pressures from ice or salts in microcracks and pores, the other being dimensional instability and consequent eventual cracking due to a significant presence of clay or other deleterious (usually secondary) minerals. To accommodate the first possibility, the water absorption test is mandatory. For the second, knowledge of the rock type(s) may negate the need for mandatory tests for methylene blue absorption and the Sonnenbrand effect (see Table 1).

If in the unlikely event that the rock type is not determined, then tests for methylene blue absorption and the Sonnenbrand effect (a boiling test) are mandatory. In addition, the manual recommends that these mandatory tests should normally be supplemented with either a freeze–thaw test or a magnesium sulphate test, the specifier being given the choice. Guidance on the most appropriate choice, which considers the climate in which the rock is to be used, is given in the main text of the manual. Note also that a water absorption value of 0.5% or under is said in the manual to satisfy the requirement for freeze–thaw resistance. However, no equivalent water absorption clause is given for satisfying the magnesium sulphate test, an inconsistency which has been rectified in the 16th draft CEN specification.

Methylene blue test
This test detects undesirable sheet silicates and points to a potential for weathering deterioration. It has, however, been pointed out that the test is typically as expensive as X-ray analysis of the sample, which will provide more data about the presence of unacceptable sheet silicates. The specified methylene blue test method is the one described in an appendix of the manual.

Magnesium sulphate test
This non-mandatory test provides a measure of the resistance of the material to weathering, particularly salt weathering, or wetting and drying damage or frost damage. It requires much less test material and is less time consuming than the freeze–thaw test. The manual allows alternative size aggregate pieces to be tested.

Water absorption
In the CIRIA/CUR test individual pieces of 50–150 ml are tested using the principle of atmospheric pressure saturation to constant mass. The test is a mandatory test firstly in order that the saturated density of armourstones can be calculated for design purposes (using the oven dry density and water absorption) and, secondly, because it is the single simplest and most indicative test for resistance to weathering in spite of documented exceptions such as limestones with large free-draining pore structures (Clark 1988). Note, however, that the acceptance criterion for the average water absorption is less than 2% or less than 6%, depending on the designer's choice of acceptable quality, which, in turn, should be based on their judgement of the aggressiveness of the site environment.

Freeze–thaw test
This non-mandatory test is a complex and difficult test for the resistance of the material to occasional very low temperatures. It requires the use of a powerful freezer cabinet and large pieces of rock which are intact and have no visible flaws. When freeze–thaw resistance is to be tested, the water absorption test is taken as the first screening stage whereby a water absorption value of less than 0.5% is taken to mean that the specimen is freeze–thaw resistant. The CIRIA/CUR method involves saturation to constant mass in preference to a fixed 24 hour period, thus giving greater confidence in the assertion of freeze–thaw resistance when a result of under 0.5% absorption is obtained. This staged approach has implications for the sample preparation, which have rarely been spelled out to the sample supplier. For consistency and sampling rigour, test material for the water absorption test should be derived from the same individual parent piece of armourstone as the larger (10–20 kg) test pieces required for the freeze–thaw test.

Sonnenbrand effect
A test for the phenomenon relatively unknown in the UK, but long recognized in Germany, is the test for the 'Sonnenbrand' or 'sunburn' effect. The cracking resulting from this phenomenon is a highly destructive result of what is believed to be the instability of certain minerals such as primary feldspathoides, zeolites and glass, as well as secondary zeolites (e.g. analcime) and

smectites (swelling clay minerals), found in a narrow class of basaltic rocks. Temperature accelerates the decomposition of unstable constituents and therefore the test is based on a boiling procedure and a visual examination for star-shaped spots with hair cracks on a drying surface. The discovery of so-called 'Sonnenbrenner' as the first indication of the rock's instability is discussed in Kuhnel (1985), where a more elaborate test method than the boiling test is recommended. In both the manual and the 16th draft CEN specification, this boiling test is intended to be mandatory if the rock is of the basaltic type.

Specification problems arising from the lack of a petrographic description clause
This last sentence above raises a difficulty for manual specification users. It is strongly implied in the manual that a petrographic examination and classification by an experienced and qualified geologist (e.g. a chartered geologist) using a specified acceptable (e.g. BS or ASTM) procedure should first be carried out to ascertain its rock type and thus whether it is of a basaltic type. Alternatively, but certainly less desirable than a mandatory petrographic examination, it could be argued that, from the wording in the manual, the quarry industry's accepted classification for trade purposes (which includes basaltic and other distinct types) may be deemed a satisfactory basis for whether to invoke the boiling test in the specification. Such problems would be instantly solved by introducing a mandatory petrographic description according to a set method that classifies the rock type as a first stage to testing. This has, in fact, been done in the 16th draft CEN specification, where the rock classification name, taken from CEN's new simple petrographic description procedure, must accompany any sample.

The manual specification contains a note to indicate those rock types which are unlikely to have deleterious secondary minerals. In principle, this is useful information for specification users as it can give a prediction of a likely test outcome. However, because 'experienced geologist' and the petrographic procedure were not objectively defined in the manual, it is advisable that this type of exemption should, in future, be discounted when adopting the specification or alternatively, an appropriate reference to standard procedures is given. This will ensure that *ad hoc* rock classification procedures cannot act as 'get-out clauses' for certain tests.

With respect to the problem of preventing degradation due to clay minerals, the current majority view expressed within the European working group suggests that mandatory test requirements and appropriate acceptance values for a wet milling abrasion test (e.g. wet micro-Deval) and a wet intact strength test would normally act as a fail-safe test to pick out potential in-service weakness due to slaking and the presence of swelling clay minerals. If not, then the resistance to weathering clauses should provide adequate further assurances. The group has

therefore suggested that a specific test for clay minerals, such as the methylene blue test, is therefore unnecessary, particularly as there is scope within CEN's new simple petrographic description procedure to indicate the presence of clay minerals. However, the author warns that there should be no illusions as to the superficial nature of the simple examination procedure just referred to, which falls far short of what a truly diagnostic petrographic examination by an experienced engineering petrographer would entail.

Resistance to breakage

One common way for armourstone blocks to break is by splitting into major pieces along geologically formed planes of weakness or blast-induced cracks. The author has distinguished this as type 1 breakage (Fig. 1). Guarding against excessive type 1 breakage, which in practice means the prevention of a large proportion of poor integrity blocks arriving on site, should ideally be addressed with an objective quarry-based test that applies to a representative sample of whole blocks. The manual specification retains a subjective clause based on visual criteria, but strongly urges the use of a separate objective test for block integrity. It proposes a new direct and objectively defined test for the 'whole block strength'. It is known as the drop test and the sample's breakage parameter that is determined is called the drop test breakage index. It is described in the manual appendix and further investigated in Latham & Gauss (1995), where it was suggested that the index definition could be improved to better describe a rock block's fragility. This is a distinctive property of a sample of source blocks which needs to be tested in addition to intact strength. The intact strength tests strictly measure the mineral fabric strength within a hand-sized specimen, which is often poorly correlated with block integrity.

The resistance of the mineral fabric to breakage caused by impact is a strength property that is not sensitive to the possibility of flaws that may partially or fully traverse blocks (i.e. the block integrity). Instead, it relates to the strength to resist new breakages through the mineral or grain fabric (type 2 breakage; Fig. 1), which typically occurs at the corners and edges of blocks when knocked during handling and in service. This, in turn, may lead to the progressive loss of interlock, size reduction and rounding and the generation of a large proportion of useless fines and fragments during handling and transportation. To measure resistance to type 2 breakage, the CIRIA/CUR specification indicates that any combination using at least one of the following three tests – fracture toughness, point load strength or wet dynamic crushing value – can be used to varying degrees of effectiveness. The first two use hand-sized specimens while the third uses 10–14 mm size aggregates.

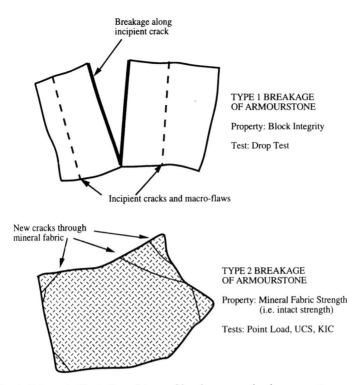

Breakage along
incipient crack

TYPE 1 BREAKAGE
OF ARMOURSTONE

Property: Block Integrity

Test: Drop Test

Incipient cracks and macro-flaws

New cracks through
mineral fabric

TYPE 2 BREAKAGE
OF ARMOURSTONE

Property: Mineral Fabric Strength
(i.e. intact strength)

Tests: Point Load, UCS, KIC

Fig. 1. Schematic illustration of types of breakage occurring in armourstone.

Fracture toughness
The fracture toughness test is recommended in the manual as the best test to establish resistance to type 2 breakage. The model specification refers to the ISRM (1988) test methods (at level I). These methods encourage a new crack to grow naturally from a ligament of rock that is highly stressed in a standardized fashion rather than from a chance occurrence of a pre-existing flaw. The test measures the stress intensity ahead of the crack tip that is required for catastrophic crack propagation. It is an ideal test parameter for classification purposes, but has yet to gain widespread recognition, while such few geomaterials testing laboratories have the necessary testing set-up. An appropriate and even simpler fracture toughness test method that loads a rock disc in compression has been reported (Fowell & Chen 1990), and has now been further investigated by the ISRM commision on testing materials (ISRM 1995) so that relative costs for obtaining this parameter for a set of test specimens may come down in the future. (Currently, though fewer laboratories do the test, per specimen it is of comparable cost to the uniaxial compressive strength test.) The manual indicates that other intact strength measures have higher test variability, a point taken up later in the paper, and the manual specification gives clear-cut requirements based on a test sample of at least six test specimens. That the tests should be carried out on saturated specimens, i.e. the engineering condition in which they must perform, is not explicitly stated, but is noted in the ISRM method descriptions for both fracture toughness and point load strength index.

Point load strength
The point load strength test is recommended in the manual as the second best test to establish the resistance to type 2 breakage. In many respects the point load strength index would appear to be the ideal practical method to use for the mineral fabric strength. This is because the testing apparatus is simple and portable and the specimen preparation and testing is rapid. Field testing using irregular lumps from the quarry face is ideal for quarry evaluation and production control. To sample the variability of properties in an armourstone stockpile, particularly in a quarry with visibly differing sedimentary horizons, there will always be a desire to obtain test specimens from a relatively large number of blocks. For production control testing and even specification conformance testing, the use of the uniaxial compressive strength test would seem prohibitively expensive. At approximately four times the cost of the point load test per specimen, based on machine operator time and the

tolerances required, the compressive strength test was not considered in the manual specification.

The ISRM (1985) point load strength test is the test method referred to in the manual specification. However, certain conditions for reporting results are included to override and improve on those given in the ISRM for the purposes of armourstone specification. For anisotropic rock, the strength parallel to the plane of anisotropy is required for the reported result. Also, the number of valid test results is required to be at least 12, these originating from at least 10 separate randomly selected armourstones. This has sometimes lead to confusion as the number of invalid failures is unpredictable. Therefore a number of reserve specimens may be needed and enough sample material must be available. Another less significant difference with the ISRM reporting of results is the discounting of the top and bottom results before calculating the average strength rather than excluding the top two and bottom two results as suggested in the ISRM method. It is also the intention that for specification conformance testing the irregular lump test should not be considered as a valid specimen geometry option for the point load test as it unnecessarily increases test variability through inaccurate size determination.

Aggregate impact strength tests

The wet dynamic crushing test method (WDCV) is fully described in an appendix of the manual and is the least preferred of the three tests for resistance to type 2 breakage given in the manual specification in terms of the information it yields. It takes the essential features of the BS 812 (1975) AIV test, but improves its relevance to armourstone by controlling the shape of the aggregates – flaky and equant pieces are removed by slotted sieves and aggregates are tested in a saturated condition which can show up a susceptibility to water weakening. The specification attempts to ensure that samples are representative of the material in the armourstone stockpiles by requiring that the aggregate is derived from separately crushed parts of randomly selected armourstone. The main objection for using aggregate impact tests for the mineral fabric strength is the exclusion of good quality armourstone that would result. Some of the most ideal armourstone sources are from coarse-grained igneous rocks which will tend to perform unrepresentatively in the standard and related AIV tests, with results between 20 and 30 being common. This is thought to be because unfavourably oriented crystal cleavage planes have a proportionally greater influence as the crystal size approaches the test aggregate size.

Another disadvantage that applies to all aggregate tests is that sample preparation will need to be standardized. It will also be time consuming and expensive to prepare a representative sample from separate armourstones unless aggregates taken from

the aggregates production crushing plant are deemed representative by the purchaser. However, by no means will all armourstone supplying quarries be aggregate producers, e.g. dimension stone quarries, so that test aggregate samples will have to be made anyway. The sample preparation procedures for the test aggregate can influence the occurrence of micro-fractures. Therefore, the effect of preparation will not necessarily be comparable from different sources unless a prescribed method (e.g. laboratory jaw crusher and incremental size reduction settings) is always used. This problem has also been recognized in the 16th draft CEN specification, in which test aggregate is needed for the micro-Deval and magnesium sulphate tests.

Because of the popularity and simplicity of the AIV type test, the WDCV test was included in the manual specification. It enables a cheap, reproducible and rapid test on a less bulky test sample. However, it is the least preferred of the three tests. As with any test, the sampling method indicating the representativness of the test sample should be detailed in the test report. In spite of the explicit points in the manual, this rarely takes place in practice. Samples usually arrive with no such details and an independent sample taker is rarely commissioned for this work as the aggregates production stockpile is usually deemed sufficiently representative for the supply of aggregate test samples, sometimes even without the client's consent or awareness.

The manual specification simply states that one or a combination of the three mineral fabric strength tests shall be specified. However, it is implicit (but not as clearly set out as in Table 1) that if two tests are specified and one of these two tests fail (e.g. WDCV), while another passes (e.g. point load), then the material fails to meet specification approval.

Resistance to abrasion

This is another property of the mineral fabric strength. The relatively new QMW mill abrasion test is the mandatory test. It was included as it was believed to be a superior test to existing standard tests in many respects, both for discriminating suitable rocks including marginal and poor ones, and for predicting in-service performance. The mill abrasion testing machine was under active consideration by a leading international testing machine manufacturer at the time the manual was going to press in 1991, and would therefore have become widely available to testing laboratories had the manufacturer gone ahead with its production. However, in the 16th draft CEN specification the wet micro-Deval test has been chosen instead.

The discriminating power and physical interpretation of the QMW mill abrasion test results are best seen when different rock samples are superimposed on a plot of fraction of weight remaining versus revolutions in the

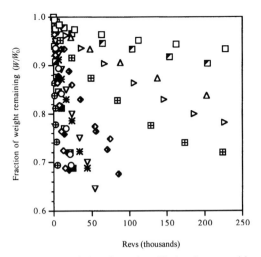

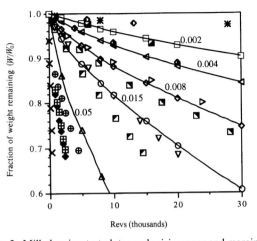

Fig. 2. Selection of plots from the mill abrasion test with precise results for MAV (k_s) as follows: □, gneiss, 0.000180; ◇, porous sandstone, 0.0245; ○, porous sandstone, 0.0147; △, granite, 0.000688; ⊞, weathered granite, 0.00135; ◈, hard chalk, 0.0179; ⊕, Cretaceous ironstone, 0.0656; ▽, oolitic limestone, 0.00703; ◪, muddy limestone, 0.0110; ◧, sandy limestone, 0.00405; ✳, weathered dolerite, 0.00784; ▷, recrystallized sandstone, 0.000831; ◿, andesite, 0.000330; and ◇, dolerite, 0.00286.

Fig. 3. Mill abrasion test plots emphasizing poor and marginal materials. Bands show typical plots for the MAV (k_s) categories given in the manual with precise results as follows: ⊞, Bayadat limestone, 0.120; ◈, Bayadat limestone, 0.123; ⊕, Cretaceous ironstone, 0.0656; ▽, hard chalk, 0.0179; ◪, Carboniferous limestone, 0.00256; ◧, sandy limestone, 0.00405; ✳, augen gneiss, 0.000180; ▷, oolitic limestone, 0.00703; ◿, Bunter sandstone, 0.0245; ◇, granite gneiss, 0.000191; ×, soft chalk, 0.818; and ◣, Roach limestone, 0.0107.

mill (see Figs 2 & 3). The test method and relative merits of this novel test have been presented previously (Latham 1991, 1993).

Test programme for the correlation study

Rock sample suites

Rock samples numbered 1–23 were obtained from UK and Scandinavian sources. They consisted of 13 sedimentary rocks, with sandstones ranging in strength from an ironstone of Cretaceous age (mi) to a re-crystallized Devonian sandstone (ts), and limestones ranging in strength from a hard chalk (mc) to a typical Carboniferous limestone from the Mendip area (wl). There were ten igneous and metamorphic rocks, including samples from weathering grades II and III, as well as four Scandinavian rocks now found in UK coastal structures. These included an augen gneiss (ag), a granite–gneiss (eg) and a syenite (ls). Rock samples numbered 24–28 represent overseas rocks submitted under a PIANC (Permanent International Association of Navigational Congresses) working group initiative to the QMW laboratories for mill abrasion and fracture toughness testing. Numbers 29–32 represent a group of very weak limestones, including duricrust from the Middle East (bl) and soft chalk (dc) from the Dover area. Numbers 33–39

represent an earlier suite of rocks that were investigated before building the new mill abrasion apparatus. A conversion factor yields the equivalent new mill abrasion results (Latham 1993).

Test programme

An SERC funded research project of 1988–1990 was set up with the welcomed agreement of financial support for materials testing given by one major quarry company. Unfortunately, their testing facilities were later to be decommissioned and only one set of wet attrition tests were carried out there before closure. The programme was consequently severely disrupted. The redesign and construction of the QMW abrasion mill apparatus was successful, but slower to materialize than anticipated. Material preparation for the intact rock and aggregate tests was relegated to low priority work in an already over-stretched geomaterials testing laboratory. Four overseas samples from the PIANC working group members remained in storage for over three years.

The overall investigation can be divided into five topics; (1) abrasion resistance tests; (2) soundness tests; (3) aggregate impact tests; (4) mineral fabric strength tests; and (5) overseas samples. It was not possible to subject all samples to all tests. The subjects reported in this paper will be confined to topics (1) and (4), whereas other topics will be reported in future publications.

Abrasion resistance series

Considerable effort has focused on the new mill abrasion test (Latham 1991, 1993) developed at QMW, which gives an abrasion resistance index, k_s, or mill abrasion value (MAV) that indicates the fraction of weight lost per thousand revolutions for rock particles tumbled in a cylindrical drum. Between 10 and 20 samples have been used to correlate MAV with: (1) the aggregate abrasion test value (AAV) defined in BS 812 (1975); (2) the wet attrition test value (WAV) described in BS 812 (1951), which is similar to the French wet Deval test; and (3) the wet micro-Deval test value (MDE), which has been a standard in France for some 20 years (AFNOR 1990; NF P 18-572).

An examination of the MAV with certain physical and other strength properties was also included for completeness.

Intact strength compared with aggregate impact strength series

In the UK, mineral fabric strength testing for armourstone has traditionally followed the recommendations of BS 6349 (1984) of using the aggregate strength tests AIV, ACV, 10% fines, but there are reasons, discussed earlier, for preferring an intact strength test. The fracture toughness test value, K_{IC}, and point load strength index $I_{s(50)}$, were in need of further evaluation through correlation studies with AIV as spurious results and a poor correlation have long been suspected.

Results of correlation study

In considering the nature and quality of any apparent relationships between different tests for this diverse suite of rocks, the raw scatter plot is first examined. Any results that can be treated as outliers or results groupings according to rock type can then be considered. Best-fit equations that omit outliers may be more meaningful than those for the whole set which include the outliers.

The two main sections of results which are concerned with abrasion resistance and resistance to breakage are now given.

Abrasion resistance tests

Aggregate abrasion value versus mill abrasion resistance index

Sometimes a potential source has test results available for AAV, but not for MAV, which is the specified CIRIA/CUR test for abrasion resistance. Once a reasonable cross-section of rock types and strengths has been subjected to both tests, a correlation study using regression analysis can be used to derive a prediction of the MAV result from any given AAV result. Under

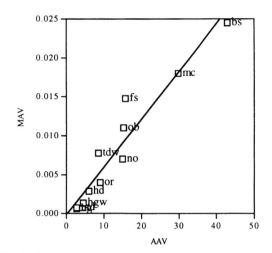

Fig. 4. Aggregate abrasion value (%) versus mill abrasion value, k_s (fraction lost per 1000 revs).

certain assumptions, which are often reasonable, it is possible to attach confidence bands to this estimate.

In Fig. 4, which includes 12 rock samples (i.e. $n = 12$), a linear-regressed scatter plot with one outlier (mi) removed gives a reasonably high r-squared correlation of 0.921. However, predicting the MAV from AAV results using the regression equation could be misleading (e.g. compare fs, ob and no, which have similar AAV values of about 15, but widely varying MAV). It appears that the wet mutual tumbling environment of the mill abrasion test has revealed a much poorer performance for the weathered dolerite (tdw) than would be predicted from the regression equation using the AAV test result which assesses resistance to the grinding action of a dry sand.

Wet micro-Deval versus mill abrasion resistance index

These results are of particular interest for the CEN specification of armourstone and the move to adopt the wet micro-Deval test with its long history of use in France. Note that this paper only considers the wet version of the micro-Deval throughout. The scatter plot in Fig. 5 shows an exceptionally good correlation over the full range of rock strengths (excluding mi), with an r-squared value improving from 0.948 to 0.967 when a power law is fitted in preference to a linear regression. Both sets of regression equation constants based on $n = 18$ are given in Table 2. The high degree of correlation can be explained by the similarities of the mutual surface grinding effects of the wet mill abrasion process in both tests. The high correlation also suggests that the steel balls in the micro-Deval test do relatively little to actually fragment the particles, but they simply speed up the test, giving larger surface losses in a shorter

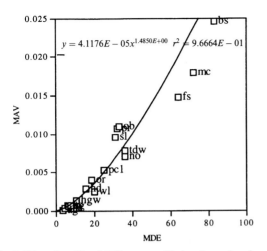

Fig. 5. Wet micro-Deval (%) versus mill abrasion value, k_s (fraction lost per 1000 revs).

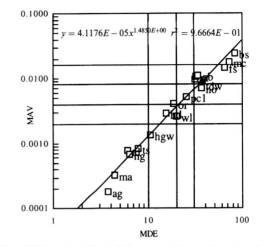

Fig. 6. Wet micro-Deval (%) versus mill abrasion value, k_s (fraction lost per 1000 revs) on logarithmic axes.

test duration. The relative lack of fragmentation in the micro-Deval test is further indicated by the poor AIV versus MDE relationship described later.

Requirements for CEN specification of armourstone abrasion resistance
Much discussion of the micro-Deval test for specification of armourstone is given in the French report *Les Enrochements* (LCPC 1989). Further research on the micro-Deval test can be found in Tourenq (1971) and the Dutch report by Maase (1993).

The reference test in the CIRIA/CUR manual specification for armourstone is the mill abrasion test and the acceptance categories applicable to different environments of use were previously reported (Latham 1991, 1993; CIRIA/CUR 1991).

The 16th draft CEN specification for armourstone can now be given in the light of data in the Maase (1993) report, together with previous French recommendations based on their longer experience of categories for MDE (LCPC 1989). It draws upon the excellent correlation and data presented in Figs 5 and 6. The acceptance

Table 2. *Correlation and regression analysis statistics*

Tests compared x v y	Best fit relations*							
	Linear y = a + bx				Power law y = Ax^B			
	a	b	n	r^2	A	B	n	r^2
AAV v MAV, Fig. 4	−0.00019	0.000614	12	0.921				
MDE v MAV, Fig. 5, Fig. 6	−0.00115	0.000283	18	0.948	0.0000412	1.485	18	0.967
MDE v MAV, (excludes bs, mc, fs)	−0.00137	0.000299	15	0.864	0.0000306	1.614	15	0.968
WAV v MAV, Fig. 7	−0.00336	0.000719	13	0.815	0.0000854	1.570	13	0.951
WAV v MDE, Fig. 8	−6.321	2.510	13	0.819	1.360	1.128	13	0.915
MDE v AIV, Fig. 9	1.989	0.314	20	0.698	6.145	0.381	20	0.617
K_{IC} v MAV, Fig. 10	0.016	−0.007	16	0.549	0.004	−1.862	16	0.559
$I_{s(50)}$d v $I_{s(50)}$w, Fig. 12, Fig. 13	−0.888	1.029	20	0.951	0.528	1.244	20	0.975
$I_{s(50)}$d v K_{IC}d	0.389	0.167	10	0.704				
$I_{s(50)}$w v K_{IC}w, Fig. 14	0.151	0.215	7	0.873	0.185	1.111	7	0.945
$I_{s(50)}$w&d v K_{IC}w&d, Fig. 15	0.340	0.164	14	0.669	0.288	0.836	14	0.793
AIV v K_{IC}w&d, Fig. 15	3.112	−0.077	15	0.700	28.315	−1.045	15	0.663
AIV v $I_{s(50)}$w&d, Fig. 16	13.698	−0.360	24	0.608				
AIV v WDCV, Fig. 17	−1.234	1.000	17	0.934				

* Calculated using CA Cricket-Graph III Version 1.5.

Table 3. *Specified abrasion resistance categories*

CIRIA/CUR (1991) categories	CIRIA/CUR (1991) mill abrasion value (k_s or MAV)	CIRIA/CUR (1991) equiv. micro-Deval (MDE)	Draft CEN (1996) micro-Deval (MDE)	LCPC (1989) micro-Deval (MDE)
Excellent	<0.002	≤14	≤10	<16
Good	0.002–0.004	14–22	≤20	<20
Upper marginal	0.004–0.008	22–35	≤30	<27
Lower marginal	0.008–0.015	35–53		
Poor	>0.015	≥53		

16th Draft CEN (1996) categories	16th Draft CEN (1996) description of suggested end-use environments	16th Draft CEN (1996) micro-Deval (MDE)	Equiv. mill abrasion value (k_s or MAV)
A	Very highly abrasive, e.g. often stormy seas with shingle foreshore attack or dynamic armour design concept	≤10	≤0.0013
B	Highly abrasive, e.g. occasionally stormy seas with shingle or sandy foreshore	≤20	≤0.0035
C	Moderately abrasive, e.g. occasional significant wave or current action of suspended load	≤30	≤0.0064
D	No requirement, e.g. for underlayer, core or extremely mild conditions		

categories in the specification apply to armourstone in a top layer which is known to be subject to abrasion by sediment. They are shown overlaid in Fig. 6 and are given in Table 3.

Tourenq has shown (see fig. 3 of his paper) that MDE can increase from about 5 for equant-shaped aggregate to a value of about 20 for aggregate that is 100% made up of platy-shaped aggregate. For the specification of the wear resistance of armourstone, a result which depends on the test aggregate shape or even the preparation method used to obtain the test aggregate is not wanted. A note requiring standardized sample preparation is therefore included in the 16th draft CEN specification for armourstone under the section referring to the micro-Deval test.

Apart from this shape effect, the wet micro-Deval test appears ideal for specification purposes, whereas the mill abrasion test remains more suitable for modelling degradation (Latham 1991; Tomasicchio *et al.* 1995) and predicting service life.

For category A, the values of ≤10 will effectively exclude all but the most abrasion-resistant igneous and metamorphic rocks and re-crystallized sandstones. Only an exceptional limestone would pass. Note that one slightly weathered granite (hgw) failed to reach this category, which is reassuring. It is, however, important to recognize that field data are limited and that category A is probably only necessary for a no maintenance design in a highly abrasive environment, for example, where fierce shingle attack is frequent, or where armourstone is expected to reprofile as in a dynamic design.

The range of MDE for category B will exclude many limestones, except those typical of the Carboniferous in the UK and those which are relatively pure and have a large proportion of re-crystallized spary calcite cement. Poorly cemented sandstones, micritic, porous or impure limestones, as well as severely altered or weathered igneous and metamorphic rocks, will normally be excluded. This range has given ample protection from abrasion in most north European sites and will normally be the most suitable specification category in such regions.

Experience with the five rock types with MDE values of between 30 and 40 suggests that they should all be excluded from category C, their use being only acceptable if there is no risk of active abrasive agents and if the water is almost permanently calm. These recommendations broadly follow those given by LCPC, except the specification of category A (≤10). In northern Europe, especially the UK, and overseas, a high performance rock may be needed in the aggressive shingle environments and for berm breakwaters incorporating armour displacements, so that a value of 16 is much too high. The boundary value of 20 seems to allow a large number of perfectly satisfactory limestones which are generally available and are widely used at present into category B. For simplicity and rounder numbers there is no apparent good reason for not extending the LCPC value of 27 up to 30, but no further.

It should be noted that these recommendations are based on results with the normal test samples that could have included unusually flaky or equant materials. In general, the results using test samples with flaky and equant pieces removed will give slightly lower MDE values than previously measured, but the differences are unpredictable. The sampler should be aware that the extra shape control with slotted sieves means that more test material is required and that simply sending a normal production aggregate for the test will not yield a result that is always considered valid for armourstone specifications. Therefore some detailing of sample preparation from armour blocks will be necessary. In this respect, the type of wording for the preparation of test aggregate under consideration in the CEN draft is: 'The test portion shall be obtained by crushing at least 6 separate pieces of armourstone or parts thereof for which the masses mutually differ by not more than 25%'.

Further correlation analyses relating to abrasion resistance

Wet attrition value versus mill abrasion resistance index. A weakly non-linear power law which describes this relationship is shown in Fig. 7. As the testing environment (autogenous milling with no steel balls) is similar in the two tests except that the MAV removes non-linear effects, a good correlation is to be expected, particularly for the stronger rocks (see also the discussion in Latham 1993).

Wet attrition value versus wet micro-Deval. From Fig. 8, the best-fit relation can be seen to be weakly non-linear, as reported by Tourenq (1971).

Wet micro-Deval versus aggregate impact value. It is of interest that the scatter plot ($n = 20$) of Fig. 9 clearly indicates that the micro-Deval value does not correlate particularly well with AIV (nor the Los Angeles abrasion value), which measures resistance to fragmentation. As suggested earlier, the data confirm that these two

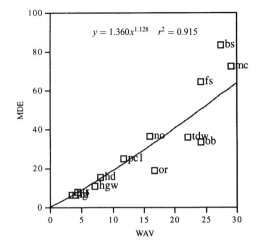

Fig. 8. Wet attrition value (BS 812, 1951) (%) versus wet micro-Deval (%).

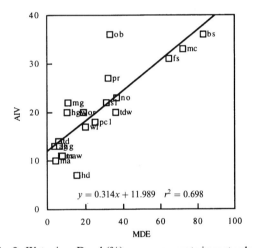

Fig. 9. Wet micro-Deval (%) versus aggregate impact value (BS 812, 1951) (%).

aggregate tests measure two very different mechanical properties, both of which are relevant and need separate specification to properly safeguard the performance of unbound aggregate and armourstone in different end use situations (see, for example, data points hd and ob).

Fracture toughness versus mill abrasion resistance index. As shown in Fig. 10, the abrasion action typical of the MAV is poorly correlated with K_{IC} (r-squared = 0.559), although a greater degree of correlation with K_{IC} was noted with the abrasive action reflected in the AAV test. A better correlation with K_{IC} might be expected for prototype coastal or laboratory sand blasting action, which involves fatigue with predominantly tensile brittle failure mechanisms (see Verhoef 1987).

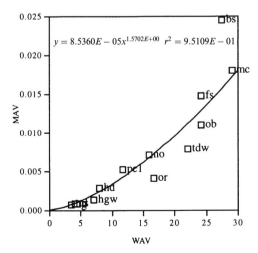

Fig. 7. Wet attrition value (BS 812, 1951) (%) versus mill abrasion value, k_s (fraction lost per 1000 revs).

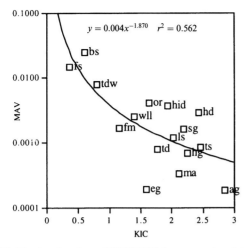

Fig. 10. Fracture toughness (ISRM 1988) (average wet and dry) versus mill abrasion value, k_s.

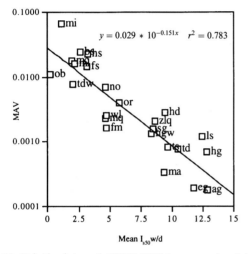

Fig. 11. Point load strength (ISRM 1988) (average wet and dry) versus mill abrasion value, k_s.

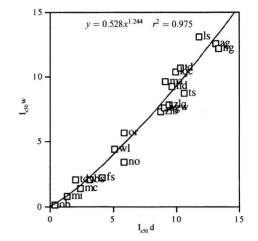

Fig. 12. $I_{s(50)}$ dry versus $I_{s(50)}$ wet.

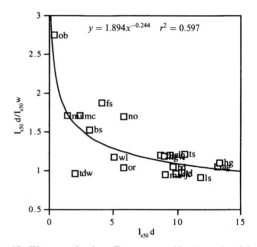

Fig. 13. Water weakening effect expressed by the ratio of dry to wet point load strength $I_{s(50)}$.

Point load strength index versus mill abrasion resistance index. The scatter plot shown in Fig. 11 is of interest because of the much higher correlation than with with fracture toughness shown in Fig. 10 (r-squared $= 0.783$). The exponential equation may be of value in the prediction of MAV and thus abrasion losses when only $I_{s(50)}$ values are available.

Resistance to breakage of the mineral fabric

Effect of water saturation
It is important to recognize that rock strength is often influenced by the degree of saturation. An extensive study of point load strength index $I_{s(50)}$ for both wet (i.e. 48 h tap water saturation at room temperature) and dry samples ($n = 20$) revealed that a weakly non-linear power law helps to account for the more pronounced water weakening at lower strengths (see Fig. 12). If the ratio of dry to wet strength is examined (Fig. 13) for dry strengths below 5 MPa, the dry strength may be 1.2–2.5 times the wet strength, depending largely on porosity.

When the wet fracture toughness K_{IC} is compared with the wet $I_{s(50)}$, high correlations are obtained for linear and power law forms (see Fig. 14), whereas the same plot for the dry case shows more dispersion and a lower r-squared coefficient.

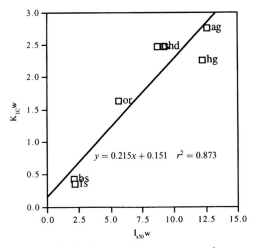

Fig. 14. Wet point load strength $I_{s(50)}$ versus wet fracture toughness K_{IC}.

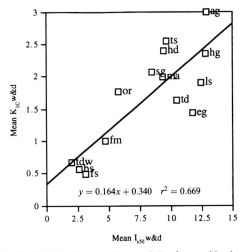

Fig. 15. Relation between $I_{s(50)}$ and K_{IC} for combined wet and dry results plotted as an average.

The data set for K_{IC} includes 16 samples, of which only three were tested both wet and dry, but a relation of the same form as with $I_{s(50)}$ (see Table 2) can probably be justified (due to the similar failure mechanisms), which was then used to interpolate missing wet or dry K_{IC} data. In the following correlation analyses the $I_{s(50)}$ and the K_{IC} values reported for each rock sample are the average of their wet and dry values to generate more reliable equations to relate K_{IC}, $I_{s(50)}$ and AIV.

Point load strength index versus fracture toughness
Consider first the test variability. The mean value of the point load strength reported for each rock sample tested both wet and dry is derived from typically ten test specimens. Thus with 20 rock samples, approximately 400 pieces were tested in all.

Statistics on the coefficient of variation (CoV) for each sample are given in Table 4. The CoV for fracture toughness, based on a smaller data set of nine wet and six dry samples with typically five specimens in each

Table 4. *Comparison of the coefficient of variation for different intact strength tests*

Statistic	Coefficient of variation (%)*	
	Fracture toughness K_{IC} wet ($MPa\,m^{0.5}$)	Point load $I_{s(50)}$ wet (MPa)
Mean	8.0	23.5
Range	0.3–17.2	9.4–50.0
Count (i.e. no. of rock types)	9	20

* Coefficient of variation (%) = 100 × standard deviation/mean.

(a total of 46 wet and 30 dry test pieces) is also given in Table 4. It should be noted that the CoV may not be significant with only a few test pieces in the sample. However, the startling point to note is the low test variability of the K_{IC} test (typically below 10%) and for $I_{s(50)}$ it is only just above 20% overall. Gunsallus & Kulhawy (1984) reported overall values for the CoV of a range of sedimentary rocks as 18, 27 and 33% for K_{IC}, uniaxial compressive strength and $I_{s(50)}$, respectively.

The appropriate scatter plot is shown in Fig. 15. It is interesting to note the similar values of $I_{s(50)}$ of two different gneisses (ag and eg), which, according to their different K_{IC} values, exhibit very different resistance to crack propagation. Gunsallus & Kulhawy (1984), reporting on ten typically rather weak sedimentary rocks, obtained the following relation with r-squared of 0.67

$$K_{IC} = 0.0995 I_{s(50)} + 1.11$$

For the results of this study, the best linear relation for 14 different sedimentary, igneous and metamorphic rocks spanning a wide strength range was

$$K_{IC} = 0.164 I_{s(50)} + 0.340$$

with r-squared also of 0.67. For a sample size of $n = 14$, the correlation coefficient of 0.67 is significant at a 1% level. Although it is clear that the K_{IC} test measures a different property to the point load test, proof that it has a significantly greater relevance to predicting the long-term performance of armourstone in service is unlikely to be forthcoming.

Aggregate impact value versus fracture toughness
The scatter plot with $n = 15$ is shown in Fig. 16. The weathered dolerite (tdw) point was particularly

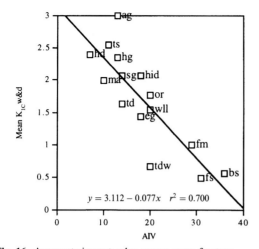

Fig. 16. Aggregate impact value versus mean fracture toughness K_{IC} for combined wet and dry results plotted as an average.

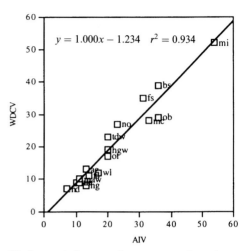

Fig. 18. Aggregate impact value versus wet dynamic crushing value.

conspicuous. The K_{IC} test clearly showed it to be very weak for an igneous rock, whereas with the AIV test no concern would have been expressed. The data for the gneiss (ag) reveals a much greater resistance to fracture than suggested by the AIV test. This is further indication of a severe limitation of the AIV test for predicting the mechanical performance of a coarse crystalline rock in any form other than when it is to be used as aggregate. It is perhaps of interest to speculate from the r-squared value of 0.70, and an examination of Fig. 16, whether the dynamic strength behaviour tested by the impact method is also reflected in the K_{IC} value.

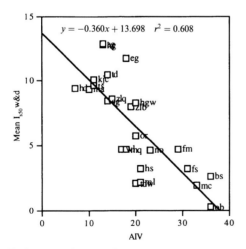

Fig. 17. Aggregate impact value versus mean point load strength $I_{s(50)}$ for combined wet and dry results plotted as an average.

Aggregate impact value versus point load strength index
It can also be seen from the r-squared value of 0.61, and an examination of Fig. 17, that the AIV is not a good predictor of point load strength. It may therefore be suggested tentatively that if an intact strength test is sought which reflects dynamic strength behaviour, which seems appropriate for armourstone, the fracture toughness test is probably preferable to the point load test.

Aggregate impact value versus wet dynamic crushing test
Because of the popularity of the AIV type test, the WDCV was introduced in the rock manual specification. The subsequent research experience since 1991 has shown that the two tests are highly correlated and the WDCV and AIV values are practically interchangeable, as indicated by the regression slope of 1.00 (see Fig. 18).

Requirements for specification of resistance to breakage of armourstone
A concerted move away from aggregate tests for strength specification was made in the manual. The 16th draft CEN specification has continued with this need and has adopted the compressive strength test because of its more universal recognition within Europe compared with the point load test.

    The apparent expense, lack of widespread access to apparatus and lack of experience with the fracture toughness test still prohibit its widespread use in specification documents. This is unfortunate when considering its high repeatability, relevance to fracture mechanism and true cost of the test. The plots in Figs 16 and 17 indicate regression equations which, in general, show that the $I_{s(50)}$ requirements, for all categories in the rock manual are less severe than the equivalent K_{IC} and

Table 5. *Specified breakage resistance categories*

Categories	CIRIA/CUR (1991)					16th Draft CEN (1996)	
	K_{IC} $(MPam^{0.5})$	$I_{s(50)}$ (MPa)	$(\sim K_{IC}$ equiv.) $(MPam^{0.5})$	$WDCV$ $(\%)$	$(\sim K_{IC}$ equiv.) $(MPam^{0.5})$	Compressive strength (MPa)	$(\sim I_{s(50)}$ equiv.) (MPa)
Excellent	>2.2	>8.0	(>1.65)	<12	(>2.19)		
Good	>1.4	>4.0	(>1.00)	<20	(>1.57)	>80	(>3.6)
Marginal	>0.8	>1.5	(>0.59)	<30	(>0.80)		

WDCV requirements, which show roughly equal severity. The data in this study suggest the K_{IC} remains the most suitable test, but with fears of expense and obscurity, the point load test appears at present to be the obvious choice of strength test, although it was not possible to evaluate the compressive strength test in this study (Table 5).

The 16th draft CEN specification proposes the familiar compressive strength test in line with the specification for natural building stone and European tradition. Only one requirement category for all armourstone applications is given in the CEN draft and this is set at a relatively mild acceptance level of 80 MPa for the compression test. Scant regard has been paid to the argument that compared with the point load test, the compressive strength test is perhaps about four times as expensive to conduct, but appears to have comparable test variability (Gunsallus & Kulhawy 1984).

16th Draft CEN specification (1996): recent developments

According to the 16th draft, tests for density and resistance to breakage (using a compressive strength test) will be mandatory and are to be determined by testing individual stones. Block integrity cannot be specified other than by subjective clauses or by the unofficial tests such as the drop test and sonic velocity test to be referred to in an informative annex. In most cases resistance to wear, which is to be tested by the wet micro-Deval test, and resistance to weathering will be mandatory, but the purchaser has the possibility of not specifying a requirement for either or both of these two properties.

The resistance to weathering of armourstone, according to the 16th draft CEN specification, refers directly to only three properties: resistance to freezing and thawing; resistance to salt crystallization; and the presence of signs of sonnenbrand. Little guidance is given in an informative annex to help the specifier select the most appropriate choice depending on different climatic and exposure zones. When there are satisfactory service records (a condition for which a definition and specific criteria unfortunately could not be agreed), the possibility exists for the specifier to choose only the requirements considered to be essential for the particular armourstone use. Petrographic reports from representative samples that indicate excellent or potentially deleterious material, however, do not appear at present to have any real influence on the approval process set out in the 16th draft CEN specification (see Table 6). The final CEN approach compared with the CIRIA/CUR approach is therefore certain to be a significant improvement in terms of clarity of guidance, but may again neglect the potential role of petrographic analysis. The lack of a specific test for the presence of clay minerals is due to the likelihood that such weakened materials will fail on criteria required in other tests, particularly the wet micro-Deval test.

To overcome sample taking difficulties, the 16th draft CEN document has an informative annex, which includes a table. The actual phases of the programme of testing for source approval to CEN requirements would depend on the precise choice of clauses chosen by the client. For example, it might be possible to assess the resistance to weathering in a hot country with no significant risk of freezing using, firstly, petrographic examination, secondly, water absorption and, thirdly, magnesium sulphate if necessary. Alternatively, according to the 16th draft, it is also possible that a producer seeking approval as an armourstone supplier would be allowed to simply follow CEN approved quality control procedures and provide the client with the certification of procedures in place and a complete suite of recent test results. These test results would need to be updated at the necessary intervals which have been stipulated under factory production control in yet another normative annex of the 16th draft.

Conclusions

Regarding rock quality, the CIRIA/CUR specification for armourstone has a number of defects that stem mainly

Table 6. *Mandatory and optional tests in the draft CEN specification*

Type of properties	Mandatory tests	Further non-mandatory tests
Physical properties	Density	
Resistance to weathering	'No requirement' may be chosen – specifier advised in annex to choose tests and requirements after consideration of: service record; petrography*; site climate and exposure zone; then to employ the following tests as necessary: water absorption; magnesium sulphate; freeze–thaw; boiling test	
Resistance to breakage (type 2 breakage)	Compressive strength	Point load strength is recommended for factory production control (in an annex to the compressive strength test)
Resistance to abrasion	'No requirement' may be chosen Micro-Deval	
Block integrity (type 1 breakage)	Visual examination (subjective)	Drop test breakage index and sonic velocity tests are described in an annex

* Simplified petrographic description to the 16th Draft CEN method is mandatory, but may in practice yield little more useful information than the rock name.

from practical difficulties in its detailed implementation rather than from inappropriate principles and tests.

The correlation studies suggest that, for specification purposes, the wet micro-Deval test will be an appropriate alternative to the QMW mill abrasion test and the equation presented in Table 1 may be used to estimate one test value from the other. The mill abrasion test remains the more suitable test for modelling natural abrasive processes, with accurate results for rock types spanning at least three orders of magnitude (MAV or $k_s = 0.00018$ for a weathered chalk, to MAV or $k_s = 0.00018$ for an augen gneiss, with a value of 0.0000125 for flint shingle).

The wet micro-Deval value, although incorporating a charge of steel balls, has a relatively poor correlation (0.70) with the AIV. The surface rounding and fine rock flour produced during the test also indicate that during the micro-Deval test any breakdown by fragmentation that may occur (as tested by AIV) is subordinate to the surface grinding mechanism and the test is a truly abrasive test (*cf.* the Los Angeles test, which is truly a test of fragmentation resistance).

The fracture toughness test exhibits good repeatability, as indicated by low coefficients of variation. It appears more likely to be able to asses the resistance to dynamic loading experienced by armourstone during construction and in service than other pseudo-static strength tests such as the point load test. The problem of strong grain size dependence and poor discrimination of weathered rock in the AIV test confirms the lack of

confidence in using an aggregate strength test for specifying armourstone.

Water weakening is generally more pronounced the lower the dry strength is. Point load strengths below 5 MPa for dry samples, may be 20–250% stronger than their saturated equivalents, so it is important to specify clearly that saturated conditions are to apply to the testing of armourstone.

The relation between aggregate strength test results obtained from crushing blocks in the laboratory compared with the intact strength test results obtained directly from test pieces cored from such blocks has rarely been reported, presumably because of the high cost involved in specimen preparation and the previous lack of an application for the results. This paper provides such a study and a scientific basis for shifting armourstone specification tests for strength away from those based on aggregates tests as given in BS 6349: Part 1: 1984 and towards intact strength tests as preferred in the CIRIA/CUR manual and the 16th draft CEN specification.

Recommendations to specifiers

Specifiers may wish to adopt the most recent available draft (16th) of the CEN specification for armourstone. A similar earlier 1996 draft was discussed at a recent armourstone meeting held at H R Wallingford, UK. However, it is likely that not all the related documents and an obligation to specify using the approved EN specification will be in place much before the year 2000. The opportunity therefore remains to sharpen up the existing CIRIA/CUR specification broadly as follows:

(1) Adopt the micro-Deval categories for wear resistance of armourstone given in the CEN draft.

(2) Retain the wet point load for resistance to breakage with an acceptance value at 4.0 MPa. However, the specification clause should perhaps have a control on the spread of results, such as stating that for separate pieces of armourstone the average $I_{s(50)}$ of nine specimens after striking out the lowest of 10 specimens shall be $\geqslant 4.0$ MPa and no more than two specimens out of 10 shall have an $I_{s(50)}$ of <3.0 MPa.

(3) Specification with the fracture toughness test (ISRM) is still to be encouraged as an alternative and superior test with high reproducibility provided there is sufficient interest in controlling the performance with respect to corner breakages and loss of angularity. However, it cannot be generally recommended until the test has wider acceptance and is more commonplace within normal testing rather than specialized geomaterials or research laboratories.

(4) Block integrity specification using the CIRIA/CUR drop test is to be encouraged, especially as it is mentioned, but not mandatory, within the 16th draft CEN specification on the grounds of insufficient experience and research data. It will be in the client's interest to have taken some objective measures to ensure cracked and flawed material is not purchased and the drop test should ideally be coupled with appropriate sonic velocity surveys before and after the blocks are dropped.

(5) Specification and testing for the resistance to weathering should proceed from petrographic examination using the simplified CEN test method for petrographic description of aggregates, but preferably a more detailed analysis, in an ordered logical progression. It should only end up with expensive freeze–thaw testing if absolutely necessary. The type of guidance given in annexes of the 16th draft CEN specification for armourstone, together with that of a chartered geologist, should help ensure that the testing is appropriate for the service record, petrographic type, end use and climate.

(6) That samples to be sent to the laboratory must be representative of the consignment is obvious, but cannot be over-stated. The need therefore to take test specimens from material originating from a number of separate randomly selected pieces of armourstone is essential. Some guidance on sample and test piece sizes that may have been obscure in the manual is given in the appendix to this paper.

Appendix: recommendations for field examination, sample taking and laboratory test programme

Importance of field investigation

Experience of problems in recent years has led to the following general guidance. The first approach to assessing armourstone quality must be based on field assessment. The examination of a new rock source should provide the following information.

- A list of the rock types available, their properties, any potential problem areas in the source and recommendations for quarry-based testing.
- An estimation of the results to be expected of tests on the rocks.
- A recommendation for sampling and for the standard (CIRIA/CUR or CEN) laboratory test strategy. This should be designed to optimize the joint benefit of laboratory and field work and the costs involved.

A good balance is required between field observation and test programme and this should minimize the overall cost. The data obtained should be such that the source is assessed for long-term use and should indicate a list of tests that need to be repeated at regular intervals to provide some form of quality control. A normative annex to the 16th draft CEN specification has been included which identifies test frequencies and procedures for factory production control.

In addition to intrinsic rock properties, an assessment should no doubt be made of the potential block integrity, shape and mass distribution of the blocks likely to be available, but discussion of these properties is not the main concern of this paper.

Laboratory test programme

The laboratory test programme for assessing rock quality should be carried out in stages with the continuance of the programme depending on acceptable results being obtained in the earlier tests. Where a quarry or other source is to be approved for armourstone supply according to the CIRIA/CUR (or forthcoming EN) specification, or if an armourstone consignment is to be approved, it is desirable that the whole range of tests is carried out.

The laboratory testing can be based on samples taken from armourstone blocks either as bulk pieces or as prepared smaller samples. It is usually more economical to take smaller samples of various types from the quarry, if these can be obtained, as the sample reduction from large blocks delivered to the laboratory can be time con-suming and expensive. Interpretation of the manual's text on sampling leads to the following expanded recommendations on the subject of sample taking, which accommodates most of the 16th draft CEN sampling needs.

The test strategy can be divided into three parts. The first includes the petrographic study, measurement of the density and water absorption of pieces of rock, the methylene blue test and the aggregate impact value. This provides basic information on the potential for weathering, the resistance to breaking and resistance to frost damage and chemical deterioration. The wet micro-Deval test, the magnesium sulphate test and the point load index test provide a second suite of tests that might be considered. A third suite of tests represented by the mill abrasion resistance index, the freeze–thaw test and the fracture toughness test is suitable for the primary, i.e. most indicative description, of source material and this information will allow calibration of the data from the less expensive quality control tests.

For each physically distinctive rock type in the quarry a separate sample is required and pieces should be removed from 20 randomly selected armourstone blocks. It may be advantageous to take these pieces from blocks sampled for grading tests. These pieces should be about 30 kg. If no further sample reduction on-site is planned, some 600–1000 kg of rock will have to be transported to the laboratory to provide the basis for the test programme. From these large pieces the laboratory will need to cut, break or core the working subsamples. The residue of rock fragments from which intact specimens have been taken must then be crushed to provide aggregate-sized particles for the other aggregate based tests referred to (from micro-Deval, magnesium sulphate and, possibly, WDCV, AIV and QMW mill abrasion). Hence in most instances it is advised that individual sample requirements be met directly by taking appropriately sized pieces and sample types from the armourstone blocks in the quarry.

Samples for dispatch to the laboratory

In many quarries where the rock has been crushed for purposes other than armourstone production an adequate source for the test material may be readily available, but its representativeness may be questioned. The detailed subsample requirements for each test that may be chosen from the manual specification are as follows.

Petrography, water absorption and density

Ten test specimens need to be examined. These can be 10 cores of about 70 mm length and 50 mm diameter or 10 intact lumps of roughly the same volume. The volume should be between 50 and 150 cm³. The same test specimen can be used for all three determinations and may also be satisfactory for the point load test, which can be performed last. It is suggested that 15 pieces are dispatched.

Methylene blue and wet dynamic crushing value

These tests are carried out on crushed rock in the size range 10–14 mm. A sample of 5–10 kg of the crushed rock is required. This sample must represent the range in quality of armourstone blocks, but could be obtained from a production stockpile of 20 mm aggregate if the client agrees this is representative. For the WDCV test the test sample also needs to fall within a certain flakyness sieve range, a requirement best met by prepa-ration in the laboratory. However, the well-established correlation with AIV reported earlier should halt further requests for the manual's WDCV tests.

Micro-Deval and mill abrasion resistance

For the QMW mill abrasion test, a minimum of 14 kg of 25–31.5 mm aggregate deemed representative of the quarry or crushed to this size range from selected blocks is required. However, the excellent correlation with the micro-Deval reported earlier should promote the more modest request for a wet micro-Deval test which requires a 6 kg sample.

Magnesium sulphate

The test can be applied to either about 1 kg of 10–20 mm crushed rock aggregate or to 10 pieces falling in the size range 63–125 mm diameter. The choice depends on the purpose.

Normally about 75 kg of 20–40 mm aggregate will provide enough material for all the various aggregates tests for the manual specification. This mass will be greatly reduced for the proposed suite of tests given in the 16th draft CEN standard, which includes only the micro-Deval and a magnesium sulphate aggregate test.

Freeze–thaw test

This test requires the analysis of 10 or 20 pieces each in the size range 10–20 kg. This test is not required, according to the manual and the 16th draft CEN specification, if the water absorption is less than 0.5% in all of the first 10 pieces tested.

Point load test

This test requires 15 cores, each about 50 mm in diameter and about 70 mm in length, or roughly rectangular saw-cut blocks measuring about $30 \times 40 \times 50$ mm. Note that these test specimens may be ideal for water absorption and density tests.

Fracture toughness

For this test using the short rod method, 10 core samples, each about 50 mm in diameter and 80 mm in length, are required. Of these, eight valid test results are required. The cores must be taken with their long axis parallel to any visible foliation.

Note that for both the point load test and the fracture toughness test, if cores cannot be taken on site, the cores or cut blocks are best taken in the laboratory from rectangular sectioned pieces measuring about 200 × 100 × 100 mm. Altogether, about 20 such pieces would be required to yield specimens for both fracture toughness and point load strength tests, and the petrography, density and water absorption.

Acknowledgements. The author wishes to acknowledge the support and co-operation from the former Science and Engineering Research Council (SERC) amd the Permanent International Association of Navigational Congresses (PIANC). Curing several years of research, particularly fruitful discussions were held with W. J. French, G. J. Laan, J. D. Simm and many others. Views expressed in the paper are, however, personal interpretations of data and do not represent a formal consensus.

References

AFNOR 1990. *L'association Francaise de normalisation (AFNOR P 18–572). Essai d'usure micro-Deval.* AFNOR, Paris.

BRITISH STANDARDS INSTITUTION (BSI) 1951, 1975. *Sampling and Testing of Mineral Aggregates, Sands and Fillers: BS 812.* BSI, London.

——1984. *Code of Practice for Maritime Structures: Part 1, General Criteria: BS 6349.* BSI, London.

CIRIA/CUR 1991. *Manual on the Use of Rock in Coastal and Shoreline Engineering.* Construction Industry Research and Information Association Special Publication, 83, London/Centre for Civil Engineering Research, Codes and Specifications, Report 154, Gouda.

CLARK, A. R. 1988. The use of Portland Stone rock armour in coastal protection and sea defence works. *Quarterly Journal of Engineering Geology*, **21**, 113–136.

FOWELL, R. J. & CHEN, J. F. 1990. The third chevron-notched rock fracture specimen – the cracked chevron-notched Brazilian disc. *In: Proceedings of the 31st US Rock Mechanics Symposium.* Balkema, Rotterdam, 295–302.

GAUSS, G. A. & LATHAM, J.-P. 1995a. The measurement of layer thickness and the estimation of as-built bulk density and void porosity in a rock armour revetment at Beesands, South Devon. *Proceedings of the Institution of Civil Engineers, Water Maritime and Energy*, **112**, 326–335.

—— & ——1995b. The onsite quality control of the as-produced properties of armourstone during construction of a rock revetment in South Devon. *Geotechnical and Geological Engineering*, **13**, 29–49.

GUNSALLUS, K. L. & KULHAWY, F. H. 1984. A comparative evaluation of rock strength measures. *International Journal of Rock Mechanics, Mining Science and Geomechanics Abstracts*, **21**, 233–248.

INTERNATIONAL SOCIETY OF ROCK MECHANICS COMMISSION ON TESTING METHODS 1985. Suggested method for determining point load strength (revised version). *International Journal of Rock Mechanics, Mining Science and Geomechanics Abstracts*, **22**, 51–60.

——1988. Suggested method for determining the fracture toughness of rock. *International Journal of Rock Mechanics, Mining Science and Geomechanics Abstracts*, **25**, 71–96.

——1995. Suggested method for determining mode I fracture toughness using cracked chevron notched Brazilian disc (CCNBD) specimens. *International Journal of Rock Mechanics, Mining Science and Geomechanics Abstracts*, **32**, 57–64.

KUHNEL, R. A. 1985. *Development of a New Technique for the Recognition of Tendency to Rock Decay.* T. E. Delft, afdeling Mijnbouwkunde, 11th April.

LATHAM, J.-P. 1991. Rock degradation model for armourstone in coastal engineering. *Quarterly Journal of Engineering Geology*, **24**, 101–118.

——1993. A mill abrasion test for wear resistance of armourstone. *In:* McELROY, C. H. & LIENHART, D. A. (eds) *Rock for Erosion Control.* ASTM, Philadelphia, 46–61.

—— & GAUSS, G. A. 1995. The drop test for armourstone integrity. *In:* THORNE, C, A. R., ABT, S. R., BARENDS, F. B. J., MAYNARD, S. T. & PILARCZKY, K. W. (eds) *River, Coastal & Shore-line Protection.* Wiley, Chichester.

LABORATOIRE CENTRAL DES PONTS ET CHAUSSÉES (LCPC) 1989. *Les enrochments, ministère de l'équipment, du logement, des transports et de la mer.* LCPC

MAASE, T. 1993. *The Micro-Deval Test.* Memoirs of the Centre for Engineering Geology in the Netherlands, **106**.

SIMM, J. D. & LATHAM, J.-P. 1994. Integrating rock materials technology into coastal structures and breakwaters. *Proceedings of the Institution of Civil Engineers, Water Maritime and Energy*, **106**, 371–376.

——, —— & ORBELL-DURRANT, C. 1992. Standardizing the approach to specifying quarried rock in coastal structures and breakwaters. *In: Proceedings of the ICE Conference on Coastal Structures and Breakwaters.* Thomas Telford, London, 17pp.

TOMASICCHIO, G. R., LAMBERTI, A. & GUIDUCCI, F. 1995. Stone movement on a reshaped profile. *In: Proceedings of the International Conference on Coastal Engineering, 1994.* ASCE, New York

TOURENQ, C. 1971. L'essai micro-Deval. *Bulletin de Liaison Laboratoires Central des Ponts et Chaussées*, **54**, 69–76.

VERHOEF, P. N. W. 1987. Sandblast testing of rock. *International Journal of Rock Mechanics Mining Science and Geomechanics Abstracts*, **24**, 185–192.

Meeting the demand for rock armour and its grading specification

R. G. Rees-Jones[1] & E. Storhaug[2]

[1] Woodstock Deering Ltd, 42 Friar Gate, Derby, UK
[2] Fjordstein, Larvik, Norway

Abstract. An analysis of tenders for contracts requiring armourstone issued since 1991 has been carried out. The results show the market size, the impact of major projects, the proportion of deliveries by sea and the extent to which the CIRIA/CUR specifications have been adopted. Proposals from the CEN armourstone committee regarding grading and shape are discussed, together with developments in quality control procedures at the loading port.

The demand for rock armour in the UK grew strongly through the 1980s as clients became more confident in both its design and its performance. This paper describes the estimated market size between 1991 and 1995.

The publication of the CIRIA/CUR manual in 1991 brought together a wide ranging collection of data and research on the use of armourstone. This was an important milestone, particularly as it offered a model specification which has generated considerable interest. However, this has not yet been fully translated into the specifications for actual contracts and this paper describes the extent to which this model specification has been adopted. In practice, the grading test presented particular difficulties and this issue has now been addressed in the CEN armourstone committee. This paper also discusses the specification of armourstone shape factors and some aspects of quality control adopted by one of the dedicated suppliers of armourstone.

UK armourstone market

Previous attempts to measure the market size for rock armour have relied on a combination of import statistics, surveys of local inland quarries and contractors' site records. It has been recognized that such methods run the risk of both duplication and omission.

Import statistics, in particular, are unreliable because there is no specific category for armourstone and because the use of kg rather than tonnes increases the possibility of incorrect entries. As the product does not attract duty, there is limited pressure to correct such errors.

Because imported stone represents less than half the total market size it is necessary to combine import statistics with market research from the numerous inland quarries which supply rock armour. These figures then need to be correlated with records from the contracts themselves as several quarries will often supply the same contract. Such an exercise has a high potential for inaccuracy.

Since 1991, Larvik in Norway has become a major source of armourstone. As a dedicated supplier of armourstone the company has received tender details of over 150 rock armour contracts and these are estimated to represent at least 90% of the total UK market. By summarizing the quantities of armourstone required for each contract an estimate of the overall market size can be obtained. However, because tender documents do not always reflect the scope of the completed job, or indeed whether the job even went ahead, some adjustments based on market knowledge are still needed. The adjustments that have been included in the totals presented here include: variation from tender documents of tonnage of armourstone actually supplied; deletion of contracts which did not proceed; and allocation of tonnage to later years because of contract delays.

The overall market size shown in Fig. 1 is in excess of 1.5 million tonnes per year. However, the pattern is uneven and is distorted by a number of major projects (>200 000 t) which have arisen each year. For example, in 1993 a project to construct four offshore reefs at Happisburgh on the Norfolk (UK) coast used over 250 000 t. Similarly, the La Collette land reclamation scheme at Jersey (Channel Islands) required 600 000 t in both 1994 and 1995. Other large projects (>100 000 t) have contributed around 500 000 t per year, with smaller contracts totalling another 750 000 t. This latter group have an average contract size of around 25 000 t.

The importance of deliveries by sea is reflected in Fig. 2. Several market factors can be identified which affect the proportion of deliveries by sea: environmental pressures on inland quarries; local objections to deliveries by road; awareness of the risks in sea deliveries leading to increased costs; and ship and barge availability. Unfortunately, past experience is not a reliable indicator as to the relative importance of each of these factors. It is interesting to note the variation in the percentage of sea deliveries (Fig. 2, right-hand axis), which reflects a fairly static market size, but with barge

REES-JONES, R. G. & STORHAUG, E. 1998. Meeting the demand for rock armour and its grading specification. *In*: LATHAM, J.-P. (ed.) 1998. *Advances in Aggregates and Armourstone Evaluation*. Geological Society, London, Engineering Geology Special Publications, **13**, 87–90.

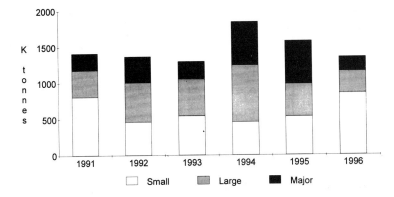

Fig. 1. The UK armourstone market.

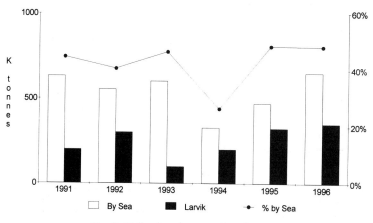

Fig. 2. Deliveries of armourstone by sea.

capacity influencing the market share. Imports of armourstone are dominated by supplies from Norway, with Sweden and France ranking behind. This position reflects the trend towards dedicated armourstone suppliers, both in the UK and abroad, and it is reasonable to attribute this to the publication of the CIRIA/CUR manual in 1991 and the subsequent use of its model specification. With its standard grading and shape definitions, suppliers are able to build up stockpiles of armourstone, confident that they will not be left with unsaleable stone.

Adoption of CIRIA/CUR manual

Whether this trend towards dedicated suppliers continues may depend on the extent to which clients and their designers adopt the recommendations of CIRIA/CUR. A further inspection of the tender documents used

in the preceding analysis to define the market size reveals the proportion that have adopted these standard specifications. For 1995 the uptake of the CIRIA/CUR model specification for grading, shape and test methods (i.e. intrinsic armourstone qualities) was as follows: CIRIA grading, 55% of tonnage; CIRIA shape, 43% of tonnage; and CIRIA test methods, 33% of tonnage.

In summary, the CIRIA recommendations were used in whole or part for 60% of the armourstone tonnage in 1995 and this represents a little under half (46%) of the actual number of contracts. However, testing based on the aggregate test methods described in BS 812 (1995) still predominate the rock quality specification of armourstone. In addition, an increasing number of tenders now include some kind of geological description of acceptable rock types.

One area where the market would benefit from still further standardization is in the definition of shape factor (or aspect ratio), where at least four different formulae are still in current use. The CIRIA/CUR manual is specific that in the majority of cases a shape factor of 1:3 would be sufficient. In fact, only 32% of the tonnage specified in 1995 used this clause, with other proportions as follows:

CIRIA, 3:1, max. 5% >3:1, 32%;
CIRIA, max. 50% >2:1, 11%;
others 3:1 type, 17%;
others 2:1 type, 40%.

Apart from the practical difficulties in supplying stone with a shape factor better than 2:1, this variety in specifications means that producers are discouraged from stockpiling armourstone in advance of orders. This inevitably leads to shortages and higher prices.

Against this background it is notable that the most recent draft of the European standard for armourstone prepared by the CEN armourstone experts group has produced a test method for 'determination of the content of stones with a length to thickness ratio greater than 3'. The exclusion of any other shape definition reflects research (Bradbury *et al.* 1990) showing that the stability of armourstone structures using a shape factor specified in this way is in no way compromised and, if anything, is improved. Also, it is possible that any specification based on a 2:1 clause will result in vast quantities of perfectly sized rock (from a functional point of view) being unnecessarily rejected. However, construction may possibly progress faster with more equant shaped blocks.

This same CEN group has also produced new recommendations for 'determination of the mass distribution', which for heavy gradings has considerably reduced the minimum number of stones on which to carry out the test as follows: 10–15 t, 25 pieces; 6–10 t, 30 pieces; 3–6 t, 60 pieces; 1–3, 100 pieces; 300 kg–1 t, 140 pieces; and light gradings, 200 pieces.

Compare this with the recommendation in the CIRIA/CUR manual which states that 'for the determination of the weight distribution the sample must contain at least 200 pieces heavier than the extreme lower class limit of the designated grading class'. On the project at Elmer, West Sussex in 1992, where 6–10 t grading was used, this meant a sample size of 1600 t.

In arriving at the new sample sizes the CEN experts group recognized the practical difficulties in handling such large samples. Although smaller samples are obviously less satisfactory from a statistical viewpoint, a risk analysis showed that the impact on the design of a change in D50 was not so great (Simm, J. D. pers. comm. 1994). Given this reduction in sample size, however, it may be prudent for specifiers to allow for the sample size to be increased in the event that a grading test on site does not meet the requirements. In this way experiences on site will show whether an optimum sample size has been selected.

Table 1. *Compliant weight distribution of loading cycle*

Size range (t)	Cumulative weight (t)	Percentage lighter
<3	45	8
<6	375	75
<9	500	100

In practice, dedicated suppliers of armourstone (e.g. Rees-Jones 1995) have found that the most efficient way of stocking the product is to pre-sort it into stockpiles with weight ranges of 1 t. A computerized record can then be kept showing the average weight and standard deviation of each stockpile. Simple instructions can then be issued at the time of loading which ensure compliance with the grading specification.

As an example, take the CIRIA/CUR manual specification for class designation 3–6 t, where y is the percentage by weight lighter on the cumulative plot:

Extreme lower class limit, $y < 2$, 2 t
Lower class limit, $0 < y < 10$, 3 t
Upper class limit, $70 < y < 100$, 6 t
Extreme upper class limit, $97 < y$, 6 t

This is converted to an instruction given to the machine operators to load in 500 t cycles comprising the following number of stones from each stockpile: 2 t, 18 stones; 3 t, 31 stones; 4 t, 25 stones; 5 t, 20 stones; and 6 t, 19 stones. As the loading proceeds, the machine operators can then produce tally sheets which verify the number of stones taken from each stockpile.

This loading cycle will give a grading curve with a W_{50} around 4.4 t and the compliant weight distribution given in Table 1. Where systems such as this work effectively, then a grading test on-site becomes largely irrelevant, except as a means of showing how much (or how little) the stone has degraded during handling. Furthermore, the twelfth draft European standard now allows up to 5% of fragments (i.e. greater than extreme lower class limit) to be excluded from the grading test. This relaxation from the 2% specified in the CIRIA/CUR manual, coupled with the absence of a block integrity test (such as the drop test), means that new specifications based on the CEN draft European standard will have to find other ways of ensuring armourstone integrity.

Conclusions

The market for rock armour can be accurately measured by analysis of the tenders issued each year.

In addition, the tender documents can be used to demonstrate the actual specifications for armourstone that designers are adopting. This gives a useful feedback both to researchers and to the designers themselves.

From the suppliers' side, increased standardization of specifications has led not only to the development of dedicated armourstone suppliers, but also to increased interest from inland quarries. In total, this has resulted in greater investment in stock levels and, in the case of one supplier, to improvements in quality control systems.

References

BRADBURY, LATHAM & ALLSOP 1990. Rock armour stability formulae – influence of stone shape and layer thickness. *In*: EDGE, B. L (ed.) *Proceedings of the 22nd International Conference on Coastal Engineering, Delft*. ASCE, New York, 1446–1459.

BRITISH STANDARDS INSTITUTION (BSI) 1995. *BS 812: Testing Aggregates*. BSI, London.

CIRIA/CUR 1991. *Manual on the Use of Rock in Coastal and Shoreline Engineering*. CIRIA/CUR Special Publication 83.

REES-JONES, R. 1995. Improvements in quality control at the loading port. *In*: *Proceedings of the 30th MAFF Conference of River and Coastal Engineers, Keele University*, 9.1.1.–9.1.6.

Rock engineering rating system for assessing the suitability of armourstone sources

D. A. Lienhart

Rock Products Consultants, 7229 Longfield Drive, Cincinnati, OH 45243–2209, USA

Abstract. The process involved in assessing and selecting a potential source of armourstone of suitable quality is one of great complexity. The process involves the inspection and evaluation of the quarry and its production methods, testing of the processed stone, evaluation of the quality of both intact and processed stone, and consideration of both the transportation methods and placement techniques. The entire process, from quarry selection to placement at the project, may be viewed as a rock engineering system. The use of a rock engineering interaction matrix simplifies an understanding of how various factors affecting the quality of quarried armourstone are interrelated. Through this understanding of the various interrelationships a weighted rock engineering rating system may be developed for the assessment of the suitability of various armourstone sources. Such a rating system is designed to pull together all the factors related to both the field and laboratory investigations of a potential source, enabling geologists at all experience levels to arrive at a well-founded conclusion concerning the potential quality of stone produced from a particular armourstone source.

Periodically, engineering geologists and coastal engineers must determine the quality of a specific source of rip-rap and armour stone based only on the results of a quarry evaluation and a set of laboratory data. The quarry evaluation may result in an intuitive feeling for the ability of a quarry to produce stone of adequate quality to meet the specifications for a certain project. An attempt to correlate laboratory test results with quarry observations, however, occasionally leads to confusion. Often the person responsible for making such a decision has either an incomplete or no understanding of exactly what the laboratory results mean or how those test results relate to the quarry evaluation. This paper seeks to correlate quarry observations, with laboratory data in such a way that each quarry will be numerically rated on the rock engineering system parameters that are pertinent to the quality and durability of both the intact and quarried rock.

Processes affecting rock armour

There are four processes that are likely to induce changes in the quality of the potential rock product being considered for use as armourstone. The four processes are: geological; production and processing; transport and placement (construction); and in-service. Obviously, each process will in some way affect the next process. For example, the geological process will affect the production methods and processing of the quarried stone. Both of these processes will affect the construction

and all three will affect the in-service life of the rock product. Specifically, each process will alter the quality of the rock product under consideration and, ultimately, the combined impact of the four processes will determine the service life of the final product. Each process is related to and affected by a number of principal factors that influence the process. Some of the principal factors may be affected by the actions of humans and, depending on how these factors are managed, the rock may either maintain intrinsic quality or the intrinsic quality may be reduced.

The geological process solely involves principal factors related to origin, orogenic and tectonic events, changes in geological environment and natural forces or physical conditions related to the derivation of a specific rock formation. Although not controlled by humans, they interact in such a way that the intact rock quality may be altered by deviations in environmental conditions.

Because of the similarity in operational conditions and the extent of human involvement in both the production and the construction processes, these processes may be combined. The principal factors pertinent to this process are related to the quality of the quarried rock as altered by both natural properties and artificial forces (blast effects, degradation due to processing, handling and construction activities). Like the principal factors of the geological process, the principal factors of the production/construction process are sensitive to changes in the environment.

The in-service process involves principal factors inherent to the rock, physical and chemical conditions such as wave impact, abrasion and salt-burst weathering, and

LIENHART, D. A. 1998. Rock engineering rating system for assessing the suitability of armourstone sources. *In*: LATHAM, J.-P. (ed.) 1998. *Advances in Aggregates and Armourstone Evaluation*. Geological Society, London, Engineering Geology Special Publications, **13**, 91–106.

other environmental conditions that may affect the ultimate durability of the stone.

Factor interrelationships and interactions

In this age of specialization, many workers have developed favoured theories for the causes for the short-term failure or deterioration of armourstone. The theories include, but are not limited to, excessive blasting energy with accompanying microfractures, depositional environment, rock type, pore structure and intrinsic rock properties. In addition to these favoured theories, a tendency exists among these same workers to try to fix the cause of deterioration on one factor. This tendency is related to a failure recognize the entirety of the problem, which is that all factors are interrelated. Hudson (1989) first addressed the failure to recognize the interrelationships by proposing the use of an interaction matrix. He further defined the use of such a matrix as a systems approach to rock engineering problems (Hudson 1992; Hudson & Harrison 1992).

To identify the pertinent rock engineering system principal factors it is useful to examine the factors in terms of an interaction matrix. Hudson (1989) suggests beginning the matrix with the operation or process of concern and positioning the process in the lower right corner of the matrix. Next, consider the main diagonal of the matrix and begin adding the principal factors that will influence the process of concern. Lastly, evaluate the interaction mechanisms. The results will reveal, in the far right column, the effects of the principal factors on the process of concern, while the bottom row displays the effects of the process of concern on the principal factors. The remaining portions of the matrix illustrate the interaction of the principal factors on each other.

Figures 1–3 depict the interaction matrices developed for the three processes: geological, production/construction and in-service (site environment). The process has been located at the bottom right corner of the matrix in all three figures and the principal factors that influence the process have been located along the diagonal. The principal factors of the geological process which have been identified by the author through this matrix are: discontinuity geometry (number, spacing and orientation of joint sets, *in situ* block size distribution); hydraulic conditions (permeability, groundwater conditions); rock mass properties (deformability, strength or failure of rock mass, effects of intercalated soft or porous strata); *in situ* stress (principal stress magnitudes and direction, effects of tectonism and continental glaciation); and intact rock quality (strength, hardness, weathering susceptibility, conditions of formation).

The principal factors of the production/construction process identified by the author are: block integrity (planes of weakness, flaws that control parting); degree of saturation (presence of quarry sap, percentage of pore

space occupied by water or degree of saturation); release of stored stress (loss of confining pressure, elastic and inelastic rebound with the development of unloading fractures and rockbursts); and quarried rock quality (block shape, strength, hardness, weathering condition and susceptibility).

The principal factors of the in-service process identified by the author are: petrological features (mineral composition, grain size, texture, genetic history, presence of microfractures); strength properties (compressive strength, tensile strength, abrasion resistance, fracture toughness, sonic velocity); density properties (specific gravity, adsorption/absorption ratio, microporosity); and rock durability (susceptibility to weathering action).

The mechanisms of interaction affecting each principal factor have been established in the remaining portions of each matrix and the influence of an interaction of one principal factor on another is in the direction of the arrows. The choice of entries is extremely subjective if assigned by a single investigator, as in this case. It is therefore recommended that the entries for the matrices are assigned by a panel of experts.

Using the 'expert semi-quantitative' method suggested by Hudson (1992) the matrices were coded as displayed in Fig. 4. Obviously these codes will vary from one expert to another; however, as Hudson (1992) indicates, categorization becomes more definite with experience. Furthermore, the system is dependent on the totals for the columns and rows, not on each specific code, and, therefore, a specific code is not critical to the evaluation of a principal factor. The following is a key to the codes: $0 =$ no interaction; $1 =$ weak interaction; $2 =$ medium interaction; $3 =$ strong interaction; and $4 =$ critical interaction.

The interaction codes may be added by rows resulting in a 'cause' value for each principal factor. The 'effect' value for each principal factor may be determined by adding the codes for each column. The net result of this procedure is a relative 'cause–effect' value (C, E) that may be plotted as coordinates on a cause–effect plot for the system or process of concern. 'C' represents the manner in which a principal factor affects the process of concern, whereas 'E' represents the way the process of concern affects the principal factor. The overall result will signify the relative importance of each principal factor. This is shown in Figs 5–7.

The relative importance or reliability of a particular principal factor may be assessed by the factor's position on the cause–effect plot as follows. Using factor 1 in Fig. 5 as an example, factor dominance is determined by scaling the perpendicular distance from the factor point to the factor intensity line. This distance is equal to $(C - E)/2^{\frac{1}{2}}$. If the factor point lies to the right of the factor intensity line, the factor dominance value will be a positive value, meaning that the factor will directly influence stone performance. If the factor point lies to the left of the factor intensity line, the factor dominance

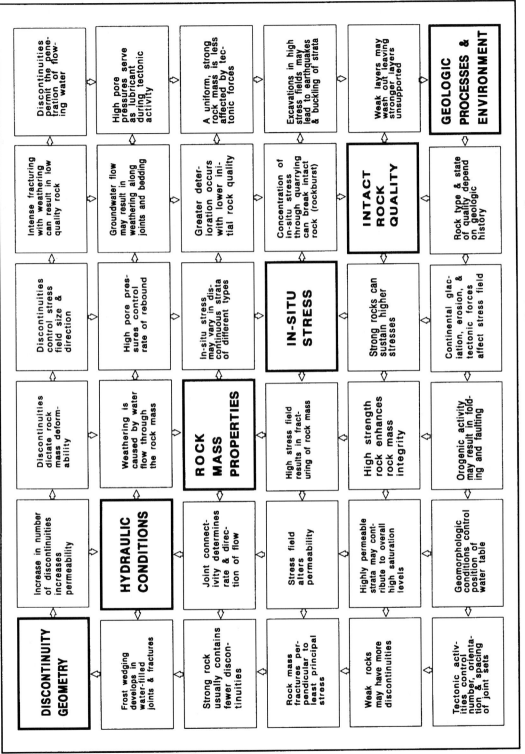

Fig. 1. Interaction matrix for geological processes affecting armourstone quality.

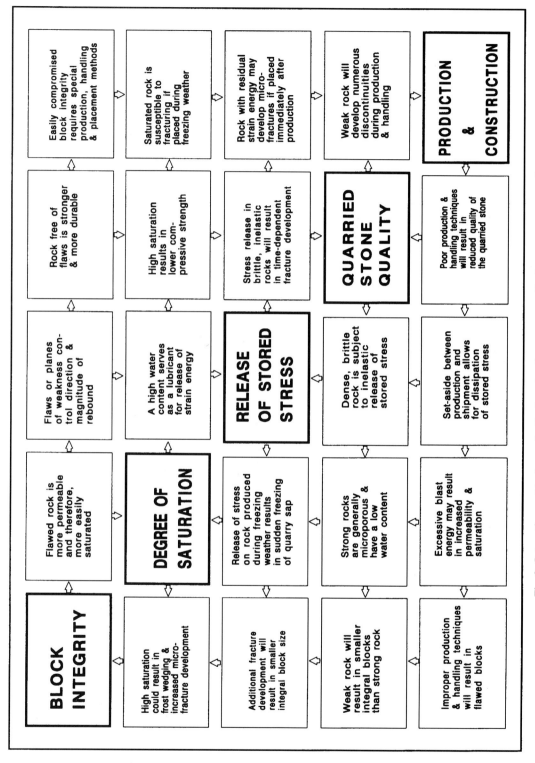

Fig. 2. Interaction matrix for production/construction processes affecting armourstone quality.

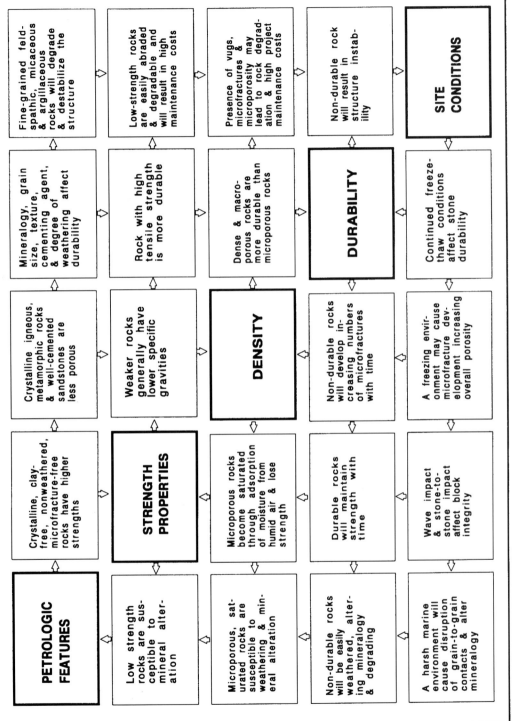

Fig. 3. Interaction matrix for in-service processes affecting armourstone quality.

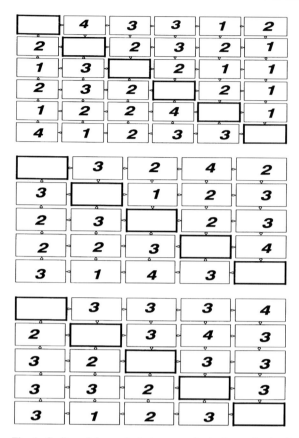

Fig. 4. Coding of the geological process (top), the production/construction process (middle) and the in-service process (bottom).

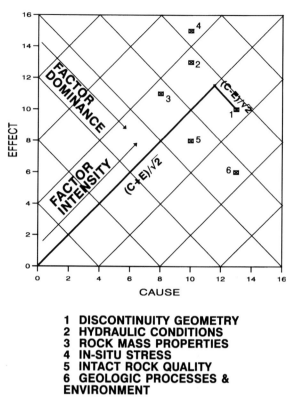

1 DISCONTINUITY GEOMETRY
2 HYDRAULIC CONDITIONS
3 ROCK MASS PROPERTIES
4 IN-SITU STRESS
5 INTACT ROCK QUALITY
6 GEOLOGIC PROCESSES &
   ENVIRONMENT

Fig. 5. Cause/effect plot for the geological process illustrating the proper method of factor assessment as recommended by Hudson (1992).

value will be a negative value and the factor will only indirectly affect stone performance. If the point lies on the factor intensity line, cause and effect are equal. Factor intensity is measured by scaling the distance from the origin to the point at which the perpendicular from the factor point intersects the factor intensity line. This distance is equal to $(C+E)/2^{\frac{1}{2}}$. The total vectorial distance (factor intensity plus factor dominance) is the factor's relative importance

$$(C+E)/2^{\frac{1}{2}} + (C-E)/2^{\frac{1}{2}}$$

= factor importance or reliability.

Though the formula $(C+E)/2^{\frac{1}{2}} + (C-E)/2^{\frac{1}{2}}$ reduces to $2^{\frac{1}{2}}C$ and appears not to take E into consideration, E is actually represented by $2^{\frac{1}{2}}$, as Fig. 5 illustrates.

Figure 5 shows a wide variation in both factor dominance and factor intensity. '*In situ* stress' has a high intensity, but low dominance, resulting in a rating identical to 'intact rock quality'. Figure 6 illustrates a

wide variation in factor intensity, but a low variation in factor dominance, indicating that the cause and effect are about equal for each principal factor. The principal factors plotted in Fig. 7 show about equal variation in factor intensity and dominance. In this case, the first three principal factors will directly influence stone performance, whereas the last two factors will only indirectly affect stone performance. The principal factor ratings are summarized in Table 1.

Rock armour quality specification

To develop a specification system for the assessment of the potential quality of armourstone, the following criteria must be established: specific information related to the geology of the quarry and quarry operations that may affect rock quality; specific information related to rock properties that may affect performance; and limits for the various qualities (excellent, good, marginal, poor) of rock.

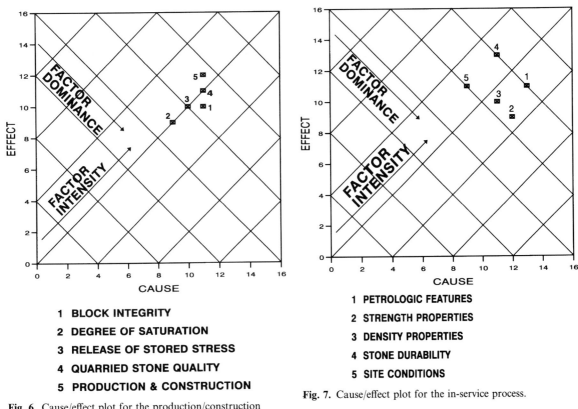

Fig. 6. Cause/effect plot for the production/construction process.

1 BLOCK INTEGRITY
2 DEGREE OF SATURATION
3 RELEASE OF STORED STRESS
4 QUARRIED STONE QUALITY
5 PRODUCTION & CONSTRUCTION

1 PETROLOGIC FEATURES
2 STRENGTH PROPERTIES
3 DENSITY PROPERTIES
4 STONE DURABILITY
5 SITE CONDITIONS

Fig. 7. Cause/effect plot for the in-service process.

In attempting to identify the specific information required, the principal factors developed for the interaction matrices must be re-examined. The matrices presented in Figs 1 and 2 are related to the quarry itself or to quarry-related factors that affect quarried rock quality and, accordingly, the information required from the quarry evaluation must be developed from these figures. Figure 3 is related to properties that may be determined in the laboratory and, hence, will be used to develop most of the requirements of the laboratory testing program.

From Figs 1 and 2 the following information is required either during the preliminary desk study or during the quarry evaluation: geological age and formation and miscellaneous geological information developed from published information; regional *in situ* stress conditions (presence of folds, faults, unloading features and their orientation to quarry face, unloading fractures in quarried stone, rockbursts in quarry floor; also see Hudson & Cooling (1988) and Sbar & Sykes (1973); rock mass conditions (lithological classification of rock type or types present, bedding or strata thickness, variability within beds or strata, stratigraphic log of working face); rock quality (block shape, degree of weathering, perme-

Table 1. *Ratings of matrix parameters*

Matrix parameters (factors and processes)	Ratings from cause–effect plot $[(C+E)/2^{\frac{1}{2}}] + [(C-E)/2^{\frac{1}{2}}]$
Discontinuity geometry	18.38
Hydraulic conditions	14.14
Rock mass properties	11.31
In situ stress	14.14
Intact rock quality	14.14
Geological processes	18.38
Block integrity	15.56
Degree of saturation	12.72
Stress release	14.14
Quality of the quarried stone	15.56
Production and construction	15.56
Petrologic features	18.38
Strength properties	16.97
Density properties	15.56
Durability	15.56
In-service conditions	12.72

ability, approximate strength); discontinuity geometry (number of joint sets and their orientation, *in situ* block size distribution, preferably using the methods outlined by Priest (1993) or Wang *et al.* (1991); groundwater conditions (position of groundwater table relative to rock strata of interest, conditions of flow, degree of saturation); block integrity (condition of quarried blocks in regards to the presence of flaws, planes of weakness, blasting fractures, microfractures); and production methods (if blasted, information on blasting methods should include number of rows of blastholes, blasthole diameter and inclination, specific charge or powder factor, type of explosive, bench height, burden distance, spacing distance, stemming material and height).

From Fig. 3 the following information is required during the laboratory testing and evaluation phase of the evaluation: petrographic analysis, evaluation and classification of the rock samples as to expected quality for the intended use (excellent, good, marginal or poor); strength and abrasion properties (sonic velocity, point load strength, Schmidt impact resistance, and LA abrasion); density properties (specific gravity, absorption, adsorption); and durability tests (sulphate soundness, wetting and drying, freezing and thawing).

Specifications based on these lists of required information and on additional information gained from the interaction matrices were developed for the various qualities of rock as shown in Tables 2–4. Portions of the rock property specifications are based on specifications from CIRIA (1991) and the U.S. Army Corps of Engineers (1990).

Table 2 consists of criteria, developed as the core of Fig. 1 that should be generated during the initial phase of the quarry evaluation. The lithological classification standard is based on data from Handin (1966) and Lama & Vutukuri (1978). Data for the *in situ* stress standard (the relation of σ_c to σ_1, where σ_c = compressive strength and σ_1 = virgin stress field principle stress) was derived from Stillborg (1986). Smith & Collis (1993) provided the information for the weathering grade model.

Priest (1993) was the initial source for the guidance on discontinuity analysis, but Wang *et al.* (1991) and CIRIA/CUR (1991) should also be consulted for information on determination of *in situ* block size distribution. The V_{80} criteria (V_{80} = 80% passing volume) as determined from the *in situ* block size distribution and the principal mean spacing data are based on a specific gravity of 2.65 and, therefore, the criterion for 'excellent' is assumed to have a mass of 18.5 t or greater. The upper limit of 7 m^3 is arbitrary and will actually depend on the project requirements, with the knowledge that even specifically tailored blasting will reduce the *in situ* V_{80} by as much as a factor of six (Latham *et al.* 1994).

The groundwater conditions are particularly important because of the influence of water on rock quality. The impact on rock quality is not only due to

weathering action, but also the decrease in rock strength with increased saturation, the increased development of microfractures during blasting and the need for 'curing' after production. The guidance for this standard is fairly simple: if everything else is equal, a 'dry' quarry is better than a quarry with flowing water.

Table 3 consists of standards that were the model for Fig. 2 and which would result from observations during the secondary phase of the quarry evaluation. The method used in the production of armourstone is of utmost importance. Non-blasting methods are preferred for producing large stones free of microfractures. If blasting methods are used, they need to be specifically tailored to the production of large stones. This is definitely a problem in the USA where large stone is repeatedly sold as a by-product of the aggregate and road metal operations. Latham *et al.* (1994) found that even with blasting methods specifically designed for armourstone production, the V_{80} size was reduced by a factor of six, but with aggregate-type blasting the V_{80} size was reduced by a factor of 20 or more. Toksöz *et al.* (1971) found that overblasting appears to activate the development of release fractures. Even the stone masons in the USA who work on the restoration of building facings have come to recognize the problem with microfracture development in rock damaged by excessive blasting energy. The development of this standard is the result of guidance from CIRIA/CUR (1991), Morhard (1987), Person *et al.* (1994), Roberts (1981), US Army Corps of Engineers (1972), US Bureau of Reclamation (1990) and Wang *et al.* (1992).

The set-aside requirement developed as a result of problems with early post-production fracturing and splitting that occurred in armourstone placed on breakwaters in the Great Lakes in the north-central USA. This fracturing and splitting developed in stone placed within a few weeks of production. There are basically three causes for this type of fracture development: production during or immediately before the onset of freezing weather; high degree of saturation with connate water (quarry sap); and stress release and relaxation of the rock block.

The need for a set-aside period was recognized over 2000 years ago by the Roman architect Vitruvius (Morgan 1960). Vitruvius specified a period of two years before the quarried rock could be used in construction. Lienhart (1975) found that a sandstone improved in durability by simply allowing it to 'cure' or to lose its quarry 'sap' over a period of three months. The set-aside is also useful for allowing the dissipation of stored stress and the development of relaxation fractures before the purchase of the stone. Microfracture development due to stress release was detected in the middle Devonian Onondaga limestone over a period of three months after the limestone was removed from the quarry face by diamond core drilling (Lienhart & Stransky 1981).

Table 2. *Quality specifications based on geological factor criteria*

Criteria	Quality specification			
	Excellent	Good	Marginal	Poor
Lithological classification	Unfoliated, coarsely crystalline igneous and metamorphic rocks, quartzite and highly silica-cemented sandstone	Crystalline dolomite, limestone and moderately well-cemented sandstone	Argillaceous limestones and sandstones, very vuggy dolomite reef rock, rhyolite and andesite	Shaly limestones, reef breccia, shale, siltstone, slate, schist, obsidian, pumice and gypsiferous carbonates
Regional *in situ* stress	Low stress, no folds, or faults $\sigma_c/\sigma_1 > 200$	Medium stress. Unloading features may be present $\sigma_c/\sigma_1 = 200\text{--}10$	High stress. Release fractures parallel to face may be present $\sigma_c/\sigma_1 = 10\text{--}5$	Very high stress. Faults may be present in quarry face. Rock bursts may be present in floor $\sigma_c/\sigma_1 = 5\text{--}2.5$
Weathering grade	IA – fresh, unweathered	IB – faintly weathered (staining on major discontinuity surfaces)	II – slightly weathered (staining persists throughout a greater part of the rock mass)	III – moderately weathered (less than half the rock mass is decomposed)
Discontinuity analysis (*in situ* block size distribution)	$V_{80} < 7, > 4.5\,\mathrm{m}^3$	$V_{80}\ 3\text{--}4.5\,\mathrm{m}^3$	$V_{80}\ 0.6\text{--}3\,\mathrm{m}^3$	$V_{80} < 0.6\,\mathrm{m}^3$
Groundwater conditions	Dry	Moist	Seepage from quarry walls	Water flowing from walls and pooling on floor

Table 3. *Quality specifications based on production and processing factor criteria*

Criteria	Quality specification			
	Excellent	Good	Marginal	Poor
Production method	Cutting, channelling or rock piercing methods – non-blasted	Specifically tailored blast using a single row of blastholes (low specific charge using explosive with low shock energy, high gas energy; bench height/burden = 2–3; spacing/burden = <1; stemming/burden = >1; blasthole diameter = 50–76 mm)	Conventional blasting using anfo and multiple rows of blastholes (bench height/burden = 1–2; spacing/burden = 1–1.5; stemming/burden = 0.75–1; blasthole diameter = 76–127 mm)	Aggregate blasting with large size stone as a by-product
Set-aside	Quarried stone is stockpiled for three months for curing and release of stored stress	Quarried stone is stockpiled for two months	Quarried stone is stockpiled for one month	Freshly quarried stone is transported directly to project site for placement
Quarried rock quality	Less than 5% of blocks have a length to thickness ratio greater than 3:1. 95% of the blocks are weathering grade IA, dense, free of vugs and cavities, and extremely high strength	5–10% of blocks have a length to thickness ratio greater than 3:1. 95% of blocks are weathering grade IB or better, dense to free-draining, very high strength	10–15% of blocks have a length to thickness ratio greater than 3:1. 95% of blocks are at least weathering grade II, either microporous or vuggy with cavities, high strength	>15% of blocks have a length to thickness ratio greater than 3:1. 95% of blocks are at least weathering grade III, argillaceous or micaceous
Block integrity	>95% of blocks are free of incipient fractures, flaws or cracks due to stress relief, rough handling, overblasting or other causes after two months set-aside in stockpile	90–95% of blocks are fracture-free after two months set-aside in stockpile	85–90% of blocks are fracture-free after two months set-aside in stockpile	<85% of blocks are fracture-free after two months set-aside in stockpile

Table 4. *Quality specifications based on rock property factor criteria*

Criteria	Quality specification			
	Excellent	Good	Marginal	Poor
Petrographic evaluation	*	*	*	*
Sonic velocity (km/s)	>6	4.5–6	3–4.5	<3
Point load strength (MPa)	>8.0	4.0–8.0	1.5–4.0	<1.5
Schmidt impact resistance (% rebound)	>60	50–60	40–50	<40
LA abrasion (% loss)	<15	15–25	25–35	>35
Specific gravity	>2.9	2.60–2.90	2.50–2.60	<2.50
Absorption (%)	<0.5	0.5–2.0	2.0–6.0	>6.0
Adsorption/absorption	<0.1	0.1–0.3	0.3–0.45	>0.45
$MgSO_4$ soundness (% loss)	<2	2–10	10–30	>30
Freeze–thaw loss (%)	<0.1	0.1–0.5	0.5–2.0	>2.0
Wet–dry loss (%)	<0.1	0.1–0.5	0.5–2.0	>2.0

*The petrographer will rate the quarried rock according to one of these categories.

There is often a difference in the quality between the observed and quarried rock. The quarried rock quality criterion addresses the particle shape in limiting the percentage of particles with a length to thickness (l/d) ratio greater than 3:1 where l = 'greatest distance between two points on a stone' and d = 'minimum distance between two parallel straight lines through which the stone can just pass' (CIRIA/CUR 1991). This standard also attempts to address the percentage of weathered particles (and weathering grade), the observed porosity and the relative strength (as determined by the sound of striking the rock particles with a rock pick).

The block integrity requirement is designed to prevent the inclusion of inferior blocks in the placement on the breakwater. The concern is for the presence of flaws (e.g. tension gashes and unloading fractures associated with stylolites; clay seams which could weather at a more rapid rate than the surrounding rock; micaceous foliated zones), incipient fractures (whether naturally occurring due to stress relaxation or to blasting or quarry processing) or other planes of weakness which may wedge apart on exposure to the elements. To eliminate some judgement variabilities in this standard, Latham (1994) proposed that the fractures or flaws be considered of significant concern only if a feeler gauge 0.5 mm in thickness can be inserted into the fractures or flaws for 1 m of the total length of the total visible fractures and flaws on the rock surface. The number of blocks to be examined will be at the discretion of the individual performing the inspection and will depend on the homogeneity of the source, but the sample size must be representative of the source.

The guidance for the rock property test standards that comprise the quality specifications of Table 4 is derived from Fig. 3. It should be noted that Table 4 includes the petrographic evaluation as one of the test standards in this set of specifications. The petrographic evaluation is one of the most effective test methods available for predicting the performance of rock as a construction material. An experienced petrographer will determine, through a petrographic analysis, the mineralogical composition, the grain size and texture, the presence of microfractures, signs of induced stress (and, therefore, possible stress release) and even the pore size distribution (using blue dye resin injection techniques); however, because the petrographic analysis is judgmental and depends strictly on the petrographer's interpretation, it is usually not included as part of a set of specifications. When the person responsible for interpreting the test results looks at the laboratory report (which usually consists of test data, a summary of the test results, descriptions of sample preparation and test methods, the petrographic evaluation report and quality control/quality assurance report), that person is more apt to consider test data than to read the petrographic evaluation report. Usually the petrographic report addresses any unique and important aspects of the rock, the quality of the rock and the expected performance of the rock. For these reasons, the petrographic evaluation is included in the rock property specifications.

Strength properties have been shown to be related to in-service durability (Fookes *et al.* 1971; 1988; Fookes & Poole 1981; Dibb *et al.* 1983; Latham 1992, 1993). Four strength/hardness property tests have been included in Table 4. Each measures a different aspect of strength/hardness which, if considered independently, would present a slightly different implication. Most of the quality specification criteria have been adapted from CIRIA/CUR (1991) and the US Army Corps of Engineers (1990).

The next group of standards included in Table 4 are related to the density/pore properties. Like the strength properties, if considered separately, there does not appear to be any relation to durability. Lienhart (1994) has shown, however, that when considered together there is a direct correlation with durability. The quality

specification criteria have been adapted from CIRIA/
CUR (1991) and the US Army Corps of Engineers
(1990).

The last group of standards in Table 4 are the dur-
ability/accelerated weathering tests. Once again, these
tests must be considered as a group and the criteria have
been adapted from CIRIA/CUR (1991) and the US
Army Corps of Engineers (1990).

Assessment of suitability

As discussed previously, relationships exist among all
factors and a proper assessment of a potential source of
armourstone cannot be accomplished by the evaluation
of a single criterion; nevertheless, an adequate assessment also cannot be obtained through a simple
evaluation of all criteria without a systematic approach.
A systematic approach must include not only an
evaluation of each criterion, but also consideration of
the relative importance of each criterion relative to all
others. It is proposed that the quality assessment of a
potential source is executed in the manner proposed in
the following discussion.

Table 5 is a proposed 'quality rating assessment
worksheet.' Column (a) lists the specification criteria

from Tables 2–4. Column (b) consists of the four quality
ratings where the appropriate rating may be entered by
checkmark based on observations, testing and evaluation of the potential source according to the specifications. The appropriate numerical rating value will be
entered in column (c). Column (d) displays the relative
importance of each criterion or group of criteria based
on the information developed in Figs 1–7 and Table 1.
An index based on column (d) is given in column (e).
Column (f) will display the weighted rating of each
criterion (c × e).

For any and every source of armourstone, each of the
quality specifications from Tables 2–4 should be evaluated, ranked 'excellent, good, marginal or poor', and
noted under the appropriate quality rating in column (b)
of the worksheet. A numerical rating of 4 (excellent),
3 (good), 2 (marginal), or 1 or 0 (poor or less) should be
entered in column (c) of the worksheet. Note that a '0'
rating (meaning less than 'poor' quality) may be
assigned for a particular specification criterion if there
is an expectation that the criterion will be especially
detrimental to the long-term performance of armourstone produced from a potential source.

The rock property criteria, other than the petrographic evaluation, is treated somewhat differently. The
rating values for each of the strength property criteria

Table 5. *Quality rating assessment worksheet*

(a) Criteria	(b) Quality rating				(c) Rating value	(d) Cause–effect rating	(e) Index (d/d$_{mean}$)	(f) Weighted rating (c × e)
	Excellent (=4)	Good (=3)	Marginal (=2)	Poor (=1)				
Lithological classification						11.31	0.74	
Regional *in situ* stress						14.14	0.93	
Weathering grade						14.14	0.93	
Discontinuity analysis						18.38	1.20	
Groundwater conditions						14.14	0.93	
Production method						15.56	1.02	
Rock quality						15.56	1.02	
Set-aside						13.43	0.88	
Block integrity						15.56	1.02	
Petrographic evaluation						18.38	1.20	
Sonic velocity								
Point load strength						16.97	1.11	
Schmidt impact resistance								
LA abrasion								
Specific gravity								
Absorption						15.56	1.02	
Adsorption/absorption								
MgSO$_4$ soundness								
Freeze–thaw loss						15.56	1.02	
Wet–dry loss								
						Mean = 15.2838	Overall rating (Σ column f/13) =	

Table 6. *Example of completed quality rating assessment worksheet*

(a) Criteria	(b) Quality rating				(c) Rating value	(d) Cause–effect rating	(e) Index (d/d_{mean})	(f) Weighted rating ($c \times e$)
	Excellent (=4)	Good (=3)	Marginal (=2)	Poor (=1)				
Lithological classification		✓			3	11.31	0.74	2.22
Regional *in situ* stress			✓		2	14.14	0.93	1.86
Weathering grade		✓			3	14.14	0.93	2.79
Discontinuity analysis		✓			3	18.38	1.20	3.60
Groundwater conditions			✓		2	14.14	0.93	1.86
Production method				✓	1	15.56	1.02	1.02
Rock quality			✓		2	15.56	1.02	2.04
Set-aside		✓			3	13.43	0.88	2.64
Block integrity				✓	1	15.56	1.02	1.02
Petrographic evaluation			✓		2	18.38	1.20	2.40
Sonic velocity				✓				
Point load strength		✓			1.75	16.97	1.11	1.94
Schmidt impact resistance				0				
LA abrasion		✓						
Specific gravity		✓						
Absorption		✓			3	15.56	1.02	3.06
Adsorption/absorption		✓						
MgSO$_4$ soundness	✓							
Freeze–thaw loss		✓			3.67	15.56	1.02	3.74
Wet–dry loss	✓							
						Mean = 15.2838	Overall rating	2.32

are noted in column (*b*) but only the average of these four values are entered in column (*c*). The same procedure is used for both the density properties and the durability properties. Once the rating process has been applied to all specification criteria, each rating value in column (*c*) will be multiplied by the pertinent index number in column (*e*) and entered in column (*f*). Column (*f*) is averaged and the result is the overall rating of a source.

Table 6 is an example of a completed worksheet for an aggregate quarry where the armourstone is sold as a by-product. In this example the rock apparently appeared to be of good quality, but the presence of unloading fractures parallel to the face were noted during the quarry inspection. Only faint staining was visible on major discontinuity surfaces and the *in situ* block size distribution indicated that the V_{80} volume was between 3 and 4.5 m^3. Groundwater was seeping from the upper part of the quarry face. The production method was by blasting for aggregate production, but the large size stone was set aside for at least two months. The particle shape of these large size particles exceeded 10% with an *l/d* ratio of 3:1 and the particles were vuggy with fist-size cavities. The quarried rock appeared to be more weathered than originally indicated by examination of the face and was actually quite stained throughout, indicating a weathering grade of II. More than 15% of

the large size blocks contained significant fractures. Based on the mineralogical composition, texture, the presence of microfractures, porosity and weathering, the petrographer classified this material as being of marginal quality. The sonic velocity was only 2.7 km/s (possibly due to the presence of cavities and microfractures), but the average point load strength was 4.5 MN/m^3. The Schmidt impact resistance was only 25% rebound, but the aggregate size sample had a loss of only 24% in the LA abrasion test. The specific gravity, absorption and adsorption/absorption all fell within the 'good quality' range. Only minor to trace losses occurred in the sulphate soundness and wet–dry tests, but freeze–thaw spalling resulted in a 0.5% loss. The resulting overall rating for this potential source is 2.32, or just slightly better than marginal quality.

Rating system evaluation

As part of a research study on the determination of causes of fracturing of armourstone, six quarries were evaluated using the proposed rock engineering rating system (Gerdsen & Lienhart 1996). The six quarries chosen had all been used at various times on break-waters in the Great Lakes area of the USA. Three quarries were limestone/dolomite quarries using blasting methods for armourstone production. One quarry was excavating Precambrian quartzite using specialized blasting methods (snake-hole) and low blast energy for armourstone production. One quarry was an architectural grade limestone being produced by wire-saw techniques and the last quarry was an architectural grade sandstone using a rotary-arm belt saw. Three breakwaters where one or more of these quarries had furnished armourstone were examined and the amount and probable cause of fracturing present in armour blocks from each of the six quarries was noted. Table 7 summarizes the basic quarry data, the rating of each quarry, the years in-service at the time of inspection on the breakwater and the actual performance of the armourstone. Examination of Table 7 reveals that the quarry ratings developed on the basis of this investigation either match or closely approximate the ratings of actual performance of the stone on the breakwater.

Conclusions

The use of a rock engineering system approach to the evaluation of armourstone sources requires the evaluator to consider all aspects of a potential source. This approach not only delineates the principal factors to be considered, but also provides an emphasis of the relative importance of each principal factor such that proper significance may be directed toward the pertinent feature. For those individuals who are not familiar with the laboratory testing aspect of this type of evaluation, the rock engineering system technique will provide the necessary guidance and will automate that portion of the evaluation for the responsible individual.

It is expected that this procedure will be especially useful for those situations where there are several equal quality armourstone sources within the expected transport range of the project site. This approach will provide

Table 7. *Application of rating system compared with actual performance of six quarries*

Quarry No.	Quarry data	Rating determined by proposed system*	Number of years of exposure on breakwater	Actual performance
1†	Silurian dolomitic reef rock and architectural grade dolomitic mudstone; low bench blasting using low energy explosive, single row of 70 mm blastholes with a spacing of 0.9 m	2.66	10+	Some fracturing of blocks, but overall performance is considered 'good'
2	Devonian dolomitic limestone with ≈15 m bench using 178 mm blastholes and 2–3 m spacing and high energy explosive	2.45	8+	Extensive fracturing. Overall performance considered to be 'marginal'
3	Devonian dolomitic limestone with 3 m bench using 70 mm blastholes, 2 m burden, 1 m spacing	2.45	8+	Extensive fracturing. Overall performance considered to be 'marginal'
4	Precambrian quartzite using 70 mm blastholes drilled horizontally along floor and low energy explosive to just lift formation	3.15	8+	Only one block found to be fractured after 8 years and this appears to be mechanical. Overall performance is considered to be 'good' to 'excellent'
5	Mississippian limestone, very porous, specific gravity of 2.40–2.50 produced by wire-saw	3.18	75+	15–20% of blocks exhibit exfoliation due to weathering, but this appears to be due to placement with bedding in a vertical position. Overall performance considered to be 'good' to 'excellent'
6	Mississippian sandstone, very homogeneous, siliceously cemented, but very porous and powders if blasted. Produced by rotary-arm belt saw and/or wire-saw	3.41	90+	Almost no sign of deterioration after over 90 years in service. Considered to be of 'excellent' quality

* Excellent = 4; good = 3; marginal = 2; and poor = or less.
† Located in an area of high *in situ* stresses and experiencing unloading due to continental glaciation.

an uncomplicated, but acceptable, comparison of the suitability of several different sources of armourstone. A preliminary field evaluation of the rating system has resulted in a close approximation of the actual field performance of the armourstone.

This study has presented a multifactorial assessment system in which the weighting of the factors was developed through the use of Hudson's (1992) factor interaction matrix approach. This is but one approach to the solution of multifactorial problems. Further work in this area should investigate the so-called *fuzzy* assessment approach for evaluation of current factor weightings. Ideally, multiple regression analyses of the various factors and factor interactions would present the best approach; however, the vast amount of data required would necessitate an inordinate amount of time.

Acknowledgements. The author thanks John-Paul Latham of the Geomaterials Unit at Queen Mary and Westfield College and Melvin Hill, engineering geologist (retired from the Bureau of Reclamation, Denver) for their review and suggestions early in the developmental stage of this work. The author also thanks his partner, Al Gerdsen, for his critique of the first draft. Finally, the author extends a special thanks to his wife, Donna, for her patience and understanding during this study and for her usual excellence in proofing the manuscript during the various stages of development.

References

CIRIA/CUR 1991. *Manual on the Use of Rock in Coastal and Shoreline Engineering.* CIRIA Special Publication 83/CUR Report 154, CIRIA/CUR, London.

DIBB, T. E., HUGHES, D. W. & POOLE, A. B. 1983. The identification of critical factors affecting rock durability in marine environments. *Quarterly Journal of Engineering Geology,* **16**, 149–161.

FOOKES, P. G. & POOLE, A. B. 1981. Some preliminary consideration on the selection and durability of rock and concrete materials for breakwaters and coastal protection works. *Quarterly Journal of Engineering Geology,* **14**, 97–128.

——, DEARMAN, W. R. & FRANKLIN, J. A. 1971. Some engineering aspects of rock weathering with field examples from Dartmoor and elsewhere. *Quarterly Journal of Engineering Geology,* **4**, 139–185.

——, GOURLEY, C. S. & OHIKERE, C. 1988. Rock weathering in engineering time. *Quarterly Journal of Engineering Geology,* **21**, 33–57.

GERDSEN, A. W. & LIENHART, D. A. 1996. *Quarry and Breakwater Investigation of Stone Deterioration.* Consultant's report prepared for US Army Corps of Engineers, Waterways Experiment Station by Rock Products Consultants, Cincinnati.

HANDIN, J. 1966. Strength and ductility. *In:* CLARK, S. P. JR. (ed.) Handbook of Physical Constants. Geological Society of America Memoir 97, 223–289.

HUDSON, J. A. 1989. *Rock Mechanics Principles in Engineering Practice.* Construction Industry Research and Information Association, London.

——1992. *Rock Engineering, Theory and Practice.* Ellis Horwood, Chichester.

—— & COOLING, C. M. 1988. In situ rock stresses and their measurement in the UK – part 1. The current state of knowledge. *International Journal of Rock Mechanics, Mining Sciences & Geomechanics Abstracts,* **25**, 363–370.

—— & HARRISON, J. P. 1992. A new approach in studying complete rock engineering problems. *Quarterly Journal of Engineering Geology,* **25**, 93–105.

LAMA, R. D. & VUTUKURI, V. S. 1978. *Handbook on Mechanical Properties of Rocks.* Vol. IV. Trans Tech Publications, Clausthal.

LATHAM, J.-P. 1992. In-service durability evaluation of armourstone. *In:* MAGOON, O. T. & BAIRD, W. F. (eds) *Durability of Stone for Rubble Mound Breakwaters.* American Society of Civil Engineers, New York, 6–18.

——1993. A mill abrasion test for wear resistance of armour stone. *In:* McELROY, C. H. & LIENHART, D. A. (eds) *Rock for Erosion Control.* ASTM Special Technical Publication 1177, 46–61.

LIENHART, D. A. 1975. *Special Study on the Effect of 'Curing' on the Durability of the Berea Sandstone.* US Army Corps of Engineers, Ohio River Division Laboratory Open-File Report #103/75.618B.

——1994. Durability issues in the production of rock for erosion control. *In:* NELSON, P. P. & LAUBACH, S. E. (eds) *Rock Mechanics, Models and Measurements, Challenges from Industry, Proceedings, 1st North American Rock Mechanics Symposium.* Balkema, Rotterdam, 1083–1090.

—— & STRANSKY, T. E. 1981. Evaluation of potential sources of riprap and armor stone – methods and considerations. *Bulletin of the Association of Engineering Geologists,* **18**, 323–332.

MATHESON, D. 1988. *Performance of Riprap in Northern Climates.* Canadian Electric Association, Montreal.

MORGAN, M. H. (translator) 1960. *Vitruvius. The ten books on architecture.* Dover, New York.

MORHARD, R. C. 1987. *Explosives and Rock Blasting.* Atlas Powder, Dallas.

PERSSON, P.-A., HOLMBERG, R. & LEE, J. 1994. *Rock Blasting and Explosives Engineering.* CRC Press, Boca Raton.

PRIEST, S. D. 1993. *Discontinuity Analysis for Rock Engineering.* Chapman & Hall, London.

ROBERTS, A. 1981. *Applied Geotechnology.* Pergamon Press, New York.

SBAR, M. L. & SYKES, L. R. 1973. Contemporary compressive stress and seismicity in eastern North America: an example of intra-plate tectonics. *Geological Society of America Bulletin,* **84**, 1861–1882.

SMITH, M. R. & COLLIS, L. (eds) 1993. *Aggregates.* Geological Society, London, Engineering Geology Special Publication No. 9.

STILLBORG, B. 1986. *Professional User's Handbook for Rock Bolting.* Trans Tech, Clausthal.

TOKSÖZ, M. N., THOMSON, K. C. & AHRENS, T. J. 1971. Generation of seismic waves by explosions in prestressed media. *Bulletin of the Seismological Society of America,* **61**, 1589–1623.

US Army Corps of Engineers 1972. *Systematic Drilling and Blasting for Surface Excavations*. Engineer Manual 1110-2-3800, 1 March 1972.

——1990. *Construction with Large Stone*. Engineering Manual 1110-2-2302, US Army Engineers, Washington.

US Bureau of Reclamation 1990. *Engineering Geology Field Manual*. US Department of the Interior, Bureau of Reclamation, Denver Federal Center, Denver.

Wang, H., Latham, J.-P. & Poole, A. B. 1991. Predictions of block size distribution for quarrying. *Quarterly Journal of Engineering Geology*, **24**, 91–99.

——, —— & ——1992. Producing armourstone within aggregate quarries. *In*: Magoon, D. T. & Baird, W. F. (eds) *Durability of Stone for Rubble Mound Breakwaters*. American Society of Civil Engineers, New York, 200–210.

—— & Poole, A. B. 1994. Rock for maritime engineering. *In*: Abbott, M. B. & Price, W. A. (eds) *Coastal, Estuarial and Harbour Engineers' Reference Book*. Spon, London, 523–539.

Opening and operation of the Pasir Panjang quarry: a dedicated armourstone quarry in the Malaysian jungle

J. A. Van Meulen

Baggermaatschappij Boskalis bv, 20 Rosmolenweg, Papendrecht, 3350 AA Papendecht, The Netherlands

Abstract. In August 1993 Baggermaatschappij Boshalis was awarded a contract for the construction of a breakwater (1400 m parallel to the coast) and four rock groynes (180 m each) in Malaysia. The award was based on the company's alternative design, which was to use 11 and 20 t concrete armour units (tetrapods) totaling $115\,000\,m^3$ of concrete and 2.1×10^6 t of rock with sizes from 50 mm to 9.0 t. The quantities of the various rock grades chosen in the alternative design were optimized to suit the assumed production possibilities of rock block sizes from sources in the area. After award of the contract, a new quarry only 8.0 km from the construction site was opened, the nearest existing quarry being 38 km away. The new quarry started deliveries on 1 April 1994 and completed them on 17 April 1995.

A case history of the quarry is presented, emphasizing the economic importance of the rock fragmentation and the logistics common to most dedicated armourstone quarry operations. It describes the tender stage, the choice of quarry location and the choice of the various specified rock gradings made during the breakwater design process. The blasting procedures used to obtain the required gradings and quantities are discussed. The particular features and problems associated with opening and operating a dedicated armourstone quarry – for example, the selection plant, the stockpiling procedures, shipping and materials quality control procedures – are amplified upon.

Historical background to the contract

In 1992 Ethylene Malaysia Sdn Bhd invited various companies to bid for the construction at Kerteh of the following: a 1400 m long breakwater (parallel to the coast); a 1100 m long revetment for slope protection; four groynes each 180 m long; $700\,000\,m^3$ dredging; $200\,000\,m^3$ beach recharge; and three jetties for berthing 50 000 t gas tankers.

The tender design asked for a total of 2 750 000 t of rock, of which 550 000 t was to be armour of 5.0–9.0 t. Baggermaatschappij Boshalis was of the opinion that it would be difficult to estimate, with any great accuracy, the percentage of large armour blocks that local quarries would yield. The estimates for the total amount to be quarried that would yield sufficient armour varied between 7 500 000 and 12 500 000 t. This meant that pricing the project correctly would be risky. Investigations into marketing the excess material (e.g. as aggregates) showed that locally there was only a market for at most 350 000 t of aggregates per year and that shipping to Singapore (350 nautical miles by sea) was only marginally economical. Moreover, selling all the excess material, between five and ten million tonnes, over a period of two years, would mean trying to obtain an unrealistically high market share in Singapore of 20–40%. Furthermore, it was doubtful whether the reserves in the 'best' suited existing quarry were sufficient to cover the maximum estimated rock requirement.

Consequently, an alternative design, incorporating artificial concrete armour units (tetrapods) was proposed, which was selected on 13 August 1993 in preference to other alternative designs presented after a re-tender. The alternative design required approximately 2 125 000 t of rock (of which 108 000 t was to be above 2.0 t) and additionally 18 000 tetrapods weighing 11 t and 1700 weighing 20 t.

Quarry selection

The Malaysian client investigated all potential quarries in the area while designing the facilities. All these quarry sites were also visited by the author and were evaluated for: (1) their distance to the construction site by sea (including the length of quaywall and draught possibilities) and by road (including road conditions and traffic frequency); (2) the reserves available; (3) the ease of quarrying; (4) the quality of the rock; and (5) the stockpile capacity.

(1) The majority of the rock required was for the off-shore breakwater, hence sea transport was preferred. Furthermore, sea transport is cheaper than

VAN MEULEN, J. A. 1998. Opening and operation of the Pasir Panjang quarry: a dedicated armourstone quarry in the Malaysian jungle. *In*: LATHAM, J.-P. (ed.) 1998. *Advances in Aggregates and Armourstone Evaluation*. Geological Society, London, Engineering Geology Special Publications, **13**, 107–120.

road transport and transporting large quantities of rock by truck on public roads has a strong negative impact in the region. The local roads were only two lanes wide and if they were to be used, congestion, pollution and probably accidents would have occurred. This would have been likely to cause problems with the local population and delayed the project.

(2) The reserves have to be sufficient to supply the required quantity and should include 'excess material'. Excess material is taken to mean material produced which does not fall within a required rock grade or is of a size grade that is by necessity over-produced and therefore left over after construction is complete. Typically large quantities have to be quarried to produce sufficient volumes of a particular grading.

(3) The reserves of the quarry should be accessible without having to change the complete layout and infrastructure of the quarry (e.g. remove overburden, construct haul roads, etc.).

(4) The quality of the rock should comply with the contract requirements. It is reasonable to assume that any existing aggregate or dimension stone quarry will have been located at a particular spot because it has good quality rock. Therefore it was assumed that armourstone quality specifications could be met from existing quarries.

(5) The stockpile capacity within the quarry or the harbour area is important. During routine production the quarry, with some small variations, will tend to produce the same daily quantities for each size range (from large to small). The consumption (use) of the rock in the construction of the project can be erratic when certain stages of the construction are carried out. There is therefore a fine balance to be found between the need to minimize the excessive production of small blocks, to have the right sizes at a given time in the construction programme and to have large stockpile areas, as amplified briefly in the following:

The construction of a marine structure requires the placement of small material first and then a stepped increase in the size of the rock when progressing to the outer layers. This means that the small sizes are required in the beginning and the large sizes towards the end of the project period. A dedicated quarry, existing solely for the purpose of one contract should take this into account. The quarry operator has the tendency to accommodate the wishes of the client and produce what they ask for at a particular moment. The quarry production should however concentrate on producing the critical grade so as to minimize the amount of excess material. When the optimum schedule for the quarry production is not acceptable to the client then it is reasonable for the client to bear the extra costs of blasting and removing the larger proportion of excess material than would otherwise be produced. A dedicated quarry operator should always be

mindful to 'save' the critical rock grades, i.e. the most difficult ones to produce, until they are needed. This requires large stockpile areas.

During the first tender phase the Kemamam quarry was used in the estimates. This quarry provided the rock for the construction of the Kemamam Supply Base (1983–1986) and is currently still in use as an aggregate quarry (yearly output of 200 000–300 000 t). The major reasons for considering this location were that it was located immediately at the coastline and that permission had been granted to use part of the quarry and to carry out the quarrying via a subcontractor or by the author's company. The quarry's disadvantages were: the distance to the construction site (38 km by sea or 45 km by road); the existing harbour facilities became completely blocked by sand and uncertainty remained about future blockages if new facilities were created; no suitable infrastructure (quarry roads + rock benches/ faces); and limited reserves.

During the tender phase the author's company was approached by a quarry owner who purported to have mining rights by the seashore only 8.0 km from the construction site, but it was considered that not enough information was available to confidently price this location. Upon award of contract the author was again approached by this quarry owner who said that he now had environmental impact approval and nearly all the permits from the various government departments to operate a quarry and to build a jetty at this seaside location. The prospect of having a quarry so close to the construction site appealed very much, although it was realized that the time was short to 'prove the quality and quantity' of the quarry and to obtain the 'last and final' permits necessary to 'open' the quarry.

Immediately, a topographical survey (8 ha beach + 20 ha hill), a borehole investigation (six holes 150 m core) and a seismic refraction survey (1600 m) were started to prove the quality and quantity of rock available. In the meantime various discussions were held with the government departments involved to obtain approval for the design of the quarryside works harbour. The progress of the surveys was slow because the quarry site was remote. The equipment could only be brought to the site by small boats and by wading through the surf zone. Reaching the site by land was not possible; there was only a small and steep jungle footpath. Time was running out quickly and a decision had to be taken to enable the opening of this quarry on time. Again, the quarry area was visually inspected, which was difficult because of the steep slope, the jungle and the huge boulders. On the basis of this visual inspection a decision was taken on 24 September 1993 to go ahead with the development of the Pasir Panjang Quarry. Should the investigations prove negative within two months, there was still time left, although very little, for the author's company to revert to the Kemamam

Table 1. *Estimated quantities in the Pasir Panjang Quarry*

	Project quarry	Concession
Overburden (bank m^3)	250 000	650 000
Rock of weathering grade III (bank m^3)	200 000	850 000
Rock of weathering grade I and II (t)	4 000 000	15 000 000

Table 3. *Gradings used in contract*

Material class name	Grading definition
Bedding material	50–150 mm
Core material	5–500 kg
Underlayer	0.5–2.0 t
Armour I	2.0–5.0 t
Armour II	5.0–9.0 t

quarry. In the weeks that followed the topographical, borehole and seismic information that became available supported the decision taken.

The overburden thickness varied between 5.0 and 10.0 m. The seismic refraction survey showed an additional layer of 5 m with uncertain quality material of weathering grade III, a quality that might or might not be satisfactory for use as core in the break-water. Tables 1 and 2 summarize the prospects for the quantities (note that the potential of the area is much higher as later more land plots were added to the concession) and quality of the granite from the Pasir Panjang Quarry.

Breakwater design

In the meantime the final design of the breakwater was being prepared and tested in The Netherlands in a physical model. The design concept was to take into account the relative proportions of the different size fractions that the quarry could deliver to minimize 'excess material'. A problem was that the recovery percentages (the fragmentation curve) for the new quarry were not known and had to be estimated from experience (e.g. of other quarry locations used for other projects).

For the design the gradings chosen were 'simple' in so far as they could all be produced with relative ease using appropriate size selection plant, while ensuring that there was no gap in the sizes that might be required, nor

any appreciable overlap in size from within different gradings. Just such a standard grading system was proposed in the CIRIA/CUR (1991) manual, whereby the grading classes were named after the range of weights for which up to 10% may be smaller and up to 30% may be greater. The chosen gradings (shown in Table 3) were based on this system, but differ slightly from the CIRIA standard gradings.

By focussing on the materials requirements and the expected fragmentation as well as the hydraulic performance, evaluations of the preliminary design showed that to deliver the required high proportion of underlayer material (0.5–2.0 t) there would need to be an excessive amount of blasting, leading to vast piles of excess material after the contract. This was a crucial factor needing correction in the ultimate design. The core in the original tender design was defined as 5–500 kg, and this range was essentially retained. To make more use of the smaller sizes, while cutting down on the need for armour sizes, the undersize of the core could be screened to produce both bedding material (50–150 mm) and aggregates (25–50 mm) which, if required could then be used as coarse aggregates for the manufacture of concrete armour units. (In fact, the subcontractor for the tetrapod production later declined to take advantage of the aggregates from the undersize of the core material on the grounds that the shape was not suitable.)

The consequences of the alternative design's volume requirements are set out in Table 4, where it can be seen that 2 550 000 t would have to be blasted to achieve the

Table 2. *Pasir Panjang Quarry test results compared with their classification of rock quality based on CIRIA/CUR (1991)*

	Test value	Units	Class range	Quality class
Rock density	2.64	t/m^3	2.60–2.90	Good
Water absorption	0.55	%	<0.50	Excellent
MgSO$_4$ soundness	0.14	%	<2.00	Excellent
Methylene blue absorption	0.20	g/100 g	<0.40	Excellent
Aggregate impact value	20.0	%	12.0–20.0	Good
Unconfined compressive strength	219	MPa	>200	Excellent
Brazilian tensile strength	9.4	MPa	6.0–12.0	Good
10% fines value	230	kN	>200	Excellent
Los Angeles abrasion value	26.6	%	25.0–35.0	Marginal
Micro Deval value (wet)	5.3	%	<10.0	Excellent

Table 4. *Blasting requirement for alternative design based on estimated yield for each grading*

Class name	Requirement (t)	Yield (%)	Blasting required (t)*
Armour II (5.0–9.0 t)	12 150	3	405 000
Armour I (2.0–5.0 t)	94 450	6	1 574 167
Underlayer (0.5–2.0)	322 700	13	2 482 308
Core (5–500 kg)	1 374 550	54	2 545 463
Bedding (50–150 mm)	311 200	15	2 074 667
Fines (0–50 mm)	0	9	–
Total	2 162 550		

*This column indicates the total tonnage of rock needed to be blasted to produce the contract requirement for the grading in question.

required grades and quantities, which is only 16% more than the requirement; in other words a design with only 16% excess material.

Quarry operation and design

On 7 October 1993 a subcontract was awarded to a local joint venture to operate the Pasir Panjang quarry. This contract included: construction of the access road; development of the quarry roads; removal of overburden; carrying out the drilling and blasting; construction and operation of two selection plants; excavating the rock from the face; selection of the armour at the face; stockpiling the various gradings; and loading of the various vessels.

Bench heights were designed to be 15.0 m as this was considered to be the optimum between the output requirement and a suitable bench height for armourstone production (which, in fact, favours smaller heights). The width of the quarry was of major concern because some private land protruded into the working area. Shortly after the development of the top face it became possible to purchase one of the most problematic plots of land. This made it possible to increase the width of the quarry considerably. The excavation area required for the project measured 100–175 m wide by 250 m long.

Two main haulroads were constructed on either side of the quarry. The north road coincided with the access road and had a gradient of 10% (in places 12%). The south road had a gradient of 10% (with the upper section at 13%). The roads had a minimum width of 12.5 m and were partly constructed on a cut, into the overburden of the hillside, and partly on fill, constructed from the overburden excavated from the quarried area.

Incorporated in the planning were a sufficient number of ditches, drains and culverts to enable monsoon rains

to drain rapidly without causing any damage. The system drained into two silt traps before discharging into the sea.

Construction of a works harbour able to ship the rocks from the quarry to the construction site and other features of the quarry site which were designed by the author's company can be seen in Fig. 1. Two breakwaters were constructed to protect the three berths against the strong northeast monsoon swells (generally caused by typhoons passing the Philippines in the direction of Vietnam and Hong Kong), which alone required 145 000 t of rock graded from 0 to 9.0 t.

Overburden removal

The removal of the overburden proved to be troublesome because of the great number of boulders at the surface and close to the bedrock. The material indicated on the seismic refraction survey as grade III material (with seismic velocities between 1700 and 2400 m/s) proved to be good quality rock, but in the form of huge boulder nests. The size of the boulders varied between 10.0 and 50.0 t. All boulders were dug free, which was time consuming, before they were broken down by 'drill-blasting'. The thickness of this boulder layer varied between 5.0 and 15.0 m.

All overburden material was transported by truck to be used either as fill for the roads and the casting yard or to waste tips. By the end of 1994 all the overburden had been removed (400 000 m^3) and all the required benches developed.

Drilling and blasting

Face development started at floor level +105 m. All rock quarried during the months of January, February and March 1994 were used for the construction of the workharbour breakwaters and for road surfacing. All large rocks in the 2.0–5.0 t and 5.0–9.0 t classes and of suitable quality and shape were put aside and stockpiled for the Kerteh breakwater in the knowledge that obtaining large rocks is often problematic. The sooner they are in stock the better and reducing their size at a later stage is relatively easy.

The techniques of drilling (in this case by Tamrock 600 hydraulic crawler drills) and blasting are always important, but more so when dealing with armourstone production. When producing aggregates blasting is only the first step in reducing the size of the rock and is followed by various stages of crushing. When producing armourstone and core materials, blasting is generally the last step. This means that all the sizes of the stones required have to come out of the fragmented blastpile.

Fig. 1. Pasir Panjang quarrybenches, haulroad, stockpiles and works harbour.

All sizes which fall outside the sizes required, generally the small sizes, are excess material and in this project could be thrown away because crushing the excess into aggregates was not permitted. Drilling and blasting for armourstone must also be carried out more carefully and more accurately because the drill patterns are large and the explosive ratios low. Inaccurate drilling and/or charging will result very quickly in 'poor' blasting results, e.g. sizes that are not required.

To keep up with the output target it was necessary to blast every day because larger blasts were not possible in the limited working space available. Even outside the monsoon period there were frequent rain showers and at all times there were significant flows of groundwater. This meant that the drillholes were generally partly filled with water. Blasting in Malaysia is only carried out with ANFO and therefore special measures had to be taken to ensure that blasting was possible every day. The blasting design and procedures adopted were developed by the author's team.

The following blast geometry (as shown in Fig. 2) was generally in use: hole diameter, 89 mm; burden, 2.75–3.00 m; spacing, 3.00 m; subdrilling, 0.90 m; and face height, 15.0 m.

The initiation of the explosives was with an electric millisecond delay detonator in the bottom of the hole. The detonator was fitted to a 100 g pentolite booster to initiate the ANFO. A 10 g/m detonating cord connected and initiated the deck charges from the bottom up. In each deck there was a 50 g pentolite booster. Generally three rows were fired in each blast with a 50 ms delay interval between each row. The following points were noted:

- All ANFO was packed into double-skinned plastic sleeves to ensure that the ANFO stayed dry.
- Because of the use of packed ANFO as a bottom charge it was not possible to increase the burden greater than 3.0 m, otherwise toe problems would have occurred.
- Emulite 150 was used in the beginning as the booster charge, but inconsistent results were obtained and therefore the switch was made to pentolite.
- The accuracy of drilling was poor and variations in the spacing (at the bottom of the face) of 2.4–3.8 m were measured when 3.0 m was required. Increasing the accuracy was rarely achieved due to lack of experience.

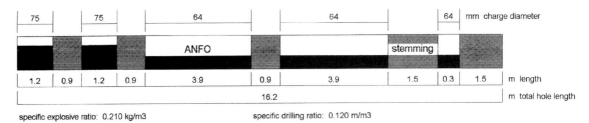

specific explosive ratio: 0.210 kg/m3   specific drilling ratio: 0.120 m/m3

Fig. 2. Typical charging plan for a drillhole.

For the reasons given above, a burden of 3.0 m was retained. Thereafter the fragmentation was controlled by the size (diameter) of the column charge and by the number of decks. To produce the relatively large quantities required for the middle size (500–2000 kg), reduced charge diameters, with consequent decoupling from explosive to borehole walls, were used to obtain an even distribution of the explosive force along the length of the drillhole. This was found to be effective. When coarser fragments were required, decks were introduced to space out the column charge.

Fragmentation results

Before discussing the fragmentation achieved, it is important to remember that the early construction phase was to put special demands on production priorities. The need to place all the bedding material (50–150 mm), which acts as the breakwater's foundation layer, in the first half of the first season caused problems. The desired rate of use of bedding material in the beginning far exceeded the production capabilities. This was foreseen during the start-up phase and the required quantity in the design was reduced by approximately 50% by using a thinner layer under the breakwater. Some material was also purchased from another quarry. Soon, however the quarry caught up with the rate of production needed for the bedding material and it continued producing bedding material until the end of the contract regardless of its need. Upon completion of the contract the estimate for the yields of bedding material turned out to be close to the actual yields and therefore the economics of a speedy start must be seen against the large quantity of bedding material which had to be 'thrown' away.

The 5.0–9.0 t armour was 'saved' from the beginning when the overburden was removed. Blasting the boulders in the overburden yielded substantial amounts of good quality armour and thus a consequent reduction in the main blasting requirement so that, somewhat surprisingly, the 5.0–9.0 t armour was never a problem to produce in sufficient quantities. Likewise the 2.0–5.0 t armour never posed a problem.

The 5–500 kg core proved to be a 'problem' during the first half of the project when large quantities were required. The percentage of material less than 5 kg proved to be higher than estimated, which reduced the percentage of material per blast that was in the core grading. In fact, all material less than 5 kg became a 'waste' product and therefore the blasting was kept relatively coarse. Any rock which was oversize (>2.0 t) was broken into core (or underlayer material whichever was wanted the most) by a hydraulic impact hammer.

One aspect of economic optimization often overlooked is the rate of digging the blastpile. The ideal fragmentation to aim for will always have to be an optimum between the sizes of the rock fragments and the 'digability' (output per hour) of the excavating machines. A blast with very coarse fragments will be hard to dig e.g. the output rate will be low. It might be better to have a slightly finer fragmentation, but with an output (of the required grades) from the production units which is higher. Even by throwing some of the material away, the final production cost for the required grades can often be lower. This is a particular consideration in a dedicated quarry when excess material cannot be used in other ways. The slowing influence of the coarse fragments can clearly be seen in the relation between the hourly output of the selection plants against the percentage of fragments >0.5 t, as shown in Fig. 3.

The 0.5–2.0 t underlayer material was only in short supply towards the end of the project. The demand from the construction site for this size grade was underestimated in the design and some additional blasting had to be carried out.

The history of the recovery percentage during the project is shown in Fig. 4. Care should be taken, however, in interpreting the graphs because the yield percentages were influenced by specific demands from the construction site for certain sizes at different stages. During the months of July, August and September 1994 the high demand was for core (5–500 kg) and this was produced by blasting. In November, December and January there was again a high demand for core material, but this was also produced by breaking oversize material with the hydraulic impact hammer. In February, March and April 1995 there was a high demand for underlayer material

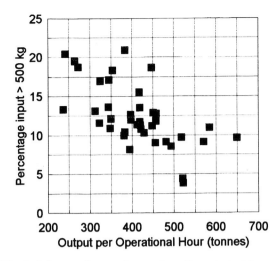

Fig. 3. Influence of coarse fragments on the output of the selection plant.

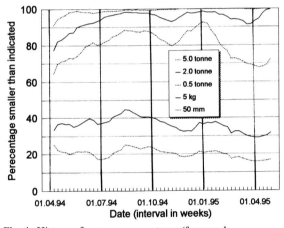

Fig. 4. History of recovery percentages (four week running average).

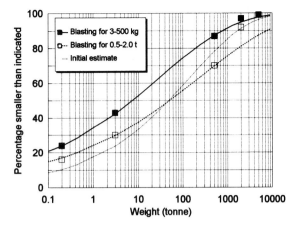

Fig. 5. Two typical fragmentation curves which were obtained in the quarry compared with the estimated curve.

Fragmentation predictions and actual production

The Kuz–Ram model (Cunningham 1987) was used to predict the fragmentation. Experience by back-analysis and by obtaining best-fit Rosin–Rammler curves showed that Cunningham's rock factor A varied between 1.75 for a lapilli tuff and 5.00 for a good quality massive granite. These conclusions were reached from analysing all the armourstone blast data. The model was found to have underestimated the amount of fines considerably and it may be suggested that the n_s value given by Cunningham's algorithm for the slope of the Rossin–Rammler equation tends to be too steep for this particular quarry application (Table 5).

An attempt was made to incorporate the influence of reduced charge diameters (decoupling) and deck charges into the Kuz–Ram model, but the approach adopted has not yet produced a more satisfactory prediction capability for the results of blasting.

Rock selection from the face

After the blast, blocks inside the blastpile were put aside by a CAT 245 face shovel and then inspected by a checker, who would usually mark each block that appeared to be greater than 2 t (i.e. of armourstone class I or II) while taking into account the rock quality, the integrity of the block (fractures), the visual appearance (surface weathering) and the shape. A marking scheme was used to indicate either the armourstone class for the acceptable blocks or the reason for rejection for the unacceptable blocks. Those boulders and blocks which were unsuitable or of sizes no longer required were loaded and carried (by a CAT 988B wheel-loader) to a

(0.5–2.0 t), which was produced by blasting. Figure 5 gives two typical fragmentation curves, one for blasting to obtain core material (5–500 kg) in August and one for blasting to obtain underlayer material (0.5–2.0 t) in March. Also included is the estimate of the fragmentation curve on which the alternative breakwater design was based.

The plots shown are the average of the results obtained during that particular month with best-fit curves using the Rosin–Rammler equation superimposed. Both graphs, however, are based on the product sizes sent to the site and therefore include the effect of the secondary breakage of oversized material which will have slightly altered the coarse end of the raw fragmentation curves.

Table 5. *Comparison of tonnages of different grades for (a) initial best estimate of production curve, (b) total actual production and (c) total quantities used in the project*

Class name	(a) tonnes required	Estimated yield (%)	(b) Tonnes produced	Actual yield (%)	(c) Tonnes used
Armour II (5.0–9.0 t)	12 150	3	10 359	0.4	10 105
Armour I (2.0–5.0 t)	94 450	6	98 641	3.6	97 915
Underlayer (0.5–2.0 t)	322 700	13	373 062	13.6	367 745
Core (5–500 kg)	1 374 550	54	1 240 368	45.1	1 228 794
Bedding (50–150 mm)	311 200	15	454 296	16.5	245 336
Fines (0–50 mm)	434 950	9	574 522	20.9	–
Total	2 550 000		2 751 248		1 949 895

remote spot in the quarry (Fig. 6). A CAT 245 excavator fitted with a Rammer G1000 hydraulic hammer was used as a secondary breaker to create more core and underlayer material.

Operation of the selection plants

The greatest quantity of material required was core material and to produce the required grading the +500 kg and the −5 kg blocks were taken out using two selection plants. The selection of the core could then be combined with the selection of the other grades required, i.e. the 50–150 mm bedding material and the 0.5–2.0 t underlayer material. This meant that at the face only the +2.0 t blocks had to be taken out. This could be quite easily achieved by machine operator eye selection.

Each of the twin selection plants, designed by the author (a schematic diagram is shown in Fig. 7), consisted of one vibrating grizzly feeder (1800 mm wide,

Fig. 6. Blocks removed from the face for breaking.

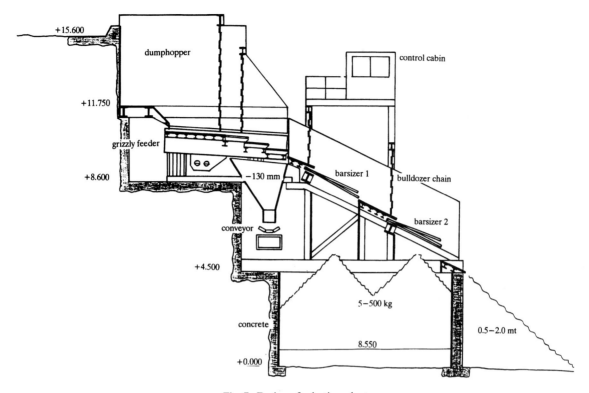

Fig. 7. Design of selection plant.

6000 mm long) with an input capacity greater than 500 t per operating hour and a double bar-sizer (3500 mm wide, 3000 mm long). The grizzly feeder took out the −5 kg (set at 130 mm) material, which would drop onto a conveyor belt and thereafter onto a vibrating grizzly screen. This screen would take out the −50 mm, thus leaving the bedding material of 50–150 mm. The double bar-sizer took out the −500 kg material, thus producing the core of 5–500 kg. The oversize would then be the underlayer material of +0.5–2.0 t (Fig. 8).

The selection of the larger bulk-handled blocks by a bar-sizer, which is a static unit, can be highly effective. The distance between the bars (i.e. the size of the material passing) can be infinitely varied so that continuous adjustments are possible. To screen large fragments with a vibrating screening unit would require much higher investments and considerable amounts of maintenance. The bar-sizer selection plant, when constructed with the right amount of steel and reinforcement, was found to require little maintenance. However, the finger bars of the bar-sizer must be of a special steel or else the bars would suffer enormous wear, tear and twisting with blocks of up to 3.0 t crashing over them.

The opening between the bars and the speed of the material across the bars is essential to the quality of the product. The optimum spacing setting for the bars (distance between tips) was found to be $1.30 \times (W^{1/3}/$ density), where W is the weight of stone at which separation is to take place (= the $W_{70\%}$ of the lower grading class = the $W_{10\%}$ of the next larger grading class).

The speed of the material across the bars depends on the size (larger material moves faster) and the moisture content (wet material moves slower) of the material. The speed of the material is controlled by the speed of the feeder and the angle of the bars (25 to 30 degrees on the upper bars). When the speed is too high the selection effect is too small and when the speed is too low the bars will block. Resetting the angle of the bars was not easy and took 2–3 h. Reducing the speed of the feeder reduces the output, so the speed of the material was controlled by chains above the bars or, more correctly, by the weights added to or taken off the chains. When the speed of the material was too high or too low, then weights were added or taken off.

The selection plants used two CAT 988Bs, one CAT 980C and one CAT 950 wheel-loader to load the material into Komatsu HD325 off-highway dumptrucks and (6 × 4) dumptrucks. The graded rocks were either brought via the weighbridge directly to the marine vessels in the works harbour, or to their respective stockpiles.

Fig. 8. Commemorating 1 000 000 t of selected material produced by both selection plants.

Stockpile regulation

Material which could not be loaded directly onto the vessels was stockpiled. The area available for stockpiling was not large and careful use of the available space was essential. All rock greater than 500 kg was stacked with either a wheel-loader or an excavator to make efficient use of the area available. Wheel-loaders cannot stack the rock any higher than 3.0 m, whereas excavators can stack material to three or four blocks high.

The stockpile of core needed special preparation and quality management. Trucks could only drive on the core when some fines were used to make a smooth surface to prevent excessive wear and tear on the tyres. Care had to be taken because segregation took place due to the wide grading and due to tipping from a height; the fines stayed at the top and the coarser material rolled to the bottom. The grading varied from coarse to fine when excavated from the bottom of the stockpile. Less segregation was obtained when the trucks tipped on top of the stockpile provided these layers were spread out immediately before the next layer was tipped. The best practice was therefore to stockpile in layers, i.e. tip by truck, level and then make the next layer. In contrast

the grading of the bedding material was relatively narrow and did not give segregation problems (Table 6).

Examining the stockpile and material consumption history of the different gradings during the project is shown in Fig. 9, where the difference between the produced and removed tonnages indicates the stockpile volume at any time. It is clearly seen that for the greater part of the period the production of core was critical as there were hardly any stocks.

The stock of 5.0–9.0 t armour which was not required was reduced by hydraulic hammer into 5–500 kg armour when this size threatened to become critical. The armourstone at the stockpile was always rechecked for

Table 6. *Capacity of stockpiles (per Ha)*

Class name	Tipping only (t)	Tipping with stacking (t)
Armour II (5.0–9.0 t)	15 000	40 000
Armour I (2.0–5.0 t)	20 000	45 000
Underlayer (0.5–2.0 t)	25 000	50 000
Core (5–500 kg)	110 000	–
Bedding (50–150 mm)	100 000	–

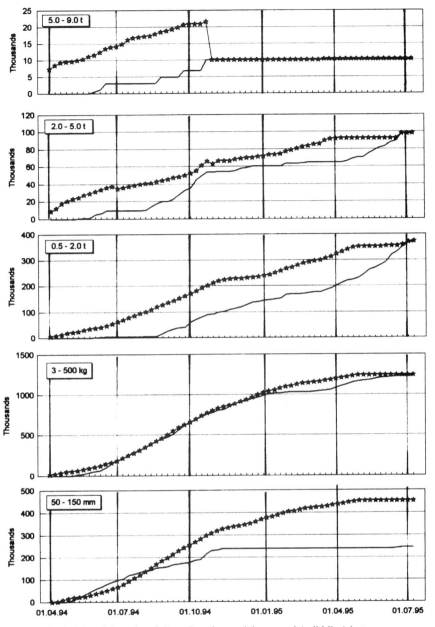

Fig. 9. Material produced ('stars') and material removed (solid line) in tonnes.

integrity and size. A weighing device incorporated in the excavator was used to carry out weight checks on individual rocks. A final visual check was carried out when the armourstone was loaded into the dump trucks using an excavator fitted with a powerfork.

When the underlayer material (0.5–2.0 t) fell from the selection plant, fragments broke off. Also, when the feed rate into the selection plant was high, then the speed of the material across the bar-sizers was high, which resulted in fines overshooting into the 0.5–2.0 t material. These fines were also moved to the stockpile, but when loaded from the stocks by a wheel-loader the small material stayed in the product. This was not acceptable and therefore the underlayer material was mostly loaded from the stockpile by an excavator fitted with a powerfork thus leaving the small material behind.

Loading the ships

The marine transport vessels to be loaded were of three types: one side-stone dumper for bedding, core and underlayer; two-split hopper barges for core; and five flat-top barges for underlayer and armour.

The trucks carried the material either directly from the selection plants or from the stockpiles and tipped the material into hoppers placed inside the berth. Two hydraulic excavators were used to excavate the rock from the hopper (with a bucket or with a grab) and to place the material into the side-stone dumper and/or the split-hopper barge. The flat-top barges were loaded by the trucks tipping directly onto the deck of the barge. The armour was brought by the (6×4) dumptrucks so the impact on the deck was limited when compared with the 35 t off-highway dumptrucks. From time to time a wheel-loader would come and stack the material to ensure that it was possible to get the required load on board.

The vessel loading requirement was 500 t/h, and when there was a second vessel for loading the second vessel was to be loaded at 250 t/h. This requirement (750 t/h) could not be met directly from the selection plant alone and so the loading had to be supplemented from the stockpiles. Loading the vessels took place around the clock, seven days each week.

Quality control

Weight distribution

For the weight distribution tests for 2.0–5.0 and 5.0–9.0 t gradings, a sample of 50 stones was taken out of a section of the stockpile and individually weighed so that a grading curve could be made. Variation in the results

occurred because the selection was made by eye, but generally it was within the tolerances.

The grades 0.5–2.0 t, 5–500 kg, 50–150 mm were made with the selection plants. Continuous gradation tests were performed when the selection plant was being calibrated for the correct bar settings on the grizzly feeder (5 kg) and the bar-sizer (500 kg) (Table 7). Once the openings between the bars were set, the grading should, in principle, stay correct for a reasonably homogeneous source material. As mentioned earlier, the quality of the 0.5–2.0 t material varied considerably and depended on the feed rate entering the selection plant.

When a test was failed, which occurred mostly for the underlayer material (0.5–2.0 t), increased attention was paid to loading that particular section of the stockpile, e.g. additional selection was carried out during loading with the powerfork excavator. The results were also fed back to the checkers and the selection plant operators to improve their working procedures. Meeting specifications was less problematic for bedding and core material, except when stockpile segregation of the core occurred at the start of the contract.

The CIRIA/CUR (1991) system for defining gradings, which was adopted here, was found to work remarkably well. The selection (by eye and by selection plant) requires that for each successive grading class the target $W_{70\%}$ of the lower grading class is the same as the target $W_{10\%}$ of the next larger grading class. The range between the $W_{10\%}$ and the $W_{70\%}$ within a grading class was also based on the CIRIA recommendation.

It was a distinct advantage that the design volume requirements did not leave out a particular size range and nor were there any overlaps in the gradings such as having, say, both 10–200 and 50–500 kg. Experience on other projects has shown that when such problematic grading combinations were specified, unbalanced gradings, were obtained.

Table 7. *Results of grading test carried out on each class*

	5.0–9.0 t		2.0–5.0 t		0.5–2.0 t		5–500 kg		50–150 mm	
	t	%	t	%	t	%	kg	%	mm	%
Max. 2% >	3.5	0.0	1.0	0.0	0.3	0.0	–	–	32	2.1
Max. 10% <	5.0	4.8	2.0	7.4	0.5	2.9	5	8.0	63	10.0
Max. 50% <	6.5	41.1	3.0	39.1	1.2	38.6	–	–	89	30.0
Max. 50% >	7.5	35.9	4.0	29.3	1.8	24.3	–	–	125	40.2
Max. 30% >	9.0	12.6	5.0	8.1	2.0	15.6	500	5.2	152	21.1
Max. 3% >	11.0	1.8	7.0	0.0	3.0	1.1	–	–	254	0.2
$W_{50\%}$ (t)	–	6.88	–	3.40	–	1.37	–	–	–	–
W_{em} (t)	–	6.78	–	3.05	–	1.14	–	–	–	–
$L/t_{50\%}$ (m)	–	1.84	–	1.83	–	1.95	–	–	–	–
$L/t_{95\%}$ (m)	–	2.45	–	2.59	–	3.00	–	–	–	–
Frequency of testing	5000 t	–	5 000 t	–	10 000 t	–	50 000 t	–	10 000 t	–
Size of sample	50 stones	–	50 stones	–	50 stones	–	10.0 t	–	350 kg	–

Table 8. *List of equipment used in the quarry and works harbour*

Overburden removal, face development
    Two CAT 300 excavators
    Five (6 × 4) dumptruck
    One 50 mm air drill crawler
Drilling
    One Tamrock 800 hydraulic drill crawler
    Three Tamrock 600 hydraulic drill crawlers
    One Tamrock 350 hydraulic drill crawler
Loading at the face
    One CAT 245 front shovel
    Two CAT 235 excavators
    Two Komatsu PC300 excavators
Secondary breaking
    0.5 19 RB crawlercrane + dropball
    0.2 CAT 245B excavator, Rammer G1000 breaker
Hauling from the face
    Seven CAT 769B offhighway dumptrucks
    Six (6 × 4) dumptrucks
Selection
    Two selection plants
    One Komatsu PC300 excavator + powerfork

Load at selection plant, haul to stock
    Two CAT 988B wheel-loaders
    Two CAT 980C wheel-loaders
    One CAT 950B wheel-loader
    Four Komatsu HD350 offhighway dumptrucks
    Four (6 × 4) dumptrucks
Load at stock, haul to works harbour
    One CAT 988B wheel-loader
    One CAT 980C wheel-loader
    One Komatsu PC300 excavator + powerfork
    Two CAT 769B offhighway dumptrucks
    Four (6 × 4) dumptrucks
Loading vessels
    One Poclain 610 excavator
    1.3 CAT 245B HD excavator
    One CAT 980D wheel-loader
    One CAT 966E wheel-loader
Auxiliary equipment
    One CAT D8N bulldozer
    One CAT D7K bulldozer
    One CAT 12G motorgrader

Fig. 10. Construction of the Kerteh marine facility with a cranebarge placing tetrapods.

Aspect ratio L/d

Of the rocks used for the gradation test, the longest length L and the shortest length (thickness) was measured to define the L/d aspect ratio. Again the CIRIA/CUR guidance was helpful in clearly defining L and d. There are still many contracts that do not give a correct description of how and where to measure these two distances, causing unnecessary confusion and arguments. When the obvious flaky and flat armour blocks were taken out it was possible to meet the $L/d < 3.0$ requirement.

Block integrity

All the armour blocks were visually examined at the quarry face for weight, shape and integrity by a checker and again at the stockpiles during stacking or during loading to the works harbour. For the bulk-handled gradings, by the time the material is on board the marine vessel it has been handled a number of times: at the face; tipped into the selection plant; loaded at the selection plant; tipped in the stockpile; loaded at the stockpiles; and tipped on the vessel. Should there be any significant fractures present, these would normally have presented themselves by the block breaking during the handling, although it is also possible to create new fractures.

The need to handle rock so many times is often under-estimated on armourstone contracts so that a lot more loading capacity is required than originally anticipated. The introduction of more equipment on site was necessary to produce a smoothly integrated flow of material. Table 8 gives a complete list of the plant used.

Summary

A large risk was taken in developing this quarry. Although its location was well suited to the breakwater project nothing of the geology of the location was known other than what could be seen visually in outcrops.

The start-up of the quarry was slow because of problems with the access road, monsoon rains, problems with the selection plant and the inexperience of the subcontractor with quarrying for armourstone. Quarrying for armourstone is very different from quarrying for aggregates and this is often overlooked. The drilling and blasting must be more precise and the size and weight of the materials require larger machines. The quality of the product in terms of grading shape and integrity is more difficult to control and requires strict procedures, for which the guidance on many aspects covered in the CIRIA/CUR (1991) manual is useful.

The major dates for this quarry were: 24 September 1993, decision to develop the quarry at Pasir Panjang; 1 April 1994, 250 000 m^3 overburden removed and production started; 17 July 1994, 500 000 t product delivered; 10 September 1994, 1 000 000 t product delivered; and 27 April 1995, 1 950 000 t product delivery complete – 2 750 000 t quarried.

It is beyond doubt that the close location was ideal in relation to the breakwater project and that the opening and effective operation of the quarry made the construction of the marine facility at Kerteh a success (see Fig. 10).

Acknowledgements. Bill Blackett (mining engineer), Oscar Render (shotfirer) and Glen Barnes (shotfirer) of Zinkcon Marine Malaysia, who all did an excellent job, are thanked for their expertise. The paper has benefited from comments in review and editing by J.-P. Latham, for which the author is grateful.

References

CIRIA/CUR 1991. *Manual on the Use of Rock in Coastal and Shoreline Engineering.* CIRIA (London) Special Publication 83/CUR (Gouda) Report 154.

CUNNINGHAM, C. V. B. 1987. Fragmentation estimations and the Kuz–Ram model – four years on. *In: 2nd International Symposium on Rock Fragmentation by Blasting, Keystone, Colorado, USA, 1987.* Balkema, Rotterdam, 475–487.

Abrasion of a series of tracer materials on a gravel beach, Slapton Sands, Devon, UK

J.-P. Latham, J. P. Hoad & M. Newton

Department of Engineering, Queen Mary & Westfield College, London University, Mile End Road, London E1 4NS, UK

Abstract. While increased attention is being paid to the use of quarried rock in groynes, revetments and breakwaters, and to beach recharge, the large volumes of materials and the associated environmental costs of obtaining these resources has begun to focus minds. Interest in the possible future use of a wider range of material sizes and qualities for beach recharge and in the use of smaller armour block sizes which move during profile adjustment has been growing. Deployment of these dynamic materials for coastal protection structures has focussed research on the long-term performance of these materials and the implications for design life. This reflects a growing concern about the more intelligent use of finite material resources.

The vast range in intrinsic resistance of different rock types to laboratory mill abrasion is well reported and these results, when presented as the QMW mill abrasion resistance index, can give relative lifetimes of differing shingle types. However, field studies and/or degradation models of the type discussed in this paper are needed to convert these relative laboratory lifetimes to prototype environmental lifetimes in years so that they are appropriate for predicting the long-term changes in beach material volumes.

The author's 1991 rock degradation model, which gives an absolute prediction of weight loss rates, was proposed for armourstone placed within structures designed for static stability. It encorporates the mill abrasion test result for the rock type in question. However, it also attempts to embrace dynamically stable rock protection structures from gravel beaches up to berm breakwaters, depending on the mobility parameter. Before this laboratory and field study, no prototype data was available to check its applicability to gravel-sized material.

This paper presents the field results for pebbles consisting of three rock types. Their rates of weight loss with respect to interactions with indigenous beach materials in both laboratory and field trials are given. Whereas weight losses from flint or gneiss pebbles in a field experiment will be negligible, their long-term losses may be predicted from experiments and observations on beaches such as Slapton Sands, where pebbles of rapidly abrading rock types have been measured.

The increasing use of loose natural rock or gravels in coastal engineering structures as an alternative to the traditional caissons, walls and statically stable concrete or rock armour units has focused engineering attention on the validity of the existing quality control and specification categories of rock materials. In particular, the typical specifications used for static armourstone may not be appropriate for the tough job expected of dynamic (i.e. reprofiling) rock armour. Similarly, aggregate specifications for concrete or flexible road pavements will not be right for gravel beaches. To understand long-term performance at a more fundamental level, both the material strengths of particles and the amount of motion arising from a given wave climate need to be studied. Only with this knowledge can the risk from excessive material wear or breakage within a given lifetime be estimated for a particular specified material quality.

A unifying concept in the study of loose rock lying on a slope subjected to wave action in coastal protection structures is the ratio between the significant wave height H_s, and the particle size (Van der Meer 1988; CIRIA/CUR 1991). Known as the stability number, but more aptly named the mobility number, N_s, it is written

$$N_s = H_s/\Delta D_{n50} \tag{1}$$

where Δ is the relative buoyant density of the rock (usually about 1.7) and

$$D_{n50} = (M_{50}/\rho_r)^{0.33} \tag{2}$$

where ρ_r is the rock density and M_{50} is the median particle mass.

LATHAM, J.-P., HOAD, J. P. & NEWTON, M. 1998. Abrasion of a series of tracer materials on a gravel beach, Slapton Sands, Devon, UK. *In*: LATHAM, J.-P. (ed.) 1998. *Advances in Aggregates and Armourstone Evaluation*. Geological Society, London, Engineering Geology Special Publications, **13**, 121–135

When H_s is smaller than ΔD_{n50}, the rock blocks or particles remain essentially stationary and most conventional rock armour designs with N_s between 1 and 3 are therefore said to be statically stable. An effective static design aims to minimize the movement for a given design storm.

As progressively smaller rock sizes compared with H_s of the design storm are considered, the mobility parameter increases. The whole range of N_s values from about 3 up to >500 can be found along our coastlines in natural or artificial structures. These could all be justifiably called dynamically stable structures because their profiles adjust to varying degrees to be in equilibrium with the wave conditions. For a properly designed dynamic structure a sufficient volume of revetment or beach material is necessary to ensure that the expected amount of reprofiling during the design storm still gives acceptable protection (see later discussion of design considerations). The dissipation of wave energy involves increasing degrees of particle movement as the stability number increases. A sand beach has an N_s of >500 and significant particle movement. The range of dynamic loose rock structures, summarized in Table 1, has been described in the *Beach Management Manual* (CIRIA 1996a), which shows that there is virtually no experience reported of rock beaches (D_{n50} of 50–500 mm). This contrasts with more extensive data for berm breakwaters (e.g. Baird & Hall 1985; Burcharth & Frigaard 1987; Tomasicchio *et al.* 1995) at the coarse end and for shingle beaches (e.g. Van der Meer 1988; Powell 1993) at the fine end of the spectrum of dynamic structures. None, however, has focussed on weight loss prediction.

Alongside the need to control costs by using the maximum width of grading produced at source, and the use of local (and thus cheaper, but possibly lower strength) rock types, there is a greater need to understand the long-term attrition behaviour of the emplaced or replenishment material in a dynamic structure. The elements of attrition, which are the processes leading to a reduction in unit mass and effective diameter, are defined by Matthews (1983). He divided these into breakage processes – which all act to decrease roundness – and abrasion processes – which act to increase roundness. Impact, grinding, crushing, cracking, splitting and spalling lead to breakage, while sandblasting and rubbing lead to abrasion.

Table 1. N_s *values for various structures and beach types*

N_s	Structure/beach type
1–4	Statically stable rock slopes/mounds
3–6	Re-shaping rock slopes including berm breakwaters
6–20	Mobile rock slopes/beaches
15–500	Shingle/gravel beaches
>500	Sand beach

A method of identifying the level of rounding and thus inferring the proportion of weight loss relative to the original mass of a particle population has been outlined by Poole (unpublished data, 1993). The method, which is only applicable to crushed rock source material, was applied to the Pensarn replenishment scheme in North Wales. This method visually compared the degree of rounding of recently placed crushed limestone with photographs of limestone aggregate at different stages and known weight losses during the mill abrasion test (CIRIA/CUR 1991). By comparing the degree of field abrasion after a certain number of years in service with the abrasion history in the mill, a scaling relationship can be used to assess the useful life of the replenishment material. This approach is clearly highly subjective and is not sufficiently discerning for already rounded material. An improved transfer function between material behaviour in a laboratory test and field behaviour is clearly required.

For structures built with higher mobility numbers (N_s) the applicability of the mill test (Latham & Poole 1988) and its use within the rock degradation model (Latham 1991) requires further examination. For example, the standard mill test simulates the mutual attrition of a given rock type by the rolling motion of individual particles under saturated conditions. A homogeneous load of test material is therefore used. However, tracer material scattered on a beach will be abraded by the indigenous rounded material and not by identical tracer rock fragments. In this paper the laboratory tests are therefore adapted to consider mixed loads so that the field abrasion response of three exotic rock type tracers undergoing abrasion on a predominantly flint shingle beach can be more accurately simulated in the laboratory and thus lead to more accurate transfer functions for the prediction of particle weight loss rates on beaches.

Engineering design of dynamically stable structures

Dynamic structures are designed to adjust their profiles until in equilibrium with the dominant conditions, while retaining a reserve volume of material seaward of the coastline feature (or breakwater core) under protection. This reserve volume must be sufficient for profile adjustment not to encroach onto the protected areas under the design storm conditions. The material's mean effective diameter, mean unit mass, grading (D_{85}/D_{15}), shape and packing must be considered to derive an appropriate design profile for the local wave climate and boundary conditions.

In an idealized situation the quantity of gravel required for the recharge of a natural shingle beach or the construction of a dynamically stable rock beach revetment is not too difficult to estimate. A greater problem is often accommodating amenity considerations and these must not be neglected. The parameters for consideration and the design methods available are reviewed in the *Beach Management Manual* (CIRIA 1996a). The three most important losses are: (i) onshore/offshore sediment movement; (ii) alongshore movement; and (iii) losses due to material wear. Gravel-sized material has a strong tendency to stay near the shoreline so there is little loss offshore. This characteristic is one of the great benefits of this type of protection. However, observations suggesting a loss of the coarser fraction in the offshore direction from certain recharge schemes and in experiments (Powell 1993) is a topic deserving further attention.

Alongshore movement of gravel-sized material is difficult to estimate, although good progress is expected as more sophisticated tracer techniques (e.g. radio-wave emitting pebbles; Voulgaris *et al.* 1994) are deployed. At the coarse end the alongshore transport rate along a berm breakwater trunk during storm attack by oblique waves has been fitted to experimental data (Frigaard *et al.* 1996) in a study that also emphasizes the importance of stone quality. For shingle, several references give a reasonably consistent picture for alongshore transport rates, e.g. Kamphuis *et al.* (1986), Johnson (1987) and Nicholls & Wright (1991).

It is probable that designers will continue to argue with some justification that major uncertainties still exist regarding short- and long-term transport. Certainly, where flint shingle is the dominant material, as along the south UK coast, its perceived relatively high resistance to abrasion (demonstrated graphically later in this paper) is justification for the research focus on shingle transport to date. However, it should be remembered that natural shingle beaches may consist of softer rock types and may be recharged using crushed rock aggregate. Limestone and slate quarries have been used to supply several schemes in North and West Wales (Penmaenmawr, Prestatyn, Pensarn and Dinas Dinlle; see CIRIA 1996a) and at Hilton Bay in Scotland. The shingle reserves which are most in demand and which have been discovered off the south UK coast are mostly flint, but locally they have important chalk, sandstone and ironstone fractions, whereas to the south of the Isle of Wight the shingle is 5–80% sandstone, but is sometimes up to 80% chalk (CIRIA 1996b).

It is therefore suggested that the main unknown losses will in some cases be those associated with rock wear and it remains impossible in such cases to develop an adequate engineering design for a dynamic revetment or shingle beach as no really convincing analysis of cost effectiveness can be made without tools for making reasonable estimates of rock wear. The main methods of calculation for assessing the required volumes of recharge materials on dynamic revetments are by Van der Meer (1988), Powell (1993) and Ahrens (1995), but none can take account of in-service wear losses in a whole

life costing. Some effects of wear losses which are more likely to be significant if the recharge material is weaker than the indigenous beach material are as follows: increased particle mobility; loss of beach volume from loss of abrasion flour; local and overall alteration of gradings and surface armouring; changes in permeability and thus stability, through changes in grading, shape and packing.

Each of these factors will alter the response of the beach section under storm conditions from those designed. Most will occur naturally on any natural beach surface starved of feed material. However, if a much weaker rock has been selected for reasons of its local availability, then the cost effectiveness may be compromised due to the shorter predictable service life when abrasion is taken into account. However, the picture may be even further complicated (where rounded land-won or sea-dredged shingle is unavailable) by the desirability of a rapidly rounding crushed rock source to maintain an amenity beach in a 'barefoot friendly' state. Possibilities also exist for dumping the recharge material deep into the beach with a thick covering of indigenous shingle. The later emergence of the recharge material may be acceptably smooth.

It is, of course, possible for quarries to supply any size distribution of rock fragments for dynamic rock revetments or beach recharge schemes if the price is right, but clearly the quarry operator seeks to minimize the processing and therefore wider gradings specifications will typically be preferred. Alternatively, the routine production of a narrow grading of coarse aggregate may be so voluminous as to make it a viable alternative to dredged gravel. Setting aside the major issue of transport costs, this introduces the engineer to the possibility of specifying a relatively coarse grading for a beach recharge or dynamic revetment design. In fact, most sea-dredged sources of shingle used for recharge are finer than those on the beach to be nourished, and so the use of material coarser than the indigenous littoral material is relatively novel. Most design guidance is based on the principle of matching the properties of the indigenous materials as closely as possible (CIRIA 1996a). Although remaining attractive from an aesthetic and environmental viewpoint, this assumption that nature knows best may be unnecessarily restrictive if coarser material can be found. An interest in using gravel- and cobble-sized material on dynamic revetments has grown in countries familiar with the effectiveness of shingle beaches as energy absorbers. Where the Upper Chalk of the Cretaceous period has dominated the geological history, flint-shingle beaches are a common feature and are currently receiving research attention to maximize their potential durability and benefits for coast protection. The work of Ahrens (1995) has also given impetus to research on dynamic revetments and their future use in the Great Lakes area of North America.

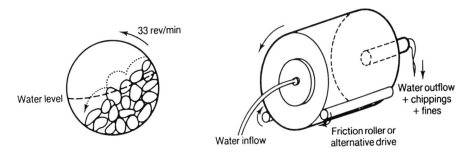

Fig. 1. Schematic diagram of QMW abrasion mill. The mill has the following specifications: inside diameter, 195 mm; inside length, 230 mm; outflow diameter, 14 mm; three plastic lifting ribs of 20 mm diameter of semicircular section, equally spaced and axially attached to the inside.

The research methodology for this study does not warrant the specialized apparatus that was designed to reproduce particle motion conditions under water current action (Keunen 1956) and surf action (Keunen 1968). In analysing the quality of rock for static armoured structures, the QMW mill abrasion test has often been used. This experimental apparatus can be used with even greater justification to analyse shingle wear as the test is more representative of the loading environment experienced by saturated pebbles which roll and slide. Their degradation in the test is dominated by abrasion rather than breakage, as is generally found in the surf zone on shingle beaches. Many other aggregate tests are available for the measurement of material quality; see, for example, Smith & Collis (1993) for a review. A highly correlated relation between the widely available micro-Deval test and the QMW mill abrasion test has been presented, together with other abrasion resistance test data (Latham 1998). It may therefore be possible to predict the mill abrasion test result from other more common abrasion tests.

QMW mill abrasion test

Standard test

The mill abrasion test, which is specified in Appendix 2.9 of CIRIA/CUR (1991) and Latham (1991), utilizes a horizontal rolling drum fitted with integral lifting bars, rotating at 33 rpm, with an axial water flow to remove the fine rock flour produced by the abrasion of the load (Fig. 1). The test is ideal for comparing the performance of different rock types undergoing mutual attrition on a shingle beach and has been used for specifying the abrasion resistance of armourstone for over five years.

The initial experiment followed the standardized procedure given in CIRIA/CUR (1991). The results of this experiment yield a plot of the fraction of the original weight remaining as a function of time or revolutions (in thousands). The process is described by Equation (3),

which may be fitted by regression to give the abrasion resistance parameters of interest.

$$W/W_0 = (1 - b)\exp(-k_f t) + b\exp(-k_s t) \qquad (3)$$

The initial rate of abrasion is expected to be greater, as indicated in Fig. 2, and can be quantified by the index k_f, which is a function of both changing stone shape and abrasion resistance and is typically about 25 to 30 times k_s. The abrasion resistance index k_s which is computed for W/W_0 (the ratio of current to initial weight) of between 0.9 and 0.7 is not a sensitive function of the initial aggregate shape and angularity. It is calculated as shown in Fig. 2. The term b is a constant of proportionality giving the relative importance of the two processes. The units of k_s are 'fraction of weight lost per thousand revolutions, i.e. per $\approx$30 minutes'. This study utilizes both the standard and a modified procedure to assess three contrasting rock types.

Modified test

For the modification of the standard method the drum was loaded to half-full with natural flint shingle and

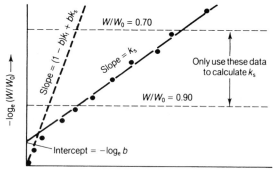

Fig. 2. Results of abrasion resistance index analysis (CIRIA/CUR 1991).

mixed with a small portion of the test aggregate in question to make up the whole test sample. The flint shingle was obtained from the beach at Reculver, Kent, where it was sieved into the range 26.5–31.5 mm as specified for the standard test.

Only 12 pieces of the test aggregate were used so that the test material would rub and grind against shingle particles during practically the whole of the abrasion action rather than against other test particles. When the total losses of weight were calculated for the test material and the shingle during each increment of the experiment, the weight loss was made up to the initial load using additional shingle particles only. All other aspects of the test conformed to the standard test method.

Previous field studies of rates of wear

Previous field applications of the mill abrasion test to the abrasion of recharge materials at Pensarn, in North Wales, UK, have focussed on photographic comparison methods (Haddon 1993; Poole pers. comm. 1993). These studies examined a beach which had been recharged with good quality Carboniferous limestone from which a value of $k_s = 0.0024$ had been determined. After three years of in-service abrasion the loss in angularity was equated from photographic comparisons to 30 000 revolutions in the mill, for which W/W_0 was 0.9. Thus Poole reported the equivalent prototype wear to be $W/W_0 = 0.9$ or 10% loss in weight (or volume) for this recharge material after three years.

Matthews (1983) studied the roundness and weight loss of beach shingle at Palliser Bay, South Island, New Zealand. It is a meso-tidal naturally fed location with a noticeable down-drift increase in beach material roundness. A tracer load of 70 tonnes of limestone from a crushing plant in the sieve size range 4–32 mm was deposited on the greywacke beaches to match the indigenous sizes of shingle. A roundness analysis using photographs which were calibrated using Krumbein's roundness scale found the rate of roundness change to be initially fast and then slowing.

Matthews also applied a rotating drum experiment to carefully considered mixed loads of crushed limestone and greywacke. Accounting for the mix of argillite pebbles on Palliser beach and the well-rounded greywacke pebbles, the natural pebbles were determined to be approximately 7.2 times more resistant to abrasion than the limestone tracer. From all this work Matthews concluded that the annual rates of weight loss were 41% (relatively exposed site, although the wave climate was not reported) and 7% (less exposed site) for the natural greywacke pebbles. His paper therefore adds to the range of data and environments studied and provides a set of rapid abrasion rate data for possible calibration purposes.

Field experiment at Slapton Sands

Principles

A tracer experiment was to be conducted at Slapton Sands, adjacent to Torcross, south Devon to directly measure the abrasion resistance of beach shingle-sized tracer particles consisting of three different rock types. Many workers (e.g. Caldwell 1981) suggest that the representativity of surface tracer data is open to question due to self-selection of the recovered population, especially when recovery depends on visual identification. Such doubts are due to the processes of surface armouring, cross-shore grading and dispersal of transported materials, which all tend to concentrate larger tracer sizes in a smaller beach section. However, these doubts are considered to be less restrictive for the narrower objectives of this preliminary study, which are to look at a method for assessing attrition losses.

The tracer materials used were deliberately chosen to be markedly dissimilar (exotic) to the indigenous particles in texture and colour, and they were also slightly larger. Therefore it was thought that the processes of armouring (Isla 1993) would assist the material to remain at the surface and allow visual identification. As with the laboratory mill abrasion tests the parameter under study was the fraction of weight remaining (W/W_0) after successive intervals of time. In an attempt to overcome the problem of not identifying each original pebble, a very narrow grading of starting weights was prepared, so that provided a reasonable number of exotic pebbles was found, the weight loss trends were of significance. Clearly the particles that contribute to the recovered data are those seen at (possibly remaining on) the surface and, as such, they represent the most rapidly wearing fraction if they are not stranded above high water level.

The purpose of the field experiment is four-fold. Firstly, to measure the loss rates and to see if the observations are in broad agreement with the relative predictions of the modified mill abrasion tests. Secondly, to use the modified laboratory tests as a simulation of the field behaviour of the three tracer types surrounded by flint shingle and thereby find three values for the equivalent wear time factor, X (Latham 1991), required to convert laboratory time (or revolutions) into days or years in the field that give the same proportionate weight loss. Thirdly, to derive the predicted X factor for this site directly from the ratings given in the degradation model and compare this with the values of X measured in the field for the surface shingle. Finally, to use the best estimate of X for this field site, together with mill abrasion test data for shingle types ranging from a friable sandstone to rounded flint, to highlight estimates of material losses through abrasive wear on our precious shingle beaches.

The field experiment was required to scale the laboratory time to prototype time in the surf zone environment at Slapton for the same amount of wear. Scaled wave tank experiments to study wear were also considered. However, due to scaling problems these were not applicable to shingle-size material processes, although such experiments were performed to study rock degradation in reprofiling breakwaters and rock beaches.

Selection of Slapton field site

The field site was selected from a number of locations which were assessed by a desk study and reconnaissance visit. The requirements were for a gravel beach with good access and with relatively high exposure to wave action (since the study was to be conducted in the summer months). A number of sites were examined including Shoreham (West Sussex), Northam Burrows (Bideford, Devon), Hurst Spit (Hampshire) and Slapton.

The Slapton site was selected as having the best combination of attributes, although the east-facing north–south orientation did give rise to some concern with regard to possible low intensity and orientation of

the incident wave energy. It is bounded by low rock cliffs and is backed by a saline lagoon. There is a channel close inshore with a bar approximately two miles offshore, which can cause storm waves to break at low water. The beach is not open to direct wave attack from the westerly channel storms and thus most incident energy is refracted around Start Point, which helps to generate a marked alongshore drift. There was a visually apparent fining of the beach sediments to the north, in the direction of the dominant drift. Figure 3 shows the view along the shoreline northward from the study site.

The site selected was at the south end of the car park at the centre of the beach, with a storage point, easy access and a wide beach at this location, free of structures in the active beach zone. The grid reference of the site is 789 443 on OS 1 : 25 000 sheet No. 20.

Figure 4 shows beach profiles for two sites which bounded the experimental area, in which a marked berm crest, below the minor cliffing of the back-beach dune line, can be seen. A comparison of the beach profile before and after a two day interval, for the profile line labelled (1), shows that there was sufficient incident

Fig. 3. View looking north along Slapton Sands shingle beach showing chalk 'injection' panel in the mid-intertidal zone on day 0, 17 July 1995.

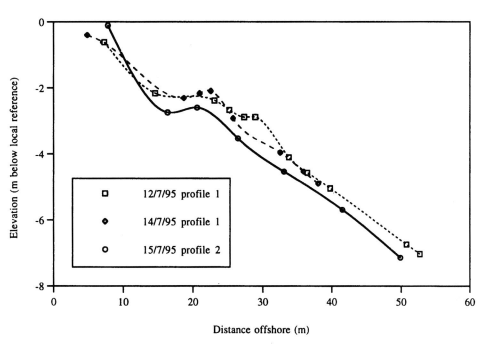

Fig. 4. Slapton beach profiles.

wave energy on the spring tide high water for some reprofiling, especially of the berm crest.

The incident wave regime was recorded for a two hour period during successive high tides of the first part of the experiment using a pressure sensor installed at the low water mark. Using the Draper–Tucker method of wave data analysis (Hardisty 1990), the incident waves at high water level were measured and found to be equivalent to $H_{max} = 0.54$ m, $H_s = 0.28$ m with $T_z = 3.1$ s, with a breaker obliquity of approximately 25 degrees from the south. The tidal range at spring tide was 4.1 m, with a neap range of 2.1 m, providing a good operating depth for the single-channel pressure transducer, which was logged using a commercial analogue-to-digital converter mounted on the parallel port of a PC. Some concern was raised by the signal to noise levels due to the power for the computer being provided by a portable generator. However, with signal smoothing and calibration checks this was found to be at an acceptable level. It has been assumed for simplicity, in the interpretation of the shingle tracers, that the wave data collected were representative of the wave conditions for the whole four-day period of the tracer deployment. This assumption seemed justified on the basis of qualitative observations of the waves.

The indigenous beach materials appeared to consist of about 20% local metamorphic rocks and slate, 10% igneous rocks (Dartmoor), with the remainder being flints with no definite origin. There is a large amount of highly resistant material on the beach due to the flint

content and the local granite and quartz pebbles. The indigenous material size at the field site was roughly estimated using three field sieves (20.0, 26.5, 31.5 mm). At the mid-tide berm (Fig. 4), $D_{100} < 32$ mm and $D_{80} \approx$ 20 mm. The material became coarser towards the storm berm with $D_{80} \approx 27$ mm and $D_{50} \approx 20$ mm (see Newton 1995). These approximate material sizes are compared with other British shingle beaches in Table 2.

Tracer materials

The tracer materials were selected on the basis of their strength, texture and colour to both provide a range of

Table 2. *Comparison of indigenous beach gravels, after Powell (1993)*

Location	Sieve size (mm)			Grading width D_{84}/D_{16}
	D_{10}	D_{50}	D_{100}	
Pensarn	6.9	15.0	50.0	4.13
Sidmouth	7.0	22.2	90.0	5.80
Chesil	23.6	30.0	–	–
Hurst Spit	6.0	20.0	63.0	4.25
Hayling Island	7.0	16.0	64.0	4.00
Seaford	6.1	13.7	38.0	2.73
Pevensey	6.6	14.3	–	3.10
Whitstable	7.6	12.6	50.0	2.41

Table 3. *Physical characteristics of test materials*

Aggregate test (mostly BS812)	Rock type and quarry source		
	Basalt Waterswallows	Chalk Melton Ross	Sandstone Hollington
ACV (crushing)	14	–	–
AIV wet (impact)	8.8, *13.0*	–	–
AIV dry (impact)	10.5, *12.0*	35.0	71.3
AAV (abrasion)	10.4	–	–
Oven dry relative density	2.85, *2.80*	2.17	2.01
SSD relative density	2.87, *2.84*	2.35	2.17
Apparent relative density	2.92	2.62	2.40
Water absorption (%)	0.85, *1.50*	7.81	8.09
Porosity (%)	–	–	*24.0*
Micro-Deval (wet abrasion)	36.0	–	–

Notes: Upright values give QMW test results on the tracer sample; italic values give production output test results supplied by the quarry.

generally low-strength characteristics (to have measurable effects within days) and to be distinguishable during visual searches of the beach. As described earlier, the field site selected was a flint shingle beach with indigenous materials dominated by black–grey, white and rust colours, and a smooth polished texture. The chosen sandstone, chalk and basalt were therefore easily distinguished on the beach surface when both wet and dry. Table 3 shows the laboratory test analysis of the three exotic source rocks obtained from the supply quarries and supplemented with additional tests performed at QMW.

Once the material sources were located, sample preparation required that the rock fragments were sieved and sorted into tight weight ranges to maximize the statistical return from the anticipated low tracer recovery rates. The injected tracers were prepared as follows:

Chalk –
    Melton Ross Quarry, Barnetby, South Humberside: 100–140 g
Basalt –
    Waterswallows Quarry, Buxton, Derbyshire: 100–140 g
Sandstone –
    Hollington Quarry, Stoke, Staffordshire: 150–400 g

The sandstone was strong enough for crushing, handling and transport while being considerably more fragile and susceptible to abrasion than the other two rock types. The size range for the sandstone (150–400 g) was set larger to accommodate the limitations of the field crusher made available by Hollington Quarry and to reduce the proportional effect of loss of mass during transport. Some loss from the blocks was experienced during transport to the field site. A small but systematic error between the laboratory measured initial weights and the weights of particles actually deposited was

noted, but was not considered worthy of inclusion in the analysis of weight loss results.

As usual, a wide range of material sizes resulted from crushing a feed of 242 kg of sandstone blocks. This amount of feed was found to generate a sufficient sample of 98 kg in the selected (150–400 g) weight range.

The chalk was an exceptionally hard type which was considerably stronger in its handling properties than the sandstone. This material was available in large quantities as it was ordered for flume tank experiments. It provides a comparison between field and flume tank abrasion. The total mass of material selected from stocks in the size range 120 ± 20 g was 222 kg. The material had a greater angularity than the sandstone as it was affected less in transport and handling. However, the material was selected from stockpiles of crushed material for cement production and had lost the appearance of a freshly crushed stone due to bulk handling in the quarry.

The basalt was a hard material selected for comparison with the other materials. The total mass of material recovered from the quarry's 40 mm crusher reject bins, in the size range specified, was 177 kg. This material was the most angular of the material samples and, after washing off the dust before weighing, it appeared the freshest of the tracer materials used.

Results

Standard mill test results

The results of the mill abrasion test are given in Table 4 and the raw data are plotted in Fig. 5 for comparison with other resistant rock types. The quality assessment (CIRIA/CUR 1991: 110; Latham 1991: fig. A4) from the k_s results classify the abrasion resistance of the

Table 4. *Standard QMW mill abrasion test results*

Best-fit parameters from regression for sample of ≈100 aggregate pieces	Rock type and quarry source		
	Basalt Waterswallows	Chalk Melton Ross	Sandstone Hollington
Slope = k_s	0.00449	0.0250	0.2967
Intercept = $(-\ln b)$	0.0244	0.0176	0.0433
r^2	0.9943	1.0000	0.9979

sandstone as poor, the chalk as marginal and the basalt as good. The higher the rate of weight loss given by k_s, the poorer is the resistance to abrasion.

Modified mill tests

The results of the modified test are shown in Table 5. Comparison with Table 4 shows that the abrasion coefficient (k_s) of sandstone has fallen from 0.296 to 0.243, whereas the coefficients of the chalk and basalt have risen from 0.025 to 0.050 and from 0.0045 to 0.014, respectively.

Figure 6 shows that whereas the rate of weight loss increases for the chalk and basalt when in a mixed load in contact with natural beach shingle, the sandstone behaves in the reverse manner. It is suggested that the poor quality and relatively rounded sandstone particles acted as a form of rough abrasive, just like sandpaper, when in contact with other sandstone particles in the standard test. This action was reduced when in contact with the harder, but smoother, beach shingle.

Intrinsic resistance to abrasion for different rock types

The vast range in intrinsic resistance to mill abrasion is clearly illustrated in Fig. 5 and again in Fig. 6 for a few different rock types and further detailed results over four orders of magnitude are given in Latham (1998). The point to note is that although laboratory studies alone can give the relative lifetimes of differing shingle types (using k_s values, for example), field studies and degradation models are needed to convert these to absolute

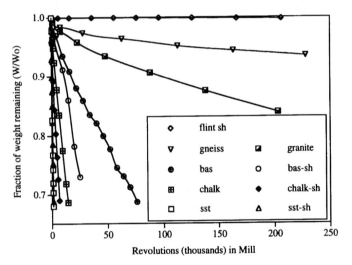

Fig 5. Mill abrasion test results. sh, shingle; -sh, result based on the modified test where the test rock is abraded in a surrounding mass of flint shingle.

Table 5. *Modified QMW mill abrasion test results*

Best-fit parameters from regression for sample of ≈100 aggregate pieces	Rock type and quarry source		
	Basalt (+ shingle) Waterswallows	Chalk (+ shingle) Melton Ross	Sandstone (+ shingle) Hollington
Slope = k_s	0.0164	0.0510	0.2439
Intercept = $(-\ln b)$	0.0906	0.0400	0.0400
r^2	0.9915	0.9998	0.9950

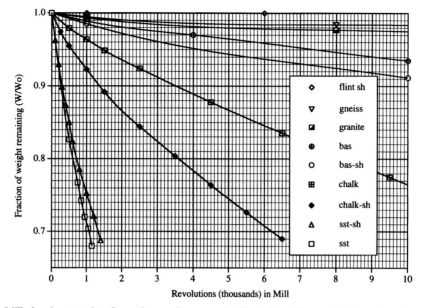

Fig 6. Mill abrasion test plots for various rock types as in Fig. 3, but with magnified *x*-axis scale and grid to enable direct comparison with observed abrasion at Slapton.

lifetimes in years for different beaches with different energies. Although weight losses from flint or gneiss pebbles in a field experiment will be negligible, their long-term losses may be predicted with experiments using pebbles of significantly abrading rock types. The question as to how long a flint shingle beach pebble will take to half its diameter can then be addressed.

Field deployment and experimental results

The exotic tracers were placed on the beach in squares, one particle deep and lightly pressed into the surface at the mid-tide elevation. A total of 334 sandstone, 1509 basalt and 1922 chalk blocks was used. Figure 3 shows a typical deployment of the tracer material at Slapton. Although this injection is considerably smaller than most tracer experiments it was an amount that was considered practical to prepare to such tight weight ranges within a few days, to transport onto the beach and to exhaustively search for during the low water period if a large recovery had been available.

Upon recovery of a pebble, the pebble was immersed and weighed saturated, but surface dried, and returned to where it was found. After two tidal periods (recovery day 1) only 23% of the sandstone, 12% of the chalk and 21% of the basalt tracer pebbles could be relocated by a visual search within approximately 200 m of the release point. Thereafter the recovery rates fell rapidly and the degree of dispersal increased so that after the second day

(four tides) the recovery rates were below 5%. The high obliquity of the waves had dispersed the material along the shore so that the typical final (fourth) day travel distances were lowest for the basalt (<300 m), intermediate for chalk (<500 m) and largest for sandstone (>800 m). The greater mobility of the larger sandstone pebbles could in part be explained by their more tabular shape, which appears to have promoted greater lift and sliding. However, size differences and density (Tables 2 and 3) also need to be considered and compared with a background relative density (estimated from rock types to be about 2.65) for the Slapton material, as these differences may also be significant for mobility.

A depth-of-disturbance rod consists of a metal ring which slides independently up and down a long metal pole. Sediment build-up or removal between tides can be deduced from measurements from the top of the pole to the sediment surface and to the buried ring (if the ring is placed on the sediment surface after each low tide). The rods showed a net gain of between 4 and 8 cm across the lower beach face over one tidal cycle, with some lowering of the upper beach surface during high water as shown by the small downward movement of the free plates. The minor profile changes at the berm observed during this period and the data from the depth-of-disturbance rods (which were installed to examine the depth of shingle activity) suggest that although some material may have been lost alongshore or offshore outside the search area, a large proportion of the tracer load may have been quickly mixed and buried when incorporated into a lower profile.

Table 6. *Numbers of recovered particles per day from field site*

Day	Status	Sandstone Slapton	Chalk Slapton	Basalt Slapton
0	Injection	338	1922	1509
1	Recovery	80	240	321
2	Recovery	4	23	29
3	Recovery	5	24	10
4	Recovery	5	13	19

Table 7. *Daily loss of particle weight and regression based estimate of rate of loss where $\pm$ symbol indicates 90% confidence intervals*

Day	Sandstone Slapton	Chalk Slapton	Basalt Slapton
0	278.4 ± 06.1	115.4 ± 0.4	119.5 ± 0.5
1	274.6 ± 13.7	118.7 ± 1.3	119.5 ± 1.1
2	237.4 ± 75.9	104.5 ± 4.2	117.4 ± 4.5
3	161.2 ± 78.6	108.7 ± 4.4	110.3 ± 8.3
4	210.3 ± 61.3	111.9 ± 5.7	119.1 ± 3.8
$(W_0 - W)/W_0$ day^{-1}	0.065 ±0.029	0.006 ±0.006	0.004 ±0.006
Percentage loss over four days	26.0	2.4	1.8

Table 8. *Results of Kolmogorov–Smirnov tests for equality of size distributions between pairs of stated days. Yes: null hypothesis (that both distributions came from the same parent population) accepted; No, null hypothesis is rejected at stated level of significance*

Pairs of days	Sandstone Slapton	Chalk Slapton	Basalt Slapton
Day 1 v Day 0	Yes	No (0.1)	Yes
Day 2 v Day 1	Yes	No (0.1)	Yes
Day 3 v Day 2	Yes	Yes	No (0.2)
Day 4 v Day 3	Yes	Yes	Yes
Day 4 v Day 0	No (0.1)	No (0.2)	Yes

A large part of the tracer population was probably hidden beneath a thin veneer of pebbles due to movement under the wave activity which was characterized throughout the experiment by low oblique surf of $H_{max} < 0.5$ m. These factors suggest that recovery rates could be substantially increased if buried tracers could be detected by remote sensing (e.g. Wright *et al.* 1978).

The weight distribution of the recovered tracer sample was analysed over the four days of the study to obtain the rate of weight loss, i.e. $(W_0 - W)/W_0$ per day, for each material type. Care was taken to refer only to saturated surface dry weights, although the time needed for full re-saturation of the recovered tracer pebbles and weighing inaccuracy has introduced errors into the individual field weight data estimated to be within ±4%.

The change in the mean weight of particles across the four recovery days is analysed in Tables 6–8. The greatest proportional change in weight is recorded for sandstone and the least for basalt, which is in accordance with their ranking from laboratory tests. Several statistical approaches for evaluating this unusual data set are helpful.

(1) Analysis of mean weight recovered on each day gives an indication of the underlying trend for typical weights of surface shingle over the four days. By making the assumption that the population of the tracer weights on each day is normally distributed (not strictly valid as truncation was used in preparing the narrow weight range bands), the significance of the mean values can be better appreciated. Using simple parametric statistics it is possible to quote a 90% confidence interval for the mean weight after each day, as given in Table 7. It is, however, reasonable to suggest that a non-parametric confidence interval on, say, the median weight would give a more robust indication of how the weights have changed each day.

(2) Regression analysis of all the individual pebble weight data for each of the three materials from the initial injection weights through all four recovery days gives the linear regression coefficients for the rates of weight loss per day. The 90% confidence limits for the regressed daily rate of loss is also given in Table 7. These weight loss rates can be used with the abrasion mill data to check the predictions of weight loss rates from the rock degradation model. The non-linear effect of shape change on rates of weight loss can be neglected for the purposes of obtaining an initial rate of loss for angular particles and in view of the marginal quality of the data set.

(3) The Kolmogorov–Smirnov test (Shaw & Wheeler 1985) is a powerful tool capable of testing the significance of the difference between any two weight distributions even if they contain substantially different amounts of data. These results suggest that although the distributions on consecutive days are mainly indistinguishable, in other cases significant differences do occur (the probability that this decision is wrong is ≤20%).

Discussion

Degradation modelling

The results of a subjective calibration of wear life from laboratory abrasion data in Matthews (1983), Haddon (1993) and Poole (pers. comm. 1993) have already been noted, but these give no account of how to predict the wear rates from a knowledge of site variables and rock type. The *degradation model* approach is to obtain mill test data and to transform the time axis of the plot of fraction of weight remaining versus mill time (1000s of revolutions) so that it represents prototype weight degradation in years. This requires finding a time conversion factor (the equivalent wear time factor X), which is simply determined from considering a number of site variables and looking up their designated ratings (x_1 to x_9). The model was first used by Latham (1991) for predicting armourstone degradation and is given as a possible technique in the *Rock Manual* (CIRIA/CUR 1991, section 3.2.4.2). If X is known for a given site, then one laboratory experiment will provide a prediction of progressive yearly weight loss on the beach or rock structure. There are therefore two ways to find X. One is to use the x-ratings from the published degradation model table. The other is to deduce the X value using results for each of the tracer rock types by directly comparing their laboratory abrasion and field abrasion rates for a given fraction of weight loss.

The result of the least-squares regression analysis given (Tables 6–8), was converted into a percentage loss rate per day over the field study period of eight tidal cycles (four recovery samples). This gave 6.5% for sandstone, 0.59% for chalk and 0.45% for basalt. Writing in terms of the mill abrasion results, the corresponding fractions of weight remaining (W/W_0) after four days are thus 0.740, 0.976 and 0.982, respectively.

Now consider the history (W/W_0 against thousand revolutions) of the modified mill abrasion test with its mixed load for each of the rock types. An equivalent time (in revolutions) for the same proportional loss of weight observed in the field, can be read from Fig. 6 for each of the three tests and the equivalent wear time factor, X which is defined as the number of prototype years equivalent to 1000 mill revolutions, for surface shingle of a given size at this site can be calculated as follows:

$$X = \text{(field time for a certain } W/W_0 \text{ in days)}/(365)$$
$$* (1000)/(\text{revs. to give same } W/W_0)$$

For example, basalt in shingle, $X = (4/365) * (1000/1150) = 0.0098$; see Table 9 for further details. These field results rank the rocks in the same order as the laboratory tests, showing that the sandstone is considerably weaker than the basalt and chalk. All the test materials are vulnerable to abrasion (Figs 5 and 6 and Table 9) when compared with a flint shingle which was also tested in the abrasion mill (Haddon 1993).

Under the assumption that the beach abrasion weight loss can be modelled by the mill abrasion weight loss, then if each field sample was subject to an identical abrasion energy, X should be the same. After correcting for the slight influence of the larger sandstone tracers (using the surface area to volume ratio and assumed surface area dependence on volume loss rates), the results for the field determination of X as given in Table 9 are 0.008, 0.010

Table 9. *Degradation analysis from laboratory and field*

Degradation analysis	Sandstone	Chalk	Basalt
Observed W/W_0 on beach in four days	0.742	0.976	0.981
Revs (000s) in mill giving an equiv. W/W_0 to four days on beach	1.05	0.25	1.15
Equivalent wear time factor (X) (years equiv. to 1000 lab. revs)	0.0078	0.0438	0.0098
Prediction for Slapton Time to reach:			
10% weight loss, i.e. $W/W_0 = 0.9$	3 days	20 days	50 days
90% weight loss, i.e. $W/W_0 = 0.1$ (crushed rocks in flint shingle, for average wave conditions of the four-day experiment, $H_s \approx 0.28$ m)	33 days	200 days	2 years

and 0.044 for sandstone, basalt and chalk, respectively. Their closeness is in some sense encouraging, although it would take an analysis of their confidence intervals to state how significantly close they are.

A reasonable explanation for the relatively small differences might be that the lower X value for the sandstones, which reflects the fact that a more abrasive environment is at work for these pebbles, has resulted from their more tabular shape. It was noted in the field that the sandstone pebbles experienced the greater alongshore transport, probably because of their greater lift and travel potential. The poor recovery of basalt on day 3 may have biased the results towards a faster apparent loss rate.

Wear rates on beaches

We now turn to the significance of these wear rate results for beaches with natural shingle or recharge materials consisting of various rock types and different energy coastlines. For the purpose of interpretation, consider shingle-size rock with an X factor of 0.01 (the rounded-off value determined from the basalt and sandstone data for the energy conditions deduced for Slapton). A surface area to volume correction for different sizes can easily be applied (see x_1 in Latham 1991). Assuming that the waves observed during the field study ($H_s = 0.28$ m) are representative of the average daily wave energy transferred to the surface shingle on Slapton Sands in one year and that the weight loss history follows that simulated in the modified mixed load mill test, then an estimate of the time to reach a given proportionate weight can be calculated as follows.

Suppose a severe failure criterion (in terms of weight loss) for the performance of the surface rock particles of a dynamically stable structure was set at $W/W_0 = 0.9$ and $X = 0.01$ was determined for the site conditions. The service life of the sandstone would be only three days (as observed on Slapton). Extrapolating the data presented in Tables 6–8 and Table 9, a relaxed service life criterion of $W/W_0 = 0.1$ (which is equivalent to approximately 50% reduction in effective diameter and a 90% volume loss in material in the active surface zones), we find that the basalt wear life is 2.0 years, that for chalk is 200 days and that for sandstone is only 33 days. In stark contrast, the wear life of a flint shingle based on Haddon's result, assuming again that $X = 0.01$, can be tentatively estimated at 200 years for $W/W_0 = 0.9$ and 2300 years for $W/W_0 = 0.1$. These results and their interpretation are compatible with intuitive guesses that have been made by beach geomorphologists. The significance to the engineer of estimating X for the site conditions and k_s for the rock type becomes clear. The relative performance of flint shingle has never been in doubt, but now it may be possible to constrain the absolute performance of different materials for beach recharge.

It is interesting to note that in looking up the degradation model ratings assessment (CIRIA/CUR 1991) for the shingle material and site conditions at Slapton Sands, an X factor of 0.0025 is obtained, which compares favourably with the observed values. This could just be fortuitous because the current degradation model was designed originally for static structures. It does not have continuously varying ratings for the particle mobility and refers to one rating value for a set range of N_s for the design storm.

The future calibration of more sensitive ratings could be achieved using more reliable, but similar, tracer methodology (e.g. cement mortar tracers) combined with wave climate data. These would give some further confidence in the ratings defined for the size effect (x_1) due to the surface area to volume ratio, the wave energy (x_4), the water-borne attrition agents (x_7) and the effect of the mobility parameter N_s (x_9), which differ substantially for shingle beach sites when compared with the statically stable armourstone structures for which the model was first derived. Indeed, the rationale for separating x_1, x_4, x_7 and x_9 will need to be reconsidered for the modelling of degradation on shingle beaches. The cumulative wave energy above a certain threshold for a period on site will need to be considered in developing a future model, rather than considering H_s of the design storm and a mobility parameter relating to these storm conditions, as in the current degradation model of Latham (1991).

Alternative field measurement methods

The field tracer methodology would be more reliable if a higher recovery rate and better understanding of the history of particles in response to wave action could be obtained. This would allow an improvement in the degradation modelling of transfer functions. However, a technique which recovered subsurface material in addition to that visible at the beach surface will require careful interpretation if it is not to distort wear life model results calibrated from laboratory abrasion in which continuous abrasion is applied to the test material, even if depth-of-disturbance data were used to weight the data.

A versatile and promising low technology improvement in the detection and recovery of tracers addressing similar objectives to this study was investigated in an unpublished research project on Hurst Spit (Collison 1996) carried out at QMW. An order of magnitude increase in the accuracy and statistical significance of the results was achieved when compared with the Slapton exotic tracer study. This latest tracer method uses cement mortar pebbles (with quantified abrasion characteristics) which have had metal cores implanted to enable subsurface detection. An alternative high technology approach would be the deployment of the radio-wave emitter pebbles developed at Southampton University (Voulgaris et al. 1994), which would allow detection, depth and identity to be established. The improvement in techniques for assessing weight loss would be three-fold. Firstly, any pebble below a given depth (defined by depth-of-disturbance rods as inactive) may not need to be recovered and, secondly, statistical analysis of the weight change of individuals (as opposed to populations) increases the value of the data enormously, whatever the recovery rate. Finally, recovery rates should be much higher as particles can be detected more reliably. These low- and high-technology approaches form a logical next step in the programme of tests.

Future theoretical models of the degradation of dynamic rock armour, rock beach and shingle beach materials will rely on a greater understanding of the hydrodynamics of how the cumulative history of wave climate relates to cumulative average particle movements, as the latter to a large extent controls degradation for a given rock type. The formulation of new theoretical approaches can be strengthened by direct measurements of particle movements and weight losses in the field while simultaneously monitoring the wave climate. The more promising field methodologies for tracer studies and a way of introducing the intrinsic strength of different rock types into theoretical models of degradation have been highlighted in this paper.

Conclusions

The standard QMW mill abrasion test (CIRIA/CUR 1991) provides an ideal basis for comparing the relative abrasion resistances of beach recharge materials that are to be placed in sufficient volume to dominate any indigenous beach shingle of contrasting rock abrasiveness and/or degree of rounding.

Where recharge materials are to be introduced on sites where the indigenous material has a significant volume for interaction and has contrasting rock abrasiveness and/or degree of rounding, then the standard mill abrasion test can be readily adapted. An appropriate test mixture consisting of a majority of indigenous beach pebbles and a small number of pieces of the rock type under consideration for recharge will yield results in the standard form.

The ratios between laboratory rates of wear during (1) mutual attrition (i.e. autogenous milling with no steel balls etc.) and (2) attrition due to rolling contacts with rounded flint shingle, are not constant and are unpredictable for different rock types. For example, it was observed that poorly cemented porous sandstone pebbles from the Keuper of the Triassic abraded faster when in contact with each other than when surrounded by flint shingle, whereas both the hard chalk and basalt abraded faster when in contact with flint shingle.

The placement of visually distinctive exotic tracers within a narrow initial weight range (to assess progressive weight loss rates) led to weight loss rate results that were of significance. The method is, however, only moderately successful in terms of the ratio of effort cost to benefit, for use on open shingle beaches experiencing rapid rates of longshore drift such as at Slapton Sands. The poor longevity of this surface experiment (which lasted only eight tide cycles) was thought to be mainly due to the mixing and burial of the tracers rather than to poor detection, judging by the beach reprofiling activity.

In spite of density differences, the susceptibility of the three different rock types to weight loss in the field was in the same sequence as that predicted from the laboratory tests.

For single-sized angular crushed rock aggregates with a D_{n50} of ≈ 40 mm placed on a shingle beach composed of dominantly rounded flint such as Slapton Sands, with a sieve D_{50} of about 15–20 mm and an inshore wave climate with a daily average H_s of 280 mm, the average rate of weight loss observed was equivalent to a 10% weight loss in three days for the sandstone, 20 days for the chalk and 50 days for the basalt.

Matching the laboratory abrasion to observed abrasion on Slapton Sands indicates that for single-sized crushed rock aggregate with D_{n50} of ≈ 40 mm, a representative equivalent wear time factor (based on results which give $X = 0.0078$, 0.0438 and 0.0098 for tracer samples of sandstone, chalk and basalt, respectively), appears to set X at between 0.005 and 0.045. This result is specific to the surface shingle conditions at Slapton Sands taken over the four day period in July 1995 for which wave heights summarized by $H_s = 280$ mm were measured. Further determinations of X at different beach sites together with wave climate data over the experimental period is needed to improve our understanding of abrasive losses and more effective ways of obtaining the data have been discussed. Application of the degradation model ratings table (Latham 1991) to the Slapton Sands site before the field experiment yielded $X = 0.0025$. The reasonable agreement between prediction and result is probably fortuitous as the model is in need of refinement for beach structures with high mobility particles such as shingle beaches.

The main conclusion derives in part from the test data of Haddon (1993) on flint shingle. The very large contrast in abrasion resistance observed in the mill test using rounded flint shingle and rock such as basalt (which is traditionally considered to be of good abrasion resistance) has been tentatively projected to give lifetime estimates. The rounded flint shingle is likely to be a vastly superior recharge material to most crushed rock sources. This conclusion could be central to strategic planning for the use of the country's finite resources of offshore shingle (see CIRIA 1996b) when contemplating its alternative use as crushed aggregate for concrete manufacture.

Acknowledgements. The authors thank Professor Howarth for improvements to the paper made during review and Win Man for help with the materials testing. The research was undertaken during a feasibility study funded by EPSRC grant GR/K17705, which is gratefully acknowledged.

References

AHRENS, J. P. 1995. Design considerations for dynamic revetments. *In:* THORNE, C. A. R., ABT, S. R., BARENDS, F. B. J., MAYNARD, S. T. & PILARCZKY, K. W. (eds) *River, Coastal and Shoreline Protection*. Wiley, Chichester.

BAIRD, W. F. & HALL, K. R. 1984. The design of breakwaters using quarried stones. *In: Proceedings of the 19th International Conference on Coastal Engineering, Houston,* ASCE, New York, 2580–2591.

BURCHARTH, H. F. & FRIGAARD, P. 1988. On the 3-dimensional stability of reshaping berm breakwaters. *In: Proceedings of the 21st International Conference on Coastal Engineering, Malaga.* ASCE, New York, 2284–2298.

CALDWELL, N. E. 1981. Relationship between tracers and associated background beach material. *Journal of Sedimentary Petrology,* **5**, 1163–1168.

CIRIA 1996a. *Beach Management Manual.* CIRIA Report 153, CIRIA, London.

——1996b. *Beach Recharge Materials – Demand and Resources.* CIRIA Report 154, CIRIA, London.

——/CUR 1991. *Manual on the Use of Rock in Coastal and Shoreline Engineering.* CIRIA Special Publication 83/CUR Report 154, CIRIA/CUR, London.

COLLISON, C. L. 1996. *A study of Hurst Spit: its geology, management and a simple experiment.* BSc Dissertation, Queen Mary & Westfield College, London.

FRIGAARD, P., HALD, T., BURCHARTH, H. & SIGURDARSON, S. 1997. Stability of berm breakwaters with special reference to stone durability. *In: Proceedings of the 25th International Conference on Coastal Engineering, Orlando, USA.* ASCE, New York, 1640–1647.

HADDON, J. R. 1993. *A study into the losses of beach nourishment material due to abrasion.* MSc Dissertation, Queen Mary & Westfield College, London.

HARDISTY, J. 1990. *Beach Form and Process.* Unwin Hyman, London.

ISLA, F. I. 1993. Overpassing and armouring phenomena on gravel beaches. *Marine Geology,* **110,** 369–376.

JOHNSON, C. N. 1987. Rubble beaches versus rubble revetments. *In:* KRAUS, N. C. (ed.) *Proceedings of the Conference on Coastal Sediments '87.* ASCE, New York, 1216–1231.

KAMPHUIS, J. W., DAVIES, M. H., NAIRN, R. B. & SAYAO, O. J. 1986. Calculation of littoral sand transport rate, *Journal of Coastal Engineering,* **10,** 1–21.

KUENEN, PH. H. 1956. Experimental abrasion of pebbles 2: rolling by current. *Journal of Geology,* **65,** 336–368.

——1968. Experimental abrasion of pebbles 6: surf action. *Sedimentology,* **3,** 22–28.

LATHAM, J.-P. 1991. Degradation model for rock armour in coastal engineering. *Quarterly Journal of Engineering Geology,* **24,** 101–118.

——1998. Assessment and specification of armourstone quality – from CIRIA/CUR (1991) to CEN (2000?). *This volume.*

—— & POOLE, A. B. 1988. Abrasion testing and armourstone degradation. *Coastal Engineering,* **12,** 233–255.

MATTHEWS, E. R. 1983. Measurements of beach pebble attrition in Palliser Bay, New Zealand. *Sedimentology,* **30,** 787–799.

NEWTON, M. D. 1995. *The analysis of weight loss resulting from attrition of beach particles at Slapton, Devon.* MSc Dissertation, Queen Mary & Westfield College, London.

NICHOLLS, R. J. & WRIGHT, P. 1991. Longshore transport of pebbles: experimental estimates of K. *In: Proceedings of the Conference on Coastal Sediments '91.* ASCE, New York, 920–933.

POWELL, K. A. 1993. *Dissimilar Sediments; Model Tests of Replenished Beaches Using Widely Graded Sediments.* Report SR 350, HR Wallingford, October.

SHAW, G. & WHEELER, D. 1985. *Statistical Techniques in Geographical Analysis.* Wiley, Chichester.

SMITH, M. R. & COLLIS, L. 1993. Aggregates: sand, gravel, crushed rock aggregates for construction purposes. Geological Society, London, Engineering Geology Special Publication 9.

TOMASICCHIO, G. R., LAMBERTI, A. & GUIDUCCI, F. 1995. Stone movement on a reshaped profile. *In: Proceedings of the International Conference on Coastal Engineering, 1994.* ASCE, New York.

VAN DER MEER, J. W. 1988. *Rock slopes and gravel beaches under wave attack.* PhD Thesis, Delft Hydraulics Communication No. 396.

VOULGARIS, G., WORKMAN, M. & COLLINS, M. B. 1994. New techniques for the measurement of shingle transport rates in the nearshore zone. *In: 2nd International Conference on the Geology of Siliclastic Shelf Seas, May 1994, Ghent.*

WRIGHT, P., CROSS, J. S. & WEBBER, N. B. 1978. Aluminium pebbles: a new type of tracer for flint and chert pebble beaches. *Marine Geology,* **27,** M9–M77.

SECTION 3

AGGREGATE TESTING AND THE USE OF ALTERNATIVE AGGREGATES

Canadian experience with the micro-Deval test for aggregates

Chris Rogers

Soils and Aggregates Section, Engineering Materials Office, Ministry of Transportation, Downsview, Ontario, Canada, M3M 1JG

Abstract. Several aggregate test methods used in evaluating the mechanical strength and predicting the performance of aggregate have been in use since the 1930s. Today there is a need for precise tests that have a demonstrated correlation with field performance. The micro-Deval test has good multi-laboratory precision and is a suitable replacement for the sulphate soundness test for fine aggregate. A micro-Deval test on coarse aggregate is a useful means of predicting performance of aggregate in concrete, bituminous pavement and as granular base.

Modern roads started to be developed in the late 1800s. Quite early on it was recognized that it was important to have suitable aggregates if the roads and bridges were to be of adequate strength and to be reasonably long lasting. Early pavements and bridges were experimental from the point of view of long-term durability. Aggregate testing was either non-existent or extremely primitive. For instance, in his report on road improvement in the province of Ontario, Campbell (1907) made the following statement:

'A practical man can judge of the qualities of a stone by applying simple tests: by breaking the stone with a hammer, wearing it on a grindstone, crushing it in a blacksmith's vice, scratching with an iron nail, breaking small pieces with the fingers: by such simple means a general idea of the stone can be readily formed, but no test is so conclusive as actual wear on the road'

The essential properties outlined by Campbell include many of the aggregate properties measured today: impact strength, abrasion resistance, crushing strength, hardness, and presence of weak particles. It was also recognized then, as now, that the best indicator was actual field performance. By the 1930s a number of empirical tests had been developed that were used for assuring that the aggregates were reasonably suitable. From time to time, poor performance was encountered that was thought to be due to some inadequacies of the aggregate. However, the reasons for the poor performance of the aggregate were not fully known because of a lack of suitable tools for post-failure examination and confusion about the mechanism of frost action. Knight (1948) gives several examples from the 1920s and 1930s of poor concrete and pavement durability thought to be caused by the nature of the aggregates.

In the 1940s alkali–silica reactions were recognized as a severe durability problem that was specific to certain types of aggregate. It was also recognized that certain definable rock types used in aggregate were frost-sensitive and could cause pop-outs or more widespread deterioration of concrete and asphalt pavements (Sweet 1940). From this point on, extensive research was conducted, particularly in North America, on the properties of aggregates, their petrography and means of separating the good from the bad. These endeavours waned somewhat in the 1970s and 1980s and were replaced with concerns about impending shortages of high-quality aggregates and the need to use marginal quality aggregates (ASTM 1976) and more recently the need to use aggregates made from waste products.

Approaching the year 2000, those of us involved in testing, selection and approval of construction aggregates are finding ourselves under considerable pressure from a number of different sides. On one hand we are being urged to find a use for recycled products as aggregate. These materials are seldom as one would wish. For instance, 'post-consumer glass' from household waste contains sugars which interfere with cement hydration and the glass itself is alkali–silica reactive and is also susceptible to asphalt stripping. On the other hand conservationist groups, in order to preserve the landscape, would sometimes like to stop extraction in areas of suitable aggregate and shift the extraction to areas where the rock may not be so suitable (Valpy 1994). At the same time, structural engineers are demanding higher quality aggregate than may be commonly available, to use in their 'high-performance concrete' of high and ultra-high strengths. Pavement engineers are also demanding aggregates of superior frictional properties to those that were commonly used in asphalt even as little as 20 years ago. To meet these challenges, we need quick test methods that are good predictors of the performance of aggregate. In addition, development of effective specifications requires they be based on test methods which have good reproducibility.

Today, the test methods available for evaluating aggregates are not very different from those available to the engineers in the 1940s. At that time, the relationship

ROGERS, C. 1998. Canadian experience with the micro-Deval test for aggregates. *In*: LATHAM, J.-P. (ed.) 1998. *Advances in Aggregates and Armourstone Evaluation.* Geological Society, London, Engineering Geology Special Publications, **13**, 139–147.

between performance in the empirical tests and field performance was not well understood and later studies have not significantly improved on this knowledge. Many of these tests have poor, or unknown, multi-laboratory precision. To deal with the increasing demands to use marginal aggregates, recycled products as aggregate, and to provide even better aggregates for structural and frictional reasons we need fast, functional, performance tests combined with a better understanding of how the results correlate with actual long-term performance.

The purpose of this paper is to provide a review of some of the Canadian developments in the use of the micro-Deval test for measuring the mechanical strength and resistance to breakdown of aggregate.

Mechanical breakdown of coarse aggregate

The classic test for resistance to mechanical breakdown of aggregates in North America is the Los Angeles Abrasion test. It has been in common use since the early 1930s and may be found in nearly every North American agency's specifications for aggregate. Despite the name, the Los Angeles test does not measure abrasion but rather impact resistance. In recognition of this, the name was changed by ASTM in the 1980s to 'Los Angeles Abrasion and Impact Test' so as to include the term 'impact'. Figure 1 shows the correlation of the results of testing in the Los Angeles apparatus with the British Aggregate Impact test (BS 812), a true impact test. The

Los Angeles test has an advantage over most direct impact tests (French, German, Swedish and British) in that a larger, and hence more representative sample may be tested.

In Ontario, it has been found that the Los Angeles test is a good predictor of susceptibility of aggregate to mechanical breakdown but little else. Losses of greater than 45% in this test indicate aggregate may breakdown during handling. This will not normally be a severe problem unless multiple handling is done, such as moving the stockpile several times, and some change in grading cannot be tolerated. Granite gneisses found in the Precambrian shield areas of Ontario may have losses in the test up to about 55% but perform satisfactorily in bituminous pavement, granular base and concrete provided precautions are taken to prevent excessive handling prior to placement. Similar problems with excessive losses with brittle granites, unrelated to their performance, have been reported in New York (Anon 1963) and Maine (Pratt & Leavitt 1941).

There are many aggregates which meet the normal Los Angeles test requirements of 60% for granular base aggregate yet are unsatisfactory. Figure 2 shows the correlation between the loss in the Los Angeles test and the micro-Deval abrasion test for granular base aggregates. Figure 2 also shows the actual field performance of the samples: 'good' aggregates were those that had many years of use with no reported failures in granular base that could be attributed to the quality of the stone; 'fair' aggregates were those that had been used at least once and some reduced service life attributed to the

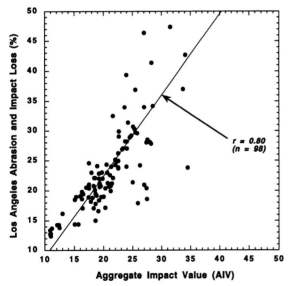

Fig. 1. Relationship between Los Angeles abrasion and impact and British Aggregate Impact Value for crushed natural gravels and crushed stone in Ontario.

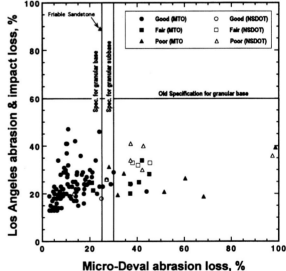

Fig. 2. Field performance ratings of granular base coarse aggregates from Ontario (MTO) and Nova Scotia (NSDOT): relation between Los Angeles and micro-Deval abrasion.

coarse aggregate had occurred; 'poor' aggregates were those which had given significantly reduced service life or were largely composed of rock types of such poor quality (shale, clayey limestone, etc) that a reduced service life could reasonably be assumed. This work is more fully described in a paper by Senior & Rogers (1991). It can be seen that the adoption of a maximum loss of 25% loss in the micro-Deval test would be far more effective at separating good from poor granular base aggregates than the Los Angeles test. There is, however, an apparent bias in the sampling. Very few aggregates were tested in the Los Angeles test with loss greater than 45% as these aggregates are rare, at least in Ontario. The reason for the apparent superiority of the micro-Deval test is that, being a wet abrasion test, it is a closer simulation of field conditions. Poorer quality rock types tend to slake or at least to have reduced strength when wet. The Los Angeles test is predominantly an impact test done on oven-dry aggregate. In the field, aggregates are rarely dry and seldom subjected to impact except in the mixing, transportation and compaction process. In the future, mechanical degradation/strength tests should be done wet rather than dry in an effort to simulate more closely exposure conditions. The Los Angeles test is very difficult to do on wet materials because of the difficulty of cleaning the drum. Tests done in the more easily cleaned micro-Deval apparatus are more useful in predicting aggregate suitability for granular base course and other applications.

Micro-Deval test method

This test was developed in France in the 1960s (Tourenq 1971). In the French test method (Anon 1990) a 500 g sample of coarse aggregate is placed in a 200 mm diameter by 154 mm long steel drum with 2.5 litres of water and a charge of 10 ± 0.5 mm diameter steel balls. Prior to testing, the aggregate is immersed in water for 24 ± 4 hours. The steel drum is rotated at 100 ± 5 rpm for two hours (12 000 revolutions) and the oven dry mass retained on the 1.6 mm sieve is measured and recorded. The loss in the test is expressed as per cent lost past the 1.6 mm sieve. The charge of steel balls depends on the size of the coarse aggregate: 2000 g for 4–6.3 mm, 4000 g for 6.3–10 mm and 5000 g for 10–14 mm. There is also a procedure using a 400 mm diameter drum for aggregates of 25–50 mm.

In the Ontario version of the micro-Deval test (Anon 1996), a 1500 g sample of coarse aggregate is placed in a 200 mm diameter by 178 mm long steel drum (about 5 litres) with 2 litres of water and 5 kg of 9.5 ± 0.5 mm diameter steel balls. Prior to testing, the aggregate is immersed in water for a minimum of one hour. The steel drum is rotated at 100 ± 5 rpm for two hours ± 1 minute. A ball mill roller, manufactured in North America is used to rotate the steel drum (Fig. 3). The mass lost past the 1.18 mm sieve is measured and recorded. The

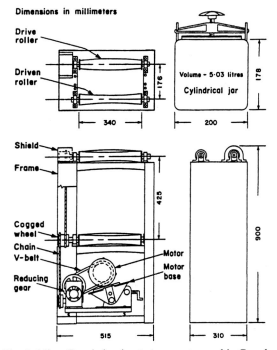

Fig. 3. Micro-Deval abrasion test apparatus used in Canada.

1.18 mm sieve was adopted because 1.6 mm is not a standard sieve in Canada. In Quebec, a 1.25 mm sieve has been adopted rather than the 1.18 mm used in Ontario. The Quebec version uses a sample mass of 500 g rather than the 1500 g adopted in Ontario. The larger sample size was adopted in Ontario following study of the influence of sample size on loss in the test. It was found that loss in the test was independent of sample mass until the sample was 2000 g. Also, because a 1500 g sample consists of three times more particles than a 500 g sample, the repeatability of the test was improved. A water volume of 2 litres rather than 2.5 litres was adopted because with the larger sample there was less space for water. The soaking time of 1 hour was adopted because it was found that after 1 hour further immersion had little affect on loss in the test with an argillaceous dolostone of moderate loss in the test. It was also desired to keep soaking to one hour so as to speed testing time.

The Ontario test also requires the periodic testing of a control or reference aggregate. A stockpile of reference aggregate is maintained by the Ontario Ministry of Transportation and made available on request. The test requires that the reference aggregate is tested every ten samples, but at least every week in which a sample is tested and the results of the last twenty tests of the reference aggregate reported to the client on a control chart.

The micro-Deval abrasion test for coarse aggregate has been adopted by the Transportation Departments of the Provinces of Ontario, Quebec and Nova Scotia for evaluating the likely performance of granular base coarse aggregates. The Province of New Brunswick has adopted the test for bituminous pavement aggregates and is thinking of adopting it for use in granular base.

Micro-Deval test for asphalt and concrete coarse aggregate

The micro-Deval test is also suitable for judging the abrasion or wear resistance of aggregate. Figure 4 shows the relationship between the micro-Deval test and resistance to abrasion measured by the aggregate abrasion value test (AAV). The AAV test (BS 812) is the modern development of the Dorry abrasion test originally developed for measuring the wear resistance of stone. Aggregate particles are held in an epoxy mould and the exposed test surface is placed down on a flat, rotating steel plate. A weight is placed on the sample and silica sand is fed onto the plate surface as it rotates and abrades the aggregate. The test is done dry. The sample mass loss on two specimens is normalized for the density of the aggregate and expressed as the aggregate abrasion value (AAV). Wear resistant aggregates give low values and soft aggregates give high values. The AAV test is time-consuming and expensive with small samples but has good repeatability and reproducibility. It is very useful for detailed investigations especially at the initial qualification stage but is not a suitable routine quality control test.

The micro-Deval test is far more suitable than AAV for quality control and assurance testing because of its low cost and relatively large sample size. In Ontario, the guidelines for surfacing aggregates for bituminous pavements with the highest traffic volume (generally AADT > 2500 per lane) require an AAV of 6 or less. The more stringent AAV value in Ontario compared to the UK (<10) is probably related to the significant abrasion that is caused by the large amounts of sand spread on the highways in the winter in order to improve friction on snow- and ice-covered roads. Figure 4 shows that the AAV of satisfactory aggregates may be as high as 17, but for pavements with lower traffic volume, a large number of aggregates with AAVs of less than 17 give unsatisfactory field performance. The AAV test by itself is therefore not satisfactory for selecting surfacing aggregates for bituminous pavements. The results show that the adoption of a micro-Deval abrasion loss of less than 17% would generally result in acceptance of aggregates with an AAV of 17 or less and also identify those aggregates which may give unsatisfactory performance. It should be noted that the aggregates of poor or fair field performance that gave low AAVs and/or low micro-Deval abrasion gave poor performance for reasons other than resistance to abrasion (they were usually frost sensitive and gave unacceptable numbers of pop-outs). The values shown in Table 1 for bituminous pavement applications were adopted in Ontario in January 1997.

Table 1 shows that, for Portland cement concrete aggregates, values of 17 and 13% loss have been adopted.

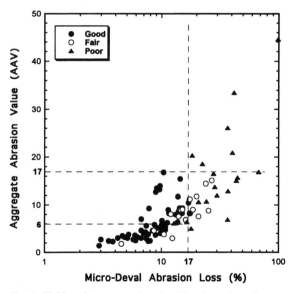

Fig. 4. Field performance ratings for bituminous bound Ontario aggregates in wearing course: relation between AAV and micro-Deval abrasion.

Table 1. *Micro-Deval specifications for coarse aggregates in Ontario*

Application	Maximum loss (%)
Granular sub-base	30
Granular base	25
Open graded base course	17
Bituminous wearing courses	
Premium[1]	5–15[3]
Secondary[2]	17
Bituminous base course	21
Structural concrete	17
Concrete pavement	13

Notes:
1. AADT > 2500 lane.
2. AADT < 2500 lane.
3. Varies with rock type, 5% for igneous and metamorphic gravel, 10% for traprock, diabase (dolerite) and andesite, 15% for dolomitic sandstone, granitic meta-arkose and gneiss.
4. These specifications were adopted in the period from 1992 to 1997.

These values were derived from a survey of aggregates of known satisfactory field performance in structural concrete and concrete pavements. Satisfactory aggregates for concrete should be dimensionally stable under the variety of conditions to which concrete is exposed. Rock types which give high losses in the micro-Deval test are generally those which are clayey or shaley, susceptible to frost action or weak. These are aggregates which do not make good concrete so the use of a test such as the micro-Deval is justified.

Mechanical breakdown of fine aggregate

A number of tests have been developed over the years to measure the susceptibility of fine aggregate to breakdown during the handling, mixing and compaction or placing process. However, none have found favour and been widely adopted by specifying agencies.

The first reported mechanical degradation test on fine aggregate was developed at Illinois Department of Highways by Roman (1915), who took the Deval abrasion apparatus for coarse aggregate and tested dry sand (4.75–0.300 mm) with a charge of steel balls. He did not attempt to use a standard grading. In 1925, this test was improved in Maine by Gowen & Leavitt (in Woolf 1929) who tested 500 g of 14 to 28 mesh sand (probably 1.40–0.64 mm) with a charge of eighteen 19 mm diameter steel balls for 2000 revolutions in the Deval machine. The amount of material passing the 0.150 mm sieve was used to express the loss by abrasion. This test was further developed by Woolf (1929) who objected to the bias introduced by testing an unrepresentative sample and proposed the use of a standard grading. Woolf also reduced the abrasive charge to ten 19 mm balls and measured loss by abrasion on the 0.300 mm sieve. He attempted to correlate the results of abrasion testing with the tensile strength of mortars but found no useful relationship. He proposed the test as a method of measuring the quality of concrete sand in conjunction with grading analysis and strength tests. It is now hard to understand why this test was not adopted.

The sulphate soundness test was adopted as a tentative test by ASTM (C 88) in 1931 and adopted as a standard test method in 1963 (Dolar-Mantuani 1978). ASTM does not give a precision statement for the fine aggregate version of the test. In repeated studies in experienced, and properly equipped laboratories the Ontario Ministry of Transportation has found that the average multi-laboratory coefficient of variation was 10.5% over a range in loss from 7% to 22%. As less well equipped and less experienced laboratories are included in multi-laboratory studies, the coefficient of variation increases to about 30%. Clearly, a test with this kind of multi-laboratory variability is not very useful as a specification test for accepting or rejecting material. In Canada, the wide variability of many aggregate quality tests has been an impediment to the acceptance of results from some private engineering laboratories by the aggregate industry.

In the late 1970s it was found that there was an interesting correlation between the wet attrition test of Davis *et al.* (1967) and the magnesium sulphate soundness test (Rogers & Bullen 1979). This was studied further and it was found that there was excellent correlation between magnesium sulphate soundness loss and the attrition test adopted by ASTM in 1990 (C 1137) provided that sands were all tested at the same gradation in the attrition apparatus (Rogers *et al.* 1991). A defect of the attrition test apparatus adopted by ASTM is a lack of robustness. The stainless steel blades which vigorously stir the aggregate/water mixture in the hexagonal tank wear rapidly and this causes a significant change in test results. It was found that, after 70 tests, the apparatus was about 20% less efficient at breaking aggregate particles (Rogers *et al.* 1991). The attrition test, while interesting as a possible replacement for the sulphate soundness test, cannot be recommended for this reason.

Micro-Deval test for fine aggregate

The micro-Deval apparatus has been used in France (Senior & Rogers 1991) for testing fine aggregates using a charge of various size steel balls and water. This 'friability' test on sand has not been formally adopted in France, perhaps because of doubts about its relevance to subsequent performance of sand. The same apparatus has been adopted in Canada (Anon 1994a) as an alternative to the sulphate soundness test for testing concrete sand. In the Canadian test, a sample of sand is washed to remove $-80 \mu m$ material, dried and 500 g is soaked in water for 24 hours. After soaking, the sample is placed in the stainless steel drum with 750 ml of water and 1250 g of 9.5 ± 0.5 mm diameter steel balls. The drum is rotated at 100 rpm for 15 minutes. The sample is then washed to remove $-80 \mu m$ material, oven dried and weighed. Loss is expressed as per cent loss in mass of the original sample. As with the coarse aggregate test, to ensure consistency between and within laboratories, the procedure requires testing of a control fine aggregate every ten samples and the plotting of the results on a control graph that accompanies test data to the client. The Ontario Ministry of Transportation maintains a stockpile of fine aggregate as a reference material and makes it available to others.

Unlike the coarse aggregate version of the test, the condition of the inside surface of the stainless steel drum can affect the results. It has been found that when the inside of the drum is polished, the loss obtained with fine aggregate can be half that obtained when the inside surface is 'frosted'. Polishing is usually caused by testing carbonate coarse aggregates in the drum. The frosted surface can be restored by periodic conditioning with a silica sand. The use of the reference aggregate is useful in detecting changes in the condition of the inside of the drum.

Micro-Deval test for concrete sand

The micro-Deval test is good at measuring the amount of weak, soft material such as shale, in a sand (Fig. 5). Preliminary data, using sands manufactured with various amounts of shale mixed with silica sand show a good relationship between drying shrinkage and micro-Deval loss (Fig. 6) (Pozderka & Pang 1993). Subsequent work has shown that natural sands with micro-Deval losses of less than about 25% give similar mortar shrinkage. When losses are above 25%, mortar shrinkage on drying becomes greater. The Canadian specification (Anon 1994b) calls for a maximum micro-Deval loss of 20% in this test for concrete sands.

Chamberlin (1966) pointed out that fine aggregate particles are smaller than the critical size needed to exert destructive volume change on freezing. As a result, sands with high sulphate soundness losses would not cause frost damage in air entrained concrete. He thought that the sulphate soundness test on fine aggregate was really measuring resistance to abrasion, presumably during the laboratory sieving process. Therefore, not surprisingly, there is a reasonable correlation between the sulphate soundness test and the micro-Deval test (Fig. 7) and also the ASTM Attrition test (Rogers & Senior 1994). Chamberlin also found a highly significant correlation between sulphate soundness loss and mortar shrinkage.

Parka & Hansen (1982) studied an Indonesian sand attrition test. The test is similar to the micro-Deval and is done by placing 100 g of sand (+0.300 mm) in a

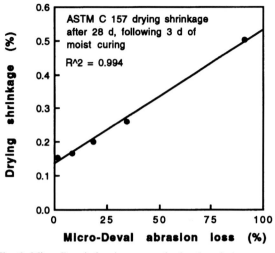

Fig. 6. Micro-Deval abrasion on sand related to drying shrinkage of mortar.

200 mm diameter porcelain jar with 200 ml of water and 100 glass balls of 17 mm diameter. The jar is rotated at 28 rpm for one hour and the sand dried and screened on the 0.300 mm sieve. The 'attrition rate' of the sand is the per cent by mass passing the 0.300 mm sieve following the test. They found that sand of a high attrition rate broke down during mixing in concrete. They also found that sands of high attrition rate (high loss) tended to give concrete of lower slump and lower strength at a fixed

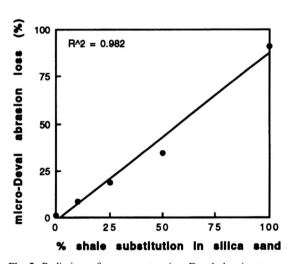

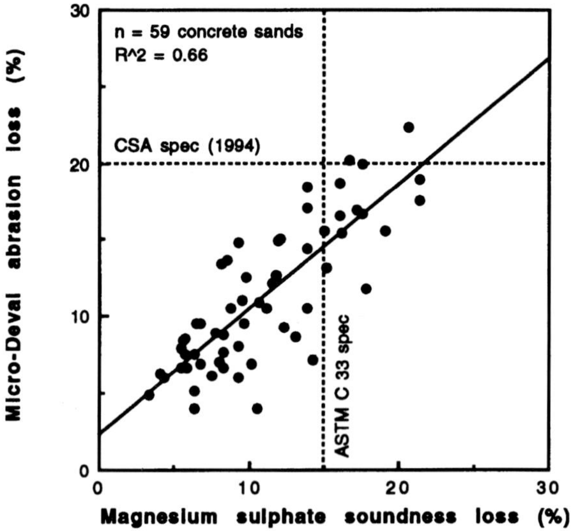

Fig. 5. Preliminary fine aggregate micro-Deval abrasion test data showing its ability to measure shale content of sand (by mass).

Fig. 7. Micro-Deval abrasion compared with magnesium sulphate soundness loss for Ontario concrete sands of satisfactory field performance.

water/cement ratio. The poorer quality sands still made satisfactory concrete but would, in general, require a higher amount of cement for a given concrete strength and workability. They reported that it was intended to introduce a specification for a maximum attrition rate for Indonesian concrete sands.

Micro-Deval test for granular base fine aggregate

Figure 8 shows the coarse (>4.75 mm) and fine (<4.75 mm) aggregate micro-Deval losses of granular base course aggregates from a variety of quarried and crushed gravel sources. Generally the fine aggregate gives a micro-Deval value which is about 20% greater than the value for coarse aggregate from the same source. Because the specification for granular base coarse aggregate is 25% (Fig. 2), an appropriate specification for the fine aggregate component of granular base should be 30%.

At present, most specifications for granular base have no physical requirement for the properties of the fine aggregate component other than a plasticity requirement. The fine aggregate component makes up a significant volume of granular base aggregate, typically 35–50%, and occasionally can have very different properties from the coarse aggregate. Typical examples would be gravel deposits where the sand contains preferentially large amounts of low durability shale compared to the coarse fraction. In Fig. 8 one of the aggregates had a very poor record of performance as granular base in both bituminous paved and also unpaved gravel roads. The other aggregate that exceeded both the fine aggregate and coarse aggregate limits was a shaley limestone that showed breakdown of the aggregate but the performance

history was limited. The plasticity of all the samples shown in Fig. 8 was assessed using the fraction passing the 425 μm sieve. Only those which had a micro-Deval loss which exceeded the coarse or fine aggregate limits had a measurable plasticity index (greater than 0). This confirms the general unsuitability of these high-loss materials, at least in the Canadian environment, where frost depths are great and plastic granular base course aggregates do not perform well. In 1996, the Ontario Ministry of Transportation adopted micro-Deval specifications for the fine aggregate component of both granular base and sub-base course aggregate to be a maximum of 30% and 35% respectively.

Micro-Deval test for fine aggregate in bituminous pavements

Specifications for bituminous pavement fine aggregate are shown in Fig. 9 and Table 2. In 1992, the Ontario Ministry of Transportation replaced the existing magnesium sulphate soundness requirements for bituminous pavement fine aggregate with requirements for the micro-Deval test. The previous specification called for a maximum magnesium sulphate soundness loss of 16% for premium surface course pavements, and 20% for secondary surface courses and all binder courses. The new micro-Deval requirements were 20% and 25% respectively. Over the past three construction seasons these new requirements have given no major problems.

In the past five years a new bituminous pavement base course made exclusively of quarried stone and manufactured sand has been used in Ontario. This 'heavy duty binder' has been designed to resist rutting. Some

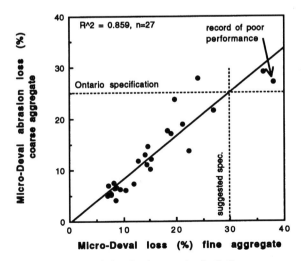

Fig. 8. Micro-Deval abrasion losses using both the coarse aggregate and fine aggregate test methods, for granular base aggregates from crushed gravel and quarry sources from Ontario.

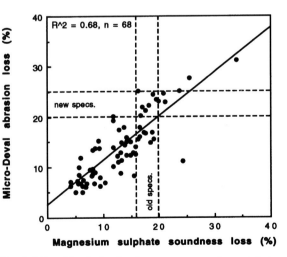

Fig. 9. Micro-Deval abrasion loss versus magnesium sulphate soundness loss for sands and crusher screenings used in bituminous pavements.

Table 2. *Micro-Deval specifications for fine aggregates in Ontario*

Application	Maximum loss (%)
Granular sub-base	35
Granular base	30
Bituminous pavement	
Premium wearing course	15[1]
Premium wearing course	20[2]
Heavy duty base course	25
Secondary wearing course	25
Normal base course	25
Portland cement concrete	20

Notes:
1. For manufactured fine aggregate for use in dense friction courses.
2. For natural sands and crusher screenings.
3. These specifications were adopted in the period from 1992 to 1997.

Table 3. *Between laboratory variation of micro-Deval abrasion tests*

Micro-Deval abrasion test	Various aggregates mean loss %	Coefficient of variation[1] %	R^2
Fine aggregate	38	2.5	2.7
	20	4.1	2.3
	10	6.0	1.7
	7	8.1	1.6
Coarse aggregate	17[3]	5.0	2.4
	12	6.4	2.2
	5	10	1.4

Notes:
1. Coefficient of variation = standard deviation/mean.
2. R = reproducibility (value below which the difference between two properly conducted test results from different laboratories may be expected to lie with a probability of 95%).
3. A study with 24 laboratories, see Fig. 10.

mixtures made with aggregates with a micro-Deval loss of 25% or more have given problems during construction because of excessive amounts of fines generated during the drying and handling process. With these mixtures it is difficult to obtain sufficient voids and small but unanticipated increases in fines content can cause severe problems in either preventing flushing or alteratively in getting enough asphalt into the mixture.

Precision of micro-Deval tests

The variability of the micro-Deval tests has been studied in a number of ways. Formal multi-laboratory studies have been conducted with eight laboratories with a variety of materials of differing abrasion loss. Table 3 shows data derived from these studies. Generally, the greater the loss in the micro-Deval abrasion test, the greater the between laboratory variation. Figure 10 shows a scatter diagram showing the results of a recent between laboratory study of two samples of a slightly shaley limestone. It can be seen that the test has good precision.

Conclusions and recommendations

There is a need for aggregate quality index tests of good precision and demonstrated correlation with field performance. The existing sulphate soundness test for both coarse and fine aggregate has poor multi-laboratory precision. The Los Angeles abrasion and impact test has poor correlation with field performance of aggregates in many applications but it is useful for identifying aggregates prone to mechanical break down.

Newer tests, such as the micro-Deval tests should be considered for adoption for evaluating mechanical strength properties of aggregates. The precision of these tests is excellent compared with many other aggregate test methods.

The micro-Deval test on fine aggregate has been adopted by the Canadian Standards Association as an alternative test for the magnesium sulphate soundness test for concrete sand. The Ontario Ministry of Transportation has adopted micro-Deval test criteria for concrete, bituminous pavement and granular base and sub-base

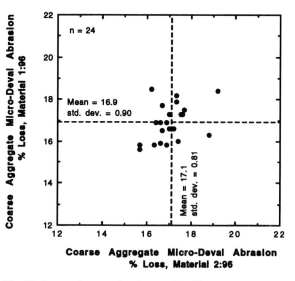

Fig 10. Scatter diagram showing results of between laboratory study of the micro-Deval abrasion test for coarse aggregate.

course applications. The micro-Deval test on coarse aggregate has been adopted by a number of agencies in eastern Canada for predicting the performance of granular base aggregates.

References

ANON 1963. *A Further Investigation of Abrasion Tests for Stone Aggregates.* New York Dept. of Public Works, Albany, Research Report 63-1.

——1990. Norme P18-572, Essai d'usure micro-Deval, Association Française de Normalisation, Tour Europe, cadex 7 92080, Paris la Défense, Paris, France, décembre.

——1994a. *CSA A23.2-23A Method of Test for the Resistance of Fine Aggregate to Degradation by Abrasion in the Micro-Deval Apparatus.* Canadian Standards Association, Toronto, Methods of Test for Concrete A23.2-94, 224–229.

——1994b. Table 3 limits for deleterious substances and physical properties, Canadian Standards Association, Toronto, Concrete Materials and Methods of Concrete Construction, A23.1-94.

——1996. *Method of Test for the Resistance of Coarse Aggregate to Degradation by Abrasion in the Micro-Deval Apparatus.* Ontario Ministry of Transportation, Toronto, Laboratory Testing Manual, Test method LS-618.

ASTM 1976. *Living with Marginal Aggregates.* American Society for Testing and Materials, Special Technical Publication **597**.

CAMPBELL, A. W. 1907. *Eleventh Annual Report on Highway Improvement in Ontario.* Legislative Assembly, Toronto, Ontario, Canada.

CHAMBERLIN, W. P. 1966. *Influence of Natural Sand Fine Aggregate on Some Properties of Hardened Concrete Mortar,* Highway Research Board, Washington, DC, Record No. 124, 18–40.

DAVIS, R. E., MIELENZ, R. C. & POLIVKA, M. 1967. *Importance of Petrographic Analysis and Special Tests not Usually Required in Judging Quality of Concrete Sand,* American Society for Testing and Materials. *Journal of Materials,* **2**, 461–486.

DOLAR-MANTUANI, L. 1978. *Soundness and Deleterious Substances,* American Society for Testing and Materials, Special Technical Publication **169B**, 744–761.

KNIGHT, B. H. & KNIGHT, R. G. 1948. *Road Aggregate: Their Uses and Testing,* Second Edition. Arnold, London.

PARKA, N. & HANSEN, T. C. 1982. On the Correlation of Consistency and Strength of Concrete to Attrition Rate of Fine Aggregate, American Society for Testing and Materials, *Cement, Concrete and Aggregates,* **4**, No. 1, pp. 24–27.

POZDERKA, S. & PANG, K. H. 1993. *Micro-Deval Abrasion Test Correlation With % Shrinkage in Portland Cement Mortars Containing Queenston Shale,* University of Toronto, Dept. of Civil Engineering unpublished report.

PRATT, H. A. & LEAVITT, H. W. 1941. *Adapting the Los Angeles Abrasion Test to Maines' Granitic Gravels,* Maine Technology Experimental Station Bulletin, 37.

ROGERS, C. A. & BULLEN, I. 1979. *The Development of an Attrition Test for Evaluating Ice Control Sand,* Ministry of Transportation, Ontario, Engineering Materials Report 26.

—— & SENIOR, S. A. 1994. *Recent Developments in Physical Testing of Aggregates to Ensure Durable Concrete,* Proceedings, Advances in Cement and Concrete, American Society of Civil Engineering, New York, pp. 338–361, July.

——, BAILEY, M. L. & PRICE, B. 1991. *Micro-Deval Test for Evaluating the Quality of Fine Aggregate for Concrete and Asphalt,* Transportation Research Board, Washington, DC, Transportation Research Record 1301, 68–76.

ROMAN, F. L. 1915. Wearing Tests for Sand and Gravel, *Good Roads,* **9**, p. 186, May.

SENIOR, S. A. & ROGERS, C. A. 1991. *Laboratory Tests for Predicting Coarse Aggregate Performance in Ontario.* Transportation Research Board, Washington, D.C., Transportation Research Record No. 1301, 97–106.

SWEET, H. 1940. *Chert as a Deleterious Constituent in Indiana Aggregates,* Highway Research Board, Washington, D.C., Proceedings, **20**, 599–620.

TOURENQ, C. 1971. L'Essai Micro-Deval, *Bulletin Liason Laboratoire,* Routières, Ponts, et Chausées, Paris, No. 50, 69–76.

VALPY, M. 1994. *An Escarpment for the Saving,* Globe and Mail, Toronto, March 23, p. 2.

WOOLF, D. O. 1929. *A Proposed Abrasion Test for Sand Investigated,* Public Roads, **9**, 222–224.

Assessing the wear characteristics of aggregate exposed at the road surface

A. R. Woodside & W. D. H. Woodward

Highway Engineering Research Centre, School of the Built Environment, University of Ulster, 75 Belfast Road, Carrickfergus, Co. Antrim BT 38 8PH, UK

Abstract. This paper considers the assessment of highway surfacing aggregate wear using the Aggregate Abrasion Value and micro-Deval test methods. Their historical development is discussed. The influence of test sample preparation and number of chippings assessed is compared. Data for both methods are presented for a range of rock types. Dry, wet and soaked versions of the micro-Deval test are compared. The use of a density correction to modify the micro-Deval test value is proposed. The ability of the Aggregate Abrasion Value and micro-Deval test methods to assess heterogeneous aggregates is assessed.

Assessing the wear characteristics of aggregate exposed to in-service conditions at the road surface has long been recognized as being of crucial importance to its performance. Methods of assessment have been in existence for the last 100 years. As a consequence a number of fundamentally different methodologies have resulted in response to what conditions were perceived as being important. This may be reflected in the terms used to describe the process, e.g. wear, abrasion and attrition. This paper first traces their development from the early work of Lovegrove at the turn of this century to the use of the Aggregate Abrasion Value (AAV) as one of the main British surfacing aggregate requirements. However, the main reason for this paper is the supposed mandatory replacement of the British AAV test by a selected CEN (Comite Europeen de Normalisation) method. It is expected that this will be the French wet micro-Deval test (MDE).

In early 1993, both the British aggregates industry and Department of Transport became concerned over the future of the AAV, in their view a tried and tested test method, which together with PSV was traditionally used as the basis for all surfacing aggregate specification requirements. Although initially accepting the micro-Deval test as a possible replacement for the AAV test, their attitude soon changed following the publication by the Department of Environment of a study of High Specification Aggregate (HSA) sources for road surfacing materials (Thompson *et al.* 1993). A comparison of 52 aggregate samples indicated an apparent lack of correlation between AAV and MDE results. As Thompson explained "... *the fact that samples with Aggregate Abrasion Values of less than 10 can have micro-Deval Coefficients ranging from 12 to 40 has disturbing implica-tions for the compliance of certain existing HSA sources with any future European Specification requirements that may be based on the micro-Deval test*". In fact, only 2 of the sources had a MDE of <16. As a result, it was felt that it would be very difficult to decide upon limiting values of MDE which correspond to the current limiting values of AAV.

It was generally felt that the AAV test complemented the PSV test i.e. abrasion resistance ensures that the macro-texture of the surface is maintained, whilst PSV limits ensure that the micro-texture of the particles is maintained. Together, they ensure a satisfactory resistance to skidding and hence the safety of the road user.

In view of this concern and the potential effect it may have on the high quality British surfacing aggregate industry, the authors have carried out a comparative investigation of the BS 812 method and its proposed CEN replacement based on an examination of the factors experienced at the tyre/aggregate interface to determine whether a correlation exists between the two methods. The ability to model the factors experienced at the road/tyre interface will determine which method is the better indicator of in-service performance.

The tyre/aggregate interface – its influence on assessing wear resistance

In any form of testing, if the aim is to improve the performance prediction process, one must first consider what one is trying to assess, i.e. the wear experienced at the tyre/aggregate interface where a pneumatic tyre is in

WOODSIDE, A. R. & WOODWARD, W. D. H. 1998. Assessing the wear characteristics of aggregate exposed at the road surface. *In*: LATHAM, J.-P. (ed.) 1998. *Advances in Aggregates and Armourstone Evaluation*. Geological Society, London, Engineering Geology Special Publications, **13**, 149–157.

contact with exposed surfacing aggregate. One must first consider the basics and then try to replicate them as simply as possible in the laboratory. The typical British surfacing has a rough texture due to the application of chippings to a hot rolled asphalt or surface dressing, or by the blend of aggregates used in a bituminous macadam or thin surfacing. In each of these, the engineer expects the choice of aggregate to maintain this degree of texture and not be affected due to trafficking.

To achieve this expectation of performance the aggregate must possess certain properties. It must have a high level of skid-resistance as measured by the Polished Stone Value (PSV), a certain degree of strength to withstand the crushing effects of compaction and trafficking as measured by the Ten Percent Fines Value (TFV), soundness such as resistance to repeated freezing and thawing as measured by the Magnesium Sulphate Soundness Value (MSSV); and the ability to adhere to bitumen. The inter-relationships between these requirements are complex with the level of performance achieved at the road/tyre surface dependent on these and many other criteria. These were studied by Woodward (1995) who showed that rather than relying on existing simplistic recipe-type test criteria and national specification limits, in-service performance is considerably more complex and difficult to predict.

The authors believe that one such simplistic view is the belief that the AAV test method simulates the wear conditions experienced at the tyre/road interface. Rather than give an in-depth description of the conditions experienced at this interface, the following is a summary of basic conditions which exist in-service and which must be considered in any method of assessment:

- Due to rain, aggregate exposed at the surface gets wet. As shown by simple wet/dry strength testing, a wet aggregate is weaker than a dry aggregate. Therefore, assessment of wear must consider this as greater levels of abrasion occur due to the presence of moisture.
- Due to the texture of the road surfacing, a rubber pneumatic tyre moulds itself around individual chippings as it travels over their surface so causing an aggregate to lose its edges and corners and so eventually to wear away. Assessment must be able to simulate this fundamental property.
- Surfacing aggregate is frequently not of uniform composition, particularly the high PSV aggregates such as greywackes which may contain quite high percentages of softer shale chippings. Any assessment method must be able to expose the presence of this softer constituent which in practice will wear at a greater rate so causing premature loss of surface texture and ultimately skid-resistance.

These are just a number of basic in-service criteria which should be considered if one is attempting to simulate in-service performance.

Development of test methods to assess surface aggregate wear

A wide range of differing test methods have been developed to assess the wear characteristics of aggregate. There are two basic types of test:

- static wear tests e.g. grinding lap type tests where the test sample is held in a static position and ground using an abrasive e.g. Dorry Abrasion, Aggregate abrasion value, Icelandic Dorry;
- dynamic wear tests e.g. Lovegrove Attrition test, Deval test, Wet Attrition test, Los Angeles test, Texas Ball Mill test, Washington Degradation test, micro-Deval test.

This basic classification forms the basis of the comparative investigation presented in this paper as the AAV may be considered a grinding lap, static measure of dry abrasion using silica sand as the abrasive; and the MDE test as a dynamic method which measures the wearing action of aggregate against aggregate in the presence of water and an abrasive charge.

Static wear tests

Assessing aggregate abrasion using the Dorry grinding apparatus has changed little over the last century. The original Dorry Abrasion test assessed two cylinders of rock. Knight (1935) believed that "...*it has been found that the differences shown by this test for different stones do not necessarily agree with the practical experience of the behavior the stones under traffic*". In 1949 this method was developed into the Aggregate Abrasion Value (AAV) test which used a similar abrasion machine but assessed aggregate chippings rather than cylinders. In the 1951 revision of BS 812, the Dorry abrasion test was superseded by the AAV test. Following full-scale road-trials in the 1950s by the TRRL the AAV was included as one of the main specification requirements for surfacing aggregates, and has not fundamentally changed in the UK since that date.

Dissatisfaction with this type of testing has occurred elsewhere, such as Iceland with their version of the Dorry abrasion test. Torfason (1994) reported an extensive investigation of this method where test specimens were assessed in a dry condition after being subjected to 75% relative humidity before testing. This showed a greater degree of loss for the wet conditioned samples. He concluded that moisture in the sample has a marked effect when abrasion tests are undertaken.

Dynamic wear tests

In response to testing aggregate in a manner which he felt resembled the conditions experienced in-service,

Lovegrove (1929) developed one of the first attrition testing machines. This consisted of a steel cylinder with an internal lip into which the test sample was placed either with or without water. The cylinder was rotated for a number of hours and the weight loss determined. Analysis of 467 aggregate samples from England, Scotland, Wales, Ireland and certain countries in Europe showed a strong relationship between dry and wet versions of the method with the wet test giving approximately 1.8 times more attrition. This may be used as one of the first examples which clearly show the influence of moisture on aggregate performance. Although Lovegrove showed a remarkable understanding of the performance properties of aggregate, the industry has largely forgotten his work.

The only apparatus comparable to Lovegrove's machine at this time was the French Deval machine. A comparison of the two methods showed that Lovegrove's machine was typically more severe than the Deval, probably due to its internal lip. Knight (1935) reported that the best rocks gave values of less than 2% when tested in a dry condition. He felt that the test was a combination of impact and abrasion test as the stones were dropped from a height while the dust that was formed tended to act as an abrasive on the larger stones and as a cushion for the smaller. For this reason he felt that the dry version could give anomalous results.

In the late 1960s the micro-Deval test was developed. Many of the factors investigated are detailed by Tourenq (1971). The method was accepted as a French Norm and has since been proposed as a CEN test method. Elsewhere, the method is gaining supporters, particularly in Canada where Rogers (1990) concluded that the method should be adopted as a method to assess granular bases, concrete aggregate and bituminous bound aggregates.

Summary of the AAV test method

A 10 to 14 mm sized aggregate test portion is deflaked using a 20 mm flaky sieve to obtain cubic chippings. These are orientated flat, surfaces down in a steel mould and held together with resin. Two moulds are fixed in contact with a horizontally rotating lap and a Leighton Buzzard abrasive sand fed continuously onto the lap surface for 500 revolutions. The AAV is calculated as:

$$AVV = \frac{3 \times (\text{mass of specimen before abrasion} - \text{mass of specimen after abrasion})}{\text{saturated surface dry relative density}}$$

The mean of the two results is given as the AAV.

Summary of the micro-Deval test method

There are two versions of the micro-Deval test. One is carried out dry while the other has water added to the test container. Of the two methods the wet micro-Deval (MDE) is the preferred method. 500 g of 10 to 14 mm sized aggregate, 5 kg of 10 mm ball bearings and 2.5 litres of water are placed in a steel cylinder and rotated at 100 rpm for two hours. The remaining aggregate is dried and sieved using a 1.6 mm sieve. The MDE is calculated as:

$$MDE = \frac{\text{mass of aggregate} > 1.6\,mm}{\text{original mass}} \times 100$$

The mean of two results is given as the MDE. The dry micro-Deval test (MDS) is identical to the wet version except no water is added to the test container.

Aggregate sizes assessed

The aggregate sizes used in both tests are shown in Table 1. Both standard versions use the 10 to 14 mm size. With regard to alternative sizes, the MDE test may assess 14 to 20 mm, 6.3 to 10 mm and 0 to 5 mm sizes. Whilst the AAV method only assesses the single size, the MDE test is capable of testing a much wider range of aggregates, e.g. 20 mm pre-coats, 10 mm PSV chippings or the grading of fine aggregate used in bituminous mixes.

Preparation of test specimens

There is a marked difference between the two methods with regard to the preparation of test specimens. In the AAV test the sample preparation consists of deflaking single sized 10 to 14 mm chippings using a 14 to 20 mm flaky sieve. This may exclude a large percentage of the original bulk sample as supplied. Analysis of a wide range of aggregates found that only a maximum of 30% of the original material supplied was selected after the deflaking process.

This may have significant implications especially for heterogeneous aggregates such as greywackes containing flaky shale chippings. As shale typically crushes to produce a flaky chipping, which may be significantly weaker than the coarser grained greywacke component, its removal due to deflaking may have a considerable effect on the AAV result obtained.

Table 1. *Comparison of aggregate sizes used in the MDE and AAV test methods*

MDE possibilities	CEN – MDE	AAV
0 to 5 mm, 4 to 6.3 mm, 6.3 to 10 mm, 10 to 14 mm, 14 to 20 mm	10 to 14 mm	10 to 14 mm, deflaked using a 20 mm flaky sieve

Number of chippings tested

With regard to the number of chippings assessed, there is a wide difference between the two methods. In the AAV test, 23 chippings are typically held in a resin mould. In the MDE test a 500 g mass of chippings is free to rotate in a steel cylinder. To determine the number of chippings assessed in the MDE test, 500 g samples of 40 different aggregates were counted. The aggregates consisted of Tertiary basalt, Silurian greywacke, Carboniferous sandstone, Carboniferous limestone, flint gravel and crushed concrete. Table 2 summarizes the number of chippings assessed in each method. It also shows the ratio of MDE:AAV number of chippings for both methods.

It shows that, whereas 46 chippings were used in the AAV test, a mean of 433 chippings were used in the MDE test. This difference is a factor of 9.41 times greater and has an important implication in the AAV's ability to predict performance. In terms of probability, it is much more likely that the larger MDE test sample is more representative of the bulk sample than the specially prepared AAV sample.

This is further indicated where the minimum and maximum values shown are for aggregate from the same source. The minimum value of 336 chippings relates to a coarse-grained greywacke with a flakiness index (FI) of 17; whereas the maximum value of 668 relates to a shale of FI = 52. For a heterogeneous aggregate, the deflaking process of the AAV test would have removed practically all of this material.

Use of AAV and MDE test data as a specification requirement

Both tests are used as a specification requirement in their respective countries of origin. In the United Kingdom the maximum AAV values are quoted in HD 21/92 (Department of Transport 1992) for different traffic loadings. These are shown in Table 3. It can be seen that no distinction is made between different categories of site in terms of road layout but rather the categories are based on traffic numbers and intended use. However, in relation to traffic volumes on our busiest roads, counts in excess of 15 000 commercial vehicles have been recorded on sections of the M25. These are far in excess of the specification limits and suggest that aggregates of much greater resistance to abrasion are required to withstand the wear experienced at these heavily trafficked sites.

In France, road aggregate requirements are given in NFP18-321 (NF, 1982). This classifies aggregate quality using three basic test methods i.e. Los Angeles (LA), wet micro-Deval (MDE) and Coefficient de polissage accéléré (CPA) which is similar to the PSV test only the results are expressed in 0.xx form. Based on LA and MDE values, there are 5 categories of decreasing quality with category A having a CPA of >0.55, the remaining having a value of >0.50. The French classification used is shown in Table 4. The LA and MDE test methods are significantly different from their British equivalent. Whereas the British base their assessment on dry, static methods, the two equivalent French methods are dynamic and in the case of abrasion, is carried out in the presence of water. This is an important table as all three methods have been proposed as possible CEN standards.

Basic comparison of AAV and MDE test methods

One of the main aims of the research summarized in this paper is to determine basic information for the two

Table 2. *Number of chippings used in the AAV and MDE tests*

	AAV	MDE	Ratio MDE:AAV
Mean	approx. 46	433	9.41
Minimum	–	336	7.30
Maximum	–	668	14.52

Table 4. *French 1982 classification of aggregate for road works*

Category	Los Angeles	Micro-deval (wet)	CPA
A	<15	<10	>0.55
B	<20	<15	>0.50
C	<25	<20	>0.50
D	<30	<25	>0.50
E	<40	<35	>0.50

Table 3. *Traffic loadings and maximum Aggregate Abrasion Values for flexible surfacings*

Traffic in commercial vehicles per lane per day at design life	Under 250	251–1000	1001–1750	1751–2500	2501–3250	Over 3250
Maximum AAV for chippings	14	12	12	10	10	10
Maximum AAV for aggregate in coated macadam wearing courses	16	16	14	14	12	12
Coarse aggregate used in porous asphalt wearing courses	12					

Table 5. *Simple comparative statistics for MDS and MDE – all data*

	Number	Mean	Median	Minimum	Maximum	Range
MDS – all data	26	6.03	4.10	2.10	32.60	30.50
MDE – all data	26	28.07	22.40	8.60	95.60	87.00

methods. Initial work considered whether to use the wet (MDE) or dry (MDS) micro-Deval test method. This showed that the dry method was not as good at indicating differences in rock quality. Attention shifted towards building a data-base of MDE and AAV comparisons. The following details an investigation of the data obtained.

Comparison of wet and dry micro-deval test methods

In other types of testing such as determination of wet strength, the presence of moisture during testing gives a poorer result than a similar test sample tested dry. As stated earlier, the presence of moisture must be considered as a basic in-service test requirement. 26 sources of aggregate consisting of 13 Silurian greywackes, 9 Tertiary basalts, 2 Carboniferous limestones and 2 granites were assessed. They were chosen to represent a wide range of quality. The standard 10 to 14 mm wet (MDE) and dry (MDS) test was carried out on each aggregate. Simple comparative statistics are given in Table 5. It is apparent that a considerable difference exists between the dry MDS and wet MDE test methods. Generally, this difference may be accounted for by:

- the cushioning effect of dust coatings during the dry test;

- removal of the cushioning effect by water during the wet test so enhancing the wear experienced during testing;
- this enhanced level of wear which is a combination of stone against stone, stone against abrasive charge, and exploitation of weaknesses in the aggregate, e.g. from planes of weakness or from softer chippings being present in the bulk sample.

The data are plotted in Fig. 1. It is apparent that the wet data are significantly poorer than the dry data. This raises serious doubts about the ability of this dry wear test method to predict performance given that a road is frequently wet. It also raises doubts concerning the ability of dry tests in general. It can also be seen that a ranking based on rock-type exists with the basalt data having poorer MDE values.

The soaked micro-Deval test

Tests were carried out to determine if soaking in water had an effect on the resulting micro-deval value. It had been expected that this may have had a weakening effect similar to soaked strength testing. 21 sources of aggregate consisting of 11 Silurian greywackes, 8 Tertiary basalts and 2 granites were soaked in water at 20°C for 24 hours and tested using a technique similar to the

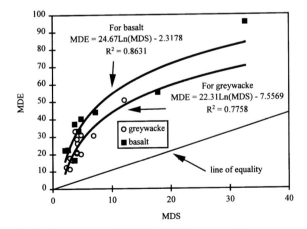

Fig. 1. Comparison of MDE and MDS test methods.

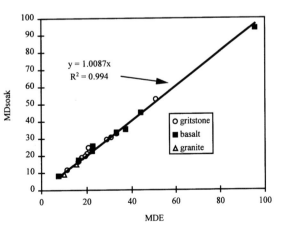

Fig. 2. Comparison of MDE and MD_{soak}.

MDE method. Their oven-dried mass after testing was used to calculate MD_{soak}. The results are plotted in Fig. 2 and show no significant difference between the two methods.

Statistical investigation of AAV data with respect to rock type

The basic statistics obtained using the standard AAV test are shown in Table 6. The majority of data meet the requirements for AAV with the mean, median, lower quartile and upper quartile all less than 11. The only exception is the column of maximum AAV values.

Statistical investigation of MDE data with respect to rock type

The basic statistics obtained for 10 to 14 mm sized aggregate using the MDE test are shown in Table 7. Using the French limit for Class A of <10 it is obvious

that the important types of surfacing aggregate such as gritstone and basalt, with means of 21.69 and 38.87 respectively, are much more susceptible to wear. In contrast, the low PSV but hard aggregates i.e. flint, granite, quartzite and porphyry are within or close to the French limit. Another point which needs to be highlighted is the range of values obtained within a single group of aggregate. This was 61.32 for gritstone and 91.51 for basalt. These are considerably greater than for the AAV test and suggest that wet dynamic testing is predicting greater levels of in-service loss than the dry AAV test.

Correlation of AAV and MDE

Linear regression and correlation analyses were performed to indicate the strength of the relationship between the two methods. The scatter plot of the complete data set is shown in Fig. 3. Correlation was first determined for 133 pairings of a wide range of rock types with further correlation determined for the gritstone and basalt. These are shown in Table 8. Contrary

Table 6. *Standard AAV test statistics*

Group	Number	Mean	Median	Min.	Max.	Range	Lower quartile	Upper quartile
all	477	7.04	6.02	0.40	40.75	40.35	4.39	8.44
artificial	9	3.93	2.69	1.02	9.9	8.88	1.45	4.80
basalt	127	8.29	7.19	1.60	33.31	31.70	5.43	9.10
flint	3	0.467	0.50	0.40	0.50	0.10	–	–
gabbro	3	3.87	4.90	1.80	4.90	3.10	–	–
granite	14	4.79	4.15	2.78	10.60	7.82	3.30	4.85
gritstone	161	6.95	6.02	2.43	38.40	35.97	4.50	7.83
limestone	55	9.34	9.30	1.70	40.75	39.05	6.20	11.00
porphyry	8	2.72	2.41	0.64	5.40	4.76	1.94	3.54
quartzite	9	5.76	5.92	3.10	8.38	5.28	4.68	6.10
schist	1	4.50	–	4.50	4.50	–	–	–
gravel	12	4.18	4.47	1.67	8.10	6.43	2.44	5.14

Table 7. *Standard MDE test statistics*

Group	Number	Mean	Median	Min.	Max.	Range	Lower quartile	Upper quartile
all	181	23.78	18.02	2.00	98.90	96.80	12.40	31.12
artificial	5	11.69	13.91	2.00	18.40	16.48	2.00	14.01
basalt	49	38.87	33.80	7.29	98.80	91.51	23.11	41.31
flint	4	6.14	4.05	3.26	13.20	9.94	3.54	8.74
gabbro	4	12.26	12.81	5.60	17.80	12.20	8.71	15.80
granite	10	11.50	7.95	2.66	28.16	25.50	3.84	12.70
gritstone	66	21.69	18.16	5.88	67.20	61.32	13.00	27.49
limestone	29	16.27	15.10	5.30	68.08	62.78	8.76	17.47
porphyry	3	6.06	6.60	2.17	9.40	7.23	–	–
quartzite	4	17.92	17.71	11.65	24.59	12.94	11.98	23.86
gravel	7	22.86	17.20	4.00	54.27	50.27	13.80	34.25

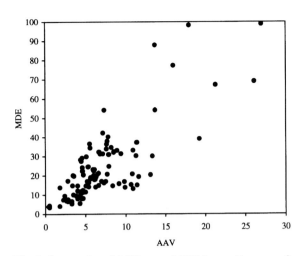

Fig. 3. Scatter plot of AAV versus MDE for a wide range of rock types.

Table 9. *Effect of density correction on the relation between MDE and AAV*

Variables	Equation	r^2
MDE, AAV	$MDE = 1.178 + 3.152\,AAV$	0.64
MDE_{dc}, AAV	$MDE_{dc} = -1.386 + 3.93\,AAV$	0.67

between the two methods. Although this density correction is insignificant at low values, as MDE increases then so does the corrected value. In practice, there will be greater degrees of chipping volume loss for high PSV surfacing aggregates that typically have poorer MDE values and lower density.

to a lack of correlation previously assumed, a significant correlation ($r^2 = 0.63$) was found to exist at a 95% level. By limiting the correlation to a single rock type it was found that the degree of correlation was greater.

The need for a density corrected MDE

During its in-service life, a combination of factors cause exposed surfacing aggregate to become rounded and, or, to be worn away. This has the effect of reducing its initial volume. This may affect surfacing performance due to loss of texture depth and skid-resistance. However, MDE simply determines the percentage loss in mass of the test sample. The authors believe that aggregate density could be incorporated into the calculation of MDE just as it is used in the AAV test method. A total of 135 MDE values for a wide range of rock-types and qualities were corrected for density.

It can be seen in Table 9 that this has improved the degree of correlation from $r^2 = 0.64$ to $r^2 = 0.67$

Use of equations to predict AAV and MDE limits

The equations obtained in Table 8 were used to predict equivalent MDE and AAV limits. This is particularly important as a MDE limit for the proposed method does not exist for British aggregates. Table 10 shows predicted values based on each test method.

If one compares the data shown in Table 10 with the French MDE limits shown in Table 4, there is a considerable difference between the results obtained and the French limit. For all data, a MDE of 32.7 is predicted for an AAV of 10; whilst this rises to 41.8 for all basalt data and drops to 30.6 for all gritstone data. This shows the influence of rock type and the need to acknowledge this if limits are to be accepted. Using the equations a MDE of 10 is equivalent to an AAV of 4.2 for all data, 2.9 for all basalt and 3.7 for all gritstone.

This correlation of test methods has important implications in the future specification of surfacing aggregate. It basically concludes that there is a contradiction in the amount of wear experienced by an aggregate. The AAV test would be conservative in its degree of prediction. In contrast, the MDE test indicates much higher levels of wear.

Table 8. *AAV and MDE correlations with regressed equations*

Type	Number	Equation	r^2
all data	133	$MDE = 1.178 + 3.152\,AAV$	0.63
all data	133	$AAV = 2.149 + 0.203\,MDE$	0.63
all gritstone data	49	$MDE = 3.605 + 2.703\,AAV$	0.68
all gritstone data	49	$AAV = 1.205 + 0.250\,MDE$	0.68
all basalt data	35	$MDE = 4.310 + 3.752\,AAV$	0.80
all basalt data	35	$AAV = 0.794 + 0.213\,MDE$	0.80

Table 10. *Prediction of AAV and MDE equivalent values*

	Predicted MDE				Predicted AAV			
	AAV = 10	AAV = 12	AAV = 14	AAV = 16	MDE = 10	MDE = 15	MDE = 25	MDE = 35
Predicted value – all data	32.7	39.0	45.3	51.6	4.2	5.2	7.2	9.3
Predicted value – all basalt data	41.8	49.3	56.8	64.3	2.9	3.9	6.2	8.2
Predicted value – all gritstone data	30.6	36.0	41.4	46.8	3.7	5.0	7.5	9.9

Ability of the AAV and MDE test methods to assess heterogeneous aggregates

Sample heterogeneity or in-homogeneity is a factor which many types of assessment have problems accounting for. Frequently, the assumption is made that the material in use is homogeneous in composition and as such behaves in a uniform and predictable manner. However, this is rarely the case. The authors believe that a surfacing's level of performance will be seriously affected by the properties of the weakest material present. If a method cannot predict the presence of a weaker constituent, i.e. because its presence is masked by a stronger constituent, then the method is seriously flawed if the aim is to predict performance. The ability of the two methods to determine which was better at assessing heterogeneous aggregates was assessed. Three different surfacing aggregate combinations were chosen to represent actual problems which are typical of certain aggregate sources, or which occur in-service. These were:

• surfacing aggregate consisting of a mixture of sound and unsound basalt

• surfacing aggregate consisting of high PSV greywacke and anorthosite
• surfacing aggregate consisting of medium grained greywacke and shale.

The aggregates used in each experiment were of uniform composition. Ten different ratios of each were assessed using the MDE test. AAV moulds were prepared using at least five different ratios. The loss in mass of these was corrected on a ratio basis depending on the density of the chippings used.

An example of the results obtained is shown in Fig. 4 for a sound (MSSV = 98.8) and unsound basalt (MSSV = 16.4) combination. Although a strong linear relationship was found for both methods the AAV test fails to warn of the presence of unsound constituents.

The gradient for each aggregate combination is shown in Table 11. In each case, a steeper gradient occurs for the MDE test suggesting that this method is better at predicting the presence of the weaker constituent. This suggestion is all the more reasonable considering that the AAV and MDE tests have comparable reproducibility of 2 to 3%. The almost flat gradients of the AAV test suggest that it is not able to highlight the presence of this material. The gradient defining the change in MDE with increasing contaminant proportion may be used to express the influence of the contaminant on predicted performance. When comparing gradients, the lowest gradient would be expected to give the best in-service combination. This simple approach could provide a performance indicator where low gradients would indicate that the contaminant does not have an influence on performance and so could be acceptable for use.

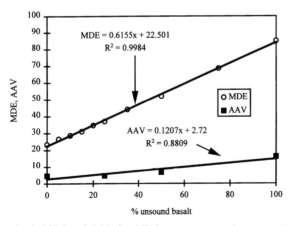

Fig. 4. MDE and AAV for differing percentages of sound and unsound basalt.

Table 11. *Comparison of AAV and MDE gradients*

Test combination	AAV gradient	MDE gradient
Sound basalt/unsound basalt	0.1207	0.6155
high PSV greywacke/anorthosite	0.1373	0.3493
greywacke/shale	0.0638	0.1373

Conclusions

The aim of this paper was to investigate two test methods which are under consideration by the highway industry at large to quantify the wear characteristics of surfacing aggregate. Basic test data, correlations and simple comparative experiments have been put forward as evidence to determine which method gives the truer indication of quality. Given the implications of the test differences for the use of aggregate in the British Isles and the levels of trafficking experienced on some of our motorways, it is important that the effect of these differences be known if the industry is to obtain the most accurate prediction of in-service wear.

Since 1992, a comparative data-base of MDE and AAV test results has been compiled with both methods investigated using a wide range of rock-types and factors thought to influence their ability to predict the performance of surfacing aggregate. The traditional view of the AAV test as a tried and dependable method to predict performance should be regarded as unsupportable.

Due to preparation of the AAV test specimen, less than 30% of the total sample is actually tested. The MDE test assesses approximately ten times as many chippings as the AAV method.

Abrasion loss during the AAV test is controlled by the harder aggregate leaving the presence of softer aggregate protected or masked. During the MDE test, each individual chipping is susceptible to the effects of wear so that this protection or masking does not occur. A correlation of $r^2 = 0.64$ was shown to exist between the two test methods.

Comparing wear as assessed by the AAV and MDE tests, there would appear to be a basic contradiction in the amount of wear. The AAV test would be conservative in its prediction, often allowing high PSV aggregates to meet specification requirements for wear resistance. In contrast, the MDE test indicates much higher levels of wear would occur. Based on regressed relations between the two tests, MDE limits of 41.8 for basalt and 30.6 for greywacke equate to the current national specification AAV limit of 10.

The MDE test is preferred to the AAV test as a method to test heterogeneous aggregates.

In conclusion, a considerable amount of information has been presented which favours the MDE test as the method which can best re-create the conditions that cause aggregate to be worn away at the road surface.

References

BRITISH STANDARDS INSTITUTION 1990. *BS 812: Part 113. Method for the Determination of Aggregate Abrasion Value.* BSI, London.

CEN 1991. *Draft Method for Determination of the Resistance to Wear of Aggregates: Micro-Deval test.* CEN/TC154/SC6.

DEPARTMENT OF TRANSPORT 1992. *Highways, Safety and Traffic Directorate, Departmental Standard, HD 21/92.* HMSO, London.

KNIGHT, B. H. 1935. Road aggregates, their use and testing. The Roadmakers Library, Vol III, Edward Arnold and Co. London.

LOVEGROVE, E. J., HOWE, J. A. & FLETT, J. S. 1929. *Attrition Tests of British Road-stones.* Memoirs of the Geological Survey and Museum of Practical Geology, HMSO, London.

NORME FRANCAISE 1982. Aggregate – characteristics of aggregates intended for road works, NF P 18-321.

——1978. The micro-deval attrition test, NF P 18-572.

ROGERS, C. A., BAILEY, M. & PRICE, B. 1991. Micro-Deval test for evaluating the quality of fine aggregate for concrete and asphalt. Ontario Ministry of Transportation, Engineering Materials Office, Report Number EM-96, June.

THOMPSON, A., GREIG, J. R. & SHAW, J. 1993. *High Specification Aggregates for Road Surfacing Materials: Technical Report.* Department of the Environment, London.

TORFOSEN, K. 1994. Wear resistance. *The Icelandic Aggregates Committee Symposium,* 37–48, March, Reykjavik, Iceland.

TOURENQ, C. 1971. L'essai micro-Deval. *Bulletin de Liaison Laboratoires Central des Ponts et Chaussées,* **54,** 69–76.

WOODWARD, W. D. H. 1995. *Laboratory Prediction of Surfacing Aggregate Performance.* DPhil Thesis, School of the Built Environment, University of Ulster.

Possible problems with high PSV aggregate of the gritstone trade group

A. R. Woodside, P. Lyle, W. D. H. Woodward and M. J. Perry

Highway Engineering Research Centre, School of the Built Environment, University of Ulster, 75 Belfast Road, Carrickfergus, Co. Antrim BT 38 8PU, UK

Abstract. This paper considers the methods of assessment of high PSV greywacke aggregate from the Longford Down Massif. It reviews current specification requirements concluding that PSV is regarded as the most important surfacing aggregate property in the UK. Using a set of data, PSV is correlated with other test properties including AIV, TFV, MSSV, AAV and MDE. Despite poor correlations, the data shows general trends between properties indicating that PSV is achieved at the expense of other test properties.

The resistance to skidding of a road surface, particularly when wet, is a serious problem to the British highway engineer. According to Young (1985), skidding was reported in 28% of accidents occurring on wet roads in 1980. Hosking (1986) calculated that an increase of 0.10 in sideways force coefficient of the road surface skidding resistance would lead to a 13% reduction in the wet road skidding rate. Traditionally skid resistance is regarded as the most important property required of a road surface to ensure an adequate level of safety for the road user.

In the British Isles the ability of aggregate to maintain an adequate level of skid resistance is assessed using the Polished Stone Value (PSV) test method (BS 812, 1989b). This value of skid-resistance is considered to be the most important property of a surfacing aggregate and forms the basis for specification requirements. Rather than accepting the view that high PSV is the aggregate's main property, the authors of this paper dispute this accepted philosophy. Using a new set of data this paper examines how reliance on a single test method may be resulting in the use of aggregate that may not be providing the most cost efficient, durable and safe road surface.

The role of texture

Aggregate makes up more than 90% by mass of bituminous surfacing materials. The resulting level of skid resistance is largely dependant on the type of aggregate used (Dahir 1979). One of the main aggregate factors influencing skid resistance is texture i.e. the macro texture (0.5–15 mm scale) or texture depth of the road surface and the micro-texture (<0.5 mm scale) of the aggregate surface. These two types of texture influence the adhesion and hysteresis properties between tyre and road and hence its safety to the road user (Adul-Malak et al. 1988). The adhesion component is considered to be the shear strength developed in the area of actual contact of the rubber tyre with the surface of the aggregate. The hysteresis component is caused by damping losses within the rubber as the tyre rolls over and around the aggregate on the surface.

The micro-texture controls the adhesion component and the macro-texture controls the hysteresis. A drop in skid resistance occurs with increasing speed on wet surfaces. This is minimized where drainage paths for the water exist. These are provided by the tyre tread pattern and the surface texture of the road. Therefore, macro-texture also governs the drainage capacity of the surface. It is important that excess water is removed so that only a thin film of water remains that can be penetrated by the vehicle tyre insuring dry contact at the interface. To provide this property, a road surface in the British Isles should have an average texture depth of least 1.5 mm and is created by the use of coarse aggregate in a macadam mix, 20 mm chippings applied to hot rolled asphalt, or by surface dressings.

Micro-texture is provided by the surface of the exposed aggregate. Small-scale asperities on the aggregate surface are necessary to break through the film of water between road surface and tyre. Neville (1974) showed that micro-texture has important effects on the low speed skid resistance of aggregate exposed to traffic. It is the polishing from vehicle tyres that reduces the micro-texture. Sabey (1966) showed that at speeds up to 30 mph, the coefficient of friction is largely dependant on the state of polish i.e. micro-texture is more important than macro-texture. The macro-texture becomes important at higher speeds where the penetration of the water film is less successful due to the reduced contact time.

Traditional selection of surfacing aggregate in the British Isles

Recently, Travers Morgan Ltd. (Thompson et al. 1993) compiled a report for the Department of Transport of

WOODSIDE, A. R., LYLE, P., WOODWARD, W. D. H. & PERRY, M. J. 1998. Possible problems with high PSV aggregate of the gritstone trade group. In: LATHAM, J.-P. (ed.) 1998. Advances in Aggregates and Armourstone Evaluation. Geological Society, London, Engineering Geology Special Publications, **13**, 159–167.

the United Kingdom concerning sources of High Specification Aggregate (HSA) in the British Isles. The basic finding of this was that the predominant source of such aggregate belonged to the gritstone trade group of BS 63 (1987). In this survey, the main aggregate requirement used was PSV. However, it may be argued that a misleading picture of HSA has been painted. The research summarized in this paper, including that of the TRRL and other researchers, has indicated that the highest levels of PSV are only achievable at the expense of other properties such as abrasion resistance, strength and durability.

If one was to review aggregate research, particularly that concerning those types of aggregate that can give high PSV, many of the conclusions are contrary to what the industry would like to think. Hopkins (1959) considered the problem of providing non-skid surfacing aggregate which even at this time was being sought to the exclusion of everything else. However, Hopkins believed that "...*many good properties are necessary to make a good roadstone ... all aggregates polish under traffic, in varying amounts, except the gritstones, which disintegrate, and so continue to present fresh edges to the passing tyres until worn away*".

In relation to accelerated polishing tests only giving high results for gritstones, Hopkins pointed out that being "...*somewhat soft ... they ... might not be suitable for use on the road, especially on difficult sites. It is of little use having a stone of high P.S.C. if its rate of wear under traffic is so high that its life is very short.*"

As regards availability of aggregates to meet the highest specified requirements, Hopkins believed that the "...*necessary aggregates are not available ... it may be that we have arrived now, or shall arrive in the near future, at a state where we shall have done all we can with the natural resources available, and the responsibility will then rest on the shoulders of the road designers, and drivers*".

This was written in 1959, long before the levels of trafficking and stress now experienced by aggregate in modern types of surfacing material. It is interesting to note that in 1959 it was recognized that a limit of performance had been achieved. Hopkins saw that the only way to achieve improvement was by the use of new mixes and uses of aggregate. Almost 35 years later, Hot Rolled Asphalt (HRA) is still dominant with a growing interest in new mixes from the more progressive surfacing contractors.

This identification of certain aggregate types, as termed of the highest quality in the Travers Morgan report (Thompson *et al.* 1993) of being susceptible to in-service problems was however known long before Hopkins. Knight (1935) concluded that "*the sedimentary rocks of this country are, as a whole, definitely inferior for the use as macadam and chippings ... this is shown not only by the physical tests, but also by their behaviour under service conditions ... the sedimentary rocks are,* however, *suitable for use on roads where the traffic is sufficiently light, such as estate roads and unclassified roads*". In the time of Knight more emphasis was placed on physical properties such as strength and attrition. Prior to this, Lovegrove *et al.* (1929) had also indicated that sedimentary rocks, in particular the Pennant Sandstones as highlighted by Thompson *et al.* (1993) were susceptible to greater levels of attrition loss.

Sources of aggregate used

In Northern Ireland, Silurian greywackes from the Central Belt of the Longford Down Massif are extensively quarried as an important source of gritstone aggregate. The greywackes consist of mostly medium sand-sized grains held together by a matrix of mostly clay and chlorite minerals. After deposition, the Central Belt suffered regional metamorphism to 350°C and pressures equivalent to a burial depth of 9–14 km. This combination of heating, compaction and rough sandpaper type texture has resulted in an aggregate with good hardness, durability and skid resistance. Over 50 samples were taken from 11 quarries. The majority were collected from production stock-piles with the remainder being selected lump samples which were crushed in the laboratory.

Test methods used

The following test methods were used:

- Polished Stone Value (PSV) BS 812: Part 114 (1989*b*)
- Water Absorption (WA) BS 812 : Part 2 (1975)
- Aggregate Impact Value (AIV) BS 812: Part 112 (1989*c*)
- Ten Percent Fines Value (TFV) BS 812: Part 111 (1989*d*)
- Aggregate Abrasion Value (AAV) BS 812: Part 113 (1989*e*)
- Magnesium Sulphate Soundness Value (MSSV) BS 812: Part 121 (1989*a*)
- Micro-Deval (MDE) CEN TC154 TG7/09/5 (1991)

British Standard BS 812 contains many of the test methods currently specified to assess aggregate. Most of the tests are performed on 10 to 14 mm aggregate. The main exception is PSV which tests the −10 mm size. The PSV test assesses the relative resistance of aggregate to polishing under conditions similar to the action of vehicular tyres on the road surface. Aggregate samples are first subjected to the polishing action of an accelerated polishing machine. The state of polish obtained is measured by a friction test and expressed as the PSV.

As the name implies, WA is a fundamental property of aggregate. AIV gives a relative assessment of its resistance to a sudden shock load when a sample of 10 to

Table 1. Minimum PSV of chippings related to site categories and traffic (Department of Transport 1992)

Site category	Site definition (commercial vehicles/lane/day)	100	100–250	251–500	501–750	751–1000	1001–1250	1251–1500	1501–1750	1751–2000	2001–2250	2251–2500	2501–2750	2751–3250	3250+
I A	Motorway	55								57		60		65	68
B	Dual carriage non-event sections														
D	Dual carriage minor junctions														
II C	Single carriage non-event sections	45	50	53		55	57		60	63		65		68	
E	Single carriage minor junctions														
III F	Approaches to and across major junctions	50	55	57	60		63		65		68		>70		
G1	Gradient 5% to 10% longer than 50 m, dual (downhill) single (uphill and downhill)														
H1	Bend radius 100–124 m														
L	Roundabout														
IV G2	Gradient >10% longer than 50 m, dual (downhill) single (uphill and downhill)	55		63		65		68		>70			artificial		
H2	Bend radius <100 m														
V J/K	Approaches to roundabouts, traffic signals, pedestrian crossings or similar	63	65	68		>70							artificial		

Table 2. *Traffic loadings and maximum Aggregate Abrasion Values (HD 21/92)*

Traffic in commercial vehicles/lane/day	Under 250	251–1000	1001–1750	1751–2500	2501–3250	Over 3250
Maximum AAV for chippings	14	12	12	10	10	10
Maximum AAV for aggregate in coated macadam wearing courses	16	16	14	14	12	12
Coarse aggregate for use in porous asphalt wearing course	12					

14 mm chippings is subjected to a sudden load 15 times. The amount of fines generated is measured and expressed as the AIV. The greater the amount of fines, the larger the AIV. TFV is the force in kN that is required to produce ten percent of fine material that will pass the 2.36 mm sieve from an original 10 to 14mm sample. The aggregate is crushed under a gradually applied compressive load.

AAV is a measure of aggregate resistance to abrasive wear of specially prepared moulds that are abraded using a grinding lap in the presence of abrasive sand. The loss in weight is described as the AAV. The MSSV test is used to assess the soundness of aggregate. Samples of 10 to 14 mm aggregate are placed in wire baskets and subjected to five cycles of immersion in a saturated solution of magnesium sulphate followed by oven drying. The samples are then sieved on a 10 mm sieve and the MSSV calculated as the percentage of material retained.

At present the testing of aggregate within Europe is under discussion and an attempt at selecting a range of most appropriate European test methods under progress. The French MDE test has been proposed to replace the AAV test for the assessment of wear and so was included in the investigation. The MDE assesses the wear produced by friction between an aggregate sample and an abrasive charge in a rotating drum. A test sample of 500 g of 10 to 14 mm aggregate is placed in a drum with 5 kg of 10 mm ball bearings and 2500 ml of water and the drum rotated for two hours. MDE is given by the percentage of material lost through wear as determined from the material greater than 1.6 mm in size after testing.

Specifications and recommendations for surfacing aggregate

In the British Isles the main specification for surfacing aggregate is the Specification for Highway Works (SHW). This is published as Volume 1 of the Manual of Contract Documents for Highways Works (Department of Transport 1991). The SHW is a national specification that aims to cover all highway contracts from the provision of new, to the improvement or reconstruction of existing roads.

The current guidelines for specification requirements for bituminous bound road aggregate are given in

Clause 901 of the SHW and in the Highways, Safety and Traffic Directorate Departmental Standard HD 21/92 (Department of Transport 1992). HD 21/92 defines the specification requirements for PSV and AAV for new bituminous surfacing. Requirements for PSV at different categories of highway layout and different traffic flows are given in Table 1. The PSV values given in Table 1 are for coarse aggregate used in HRA, surface dressing chippings and in porous asphalt surfacings.

The requirements for AAV at different traffic levels are given in Table 2 from HD 21/92. No distinction between different site categories is made, however distinction is made on traffic numbers and the intended surfacing material the aggregate is used in. It can be seen that a maximum AAV of 16 is permitted for lightly trafficked roads; this reduces to 10 for heavily trafficked sections. The minimum requirements used in the Travers Morgan report (Thompson *et al.* 1993) for High Specification Aggregate (HSA) are given in Table 3.

The required values for PSV given in Table 1 are five points higher than the values needed to maintain the associated levels of skid resistance according to the investigation of Thompson *et al.* (1993). This may be due to the following reasons:

- the natural variability of aggregate
- the lack of precision of the PSV test
- variations in estimating traffic flows
- the effect of turning movements and traction forces at major junctions and on gradients
- the deterioration of skid resistance with time

It can be seen that the PSV requirement increases with traffic levels and with the relative risk at each site category. In fact a PSV of 68 or greater is specified for

Table 3. *Minimum requirements for High Specification Aggregate (Thompson et al. 1993)*

Property	Limiting value
Polished Stone Value (PSV)	⩾58
Aggregate Abrasion Value (AAV)	⩽16
Aggregate Impact Value (AIV)	⩽30
Ten Percent Fines (TFV)	⩾140 kN
Magnesium Sulphate Value (MSSV)	⩾75%

the most heavily trafficked sections whatever the road site definition and skidding risk. In summary the specifications require the highest PSV aggregate to be placed wherever trafficking is greatest, i.e. an aggregate must be able to provide skid resistance whilst satisfying other criteria such as abrasion resistance. It is this necessary combination of properties that was examined by the authors in order to see whether a high PSV tends to imply a loss of durability.

Correlation between PSV and other test methods

The degree of correlation between PSV and the other properties was examined. Using the regression equations obtained for each relationship, PSV values were predicted based on currently used specification limits of other test methods. The aim of this was to determine whether high PSV aggregate might in-service be suspect or likely to be subject to excessive wear and poor durability according to the results of various other tests that measure wear resistance and durability.

PSV against WA

In Fig. 1, the PSV obtained from 44 aggregate samples is plotted against WA. The relationship is best described using the following equation:

$$PSV = 4.43WA + 54.9$$

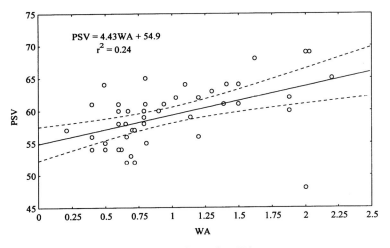

Fig. 1. PSV against WA.

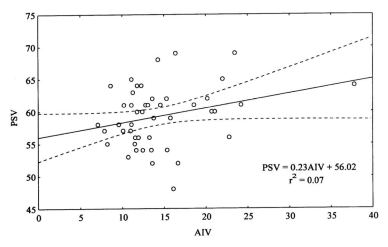

Fig. 2. PSV against AIV.

The r^2 correlation coefficient was 0.24 with a considerable scatter of the data. Using a maximum limit for WA of 2 to predict PSV from the above equation a PSV of 64 was derived. This would suggest that greywacke aggregate with PSV greater than 64 may have suspect durability.

PSV against AIV

In Fig. 2, PSV is plotted against AIV. If the outlying points are included the relationship is best described by the following equation:

$$PSV = 0.23AIV = 55.02$$

R^2 was found to be 0.07 which is low and non-significant at the 95% level and would indicate that PSV may not be predicted from its AIV.

PSV against TFV

Figure 3 is a plot of PSV against TFV. The best-fit linear relationship is as follows:

$$PSV = -0.03TFV + 70.13$$

The relationship has a r^2 value of -0.22. Again this suggests a poor relation between PSV and strength as measured by the TFV test. However, using this equation, a TFV of 140 kN would equate to a PSV of 66.

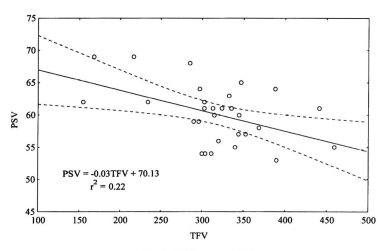

Fig. 3. PSV against TFV.

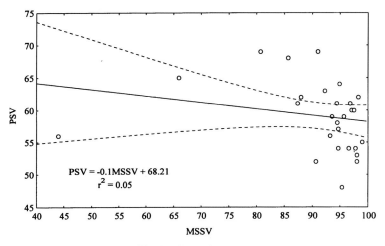

Fig. 4. PSV against MSSV.

PSV against MSSV

In Fig. 4, PSV is plotted against MSSV. The data is very unevenly distributed and with a standard linear regression analysis, the low MSSV results have an unrepresentatively large influence. This best-fit linear equation is:

$$PSV = -0.1MSSV + 68.21$$

The relationship has a r^2 of 0.05. Using a maximum limit for MSSV of 75, the above equation predicts a PSV of 61 although very little confidence can be attached to this prediction.

PSV against AAV

Figure 5 is a plot of PSV against AAV. The best-fit linear relationship is as follows

$$PSV = 1.08AAV + 53.23$$

This relationship has a r^2 of 0.34. Using the a limit for AAV of 10 a PSV of 64 was predicted. This indicates that an aggregate with a PSV greater than this may not have sufficient resistance to wear caused by high traffic loadings.

PSV against MDE

Figure 6 plots PSV against MDE. The best-fit linear relationship is as follows

$$PSV = 0.30MDE + 53.35$$

The relationship has a r^2 of 0.46. This was the best correlation of the different test methods with PSV. Using a MDE value of 30, a PSV of 62 was predicted which is slightly lower than that predicted using AAV.

Discussion

The coarse aggregate used in a wearing course must have a combination of properties to maintain both macro- and micro-texture. The investigation was based on greywacke aggregate from the Longford Down Massif. Although poor correlations were obtained, they all clearly indicate that improvement in PSV is achieved at the expense of all other aggregate properties. Table 4 is a summary of the relationships obtained between PSV and other aggregate properties. The table includes limit values which in the authors' experience are often quoted for high specification road surfacing aggregates where quality is based on tests other than PSV. These 'other' test limits have been converted to equivalent PSV limits using the equations shown.

It is apparent that these somewhat tentative equations are predicting a maximum acceptable PSV for this type of gritstone group aggregate to lie somewhere between 61 to 66 i.e. an aggregate with a PSV greater than this may be susceptible to insufficient strength, poor durability or some other type of failure. Even if the low confidence in the equations is to be acknowledged, the high variation in test values occurring with small variation in the PSV is remarkable (see Figs 1, 5 & 6).

These findings bring into question the philosophy of national surfacing specification limits for all types of aggregate used in the British Isles. HD 21/92 sets out the requirement for PSV greater than or equal to 68 for heavily trafficked, high risk site categories. It is apparent from the work outlined in this paper that such aggregates are more likely to have strength and durability problems.

Conclusions

This paper has considered the implications of the possible over-reliance of a single aggregate test property i.e. skid resistance as measured in the laboratory using the PSV test. The data obtained indicates that the specification and use of very high PSV aggregate in a heavily trafficked modern road environment may result in premature failure. In the rare cases where high PSV is combined with excellent performance in the tests for durability and strength, there is no problem; but these materials are scarce for the physical reasons that endow high PSV properties.

Table 4. *PSV correlations and regression equations*

Variables PSV, 'OTHER'	Number of samples	Equation obtained	R^2	Acceptance Limit for 'OTHER' test	Predicted Acceptance Limit for PSV
PSV, WA	44	PSV = 4.43WA + 54.90	0.24	⩽2	⩽64
PSV, AIV	46	PSV = 0.23AIV + 56.02	0.07	⩽30	⩽63
PSV, TFV	28	PSV = −0.03TFV + 70.13	0.22	⩾140	⩽66
PSV, MSSV	28	PSV = −0.10MSSV + 68.21	0.05	⩾75	⩽61
PSV, AAV	38	PSV = 1.08AAV + 53.23	0.34	⩽10	⩽64
PSV, MDE	35	PSV = 0.30MDE + 53.35	0.46	⩽30	⩽62

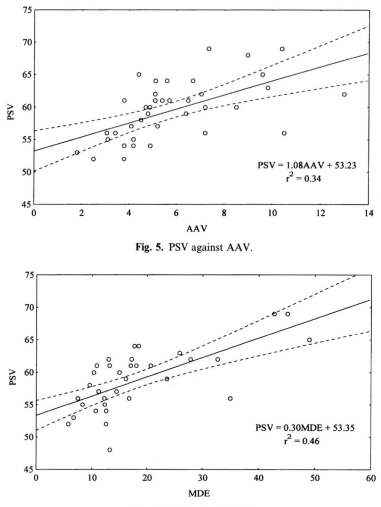

Fig. 5. PSV against AAV.

Fig. 6. PSV against MDE.

If one first considers the PSV test method, it is about 50 years old and has changed relatively little in that period. This is in contrast to modern trafficking conditions which have changed significantly. Although the test simulates in-service factors such as water, traffic loading, presence of detritus etc. it cannot adequately simulate real in-service conditions were there is great variation in traffic conditions, stressing, and types of aggregate use. Rather than predicting performance, the method simply ranks one aggregate with another within the laboratory or between laboratories, with relatively low confidence limits for an aggregate test.

Due to the British philosophy of regarding skid-resistance as the most important property for surfacing aggregate it may also be possible to suggest that too much emphasis is placed on the importance of PSV as a specification requirement. As a result, the test has favoured the use of a single type of surfacing aggregate i.e. gritstone, with many types of aggregate that are important in other countries being excluded. This has the effect of severely limiting the number of sources available, particularly if the aggregate industry is to supply aggregates conforming to the highest specification category.

Based on the investigations reported in this paper it would appear that small increases for higher PSV aggregates correspond to large decreases in the other desirable properties. Adequate in-service performance and skid related accident reduction is a combination of both macro- and micro-texture and both must be acknowledged if a cost-effective and long-lasting road surface is the aim. Rather than create a short-term high skid-resistant surfacing, it has been shown that if greywacke aggregate in the range 60 to 65 is used, then it will create a longer lasting surfacing whilst maintaining skid resistance.

In conclusion, the work indicates that the specification of surfacing aggregate needs to be reviewed. The authors recommend that rather than relying on national specification limits, there is a need to set acceptable and realistic limits based on specific rock types if the aim is to produce a safe, economic and long-lasting road surfacing.

References

ADUL-MALAK, M. U., PAPALEONTIOU, C. G., FOWLER, D. W. & MEYER, A. H. 1988. *Investigation of the Frictional Resistance of Seal Coat Pavement Surfaces.* Research Report 490–1, University of Texas.

BRITISH STANDARDS INSTITUTION 1975. *BS812: Part2– Methods for determination of physical properties.* BSI, London.

——1987. *BS63: Part 1 –Specification for Single Sized Aggregate for General Purposes*, BSI, London.

——1989a. *BS812: Part 121 – Method for the Determination of Soundness*, BSI, London.

——1989b. *BS812: Part 114 – Method for the Determination of Polished Stone Value*, BSI, London.

——1989c. *BS812: Part 112 – Method for the Determination of Aggregate Impact Value*, BSI, London.

——1989d. *BS81: Part 111 – Method for the Determination of Ten Percent Fines Value*, BSI, London.

——1989e. *BS812: Part 113 – Method for the Determination of Aggregate Abrasion Value*, BSI, London.

CEN TC 154 TG7/09/5:1991. Draft test method: Determination of resistance to wear (Micro-Deval).

DAHIR, S. N. 1979. A Review of Aggregate Selection Criteria for Improved Wear Resistance and Skid Resistance of Bituminous Surfaces. *Journal of Testing and Evaluation*, **7**, 245–253.

DEPARTMENT OF TRANSPORT 1976. Specification requirements for aggregate properties and texture depth for bituminous surfacings to new roads. Technical Memorandum H16/76.

——1991. *Specification for Highway Works*, 7th edition. Manual of Contract Documents for Highway Works, Volume 1. HMSO, London.

——1992. Highways, Safety and Traffic Directorate, Departmental Standard, HD 21/92.

HOPKINS, L. C. 1959. The problems with providing aggregates for road surfacing materials which have good non-skid properties. Institute of Highway Engineers.

HOSKING, J. R. 1986. Relationship between skidding resistance and accident frequency: Estimates based on seasonal variation. Research Report 76. Transport and Road Research Laboratory, Crowthorne, Berkshire, UK.

KNIGHT, B. H. 1935. Road aggregates, their use and testing. The Roadmakers Library, Volume III, Edward Arnold and Co. London.

LOVEGROVE, E. J., HOWE, J. A., FLETT, J. S. 1929. *Attrition Tests of British Road-stones*. Memoirs of the Geological Survey and Museum of Practical Geology, HMSO, London.

NEVILLE, G. 1974. *A Study of the Mechanism of Polishing of Roadstones by Traffic*. Department of the Environment, TRRL Laboratory Report LR 621. Transport and Road Research Laboratory. Crowthorne.

SABEY, B. E. 1966. *Road Surface Texture and the Change in Skidding Resistance with Speed*. Ministry of Transport, RRL Report LR 20. Road Research Laboratory. Harmondsworth.

THOMPSON, A. GREIG, J. R. & SHAW, J. 1993. *High Specification Aggregates for Road Surfacing Materials: Technical Report*. Department of the Environment , London. Travers Morgan Ltd., East Grinstead.

YOUNG, A. E. 1985. *The Potential for Accident Reduction by Improving Urban Skid Resistance Levels*. PhD Thesis, Queen Mary College, University of London.

A statistical study of aggregate testing data with respect to engineering judgement

Richard J. Howarth[1] & William J. French[2]

[1] Department of Geological Sciences, University College London, Gower Street, London
WC1E 6BT, UK
[2] Geomaterials Group, School of Engineering, Queen Mary and Westfield College, Mile End Road,
London E1 4NS, UK

Abstract. Aspects of product-testing and measurement uncertainty are addressed with the intention of providing guidelines to enable engineering judgements to be made which are based on valid scientific criteria. Suggestions are made to enable improved estimates of: (1) the critical range when defining measurement uncertainty; (2) the number of tests required to ensure, with a stated probability, that there is a 95% probability that the estimated mean lies within a stated absolute amount of the underlying population mean; (3) confidence intervals for a *single* determination; (4) confidence intervals on observed abundance in point- or grain-counts, including an *exact* upper bound on the proportion of a constituent which could be present (e.g. opal or chert as a contaminant) when no occurrences have been observed; (5) confidence interval on the proportion of sub-standard product present in a source of bulk material, on the basis of routine testing of a continuously delivered product. *J*-charts for the mean and range are also introduced as an aid to quality assurance. These have excellent performance compared to the better-known Shewhart and cusum charts and are well-suited to manual implementation at a 'shop-floor' level.

Although modern structures may be written off, both by accountants and in practice, in a few decades, a design life of some 200 years or more may be specified. To make modern construction materials of such durability requires critical assessment of materials tests and statistical appraisal not only of the plausible life-expectancy, but also of the associated coefficient of variation of the materials quality. This paper is concerned with aspects of the ways in which product-testing and related specifications can be considered so that engineering judgements can be made which are based on valid scientific criteria. Coefficients of variation can be very large and assessments based on current test procedures can easily be a triumph of hope over realistic judgement. The way in which tests are carried out and the associated errors means that, at least in some cases, the results may be only accidentally valid. Anyone who still believes that BS 5750 (ISO 9000) accreditation by a supplier is in-itself an adequate guarantee of product quality should read the illuminating discussion in Stickley & Winterbottom (1994).

It is suggested that there is a need for at least higher levels of replication than are currently recommended and in some cases, the tests themselves may need significant improvement. Diagnosis of the potential for aggregate instability, for example, requires a substantial investigative programme before concrete mixes are designed or specified. Consideration is given to the factors influencing the magnitude of such test results and to the additional natural diversity provided by the sources of materials.

Measurement uncertainty

Two main categories of error may arise in using a particular test procedure. These are *random errors*, which cause random positive and negative deviations about the underlying population mean, and *systematic errors* which contribute to a shift in the mean of many determinations away from the true (but usually unknown) value of the attribute whose value is being determined. Systematic errors may be of either short-term or long-term duration and their existence contributes to the degree of overall bias (i.e. the difference between the true and measured result) in the test procedure. If the bias is small, the test method is regarded as being accurate; if the amount of variance in the test procedure is small, then it is regarded as being precise. It is a common misconception that a test method that is precise will also be accurate.

It is possible to quantify the precision of a test method on the basis of its *repeatability*, characterized by a measure of the total within-laboratory (sample preparation plus test) variance, based on identical samples tested under essentially identical conditions; and *reproducibility*, a measure of the between-laboratory variation achievable

HOWARTH, R. J. & FRENCH, W. J. 1998. A statistical study of aggregate testing data with respect to engineering judgement. *In*: LATHAM, J.-P. (ed.) 1998. *Advances in Aggregates and Armourstone Evaluation*. Geological Society, London, Engineering Geology Special Publications, **13**, 169–183.

when testing a standard reference material (Technical Committee CEN/TC 154 1994, 1995a). The magnitudes of the reproducibility and repeatability of the test procedure are expressed in terms of the standard deviations of the various contributory stages (e.g. sampling, bulk-sample reduction, laboratory-sample reduction, and within- and between-laboratory testing) as determined by a formal analysis of variance procedure based on a well-designed series of experiments. The only way that an estimate of the reproducibility of a particular test method can really be assessed is through an inter-laboratory trial involving at least six laboratories; trueness can only be assessed using a prepared (e.g. spiked) reference material. Considerable effort has already been expended by the analytical chemistry community to determine the most effective procedures for undertaking 'round robin' collaborative trials (using a prescribed method) and co-operative trials (using methods which are not prescribed) and methods for organisation and proficiency testing of laboratories (Analytical Methods Committee 1987, 1989a, b, 1992; Mandel 1991). New approaches, such as the use of robust analysis of variance (an analysis of variance procedure which down-weights the influence of any outlying results) have proved very effective (Analytical Methods Committee 1989a, b, 1992) and could be advantageously adopted for use in analysis of collaborative trials in the aggregate-testing field.

One frequently encounters in published papers, reports, and even the current draft European Standards for aggregates, expressions of measurement uncertainty (or required working conditions, such as variation in a controlled temperature environment) given simply as $x \pm \delta$ without any indication as to how δ is defined. It is suggested that, in order to avoid any chance of misunderstanding by a reader as to what δ implies (e.g. the half-range, 1.0-, 1.96- or 2.0-times the standard deviation, standard error of the mean, probable error, uncertainty, expanded uncertainty, or plain guesswork, etc.), the meaning of the uncertainty parameter should be explicitly defined the first time it is used in any article or report, a point which has been made repeatedly in the past (e.g. Eisenhart 1968). A recent trend, derived from the science of metrology and becoming enshrined in the new European Standards (Analytical Methods Committee 1995; Technical Committee CEN/TC 154 1995a), is to express the uncertainty of results in the form of a prediction interval. The *critical range* (otherwise known as the *expanded uncertainty*) is defined as $\delta = k\sigma_a$ where k is the coverage factor. In this case, δ is the value within which the range of n future determinations made to obtain a test result using the same procedure could be expected to lie, with a probability of 95%, given an estimate of the standard deviation of a single determination (σ_a) based on m prior observations.

The draft European Standard defining repeatability and reproducibility for use in aggregate testing (Technical Committee CEN/TC 154 1995a) does not explain

on what basis the coverage factor quoted (*ibid.*, Table 1, p. 6) is derived, nor does it cite the source of the table. Comparison with Table A13 of Hahn & Meeker (1991) shows that the factors given match those for a two-sided $100(1 - \alpha) = 95\%$ prediction interval, where α is the desired level of risk, based on the normal distribution; the prior estimate of the standard deviation corresponds to a sample-size of six observations; and the intervals apply to $n = 1$ to 5 future observations (*not* 2 to 6, as stated in the draft standard).

Other values of the coverage factor should be applied if different prior sample sizes are used. A slightly conservative approximation to the tabled values (Hahn & Meeker 1991) is given by

$$k_{1-\alpha;m,n} \cong (1 + 1/n)^{0.5} t_{1-\alpha/(2m),n-1} \qquad (1)$$

where $t_{1-\alpha/2m}$ is $100(1 - \alpha/2m)$th percentile of 'Student's' (W. S. Gossett) t-distribution with $(n - 1)$ degrees of freedom.

How many tests?

Judgement of the number of tests required to obtain a given result is dependent on the *a priori* judgement of the precision required. If the judgement is that the magnitude of the precision needed is, say, an order of magnitude worse than that given by the test method, it is obvious that a single test might suffice for the given purpose. Where the source of material might be varied, or the test complex, or the resultant precision is of a magnitude of the same order as that required, the number of test results required needs to be calculated with care.

A common practical requirement in undertaking an experimental programme aimed at measuring the variance inherent in a new procedure, or to determine whether a critical limit has been exceeded (e.g. the expansion of concrete bars as a result of alkali-aggregate reaction) etc. is to estimate how many tests should be made to be $100(1 - \alpha)\%$ certain that the observed result, computed on the basis of n experiments, will lie within an absolute amount (Δ) of the population mean (μ). The classical formula used to solve this sample-size problem (equation (2)), given in many statistical textbooks as well as the recent *Aggregate Handbook* (Marek 1991) is:

$$n = (z_{1-\alpha/2}\sigma_0/\Delta)^2 \qquad (2)$$

where $z_{1-\alpha/2}$ is the $100(1 - \alpha/2)$th percentile of the cumulative normal distribution, e.g. if $\alpha = 0.05$, $z_{1-0.025} = 1.96$; and σ_0 is a prior estimate of the standard deviation of the process available either from analogues or, preferably, from the results of earlier experimental work. The formula assumes that the frequency distribution for the random errors inherent in the process is normal. However, Kupper & Hafner (1989) showed that since this widely used formula is based on a large-sample approximation, it gives sample sizes that are too small; an effect which becomes noticeably worse as the estimated value of n becomes smaller (Fig. 1). Indeed, they consider that the sample sizes given by (2) behave so poorly 'in all instances' that its 'future use should be strongly discouraged.' In general, given a sample of n independent values of a variate conforming to a given distribution, a tolerance probability (β) enables one to assert with confidence β that a proportion γ of the population will lie between stated upper and lower bounds. A satisfactory approximation to their tabulated corrected sample sizes, which have an associated tolerance probability β, chosen by the user, that μ will lie within the computed 95% confidence interval, is given by the appropriate values of (3), rounded up to the nearest integer.

$$n_{adj} = n + \begin{cases} 2.261n^{0.309}; & \beta = 70\% \\ 3.122n^{0.449}; & \beta = 95\% \\ 4.027n^{0.459}; & \beta = 99\% \end{cases} \quad (3)$$

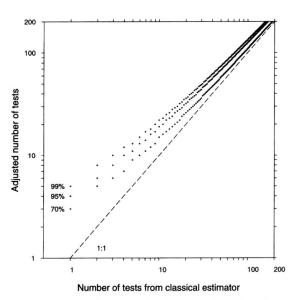

Fig. 1. Kupper–Hafner correction for the total number of tests which should be made to be 70, 95 or 99% confident that there is a 95% probability that the observed result computed on the basis of n tests, given by the classical formula (equation (2)), will lie within an absolute amount (Δ) of the population mean (μ). Choose the desired tolerance level; enter abscissa with the number of tests given by equation (2); project vertically up to the required set of points; read off the adjusted number of tests from the ordinate. For example, if the initial estimate from equation (2) is 1 test, a total of three tests will actually be required in order to have 70% confidence that the requirements of the test programme will be met.

Suppose that Point Load Tests on three granite specimens from a quarry produced a mean Is_{50} value of 6.14 MPa and a standard deviation(σ_0) of 0.67 MPa. Based on this prior information (and assuming that the random errors attributable to sampling plus measurement follow a normal distribution) what is the total number of tests which should should be carried out to ensure that the estimated mean Is_{50} value is within 0.5 MPa of the population mean? Classical theory (2) suggests that seven tests should be adequate, whereas the Kupper–Hafner correction (3) indicates that for one to be 90% confident that there is a 95% probability that μ is estimated to within ±0.5 MPa, 14 tests are actually necessary. Even a 70% tolerance probability would still require 11 tests in total, so if the time and/or cost of carrying out so many tests is not warranted, then the required bound is unrealistically tight.

Confidence intervals on a single determination

Consider a situation in which only a *single* experimental observation (x) has been obtained and it is required to estimate a $100(1 - \alpha)\%$ two-sided confidence interval on the mean. A situation in which this might naturally arise is if a 365-day concrete expansion or strength measurement has been obtained and there is not the available time to run a similar lengthy test. If possible, we first assume that the observation is drawn from a normal distribution which has a standard deviation (σ_0) of the same magnitude as one previously estimated from a separate earlier series of n comparable observations. An approximate $100(1 - \alpha)\%$ two-sided confidence interval can be obtained by inverting the equivalent prediction interval for a single future observation from a normal distribution to give:

$$x \pm z_{1-\alpha/2}\left(1 + \frac{1}{n}\right)^{0.5}\sigma_0 \quad (4)$$

where $z_{1-\alpha/2}$ is the $100(1 - \alpha/2)$th percentile of the cumulative normal distribution.

However, some situations may arise in which *no* assumptions can be made regarding the shape of the frequency distribution from which the single observation x derives, apart from guessing that the distribution must be symmetrical about its mean. A remarkable theorem (Machol & Rosenblatt 1966; Blachman & Machol 1987) has shown that, given this assumption, it is still possible to construct a $100(1 - \alpha)\%$ two-sided confidence interval on the mean:

$$x \pm \left(1 + \frac{0.484}{\alpha}\right)|x - x_0| \quad (5)$$

where x_0 is a 'reasonable' estimate of the expected value of x (which *must* be made prior to the actual observation being obtained) and $||$ denotes taking the absolute value, i.e., ignoring the sign of the difference $(x - x_0)$. The 80% and 95% Machol–Blachman (M–B) confidence intervals are respectively:

$$\left.\begin{array}{ll} x \pm 3.42|x - x_0|; & 80\% \\ x \pm 10.68|x - x_0|; & 95\% \end{array}\right\}. \qquad (6)$$

As an example of their application, consider the determination of the expected 72-week expansion of a mortar, as measured by the ASTM C227–81 (Mortar Bar Method), in order to evaluate the susceptibility of the aggregate to long-term alkali–silica reactivity. Imagine that a series of tests were carried out five years ago using a similar mix-design to that expected to be used in the current contract consisting of a specified low-alkali cement, a fine aggregate and a coarse aggregate, and 40% added PFA. A series of tests were undertaken using two different types of fine aggregate, while the other variables remained unchanged. The observed 72-week response was found to be an average expansion (five mortar bars per mix) of the order of 0.06% across the various mixes. Suppose that now the expansion of the same mix design, but using a different fine aggregate, is measured, but there is only time to perform one 72-week test. This results in an average expansion (five bars) of 0.093%. It is axiomatic that between-sample sources of variation will always contribute more to the overall variance than will within-sample variation. Hence the mean resulting from the current test can be thought of, for predictive purposes, as a 'single' result.

The 80% and 95% M–B confidence limits (6) are therefore $\{-0.02, 0.21\}\%$ and $\{-0.26, 0.45\}\%$ respectively. The width of these M–B intervals is a consequence of the minimal assumptions made about the nature of the unknown frequency distribution from which the sample has been drawn, as opposed to the convenient but possibly erroneous assumption that the underlying unknown frequency distribution is normal.

Clearly, if reduction in the width of the confidence interval is of paramount importance, then there would be a beneficial trade-off in carrying out more than one long-term test. For example, if a second, completely independent, 72-week test in which *all* aspects of the experimental design, from sampling the source materials to replicating the mortar bars is completely duplicated, gives a mean expansion of 0.08%, then the half-width of the classical 95% confidence interval is given by:

$$\bar{x} \pm t_{1-\alpha/2, n-1}(s/\sqrt{n}). \qquad (7)$$

The t-distribution is used here rather than the normal distribution, since both the mean $\bar{x} = (x_1 + x_2)/2$ and standard deviation s are estimated from the two

observations themselves. For a duplicate pair of observations, the best (slightly conservative) estimate of s is given (ASQC Statistics Division 1983) by:

$$s = 0.8865|x_1 - x_2|. \qquad (8)$$

Hence $\bar{x} = 0.07\%$, $s = 0.0089\%$ yielding a conventional 95% confidence interval (7) of

$$0.07 \pm 12.7062(0.0089/\sqrt{2}) = \{-0.01, 0.15\}\%$$

which is obviously tighter than the equivalent M–B interval. In general, if additional completely independent trials were to be undertaken, s should then obtained using the conventional estimator

$$s = \sqrt{\sum (\bar{x} - \bar{\bar{x}})^2/(N - 1)} \qquad (9)$$

where $\bar{x}$ is the mean expansion (or contraction) for each independent trial, $\bar{\bar{x}}$ is the grand mean, and $N\ (>2)$ is the number of trials. The confidence limits on $\bar{\bar{x}}$ are found using (7), as before.

How many points to count?

A related issue is that of the number of points to count in undertaking a modal analysis and the confidence bounds to be attached to the estimated percentage abundance of each component. Of particular interest is what upper bound should be placed on the possible abundance of a constituent (for example, opal) which is not detected in the inspection but could be present in the material from which the sample was taken.

These issues have been discussed many times in geological and related literature (Dryden 1931; Chayes 1944; Mosimann 1965, 1970; van der Plas & Tobi 1965; Thompson 1987; Patterson & Fishbein 1989; Buzas 1990) and classical theory, based on large-sample normal distribution approximation to the discrete binomial distribution has for many years been applied to the calculation of point-count and fragment- or grain-count estimates of proportions. It forms the basis for reference charts of counting-error such as those of Chayes (1944), Rittenhouse (1950), van der Plas & Tobi (1965) and Patterson & Fishbein (1989). However, recent work (Blyth & Still 1983; Blyth 1986) has shown that, unless the number of points (or grains) counted is in excess of 1000, the confidence interval for the mean proportion based on the still widely-used normal-theory approximation can be quite poor (Fig. 2). Blyth (1986) has shown that the lower and upper one-sided $100(1 - \alpha)\%$ bounds are related by:

$$100p(n)_{1-\alpha} = 100\{1 - p(N - n)^{1-\alpha}\}\% \qquad (10)$$

where $p(\ )_{1-\alpha}$ is the lower bound for one of the two or more components; $p(\ )^{1-\alpha}$ is the upper bound; N is the

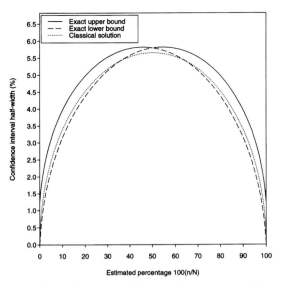

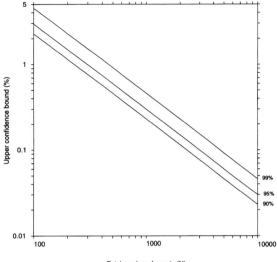

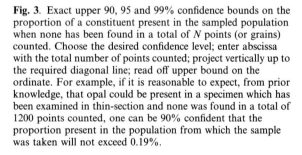

Fig. 2. Comparison of exact lower and upper 95% confidence bounds (equation 11) on an estimated percentage with the half-width given by the classical solution (e.g., van der Plas & Tobi 1965), based on a count of 300 points. Note discrepancy of the symmetrical limits based on the approximation given by the classical formula.

total number of counts made; and n is the observed number of counts for a given constituent. Very accurate approximations to the single-sided lower and upper bounds for $p(1)$ to $p(N-2)$ are obtained using:

$$\left. \begin{array}{l} p(n)^{1-\alpha} = 100B_{1-\alpha,n+1,N-n}\% \\ p(n)_{1-\alpha} = 100(1 - B_{1-\alpha,N-n+1,n})\% \end{array} \right\} \quad (11)$$

where $B_{1-\alpha,\nu_1,\nu_2}$ is the $100(1-\alpha)$th percentile of the inverse beta distribution with shape parameters ν_1 and ν_2. The beta distribution has the form

$$B(x|\nu_1,\nu_2) = \left[\frac{\Gamma(\nu_1+\nu_2)}{\Gamma(\nu_1)\Gamma(\nu_2)} \right] x^{\nu_2-1}(1-x)^{\nu_1-1} \quad (12)$$

where $0 \leqslant x \leqslant 1$, $\nu_1 > 0$, $\nu_2 > 0$ and $\Gamma(\nu)$ is the gamma function

$$\Gamma(\nu) = \int_0^\infty x^{\nu-1} e^{-x} \, dx. \quad (13)$$

Two-sided intervals on $p(n)$ are obtained by replacing α in (11) by $\alpha/2$. For the special case of $n = 0$, the *exact* solutions are:

$$\left. \begin{array}{l} p(n)^{1-\alpha} = 100\{1 - \alpha^{1/N}\}\% \\ p(n)_{1-\alpha} = 0\% \end{array} \right\}. \quad (14)$$

Fig. 3. Exact upper 90, 95 and 99% confidence bounds on the proportion of a constituent present in the sampled population when none has been found in a total of N points (or grains) counted. Choose the desired confidence level; enter abscissa with the total number of points counted; project vertically up to the required diagonal line; read off upper bound on the ordinate. For example, if it is reasonable to expect, from prior knowledge, that opal could be present in a specimen which has been examined in thin-section and none was found in a total of 1200 points counted, one can be 90% confident that the proportion present in the population from which the sample was taken will not exceed 0.19%.

Conversely, the exact lower bound when $n = N$ is $100\{\alpha^{1/N}\}\%$ and the upper bound is 100%. The exact upper bound for $n = N - 1$ is $100\{(1-\alpha)^{1/N}\}\%$. Fortunately, (11) may be evaluated using a spreadsheet package such as EXCEL™ (Anon 1992) which has very good numerical approximations for the inverse beta as well as the inverse normal, t and F distributions.

Figure 3 gives the upper bounds on zero counts as a function of the total number of points counted. Suppose, for example, that strained quartz (a contributor to alkali–silica reaction which causes undesirable expansion of concrete) is known to be a possible constituent of a rock which has been examined in thin-section. 1273 points have been counted in total, but no strained quartz grains have been observed, so what is the possible upper bound on the percentage present? It is decided that one should have 99% confidence in the outcome. Figure 3 is entered on the abscissa, for convenience rounding the total number of counts down (i.e., conservatively) to 1200, and projecting vertically up, parallel to the ordinate, until the 99% line is encountered. Reading off the horizontally-equivalent position on the ordinate, gives an upper

confidence bound of 0.38%. Based on the evidence of
this thin-section, the proportion of strained-quartz in
the sampled population must have a lower limit of zero
and an upper limit of 0.38%; the risk (α) of this decision
being wrong is 1%.

The upper bound in (11) can also be used to find the
maximum number of occurrences permitted (n) before a
threshold is exceeded. For example, if the chert content
in a product is not to exceed 2%, and the total number
of grains to be counted in a given size-fraction (N) is
1000, then the null hypothesis that the proportion in the
population sampled does not exceed 2% can be accepted
with a risk of 0.01% if $n \leqslant 5$; with a risk of 0.1% if
$5 < n \leqslant 7$; and with a risk of 1% if $7 < n \leqslant 10$; etc.

Thompson (1987) has shown that to obtain a coverage
probability of $100\gamma\%$ that the estimated proportions for
all the constituents counted simultaneously lie within an
absolute amount $\pm\Delta\%$ of their proportions in the
population sampled, the sample size required is:

$$N = c_\gamma / \Delta^2 \qquad (15)$$

where the coverage factors c_γ are as given in Table 1.
Figure 4 shows the error magnitude (Δ) as a function of
sample size and required coverage probability.

For example, if one wishes to be 99.9% sure that *all*
the constituents counted in a sample are within $\pm4\%$ of
the abundance in the population from which the samples
have been taken, then at least 1900 points should be
counted. For example, quartz, microcline, plagioclase,
biotite and total 'other' minerals were determined in a
thin-section of a granite using a count of 2000 points,
and were found to constitute 21.2, 26.4, 44.0, 6.5 and
1.9% respectively. A further 11 thin-sections of the same
rock were subsequently examined. The ranges in
percentage abundance of the constituent minerals were
found to be: {20.3, 22.8}, {25.3, 28.2}, {41.5, 45.7},
{5.1, 7.0} and {1.5, 2.4}% respectively; in no case were
the prediction limits based on the first thin-section
exceeded. In a second example, if c. 400 points are
counted per thin-section, Figure 4 shows that one can be
99% confident that all the estimates of constituent
abundance will be within $\pm6\%$ of their true values.

In order to reduce the effect of primary between-
sample variation, it is suggested that rather than rely on

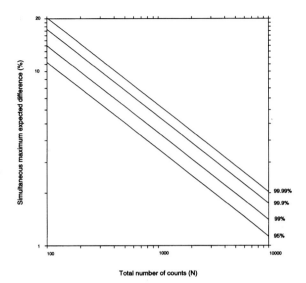

Fig. 4. Simultaneous maximum expected difference (%) from
population proportions with respect to coverage probability
(95, 99, 99.9 and 99.99%) and total points counted. Choose
the desired coverage probability; enter abscissa with the total
number of points counted; project vertically up to the required
diagonal line; read off maximum difference on the ordinate.
The procedure is reversible. For example: (a) if 400 points
are counted in a thin-section, one can have 99% confidence
that all the proportions in the population sampled of the
constituents which have been found in the thin-section will
be within $\pm6\%$ of their observed percentages. Conversely,
(b) if one wishes to be 99.9% confident that all the constituents
counted in a slide will be within $\pm4\%$ of their proportions
in the population sampled, then at least 1900 points should
be counted.

counting many points (grains) in a single thin-section or
sample (such as a polished concrete slab), one should
count, say, approximately $N/3$ points (grains) in each
of three independent sample preparations, then sum-
mate the counts for each component before determining
the confidence intervals for each percentage, as though
one were dealing with a single sample. The final bounds
will then be a more reliable estimate of the variation
inherent from all sources. In the case of point-counting
a thin-section, a useful rule-of-thumb is to use a traverse
inter-point interval of five times the largest particle
long-axis.

If grain or pebble counts are based on samples
obtained from stockpiles or conveyor belts, it is
important to remember to take steps to avoid sampling
bias caused by preferential particle segregation. Special
techniques and equipment may be required for reliable
sampling (Marek 1991; Dewar & Anderson 1992; Smith
& Collis 1993). Methods for laboratory sub-sampling are
described in Technical Committee CEN/TC-154 1995b).

Table 1. *Coverage factors for estimation of the total number
of points which need to be counted to ensure that the estimated
proportions for* all *the constituents counted will simultaneously
lie within a stated absolute amount ($\pm\Delta\%$) of their true
population proportions with a coverage probability of $100\gamma\%$
(Thompson 1987)*

$100\gamma\%$	90%	95%	99%	99.9%	99.99%
c_γ	1.0063	1.2736	1.9699	3.0289	4.1121

Monitoring a product to assess quality

Acceptance/rejection data

A commonly encountered situation is one in which batches of a product are being delivered to (or made on) a site on a daily basis and a test is performed, from which the batch is deemed either to be of acceptable quality or sub-standard (whether or not it is subsequently rejected is a different issue). The contract will almost certainly contain some statement to the effect that the proportion of apparently sub-standard batches detected by testing over the duration of the construction phase of the project shall not exceed a given threshold. Assuming that the product derives from a reasonably continuous single-manufacturer industrial process, such as a supply of crushed aggregate or mixed concrete, the questions naturally arise: 'if no failures have been observed in N tests, what is the upper confidence bound on the proportion of unacceptable (failed) lots in the population which is being sampled?' or alternatively 'if n failures have been observed in N tests, what is the confidence interval on the proportion of unacceptable (failed) lots in the population which is currently being sampled?' A *lot* is a definite quantity of a product or material accumulated under conditions that are considered uniform for sampling purposes.

A conservative two-sided $100(1 - \alpha)\%$ confidence interval on the proportion ($p = n/N$) is given by (11) or by:

$$p(n)_{1-\alpha/2} = \{1 + (N - n + 1)F_{1-\alpha/2,2(n-x+1),2n}/n\}^{-1}$$
$$p(n)^{1-\alpha/2} = \{1 + (N - n)/(n + 1)F_{1-\alpha/2,2(n+1),2(N-n)}\}^{-1}$$

$$(16)$$

where F_{γ,ν_1,ν_2} is the 100γth percentile of Snedecor's F-distribution with ν_1 and ν_2 degrees of freedom (Hahn & Meeker 1991). Computationally, the two solutions are identical. Figure 5 shows the upper 90%, 95% and 99% confidence bounds on the possible percentage of defects in the sampled population when *none* have been found in the sample of N units inspected. The lower bound is, of course, zero.

For example, measurements of uniaxial compressive strength and AIV have been made on specimens taken once a week from five randomly-selected, apparently fresh, quarried granite blocks for a period of 12 weeks. In no case has the saturated AIV exceeded a threshold set at 17%. Assuming that the nature of the source material has remained essentially unchanged over this period, what is the maximum proportion of substandard material which could have been present? The total number of tests carried out to date is 60. Choosing a confidence level of 95%, it is concluded from Fig. 5 that no more than 5% substandard material could have been present and remained undetected. There is a 5% risk that this decision might be wrong; however, Fig. 5 also

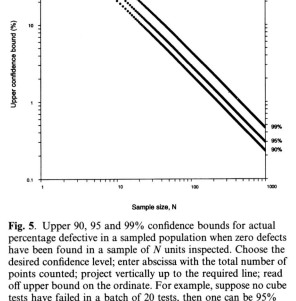

Fig. 5. Upper 90, 95 and 99% confidence bounds for actual percentage defective in a sampled population when zero defects have been found in a sample of N units inspected. Choose the desired confidence level; enter abscissa with the total number of points counted; project vertically up to the required line; read off upper bound on the ordinate. For example, suppose no cube tests have failed in a batch of 20 tests, then one can be 95% confident that the risk of failure in the population sampled is no greater than 14%.

shows that one can also be 99% confident that it could not have exceeded c. 7.6% of the product of the quarry.

Figures 6 and 7 give the lower and upper 99% confidence bounds on the true proportion of defects in a sampled population when 0, 1, 2 3, 4 5, 10, 25 or 50 defectives have been found in a sample of 1 to 100 units inspected (Fig. 6) or 100 to 10 000 inspected (Fig. 7).

In practice the number of tests it is feasible to conduct in a single day may be relatively small, and in some circumstances it may not even be possible to check every delivery. Over 10 000 28-day compressive strength tests for paving concrete were made during the construction of the Northern Illinois Toll Highway (Waddell 1961). Suppose that from the time the project began, between 15 and 20 15×31 cm concrete cylinders are made *in situ* each day from the pavement at the time the concrete is placed, and 7-day and 28-day compressive strengths are subsequently measured on all of these. Figure 8 shows that over the first 100 days the number of failures (7-day strength <20.89 MPa) never exceeds two per day. The irregularity in the upper and lower bounds is a consequence of variation in the total number of samples taken each day; in each case, the bounds are calculated using (11) or (14) with the appropriate values of n and N. Nevertheless, because of the relatively small number of daily tests, the upper 99% confidence bound on the

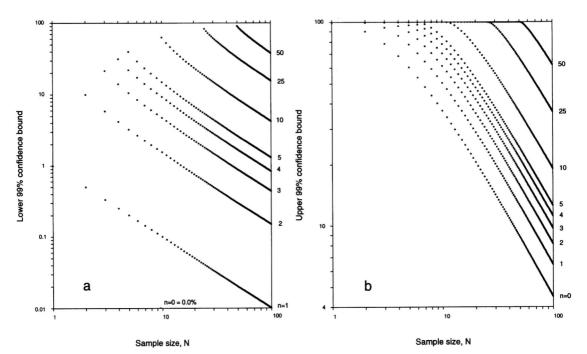

Fig. 6. 99% confidence bounds for percentage defective in a sampled population when n defects have been found in sample of $1 \leqslant N \leqslant 100$ units inspected. (a) lower bounds; (b) upper bounds. Choose the desired confidence level; enter abscissa with the sample size; project vertically up to the line corresponding to n; read off lower and upper bounds on the ordinate (a and b respectively). For example, suppose one cube test fails in a batch of 20 tests, one can be 99% confident that the underlying failure rate in the population sampled lies between 0.05 and 29%.

underlying proportion of failures which could be present in the whole of the population from which the samples have been taken (i.e., the entire road paving) never falls below $c.\,25\%$, and the lower bound remains essentially at zero.

If the bounds are instead computed from the proportion of cumulative failures relative to the cumulative number of tests made over an m-day period (17):

$$\left(\frac{n_1}{N_1}\right), \left(\frac{n_1 + n_2}{N_1 + N_2}\right), \left(\frac{n_1 + n_2 + n_3}{N_1 + N_2 + N_3}\right), \ldots, \left(\frac{\sum n_i}{\sum N_i}\right)$$

$$i = 1, 2, \ldots, m \qquad (17)$$

then convergence is rapidly achieved. Figure 9 shows that, on this basis, the upper bound for the population failure-rate falls from almost 25% to $c.\,4.5\%$ by the 20th day and both the lower and upper bounds gradually converge on the overall end-of-project failure rate of $c.\,1.5\%$.

Figure 10 shows the actual strengths for an example in which, unknown to the customer, the process mean remains on target but its standard deviation begins to drift upwards towards the end of the project lifetime. The result from monitoring seven-day strengths, as in the previous

example, is an observed gradually increasing number of failures (Fig. 11). Again, 15–20 tests per day do not enable a sufficiently tight upper bound on the underlying failure rate to be obtained. Suppose that the failure rate is instead cumulated using a ten-day moving window. This is accomplished by beginning with (17) until the 11th day, then using the updating formula (18):

$$\left(\sum_{k=m-9}^{m-1} n_k + n_m - n_{m-10}\right)$$

$$\Bigg/ \left(\sum_{k=m-9}^{m-1} N_k + N_m - N_{m-10}\right); \quad m = 11, 12, \ldots \quad (18)$$

where m is the day number corresponding to the current end of the window. This results in a much clearer picture (Fig. 12) in which the increasing proportion of failures in the parent population is now well reflected. By day 55 the lower bound is almost always greater than zero and (following a brief recovery in days 70–71), on day 72 there is an abrupt upwards shift in both the estimated underlying proportion of failures and its non-zero lower bound. This means that from day 55 onwards, one can be 99% certain that something has gone wrong with the production process. However, as in the previous

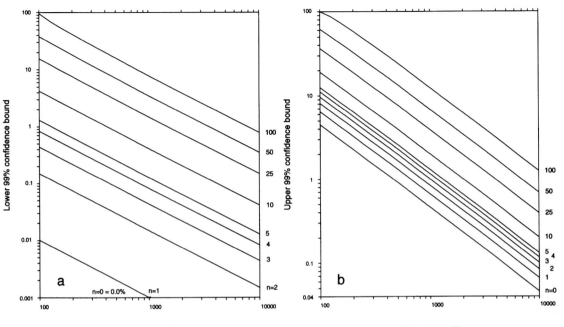

Fig. 7. 99% confidence bounds for percentage defective in a sampled population when n defects have been found in sample of $100 \leqslant N \leqslant 10\,000$ units inspected. (a) lower bounds; (b) upper bounds. Usage as for Fig. 6.

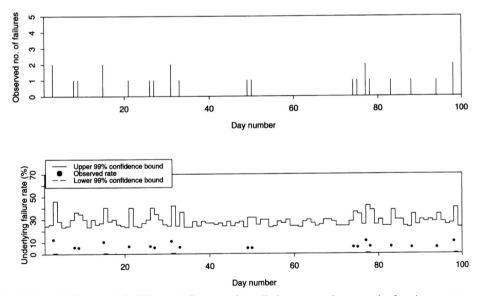

Fig. 8. (Above) Observed daily failure rate for seven-day cylinder compressive strength of paving concrete per 15–20 tests/day; (below) lower and upper 99% confidence bounds for the underlying probability of failure in the population sampled. (Artificial example based on overall statistics reported for the construction of the Northern Illinois Toll Highway; Waddell 1961).

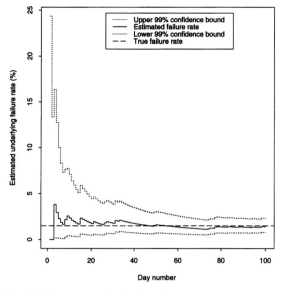

Fig. 9. Highway example (continued). Estimated failure rate and its associated lower and upper 99% confidence bounds for the underlying probability of failure in the paving concrete population sampled, based on observed *cumulative* failure rate for seven-day cylinder compressive strength of paving concrete per 15–20 tests/day. Note convergence on the true failure rate, known from overall end-of-project statistics.

example, this type of approach is most useful in situations where long-term monitoring is possible.

If detailed petrological examination for a contaminant such as opal or chert in a quarried aggregate is required and daily petrological examination in impractical, it is suggested that one could take samples of produced aggregate at regular intervals (e.g., 1 hour) throughout each 24 hour period from, say, a conveyor belt leading to the stockpile. These could be amalgamated by binning for a week, then thoroughly mixed. The composite bulk sample is then reduced by successive quartering and splitting, followed by sieving to obtain a sufficiently coarse size-fraction (e.g. >5 mm) which is then riffled and split to obtain representative sub-samples for petrological examination. It is suggested that five sub-samples are taken, crushed to 1–2 mm, embedded in resin, and a total of $N = 8000$ grains counted across the five (i.e., c. 1600 each).

Suppose the occurrence of chert-bearing grains is being counted. The upper 99% confidence bound on the percentage present in the composite sample can be found from (11) and/or (14) for $n \geqslant 0$ detections. For convenience, Table 2 gives the number of detections corresponding to selected upper confidence bounds. The worst-case, in terms of localized concentration of these grains in the source material, would be if all those found in the pooled grain-count had originated in a single one of the many samples taken throughout the 7-day week.

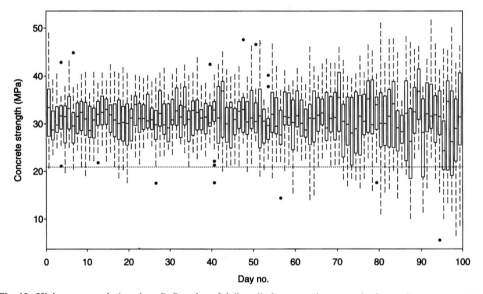

Fig. 10. Highway example (continued). Boxplot of daily cylinder strength test results for paving concrete (15–20 tests per day). Specified minimum strength of 20.89 MPa shown by horizontal pecked line. Each box encloses 25th to 75th percentiles; box centre-line is median; whiskers extend to 'furthest out' samples within 1.5 times the inter-quartile range beyond the 25th and 75th percentiles; outliers are shown as individual data points. Note the gradual increase in spread of strength distributions throughout the period monitored, owing to decrease in product quality. (Artificial example)

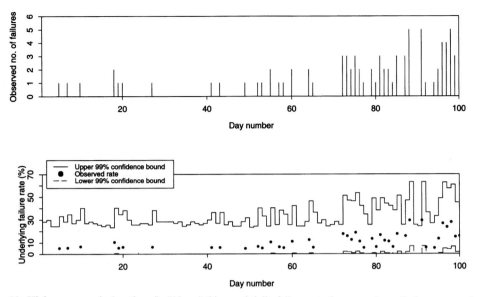

Fig. 11. Highway example (continued). (Above) Observed daily failure rate for seven-day cylinder compressive strength of paving concrete based on 15–20 tests/day; (below) lower and upper 99% confidence bounds for the underlying probability of failure in the population sampled. Data as for Fig. 10. Note gradual rise in upper bound and appearance of lower bound above zero with passage of time.

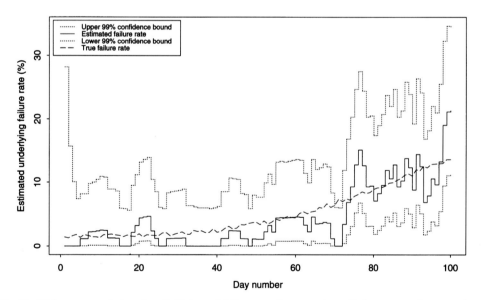

Fig. 12. Highway example (continued). Estimated failure rate for seven-day cylinder compressive strength of paving concrete and associated lower and upper 99% confidence bounds for the underlying probability of failure in the population sampled, based on observed *cumulative* failure rate in a ten-day moving window, cf. equations (17) and (18). Note how the true underlying failure rate (bold dashed line) is effectively tracked by the on-site monitoring process; the mainly non-zero lower bound following day 55 and its abrupt increase following day 72, in addition to the associated rise in estimated failure rate, indicate problems are occurring with the production process.

Table 2. *Upper 99% confidence bounds on the percentage of chert present if* n *chert-bearing fragments have been detected in a total count of 8000 fragments in a given size fraction*

No. of grains (n)	0	2	10	26	60	95	131	168
Upper bound (%)	0.06	0.10	0.25	0.5	1.0	1.5	2.0	2.5

Bounds on the proportion of failures in the population being sampled (i.e., the quarry) can be calculated using (11) and (14) or from Fig. 7. If *no* chert-bearing grains are found in, say, a total of 8027 grains counted from the sub-samples of the composite, then Fig. 7b shows that one can be 99% certain that the maximum proportion of 'failures' present in the source-material (as represented by 0 failures in $24 \times 7 = 168$ composited samples) cannot exceed 2.7%. In addition, Table 2 shows that since there were no occurrences in the $c.8000$ grains counted, the source-material quarried would, at most, contain $c.0.06\%$ chert-bearing grains.

Now suppose that 76 chert-bearing grains were found in the 8027 grains counted from the composite sample, i.e. 0.95%. From Fig. 7 or (11) the obtained upper and lower 99% confidence bounds on the likely proportion of chert in the parent material are $\{0.71, 1.23\}\%$. As mentioned above, the worst case (in potential source-concentration terms) would be if the presence of these grains had arisen from a single 'failure' in the 168 hourly samples. Hence (from 11 or Fig. 7b), the upper 99% confidence bound on the proportion of failures present in the parent material being sampled is 3.9%. Assuming that the observed chert concentration in the composite could have arisen from contributions from several of the hourly samples, then obviously more than 4% of the material being quarried could contain chert concentrations lower than 1.2%. Nevertheless, it can still be stated (with a risk of 1%) that the maximum overall concentration present cannot exceed 1.2%.

If this type of weekly monitoring were to be carried out on a long-term basis using the cumulative failure-rate approach discussed above, then it should in addition enable a long-term record of the probability of the occurrence of unacceptable material in a quarry to be established on a firm basis. Further discussion of acceptance sampling methods will be found in Montgomery (1991) and Chang & Hsie (1995).

Quantitative data

In contrast to the discrete numbers of failures in so many tests discussed in the previous section, if attributes measured on a continuous scale (e.g. cylinder or cube compressive strength of concrete or percentage passing a given size grade) are measured for each batch supplied on a daily basis and it can reasonably be assumed that the parent frequency distribution from which the samples are drawn is normal, then control-charting techniques can be used. In the case of concrete strength data, it is generally assumed that the normal frequency distribution model holds good (Erntroy 1960; Waddell 1961; Tait 1981; Balaguru & Ramakrishnan 1987; ACI Committee 228 1988; Dewar & Anderson 1992) although Hindo & Bergstrom (1985) have suggested that in cases of poor control, the lognormal model may be preferable. Re-examination of a few published concrete strength data sets ($n = 204$, Tait 1981; 1001, Balaguru & Ramakrishnan 1987; 10 268, Waddell 1961) using normal probability plots, a more sensitive tool than visual comparison of histograms, suggests that the tail-areas of the distributions can be narrower than would be expected with a normal model. However, the normal distribution is probably fit-for-purpose from the point of view of quality assurance.

Shewhart charts for the mean and V-mask cusum (cumulative sum) charts are widely used for monitoring products for quality assurance purposes (Gebler 1990; Marek 1991; Dewar & Anderson 1992) although many other approaches exist (Montgomery 1991; Howarth 1995). A useful alternative, which has some of the advantages of both but is easier to use, is the *J*-chart (Jaehn 1987, 1991), originally developed in the paper industry to enable effective process monitoring to be carried out by shop-floor personnel. Figure 13 shows an example of a *J*-chart for the 7-day concrete strength data used in Table 6.5 of Dewar & Anderson (1992).

In order to set up a *J*-chart it is necessary, as in the majority of control-charting methods, to have *a priori* estimates of the target mean and standard deviation. The value taken for the target mean (μ) may well be based on design criteria. The initial estimate of the process standard deviation (σ) may be derived from a conceptual estimate of the coefficient of variation; from prior knowledge (e.g. statistics for similar material provided to the customer by the same manufacturer in the past); or based on the mean range of, say, the first ten pairs of observations. In order to reduce the risk of obtaining a biased estimate of the standard deviation caused by autocorrelation between successive observations, this should be calculated using $|x_1 - x_2|, |x_3 - x_4|$, $\ldots$, $|x_9 - x_{10}|$ rather than $|x_1 - x_2|$, $|x_2 - x_3|$, $\ldots$, $|x_9 - x_{10}|$. The estimate of σ is then given by the mean range multiplied by the correction factor 0.8665 (ASQC Statistics Division 1983; Montgomery 1991).

The *J*-control chart (Fig. 13) consists of bands (or 'zones') of equal width, with the appropriate value ($\mu, \mu \pm \sigma, \mu \pm 2\sigma, \mu \pm 3\sigma$) written at the corresponding boundary between each. It has been found equally effective in control where the data values (x) are either individual values (as in the example discussed here) or averages. Each new value of x is plotted with the abscissa the corresponding test or day number and the ordinate at the centre of the zone (or on the zone boundary if it is

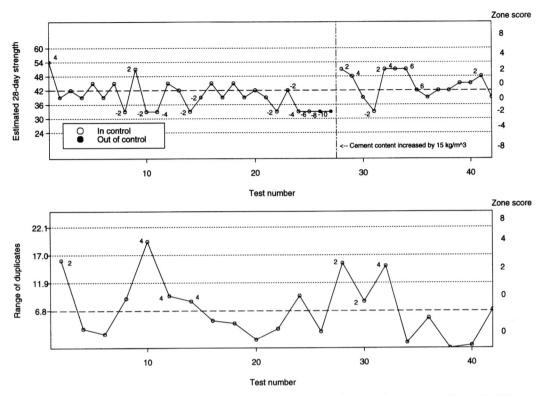

Fig. 13. *J*-charts for monitoring concrete cube 28-day strengths (data of Dewar & Anderson, 1992, Table 6.5). Target mean, 42 Nmm^{-2} and standard deviation 6 Nmm^{-2}; (above) chart for individual values; (below) chart for range of successive independent pairs. Action limit in both cases is a cumulative score of eight. See text for details of scoring method. Statistically significant fall in concrete strength detected at test 26; corrective action was subsequently taken.

exactly equal to it, usually because of round-off). Each zone has a *score* associated with it: -8 if $x \leqslant \mu - 3\sigma$; -4 if $\mu - 3\sigma < x \leqslant \mu - 2\sigma$; -2 if $\mu - 2\sigma < x \leqslant \mu - \sigma$; 0 if $\mu - \sigma < x < \mu + \sigma$; 2 if $\mu + \sigma \leqslant x < \mu + 2\sigma$; 4 if $\mu + 2\sigma \leqslant x < \mu + 3\sigma$; and 8 if $x > \mu + 3\sigma$. The sign of the score is simply used to distinguish between trends above ($+$) or below ($-$) the mean. Scores are cumulated so long as successive values of x lie either on the *same* side of the mean or are exactly equal in value to the mean, usually as a result of round-off. As soon as a new value of x lies on the opposite side of the mean, the cumulative score is reset to the appropriate zone score and cumulation begins again. Once the cumulative score becomes $-8 \leqslant$ or $\geqslant +8$, the process is deemed to be 'out of control' and a possible cause of the problem should be sought for. The *J*-chart outperforms the Shewhart chart for the mean (Jaehn 1991) and is comparable with conventional cusum charts, while being easier to use. Jaehn (1987, 1991) suggests that if very rapid detection of out-of-control situations is required, a score of 1 rather than zero, could be assigned to the zones within $\mu \pm \sigma$,

retaining the action-limit of 8, but the risk of false alarms (i.e., concluding that something has gone wrong with the process when it has not) would be increased.

Figure 13 shows the *J*-chart for daily 28-day concrete cube strengths in which the target mean is 42 Nmm^{-2} with an associated standard deviation of 6 Nmm^{-2}. It yields an identical result to monitoring using a conventional cusum approach (Dewar & Anderson 1992) who noted that once the action-limit was exceeded (test number 26), the cement content had to be increased by 15 kg m^{-3} to return the concrete to target mean strength.

Jaehn (1989, 1991) also suggested that the zone control chart approach could be used to detect an upwards shift in the observed range (r) of independent groups of $2 \leqslant n \leqslant 5$ observations, based on a prior estimate of the mean range ($\bar{R}$). In this chart, the zone boundaries are defined by: $\bar{R}$, $\bar{R} + (k\bar{R} - \bar{R})/3$, $\bar{R} + 2(k\bar{R} - \bar{R})/3$ and $k\bar{R}$, using associated scores of 0 if $r < \bar{R}$; or if $\bar{R} \leqslant r < \bar{R} + (k\bar{R} - \bar{R})/3$; 2 if $\bar{R} + (k\bar{R} - \bar{R})/3 \leqslant r < \bar{R} + 2(k\bar{R} - \bar{R})/3$; 4 if $\bar{R} + 2(k\bar{R} - \bar{R})/3 \leqslant r < k\bar{R}$; and 8 if $k\bar{R} \leqslant r$. Values of the scaling factor , which depends on

Table 3. *Scaling factors* (k) *for zone boundaries in a J-chart for range control as function of number of observations* (n) *on which the observed range is based (Jaehn 1989, 1991)*

n	2	3	4	5
k	3.267	2.575	2.282	2.115

the number of observations on which the observed ranges are based, are given in Table 3. The lower limit of the range zone chart is zero; scores are only assigned and cumulated if the observed range exceeds $\bar{R}$. As before, the action-limit is a cumulative score of 8. Figure 13 shows the J-chart for ranges applied to the independent range estimates $|x_1 - x_2|$, $|x_3 - x_4|$, ..., $|x_9 - x_{10}|$, etc. for the same series of daily 28-day concrete cube strengths as in the previous example. The cumulative sums show that unlike the drift in the mean, the 28-day strength variability remains in control.

Because these control charts merely require the zone boundaries, their delimiting values, and the associated zone scores to be given, they do not need accurate plotting of the observed values on graph paper, merely the location of the current point in the appropriate zone and cumulation of the running total score. This has helped the method to gain rapid acceptance for use by personnel at shop-floor level in a variety of industrial contexts.

Conclusions

Recent advances in statistical theory offer a variety of improved techniques for treating both field and experimental data encountered in work with aggregates and associated products.

Because many expressions for uncertainty tend to be used in practice, we recommend that reporting of results in the form $x \pm \delta$ should always include explicit definition of the meaning of δ the first time it is used; a slightly conservative approximation for calculation of the appropriate coverage factor has been given in equation (1).

Kupper & Hafner (1989) recommend that future use of the classical formula for estimating the number of tests (or measurements) required for a sufficiently precise estimation of the mean, as given in many statistical textbooks as well as the recent *Aggregate Handbook* (Marek 1991), should be 'strongly discouraged' as it is now known to seriously underestimate the number of necessary determinations when the apparent number of tests required is small. Corrected sample sizes are given by (3).

It has been shown how confidence limits can be placed on a *single* determination (5) given minimal assumptions regarding the underlying frequency distribution. This could be particularly helpful regarding tests which take a very long time to complete (e.g. estimations of long-term strength).

The classical normal-theory formula for obtaining confidence limits on a proportion (e.g. obtained by point-counting a thin-section or a count of the number of failures encountered in so many batches of a product inspected) embodied in reference charts of counting-error such as those of van der Plas & Tobi (1965) is now known to give poor results, particularly for very small or very large proportions. Much more accurate approximations for the confidence bounds can be obtained by means of the inverse beta distribution (11) and *exact* upper bounds for the proportion of an undesirable constituent of aggregate, such as chert or opal, which might be present even if no grains are found during point-counting can also be given (14).

A similar approach, but making use of the cumulative failure rate (17, 18), can be used to obtain tight bounds on the underlying failure rate when monitoring a long-term production process.

Finally, *J*-charts are shown to be a simple and effective alternative to conventional Shewhart and cusum charts, well-suited to shop-floor use, for monitoring the quality of a product by a manufacturer and/or the customer.

References

ACI COMMITTEE 228 1988. In-place Methods for Determination of Strength of Concrete. *ACI Materials Journal*, **85**, 446–471.

ANALYTICAL METHODS COMMITTEE 1987. Recommendations for the Conduct and Interpretation of Co-operative Trials. *The Analyst*, **112**, 679–686.

—— 1989*a*. Report on an Experimental Test of "Recommendations for the Conduct and Interpretation of Co-operative Trials". *The Analyst*, **114**, 1489–1495.

—— 1989*b*. Robust Statistics – How Not to Reject Outliers. II. Inter-laboratory Trials. *The Analyst*, **114**, 1699–1702.

——1992. Proficiency Testing of Analytical Laboratories: Organisation and Statistical Assessment. *The Analyst*, **117**, 97–104.

——1995. Uncertainty of Measurement: Implications of Its Use in Analytical Science. *The Analyst*, **120**, 2303–2308.

ANON 1992. *Microsoft Excel. Function Reference (Version 4.0)*. Microsoft Corporation, Redmond, WA.

ASQC STATISTICS DIVISION 1983. *Glossary and Tables for Statistical Quality Control*. American Society for Quality Control, Milwaukee.

BALAGURU, P. N. & RAMAKRISHNAN, V. 1987. Criteria for Estimating the Required Average Strength f'_{cr} to Comply with the Specified Compressive Strength f'_c. *ACI Materials Journal*, **84**, 35–41.

BLACHMAN, N. M. & MACHOL, R. E. 1987. Confidence Intervals Based on One or More Observations. *IEEE Transactions on Information Theory*, **IT-33**, 373–382.

BLYTH, C. R. 1986. Approximate Binomial Confidence Limits. *Journal of the American Statistical Association* **81**, 843–855.

—— STILL, H. A. 1983. Binomial Confidence Limits. *Journal of the American Statistical Association*, **78**, 108–116.

BUZAS, M. A. 1990. Another Look at Confidence Limits for Species Proportions. *Journal of Palaeontology*, **64**, 842–843.

CHANG, L. M. & HSIE, M. 1995. Quality acceptance sampling methods. *In*: LEMAIR, M., FAVRE, J.-L. & MEBARKI, A. (eds) *Applications of Statistics and Probability. Civil Engineering Reliability and Risk Analysis. Proceedings of the ICASP7 Conference, Paris, France, 10–13 July 1995*, Balkema, Rotterdam, 783–788.

CHAYES, F. 1944. Petrographic Analysis by Fragment Counting. I. The counting error. *Economic Geology*, **39**, 484–505.

DEWAR, J. D. & ANDERSON, R. 1992. *Manual of Ready-mixed Concrete*. Blackie, London.

DRYDEN, A. L. 1931. Accuracy in percentage representation of heavy mineral frequencies. *Proceedings of the National Academy of Sciences*, **17**, 233–238.

EISENHART, C. 1968. Expression of the Uncertainties of Final Results. *Science*, **160**, 1201–1204.

ERNTROY, H. C. 1960. *The Variation of Works Test Cubes*. Research Report, 10. Cement and Concrete Association, London.

GEBLER, S. H. 1990. Interpretation of Quality-Control Charts for Concrete Production. *ACI Materials Journal*, **87**, 319–326.

HAHN, G. J. & MEEKER, W. Q. 1991. *Statistical Intervals. A Guide for Practitioners*. Wiley, New York.

HINDO, K. R. & BERGSTROM, W. R. 1985. Statistical Evaluation of the In-Place Compressive Strength of Concrete. *Concrete International: Design and Construction*, **7**, 44–48.

HOWARTH, R. J. 1995. Quality Control Charting for the Analytical Laboratory. I. Univariate methods. A Review. *The Analyst*, **120**, 1851–1873.

JAEHN, A. H. 1987. Zone control charts: a new tool for quality control. *Technical Association Pulp and Paper Industry Journal*, **87**, 159–161.

—— 1989. *Zone control charts find new applications*. ASQC Quality Congress, Toronto. American Society for Quality Control, Milwaukee. 890–895.

—— 1991. The Zone Control Chart. *Quality Progress*, **24**, 65–68.

KUPPER, L. L. & HAFNER, K. B. 1989. How appropriate are popular sample-size formulas? *American Statistician*, **43**, 101–105.

MACHOL, R. E. & ROSENBLATT, J. 1966. Confidence Interval Based on Single Observation. *Proceedings of the IEEE*, **54**, 1087–1088.

MANDEL, J. 1991. The validation of measurement through interlaboratory studies. *Chemometrics and Intelligent Laboratory Systems*, **11**, 109–119.

MAREK, C. R. 1991. Sampling and Testing Principles. *In*: BARKSDALE, R. D. (ed.) *The Aggregate Handbook*, National Stone Association, Washington, D.C., 16.1–16.17.

MONTGOMERY, D. C. 1991. *Introduction to Statistical Quality Control*. (2nd edn.) Wiley, New York.

MOSIMANN, J. E. 1965. Statistical Methods for the Pollen Analyst. *In*: KUMMEL, B. & RAUP, D. (eds) *Handbook of Palaeontological Techniques*, Freeman, San Francisco, 636–673.

—— 1970. Discrete Distribution Models Arising in Pollen Studies. *In*: PATIL, G. P. (ed.) *Random Counts in Physical Sciences, Geoscience, and Business*, Pennsylvania State University Press, 1–30.

PATTERSON, R. T. & FISHBEIN, E. 1989. Re-examination of the statistical methods used to determine the number of point counts needed for micropalaeontological quantitative research. *Journal of Palaeontology*, **63** , 245–248.

RITTENHOUSE, G. 1950. Detrital mineralogy. *In*: LEROY, L. W. (ed.) *Subsurface Geologic Methods*, Colorado School of Mines, Golden, CO, 116–140.

SMITH, M. R. & COLLIS, L. (eds) 1993. *Aggregates: Sand, Gravel and Crushed Rock Aggregates for Construction Purposes*. (2nd edn.) Geological Society, London, Engineering Geology Special Publication, **9**.

STICKLEY, A. & WINTERBOTTOM, A. 1994. The nature of quality assurance and statistical methods in BS 5750. *The Statistician*, **43**, 349–370.

TAIT, J. B. 1981. Concrete Quality Assurance Based on Strength Tests. *Concrete International*, 79–87.

TECHNICAL COMMITTEE CEN/TC 154 1994. *Draft European Standard prEN 1744–1. Tests for Chemical Properties of Aggregates. Part 1: Chemical Analysis*. 94/109961. British Standards Institute, London.

—— 1995a. *Draft European Standard prEN 932–6. Tests for General Properties of Aggregates. Part 6: Definitions of Repeatability and Reproducibility*. 95/107263. British Standards Institute, London.

—— 1995b. *Draft European Standard prEN 932–2. Tests for General Properties of Aggregates. Part 2: Methods for Reducing Laboratory Samples*. 95/107050. British Standards Institute, London.

THOMPSON, S. K. 1987. Sample Size for Estimating Multinomial Proportions. *The American Statistician*, **41**, 42–46.

VAN DER PLAS, L. & TOBI, A. C. 1965. A Chart for Judging the Reliability of Point Counting Results. *American Journal of Science*, **263**, 87–90.

WADDELL, J. J. 1961. Quality Control in the Construction Industry. *Industrial Quality Control*, **17**, 12–15.

An investigation of some alternative aggregates for use in concrete

A. K. Butler[1] & A. M. Harrisson[2]

[1] Mott MacDonald Ltd., Special Services Division, St Anne House, 20–26 Wellesley Road, Croydon CR9 2UL, UK
[2] Rugby Cement, Crown House, Rugby CV21 2DT, UK

Abstract. The use of some waste materials as aggregate for concrete has been investigated. Three specific materials were examined, china clay waste, slate waste and pulverized fuel ash. The project investigated methods of utilising alternative materials as aggregate either by low cost processing, novel mix design or by the use of admixtures.

This paper reports on a research project commissioned by the Department of the Environment into some of the technical aspects of using some waste materials as aggregate in concrete. Alternative aggregates are regarded, for the purpose of this paper, as processed materials which do not fall within the scope of BS 882:1992 without further processing. They include industrial waste products and low grade natural materials produced as waste after mineral extraction.

The Terms of Reference for the project identified three types of waste products from the extractive and power industries for utilization as alternative aggregates: china clay waste, slate waste and pulverized fuel ash (pfa).

The purpose of the project was to develop methods of utilizing alternative aggregates in concrete primarily by low or medium cost processing, novel mix design or the use of admixtures. The approach adopted was to examine the properties of the materials selected for appraisal and to evaluate each in terms of:

- the appropriateness of improving the material for use as an aggregate in view of the current value of the material, the extent of the available supply, the projected added value and the cost-effectiveness of the process proposed for upgrading
- The technical feasibility of producing upgraded aggregate from the waste materials on a commercial scale

China clay waste

China clay is a product of the degradation of intrusive igneous rocks, particularly granites. The primary mineral of china clay, kaolinite, forms from the alteration of feldspars in the granite. As part of the china clay making process the remaining unaltered minerals, principally quartz and mica, are removed by sedimentation in a series of channels and tanks.

The waste product is of four types: coarse sand, waste rock (incompletely altered), overburden and micaceous residue. The sand is suitable for use as a fine aggregate particularly in white concrete, but has been considered uneconomic for widespread use due to the costs of transport from the locations of the waste tips (Devon and Cornwall) to the sites where aggregate is most in demand (the South East) (Department of the Environment 1991). After crushing and separation the waste rock has been shown to be suitable for use as aggregate in some applications subject to satisfactory trials and appropriate mix design (Gutt et al. 1974; Tubey 1978).

Slate waste

The waste material from slate production comprises, in the main, various sized fragments of slate. The older quarries, where waste accumulated before automation of the slate preparation process, in general produced a finer waste than the more modern quarries. Incorporated with the slate particles is a quantity of overburden, the extent and type of which is dependent on the geology of the quarry and the method of working.

It was considered possible that the slate waste may to some extent be reactive with alkalis from cement and this possibility was evaluated as part of this study. Modification of the shape of slate waste particles was investigated for general use as aggregate. It was considered that a reasonable grade of coarse aggregate could probably be produced by low cost processing provided that the other physical and chemical properties are acceptable. Higher cost modifications were therefore not considered.

Pulverized fuel ash

Pulverized coal is used as fuel in some power stations. Ash from the combustion of the coal is an alumino-silicate material. It is at first molten but solidifies on cooling. If the cooling is very rapid and occurs in the air after combustion, the resultant fine ash is glassy and pozzolanic and can be used as a cement replacement material in

BUTLER, A. K. & HARRISSON, A. M. 1998. An investigation of some alternative aggregates for use in concrete. *In*: LATHAM, J.-P. (ed.) 1998. *Advances in Aggregates and Armourstone Evaluation*. Geological Society, London, Engineering Geology Special Publications, **13**, 185–192.

concrete. Some ash does not solidify in the air but falls to the bottom of the furnace where it accumulates as the more massive, porous bottom ash. This has a use in the manufacture of lightweight concrete blocks.

Pfa can be formed into pellets and fired on a sinter strand to form a good quality lightweight aggregate. This is a relatively expensive procedure and the product is only currently used for specialised applications in the UK although its use in some other countries is more widespread. Pfa which does not meet the criteria for cement replacement can be used as a filler in some grouting applications.

Other materials

The possibility of investigating other materials was assessed during the desk study phase of the project. Such materials as waste glass, slag deposits other than from blastfurnaces, colliery shale and others may prove suitable for improvement. These did not, however, form a major part of the study and are not considered further here.

Method of approach

Desk study

The literature search examined work previously published on the use of waste materials as aggregate. Information on potential aggregates was catalogued, together with any chemical, mineralogical and physical data which could reliably be linked to a specific material at a known (and still viable) location. The material characteristics ascertained at this stage were compared with those required for concrete making. Because of the unusual nature of these aggregates this comparison was not restricted to the requirements of BS 882. This part of the programme included contacting the producers of waste materials in the particular industries involved. All the data accumulated at this stage were incorporated into a computer database using the Lotus Approach software package.

This stage of the project also involved examining the available methods of processing the aggregates and the likely costs of their application on a commercial scale.

Field studies

The location, extent and condition of the waste resources were examined during site visits to each of the potential sites identified. The team members involved had experience of geological examination of materials, including primary and secondary minerals evaluation and production, which allowed some selection to be made on site.

Small samples (about 1kg) were collected for determination of the variability within the materials by physical and chemical testing. The potential for taking larger samples for improvement trials at a later stage was also investigated.

Sample testing

The programme of testing was designed to establish the performance of aggregates in areas important for the production of concrete and to identify the properties which need to be adjusted, by processing, to allow commercial exploitation. Tests included the following:

- The chemical and physical properties of the aggregates. This involved petrographic examination, mineralogical analysis, chemical analysis, physical testing and grading to BS 812, to enable a classification of the aggregates to be made. The final classification was based on the performance of the materials and their potential for improvement. Assessment of the cost-effectiveness of the means of improvement determined the nature of further trials with each of the aggregates.
- The potential for adverse effects on strength or durability. These tests examined the potential for instability, unsoundness, alkali–aggregate reaction and freeze–thaw damage by investigating aggregate characteristics such as shape, porosity and absorption. Where possible standard test procedures were followed, for example ASTM C-1260 for alkali aggregate reactivity. In other cases test methods were developed or modified for the purposes of this study.

Classification of materials

From the results of the foregoing research, the material from each site identified was classified according to its suitability for use as aggregate in concrete by comparison with the properties required for good quality aggregate. The classification comprised the following:

1. Suitable for use, without processing, as an aggregate in conventional concrete.
2. Potentially suitable for use in concrete with adjustments to mix design.
3. Potentially suitable for use as aggregate in concrete after low/medium cost processing.
4. Potentially suitable for use as aggregate in concrete after high cost processing.
5. Unsuitable for use as an aggregate.

Possibilities for improving aggregate properties

Any materials falling into category 1 above, based on data supplied by the producers, were incorporated directly into the testing programme at the appropriate time. This included the china sand which was used in the concrete making trials.

The materials in category 2 were subjected to a series of tests to determine the viability of using them as aggregates in mixes with designs modified by the adjustment of the proportions of the various constituents or with the use of admixtures.

A selection of materials in category 3 were processed as appropriate and re-examined. This stage involved low cost techniques including physical screening (sieving) and on-site crushing. Medium cost processing involved processes such as washing, drying, blending and dry separation of fine-grained materials.

Low cost processing was found to be appropriate for the improvement of slate waste to produce a coarse aggregate with acceptable shape and grading characteristics. It was also possible to produce an acceptable fine aggregate, but the removal of excess fines took the processing into the medium cost category. The processed materials were included in the mix design trials.

The possibility of using the materials in category 4 was assessed in terms of the likely added value and the probability of encouraging investment in plant to make the process commercially viable. The prospects for lightweight aggregates production from each of the materials examined were thought to be good, particularly in association with enhanced mix designs to make the use of lightweight concrete more widespread than it is in the UK at present. The further exploration of high cost techniques was not, however, a part of the project and was not progressed. Category 5 materials were not considered further.

Laboratory examination of material characteristics with cement

Combinations of cement, aggregate and water, with and without additives and cement replacement materials, were made up to investigate the microstructure and microchemistry of the combinations. The mixes were cured at elevated temperatures (40°C) in order to accelerate the reactions which could possibly lead to problems. Six slate waste samples were examined and two china clay sands. Each was crushed and the portion between $106\,\mu m$ and $355\,\mu m$ was mixed at 2:1 aggregate to cement and 0.6 water to cement ratio to produce mortars. After three months curing, the mixes were examined for the following.

(a) Microstructural properties of the cement paste fraction. These can be affected by a number of factors, including the surface area available for precipitation of reaction products and the nature of the material of which the surface is formed. Scanning Electron Microscopic (SEM) examination with graphical presentation of elemental relationships has been used (Harrisson et al. 1986) to identify the effects on cement hydrate composition of reactive constituents other than Portland cement. In this case the technique was used to ascertain whether

deleterious reactions should be expected between the alternative aggregates and cement.

(b) Chemical stability of the aggregate in cement pastes of different compositions. Some feldspars are known to be susceptible to degradation in the high alkali environment of cement paste (Van Aardt & Visser 1977). As stated earlier, china clay is formed as a degradation product of feldspars in granite, and partly degraded feldspars will probably exist within the waste material. Slate waste contains quantities of finely divided silica and mica, the reactivity of these components in concrete needs to be identified. SEM and X-ray microanalysis of the cement hydration products was used to reveal if the chemistry of the aggregate in any way affected the reaction processes within the concrete.

(c) The nature of the cement paste/aggregate interface. Porous and irregular materials perform in a different manner in concrete to smooth and rounded materials. A microscope study of the cement/aggregate interface was used as a guide to determine which possible adjustments to mix design would improve the aggregate properties in concrete.

Physical and durability testing of concretes

The testing programme was directed towards ensuring that the aggregates do not produce concrete with physical or durability problems unsuitable for use in construction.

Tests were carried out on approximately 60 concrete mixes containing a range of cement replacement materials and admixtures. The initial mixes were made up in small quantities to assess the workability of the designs. Larger volumes were then made, sufficient to enable some strength testing to be carried out. This stage of testing established the basic parameters in order to produce good quality concrete. Durability testing at this stage was directed towards detecting and overcoming the effects of alkali–silica reaction.

Larger scale testing

A small number of mixes have been used to build larger scale trial panels designed to simulate structural elements with placement characteristics and 'constructability' recorded. The panels will be submitted to extended durability testing in a range of environments.

Results

The aggregate classification was based on the field examinations and data which were supplied for some materials by potential suppliers. The classification is shown in Table 1.

Table 1. *Assessment of the alternative aggregate sources investigated for the project*

Material quarry	Age	Particle size range	Hardness	Assessment	Category
N. Wales Slate					
Horseshoe Pass	Silurian	fine–medium	weak	not good	5
Corris	Ordovician	fine–medium	hard	possible	3 or 4
Llechwedd	Ordovician	fine–medium	mod hard	possible	3 or 4
Nantlle	Cambrian	fine–coarse	hard	unlikely	4
Dinorwec	Cambrian	mainly fine–medium	hard	good	3
Penrhyn	Cambrian	all sizes	hard	good	3 or 4
Scottish Slate					
Ballachulish	Pre-Cambrian?	fine–coarse	hard	pyrites, not good	3 or 4
Easdale	Dalradian	fine–coarse	hard	pyrites, not good	3 or 4
Aberfoyle	Dalradian	fine–medium	hard	good	3
S.W. England Slate					
Delabole	Upper Devonian				
Longford	Devonian	fine–medium	hard	good	2
Mill Hill	Devonian	fine–coarse	hard	good	2 or 3
Treviddick	Upper Devonian	fine–coarse	hard	possible	3
Lake District Slate					
Kirkstone	Borrowdale Volcanics	medium–v. coarse	hard	good	3
Elterdale	Borrowdale Volcanics	fine–medium	hard	good	3
Kirkby-in-Furness	Silurian	fine–coarse	hard	good	3
China Clay Sand					
Goonvean and	Altered Dartmoor Granite	mixed/graded	variable	good	1 and 2
Blackpool	Altered Dartmoor Granite	all graded	variable	good	1
Indian Queens	Altered Dartmoor Granite	mixed waste	variable	good	2
Pulverised Fuel Ash					
Ratcliffe on Soar		$<45\mu$–150μ	n/a	good	1 and 2
Fiddlers Ferry		$<45\mu$–150μ	n/a	good	1 and 2
Aberthaw		$<45\mu$–150μ	n/a	good	1 and 2
Ferrybridge		$<45\mu$–150μ	n/a	good	1 and 2

Slate

Sixteen slate quarries were visited (as listed in Table 1). The variability of the slate was greater than had been anticipated. As well as slates formed by metamorphism of argillaceous rocks, the materials included volcanic rocks of the Borrowdale series in Cumbria in which a slaty cleavage had been developed. The quality of material varied from good to poor in terms of the hardness of the rocks and the quantities of pyrites present. Some forms of pyrites are considered potentially expansive if included in structural concrete mixes.

The accessibility of the slate waste was variable. The economics of extraction and transportation from Penrhyn to the South East of England have been considered (Department of the Environment 1991) and the prospect of extracting and transporting waste from Kirkby-in-Furness by rail has been suggested as being eligible for grant assistance (Department of the Environment 1995). The selection of samples for testing took account of these factors where established.

Crushing trials were undertaken, using material from three slate quarries. One of these quarries is disused, at Aberfoyle in Scotland. The other two are active, one at Penrhyn in North Wales and one at Kirkby-in-Furness in Cumbria. A three-stage crushing process was utilized to improve the properties of the slate to make it acceptable in concrete mixes. The final stage of crushing involved a vertical shaft impact crusher, which is designed to improve the shape of the aggregate particles.

The results were promising, the shape of the aggregate was improved and this was verified by the reduction in the flakiness index (measure of length to width ratio). For example the Aberfoyle slate flakiness index improved from 84 (20 mm as dug) to 49 (20 mm prepared) on processing. The sand fraction of the slate aggregate was improved further by classification using a Bradley air classifier to reduce the proportion of 150 micron dust. The aggregate test results for the slates and china clay used in the concrete mixing trials are presented in Table 2. It should be noted that the Penrhyn slate waste was received as a crushed 20 mm material, so that the scope

Table 2. *Aggregate test results for slate waste and china clay sand*

	Aberfoyle				Burlington			Penrhyn			China clay	
	20 mm	10 mm	< 5mm	Dust	20 mm	10 mm	<5 mm	20 mm	10 mm	<5 mm	10 mm	<5 mm
Dry density	2755	2758	2837	2906	2748	2736	2724	2822	2821	2830	2541	2591
Saturated density	2768	2772	2848		2761	2752	2752	2831	2832	2847	2589	2630
Mineral density	2791	2786	2866		2784	2780	2800	2847	2853	2880	2670	2696
Flakiness	49	64			50	61		84	93			
Moisture content (%)	0.17	0.20	0.40	0.89	0.22	0.29	0.52	0.16	0.27	1.35	3.997	8.730
Water absorption (%)	0.50	0.69	0.36		0.48	0.58	1.00	0.32	0.41	0.61	1.909	1.504
10% fines	170				250			150				

for improvement of the shape by crushing was more limited than the other two sources from which as dug samples were obtained.

China clay waste

Samples of china clay sand were collected from three sites. The material is already used as concrete aggregate locally to the sites, but economic and technical uncertainty has limited the size of the market. A large problem is the mismatch between the quantities of fine and coarse aggregate produced from the waste.

Pfa

The extent of pfa as waste was investigated through visits to power stations where the material is stockpiled either in lagoons or in tips. The project concentrated on the use of ash for other than cement replacement, which is the main secondary use of the waste at present.

Results from SEM and X-ray microanalysis

Atomic ratios of silicon to calcium against aluminium to calcium were plotted, derived from quantitative X-ray microanalysis of several hundred locations within the cement paste fraction of the samples. Compared to the control sample, which used a standard building sand, the other mortars all showed some points indicating a slightly higher ratio of silicon to calcium in the cement hydrates, with aluminium to calcium ratios remaining constant. This is typically an indication of the presence of some alkali–silica reactivity in the sample. Some slates appeared to have been affected to a greater degree than others. The least affected of those examined was the Elterdale slate from Cumbria, the most seriously affected

was that from Nantlle in North Wales. These results do not indicate that the materials should not be used at all in concrete, but that the guidelines in Concrete Society Report No. 30 (1995) should be followed with regard to the quantity of alkali included in the concrete.

Trial mixes

Concrete mix trials have been carried out and good quality concrete has been made using each of the alternative aggregates. The mix design method used involved the measurement of void space within the various fractions of the aggregate. The optimum combination of sizes to produce the minimum voidage was calculated and the intervening space between the aggregate grains filled with cement paste, with a small amount of overfill of paste to give the mix some workability. Table 3 presents the mixes which were selected to produce the trial panels for longer term durability testing. Each of these mixes gave good characteristics when tested in smaller batches. The 28-day strength results in Table 3 confirm that good quality concrete can be made from the various mix combinations identified as being the most appropriate. The results also demonstrate that the cement content can successfully be minimized by the addition of pfa or of slate dust, while maintaining reasonable compressive strength levels. Figures 1–4 show examples of the concrete seen in sectioned cubes of the mixes.

The mortar prism testing for alkali–silica reaction revealed that the slates each had the potential for long term deleterious expansion when used in concrete with high alkali content. As described above, this was confirmed by the X-ray microanalysis results, which showed a marginal change in the calcium silicate hydrate composition when the slates were used as aggregate (Department of the Environment in prep).

Table 3. *Mix designs for the concrete trial panels*

Mix ref	Aggregate source	Proportions of constituents (kg/m³)						Litres (m³)		Mix characteristics			
		20 mm	10 mm	Sand	Dust	Opc	Pfa	Water	Plasticiser	Overfill (%)	Void (%)	Slump (mm)	28 day strength (N/mm²)
AH	Aberfoyle	502	524	737		452		226		9.5	27.5	68	38.9
AI	Aberfoyle	477	499	704		326	200	200	7	12.4	27.5	55	36.5
AAD	Aberfoyle	423	518	968	225	225		161	9	5.7	26.2	25	28.0
AAH	Aberfoyle	427	522	977		435		168	6	5.1	26.2	30	31.8
BE	Burlington	554	248	939		446		223		11.8	24.7	55	51
BF	Burlington	404	280	801		428	246	205	9	20.7	24.7	70	44.3
BH	Burlington	609	275	1035		417		163	5	5.3	24.7	15	55.7
PC	Penrhyn	419	419	785		526		263		11	32	105	40.6
PE	Penrhyn	347	347	643		525	216	254	9	20.7	32	80	44
PG	Penrhyn	483	483	906		496		179	5	2.2	32	60	46.7
CB	Ccs*	842	842	897		483		206	3	2.4	33.8	72	53.3
CE	Ccs/Aber	413	483	900		439		205	3	3.3	31.5	60	44.8

*Ccs, China clay sand

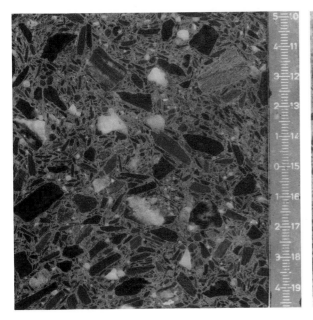

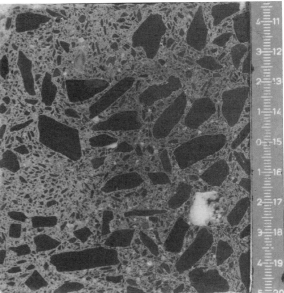

Fig. 1. Mix design AAH. Plate cut from 100mm diameter cube made using Aberfoyle crushed slate aggregate. This 10-litre mix gave a 28-day strength of 31.8 N/mm^2 with a cement content of 435 kg/m^3 and water to cement ratio 0.4. Six litres of plasticiser was needed to give a slump of 30 mm.

Fig. 2. Mix design BA. Plate cut from 100 mm diameter cube made using Burlington crushed slate aggregate. This 10-litre mix gave a 28-day strength of 51 N/mm^2 with a cement content of 446 kg/m^3 and water to cement ratio of 0.5. No plasticiser was used, the slump was 75 mm.

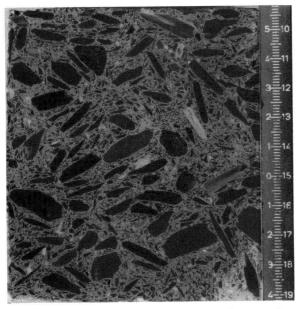

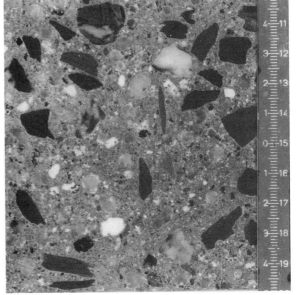

Fig. 3. Mix design PB. Plate cut from 100 mm diameter cube made using Penrhyn crushed slate aggregate. This 10-litre mix gave a 28-day strength of 33.6 N/mm^2 using 526 kg/m^3 cement and 0.5 water to cement ratio. No plasticiser was used for this mix which had a slump of 90 mm.

Fig. 4. Mix design CE. Plate cut from 100 mm diameter cube made using 10 mm and 5 mm China clay sand with 20 mm Aberfoyle crushed slate aggregate. This 10-litre mix gave a 28-day strength of 44.8 N/mm^2. The cement content was 439 kg/m^3, the water to cement ratio was 0.47 and 3 litres of plasticiser was used to give a slump of 60 mm.

It was found that the addition of dust, produced during the slate crushing, was a possible means of reducing the cost of concrete made with alternative aggregates, which in general demanded relatively high cement contents to obtain the workability and compaction required for good quality concrete. It was also found that the use of this dust in the concrete, either with or without pfa additions, was able to minimize the effects of alkali–silica reaction.

Conclusions

The results of this work have been encouraging in terms of producing good quality concrete mixes with each of the alternative aggregates.

It has been demonstrated that slate waste from some sources can be processed to create an aggregate which, in carefully designed mixes, will produce concrete with strengths comparable to normal aggregates.

For the slate aggregates it was found that there was a risk of alkali–silica reaction in the presence of high quantities of alkali in mortar samples. It has also been demonstrated that the presence of pfa will lower the risk of this reaction. It was further found that the use of the dust, produced during the crushing of the aggregate, as a partial cement replacement, was able virtually to eliminate the risk of the reaction.

Acknowledgements. This work was carried out for the Department of the Environment under the supervision of Mott MacDonald Special Services Division, who were responsible for the management, the overall direction and the reporting of the research. Aggregate testing and concrete mix design, manufacture and testing (including petrography) were all carried out by Dr French of Geomaterials Research Services Ltd with Queen Mary and Westfield College. The slate crushing trials were implemented by Construction Materials Management, under the control of Mr Paul Worters. Scanning electron microscopy was carried out by Mr Nick Winter of WHD Microanalysis Consultants Ltd. The authors are greatly indebted to all of these and to the Department of the Environment and Mott MacDonald Special Services Division for permission to publish the work.

References

BRITISH STANDARDS INSTITUTE 1992. *Specification for Aggregates From Natural Sources.*. BS 882.

CONCRETE SOCIETY 1995. *Alkali Silica Reaction, Minimising the Risk to Concrete. Guidance Notes and Model Specification Clauses.* Technical Report No. 30. The Concrete Society.

DEPARTMENT OF THE ENVIRONMENT. In preparation. *Alternative Aggregates.* Report by Mott MacDonald Special Services Division.

——1991. *Occurrence and Utilisation of Mineral and Construction Wastes.* Report by Arup Economics and Planning.

——1995. *Slate Waste Tips and Workings in Britain.* Report by Richards, Moorehead and Laing Ltd. HMSO.

GUTT, W., NIXON, P. J., SMITH, M. A., HARRISON, W. H. & RUSSELL, A. D. 1974. *A Survey of the Locations, Disposal and Prospective Uses of the Major Industrial By-Products and Waste Materials.* Building Research Establishment Current Paper CP/19/74.

HARRISSON, A. M., WINTER, N. B. & TAYLOR, H. F. W. 1986. An examination of some pure and composite cement pastes using SEM with X-ray analytical capability. *Proceedings of the 8th International Congress on the Chemistry of Cement FINEP, Rio de Janeiro.*

TUBEY, L. W. 1978. *The Use of Waste and Low-Grade Materials in Road Construction: 5 China Clay Sand.* TRRL Laboratory Report 817.

VAN AARDT, J. H. P. & VISSER, S. 1977. Calcium hydroxide attack on feldspars and clays: possible relevance to cement-aggregate reactions. *Cement and Concrete Research*, 7, 643.

An approach to the abrasion testing of individual pieces of construction materials

M. A. Eden

Geomaterials Research Services Limited, 1 Falcon Park, Crompton Close, Basildon,
Essex SS14 3AL, UK

Abstract. This paper briefly introduces the basis of abrasion testing and suggests a rapid and simple test that allows the abrasion resistance of specific materials to be evaluated. Small, individual pieces of rock, mortar, or concrete can be tested and the method has been used to evaluate the potential for surface abrasion of concrete surfaces. Many of the commonly used test methods for measuring abrasion resistance of construction materials are aggregate tests such as the QMW mill abrasion test and the ASTM Los Angeles abrasion test which measure the combined resistance of a material to impact and abrasion. Other tests such as the aggregate abrasion and polished stone value tests require a smaller number of resin mounted aggregate pieces to be studied. The ASTM surface abrasion test for concrete uses physically large flat test pieces. Like the ASTM test, the test method described in this paper measures only the abrasion resistance. However, it provides a means of comparing the abrasion resistance of small pieces of construction material and introduces quartz as a reference material.

The test uses a mixture of oil and carborundum as a grinding medium with 10 mm square test pieces held by a standard load against a rotating steel lapping wheel in a rotating jig. The results are expressed as a ratio of the abrasion rate of the test material to that of quartz tested in the same way. This comparative approach enables the test to be carried out using equipment of various designs.

This paper describes a test method developed to compare the resistance to abrasion of the surfaces of small pieces of rock or of man-made construction material such as concrete.

Abrasive wear can be described as a combination of the processes of grinding abrasion and lapping abrasion (Ulvensoen & Muller 1989) and the process of abrasive wear is discussed in detail elsewhere (Zum Gahr 1987). Grinding abrasion occurs where the abrasive particles cut across a surface. Lapping abrasion occurs where abrasive particles roll across a surface causing apex pulverization. Many factors control the rate of abrasive wear under test conditions and these include hardness differences between the abrasive and the sample, abrasive characteristics and the load on the test specimen.

Aggregate abrasion tests, which involve the tumbling action of a rotating mill such as the Los Angeles abrasion test and the QMW mill abrasion test (CIRIA/CUR 1991), measure an unknown combination of factors including the resistance of a rock to abrasive wear, mutual attrition and impact breakage. In some engineering applications such as in coastal defence, high impact breakage resistance, as well as abrasion resistance, is essential. In other situations, resistance to abrasive wear alone is the key factor of importance. An example of this might be the stone floor slab of a building which is to be subjected to foot traffic.

Table 1 lists some of the most commonly used abrasion tests and attempts to group these tests into, (i) those where the emphasis is on impact breakage as a mechanism of abrasion, (ii) ones combining impact breakage and mutual attrition with abrasive wear and (iii) ones where the emphasis is on abrasive wear.

Probably the most commonly used 'abrasion' test where impact breakage is the principal mechanism of abrasion is the Los Angeles abrasion test. This test uses steel balls in a rotating drum to impact onto the test sample which is in the form of a crushed rock aggregate. The Los Angeles abrasion test has been shown to correlate well with the British Standard aggregate impact test and has now been adopted in recent Eurostandards as the test for resistance to fragmentation.

Commonly used abrasion tests where the impact breakage, mutual attrition and abrasive wear are of some importance are the QMW mill abrasion test and the micro-Deval test (Tourenq 1971). The QMW mill abrasion test uses a crushed rock aggregate sample which is tumbled in a horizontally rotating cylindrical mill through which water is continuously passed. The micro-Deval test also uses a horizontally rotating cylindrical mill, but uses 10 mm diameter steel balls and a faster rotation rate to accelerate the rate of abrasion. The similarity in the mechanisms of abrasion of both of these tests is reflected in a good correlation between the

EDEN, M. A. 1998. An approach to the abrasion testing of individual pieces of construction materials. *In*: LATHAM, J.-P. (ed.) 1998. *Advances in Aggregates and Armourstone Evaluation*. Geological Society, London, Engineering Geology Special Publications, **13**, 193–196.

Table 1. *Current abrasion tests*

(i) Impact breakage tests

BS 812 1975 AIV – *Measures the resistance of rock aggregate to fracturing by impact with hammer blows.*

ASTM C131-89 Los Angeles abrasion test – *Measures the resistance of rock aggregate to impact breakage and to a much lesser extent abrasive wear caused by 46.8 mm diameter steel balls. The test has been applied to concrete by Sanbetta (1992).*

(ii) Attrition/Impact breakage/Abrasive wear tests

CIRIA/CUR (1991) QMW Mill abrasion test – *Uses a horizontally rotating mill through which water is passed to cause abrasion to a rock aggregate sample.*

CEN Draft pr EN 1097 (1993) – 1 micro-Deval test – *Uses a horizontal rapidly rotating mill containing water and 10 mm diameter steel balls to cause abrasion to a rock aggregate test sample.*

(iii) Abrasive wear tests

ASTM C241-85 Abrasion resistance of stone subjected to foot traffic – *Uses a lapping plate supplied with abrasive to cause abrasion to intact pieces of rock.*

ASTM C994-90 Abrasion resistance of concrete or mortar surfaces by the rotating cutter method – *Uses a rotating cutter device held in a drill press to cause abrasion to intact pieces of rock/concrete.*

ASTM C1138-89 Abrasion resistance of concrete (underwater method) – *Uses steel grinding balls which are made to roll across the surface of the test specimen underwater to cause abrasion.*

BS 812 1975 Aggregate abrasion value – *Uses a lapping plate supplied with sand as an abrasive to cause abrasion to a rock aggregate test sample.*

BS 812 1975 Polished stone value – *Uses a rubber wheel to cause abrasion/polishing to the surface of the test sample. The test is intended to simulate the polishing action of motor vehicle tyres on a road surface*

QMW mill abrasion test results and the micro-Deval test results (see Latham 1998).

Among the tests where abrasive wear is the key factor in causing abrasion are the BS 812 aggregate abrasion test and the ASTM.C-241-85 building stone abrasion test. Both tests use several pieces of rock and an abrasive to cause abrasive wear to surfaces of the test samples. The abrasive wear tests rely on a small number of selected test pieces and the average from several tests may be needed to obtain comparable reproducibility to the results achieved with aggregate abrasion tests such as the micro-Deval tests which mask any heterogeneity in the sample.

This paper describes a test developed to compare the abrasive wear of the surfaces of small samples of rock and of man-made construction material such as concrete. The test expresses measured rates of wear of the sample under test as a ratio with that of a reference material (such as single crystal quartz, soda-lime glass, or a metal). For this work, single crystal quartz was used

Abrasion resistance test method

The test described in this paper requires prisms to be cut from the material to be tested and from a reference material each measuring between 10 and 13 mm long with a cross-sectional area given by a 10×10 mm square. The test pieces are mounted in cylindrical polyester blocks with a diameter of 20 mm so that the square face of the test piece protrudes between 2 and 4 mm (see Fig. 1). The lower surfaces of the blocks are ground flat before testing, leaving the exposed face of the test pieces parallel to the reverse side of the polyester blocks.

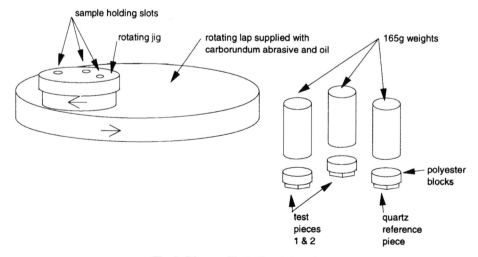

Fig. 1. Diagram illustrating test equipment.

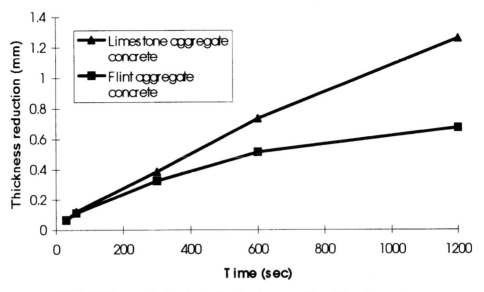

Fig. 2. Thickness reduction due to the abrasive wear of two different concretes.

The cylindrical polyester blocks with embedded test samples are fitted into a rotating jig containing three 21 mm diameter cylindrical holes. The jig is placed onto a rotating lapping plate, fed with a mixture of 600 grade carborundum abrasive and oil. The surfaces of the test samples are held against the lapping plate in the jig by three 165 g weights. The steel lapping plate is set to rotate at 60 r.p.m. The layout of the test equipment used is illustrated in Fig. 1.

The initial lengths of the test pieces and of the reference material are measured at the start of each test run and then at five minute intervals during the test up to a total of 15 minutes. The thickness measurements are made using a digital micrometer capable of measuring with a precision of 0.001 mm.

The abrasion value for the test piece is calculated as follows:

Abrasion value

$$= \frac{\text{thickness reduction (mm) for test piece}}{\text{thickness reduction (mm) for reference quartz test piece}}$$

Note: Thickness reduction is measured between 300 and 900 seconds into the test period.

Changes in rates of thickness reduction with time can also be assessed by making measurements of thickness reduction at several fixed time intervals in each test run.

Expressing the abrasion value as the ratio of the thickness reduction of the test sample to that of a quartz test piece used on the same run has the advantage that

the test method is much less dependent on obtaining precisely identical abrasion conditions during each test run.

Concrete surfaces

The test was originally developed to compare the abrasion resistance of the surfaces of small areas of flint aggregate concrete and limestone aggregate concrete containing GGBS and in particular the surface laitance of the two concretes.

The results are shown graphically in Fig. 2. For both the flint aggregate concrete and the limestone aggregate concrete there is a rapid early rate of surface thickness reduction as the surface irregularities and relatively weak surface laitance is worn away. Towards the end of the test period the contrasting wear resistance of the flint aggregate concrete and the limestone aggregate concrete becomes clear.

Rock surfaces

A selection of rock types, ranging from durable and abrasion resistant Larvik armourstone to relatively low durability Middle Eastern limestones have been tested for abrasion using the above method. The thickness reductions and the ratios of the thickness reduction to that of quartz, for each of the rock types, are listed in Table 2.

Table 2. *Abrasion test results*

Material	Abrasion value (thickness reduction relative to that for quartz)*
Middle East limestone A R1	3.067
Middle East limestone A R4	7.576†
Middle East limestone A R6	2.538
Middle East limestone A Mean	*2.803*
Middle East limestone B R1	3.898
Middle East limestone B R3	3.408
Middle East limestone B R5	4.661
Middle East limestone B Mean	*3.989*
French recrystallized limestone R2	4.522
French recrystallized limestone R3	4.242
French recrystallized limestone R5	5.974
French recrystallized limestone Mean	*4.913*
Larvik armourstone R2	2.454
Larvik armourstone R4	2.259
Larvik armourstone R6	1.476
Larvik armourstone Mean	*2.063*
Granulite R8	3.525
Granulite R8	2.562
Granulite Mean	*3.044*
Grey Flint R7	0.667
Grey Flint R7	0.812
Grey Flint Mean	*0.740*

* Ratio of thickness reduction of test sample to the thickness reduction for reference quartz run at the same time as test sample
† This test piece contained voids.

The results show considerable variation in abrasion resistance between test pieces of the same rock type and between rock types. The most abrasion resistant material tested was flint which has a higher abrasion resistance than single crystal quartz. It is interesting to note that two distinct test pieces of flint with identical visual appearance yielded results differing by some 20%.

Conclusions

This test provides a simple and rapid means of determining the resistance to abrasive wear of the outer surfaces of construction materials for use in locations where abrasive wear is the principal mechanism of abrasion. The use of a reference material which is tested at the same time as the test sample enables this approach to abrasion testing to be applied to a variety of different materials and allows for the possibility of using equipment of differing designs.

The principal advantage of this test over the other aggregate abrasion tests, such as the Los Angeles abrasion test or the BS aggregate abrasion test, is that the test is applicable to testing the smooth exposed surfaces of construction material in applications such as flooring.

References

ASTM Standard test method for abrasion resistance of stone subjected to foot traffic. ASTM Designation: C241-85.
—— Standard test method for abrasion resistance of concrete (underwater method). ASTM Designation: C1138-89.
—— Standard test method for abrasion resistance of concrete by sand blasting. ASTM Designation: C418-90.
—— Standard test method for abrasion resistance of concrete or mortar surfaces by the rotating cutter method. ASTM Designation: C944-90a.
—— Standard test method for abrasion resistance of horizontal concrete surfaces. ASTM Designation: C779-89a.
—— Standard test method for resistance to degradation of small-size coarse aggregate by abrasion and impact in the Los Angeles machine. ASTM Designation: C131-89.
BRITISH STANDARDS INSTITUTION 1989. Part 114. Method for determination of polished stone value (PSV).
——1990a. Part 112. Method for determination of aggregate impact value (AIV).
——1990b. Part 113. Method for determination of aggregate abrasion value (AAV).
COMITE DE EUROPEEN NORMALIZATION CEN pr EN 1097-1 1993. Micro-Deval test.
CIRIA/CUR 1991. *Manual on the Use of Rock in Coastal and Shoreline Engineering.* CIRIA Special publication 83, CUR Report 154.
LATHAM, J. P. 1998. Assessment and specification of armourstone quality from CIRIA/CUR (1991) to CEN (2000). *This volume.*
SANBETTA, E. 1992. New test procedure for impact resistance of industrial floor products. *ACI Materials Journal*, **89**, No 5 September–October, 495–498.
TOURENQ, C. 1971. The micro-Deval test. *De Liason de Laboratoires, des Ponts et Chaussées. Bulletin No. 54,* August–September, Reference 1034.
ULVENSOEN, J. H. & MÜLLER, K. 1989. A new and flexible test method for abrasive wear. *Hard Metal,* **39**, 463–495.
ZUM GAHR, K. H. 1987. *Microstructure and Wear of Materials,* Tribology Series 10, Elsevier, Rotterdam

Index